C0-AOE-866

Unity in Diversity

15 96
D124413872
Graduate

Unity in Diversity

INTERFAITH DIALOGUE
IN THE MIDDLE EAST

MOHAMMED ABU-NIMER, AMAL KHOURY, AND EMILY WELTY

UNITED STATES INSTITUTE OF PEACE PRESS
Washington, D.C.

0719580

The views expressed in this book are those of the authors alone. They do not necessarily reflect views of the United States Institute of Peace.

UNITED STATES INSTITUTE OF PEACE
1200 17th Street NW, Suite 200
Washington, DC 20036-3011

©2007 by the Endowment of the United States Institute of Peace. All rights reserved.

First published 2007

Printed in the United States of America

The paper used in this publication meets the minimum requirements of American National Standards for Information Science—Permanence of Paper for Printed Library Materials, ANSI Z39.48-1984.

Library of Congress Cataloging-in-Publication Data
Abu-Nimer, Mohammed, 1962-
      Unity in diversity : interfaith dialogue in the Middle East / Mohammed Abu-Nimer, Amal Khoury, and Emily Welty.
          p. cm.
      Includes bibliographical references and index.
      ISBN-13: 978-1-60127-013-9 (pbk. : alk. paper)
      ISBN-10: 1-60127-013-5 (pbk. : alk. paper)
      1. Middle East--Religion. 2. Religions--Relations. I. Khoury, Amal. II. Welty, Emily. III. Title.
      BL1600.A28 2007
      201'.50956--dc22

                                                                    2007020273

*We dedicate this book to all Muslims, Jews, Christians,
and others who have devoted their precious lives
to the pursuit of peace and justice
and who continue to sacrifice in many different ways
for all of us.*

CONTENTS

ACKNOWLEDGMENTS

There are so many people who contributed to this project over the last two years. Although our list of appreciation is not comprehensive, we would still like to thank a few of those who joined us on the journey to complete this book.

We are grateful for the financial support of the United States Institute of Peace, especially David Smock, director of the Religion and Peacemaking Program, for his patience and consistent encouragement. David has been a strong force behind many of the successful interfaith projects in the Middle East. This research would have been impossible without his leadership and commitment to creating a sustainable interfaith peacebuilding field in the Middle East. We are truly appreciative of his support. Also, Qamar-ul Huda, program officer for the Institute's Religion and Peacemaking Program, and our editor, Michael Carr, were most helpful in seeing this manuscript through to publication.

Several other institutions contributed to this project by association as well as with funds. Our sincere thanks to the American University's School of International Service, under the leadership of Dean Louis Goodman, as well as to Professor Said Abdul Aziz, director of the International Peace and Conflict Resolution Program. Both have offered their help in various ways throughout this project. This project began its first phase in 2003, when Mohammed Abu-Nimer was a Religion and Peace Fellow at the Kroc Institute at Notre Dame University. Scott Appleby, the director, offered both moral support and encouragement to pursue this project. His work on religion and peace has been an inspiring path for many in the field.

The United Religions Initiative (URI) was a central partner in this project, too. Its administrative and financial management of the grant from the Institute of Peace was crucial to the completion of the project. We are most grateful to Barbara Hartford for her excellent facilitation of this grant and for providing us with many local contacts from URI in the Middle East, too. Her encouragement and attention to detail were valuable resources for our team. Also, without URI staff and ground support, this project would have not been completed. We are also grateful to our editor, Atieno Fisher, for taking the time to thoroughly review the manuscript. Her content and style comments helped us tremendously.

Obviously our most valuable contributors to this project are the local researchers in these communities who have endured the most difficulties and faced many logistical and intellectual challenges throughout this process. We are most grateful and appreciative of their work and the risks they have taken to gather the information and provide us with enough data to write these chapters. Thank you, Rana Husseini, Jordan; Mohammed Mossad and Yasmine El Rifai, Egypt; Aref Husseini, Palestine; and Kamal Kezel and Amal Abu

Zidan, Jerusalem. We also would like to thank Mohammed Abu-Nimer's research assistants Tazreena Sajjad and Adel Ghazzel.

Finally, we are most obliged to all interviewees and organizations who opened their doors and sacrificed their time to share their views openly with us and with our local researchers. We hope that this research will bring more visibility and recognition to their valuable contribution to building a culture of peace and nonviolence in their societies.

FOREWORD

The skeptics come in at least two varieties. Secularists find it naive that anyone could actually see interfaith dialogue (IFD) as a way forward in the morass of religiously fueled intolerance and hatred that is the Middle East. Religions, they say, are a—perhaps *the*—major source of intolerance, conflict, and deadly violence in the post–Cold War world, whose dark side is overpoweringly on display in the societies the authors have selected to study: Egypt, Israel, Palestine, Lebanon, and Jordan. For exhibit A, one could point out the Muslim Brotherhood, Hezbollah, Hamas, Islamic Jihad, al Qaeda; for exhibit B, Gush Emunim, the radical Jewish "Bloc of the Faithful," who established illegal settlements in the West Bank. And for exhibit C, we have any number of crusading, messianic Americans, plotting behind the scenes, provoking Christian sentiments against Muslims, and bankrolling Israeli expansionism. Indeed, one could argue that anyone who proposes religion as the way out of this mess is scarcely less addled than the religious fanatics themselves!

And opponents of dialogue scoff with equal scorn, calling dialogue the refuge of the weak and irrelevant. They see those who lead or participate in such efforts as having no clout with the powerful, and talking across religious and cultural barriers as a noble exercise but nothing more. Even were the IFD practitioners to lead their respective "tribes" toward sustainable peace, dialogue's opponents point out, it would take very little—a rash of suicide bombings, a hate crime, the desecration of a sacred site—to wipe out years of so-called progress. And when the "fact in the field" is something as momentous as the war in Iraq, for example, the political vulnerability of religions and their would-be peacemakers is cruelly exposed.

Mohammed Abu-Nimer, Amal Khoury, and Emily Welty have heard it all before, and they remain unconvinced. Indeed, *Unity in Diversity* is their eloquent rebuttal to the so-called conventional wisdom regarding religion and dialogue. The authors of this groundbreaking comparative study of interfaith actors and initiatives in five conflict-ridden societies of the Middle East conclude, modestly but significantly, that interfaith dialogue is an underdeveloped but potentially powerful instrument in the peacebuilder's mediation and transformation tool kit.

How did they come to such a conclusion? Without assuming beforehand that IFD would prove viable, the authors interviewed practitioners in their disparate cultural and political settings and organizational contexts. In so doing, they noted and lamented the frustrations associated with interfaith dialogue, especially the marginalization of faith-based processes by secular politicians or non-governmental organizations (NGOs). Even when reporting cases where religious actors made progress, Abu-Nimer and his colleagues wisely caution that IFD alone, taken in isolation from political and economic

"Track One" diplomacy, does not provide the antidote to the complex and overdetermined conflicts bedeviling the Middle East.

Yet these intrepid researchers were able to identify patterns of effective religious interaction and develop plausible explanations for the successful cases. Several themes suggested or developed by their methodologically precise study deserve attention:

1. "Dialogue" is a set of practices, not limited to elites or to formal means of communication, which aims to foster long-term relationships based in mutual respect and caring. Dialogue is thus virtually a form of religious discipline.

Engagement with the "other" is the heart and soul of dialogue; it seeks to "know the other," not only or even primarily by exchanging official political or doctrinal pronouncements, but by listening and attending to the "meaning beyond the words." Middle Easterners, in fact, seem to specialize in communicating by multiple means, especially via the religious gesture and religious language, which speak of, and to, deeper meaning. Religious practices, such as prayer, hospitality, forgiveness, repentance, and reconciliation, express reverence for the human person. These practices, in fact, are the cultural currency of the Middle East. They give homage to the God of Abraham by paying respect to His children.

Religious symbol and ritual, in short, are a form of discourse, a self-communication that plumbs the depths of human communities. It is this dimension of human freedom that must be engaged if deadly conflict is to be deemed intolerable, if peace is to be sustained. Far from being superficial, religious discourse brings competing sides to the heart of the issues dividing their peoples, and addresses those issues via symbols and rituals charged with cultural and psychological resonance.

2. Precisely because of religion's access to the full depth of human relations, faith-based diplomacy is an effective means of democratizing and popularizing otherwise state- and elite-centered peace negotiations, settlements, and processes.

The literature on conflict resolution demonstrates that it is impossible to "resolve" a civil war or other long-term violent conflict that has caused profound suffering and displacement of peoples. Such conflicts must be gradually *transformed,* a process that unfolds beyond the solution of specific economic or political problems. The process must occur, moreover, not only among politicians and rulers but among working people and the poor—among, that is, the so-called grassroots.

Rooting negotiations between warring parties in cross-cultural, cross-religious collaboration establishes the conditions for a genuine peace process. Interfaith dialogue, the authors argue, is an effective way of building the popular support and "buy-in" that are essential to the successful implementation of a peace accord. Fruitfully, they describe the efforts of religious actors who possess the vision and courage to celebrate the internal pluralism of their own religious tradition and to welcome the diversity of religions in the larger society. Such leaders are capable of tapping what John Paul Lederach calls "the moral imagination" of populations victimized by the war. Enlarged by this moral vision, people are capable of risking the trust needed to embrace the "other."

3. The "best practices" of IFD both counteract the negative dimensions of religion and dialogue and evoke the considerable peacebuilding capacity present at the moral and spiritual core of religious traditions.

Whereas religious extremists arrogate to themselves the authority to interpret the complex and multivocal religious tradition, effective IFD participants "speak only for themselves," write Abu-Nimer, Khoury, and Welty. The participants' own experiences of the consoling and healing balm of faith, or of the efficacy of forgiveness and reconciliation, testify compellingly to the transformative power of the religious tradition and practice.

Neither do IFD participants presume to embody or comprehend the entire tradition; rather, they respect its complexity and invite their coreligionists across a spectrum of religious interpretation to join the conversation.

Moreover, the IFD exemplars presented in these pages do not interpret "dialogue" as an attempt to sort through and reshape particular religious doctrines in order find common ground or "universals" to which all religions can give assent. Rather, the common ground established by dialogue is the mutual recognition of the irreducible dignity of each person, regardless of race, ethnicity, class, or religious background. Paradoxically, however, it is precisely the religious imagination that opens one's eyes to the transcendent dignity of human beings, whatever their path to the sacred.

Interfaith dialogue, in short, is not about reducing the complex, ambiguous, multivocal religious tradition to a lowest common denominator. To the contrary, it welcomes first-order religious discourse and acknowledges the particularity and integrity of each faith tradition. Only when standing before the other on this solid ground of "untranslated" first-order religious discourse do religious actors, ironically, exhibit the confidence and courage to employ second-order language and thus to transcend their particular religious idiom in mutual action for peace.

Far from being irrelevant to the politics of social change, religious peacebuilders are capable of acting as power brokers. Moral agents and prophets, they are shrewd diagnosticians of a society's strengths and weaknesses. Indeed, religious organizations often replace or complement the state in the crucial task of providing education, health care, emergency relief, and other social services. The authors counsel practitioners of interfaith dialogue to heed their keen sociopolitical instincts when structuring the cross-religious dialogue. An imbalance of power can shatter the delicate dynamics of political and social cooperation among faith communities. Accordingly, the core participants of IFD—religious laity and local clergy drawn from the midlevel range of social and political leadership—"must pay careful attention to the location, timing, participant selection, and other dynamics of the dialogue design."

Not least among the putative weaknesses of IFD addressed in this study is the interfaith community's fragility, seen most dramatically in its vulnerability to external events (e.g., the war in Iraq, local riots, inequalities that spark intercommunal violence, and so on). The useful concluding chapters propose models for effective interfaith dialogue—patterns of communication and collaboration that can evolve into a lasting social foundation. Each of the societies studied in this volume, with varying degrees of success, has begun to build such a foundation; Abu-Nimer, Khoury, and Welty come loaded with blueprints for foundations that will endure the spasms of violence and the dualism fostered by extremists who seek to divide peoples along religious, ethnic, and class lines.

In this respect, as elsewhere throughout the volume, the authors skillfully weave together description (of IFD in the five settings), analysis, evaluation, and recommendation. The feat makes *Unity in Diversity* a groundbreaking study —the first of a series, one hopes, of systematic, scientifically sound tests and demonstrations of the limited but essential role that interfaith dialogue does and can play in the peaceful transformation of deeply rooted conflicts.

R. SCOTT APPLEBY
Professor of History
John M. Regan Jr. Director,
Joan B. Kroc Institute for International Peace Studies

Unity in Diversity

1

INTRODUCTION

Potentials and Challenges in Interfaith Dialogue in the Middle East

Since the September 11, 2001, attacks on the United States, attention to, and interest in, interfaith dialogue (sometimes also called "dialogue of civilizations") has grown. The discourse on the international political level emphasizes dualities: "us" versus "them" and "Christianity" versus "Islam." Organizing and sponsoring interfaith dialogue activities, meetings, and conferences has become more common in the United States and around the world.

The increase in interfaith dialogue is a hopeful indicator—it holds the potential to change lives, radically alter perspectives, and build channels of communication between distrustful and fearful people. Dialogue is not a replacement for the work of diplomacy or structural peacebuilding projects, but it can provide a powerful aid and basis for such work.

Like other applications of peacebuilding, interfaith dialogue and interreligious peace assume that violence and conflicts emerge and persist partly (some argue mostly) due to ignorance and a lack of constructive interaction with the "other." Thus, understanding the religion or faith of the other is a core strategy and motivation for initiating many interfaith activities. Knowing the other and getting to understand him or her has become a necessity in this age of diversity and transnational, global interactions.

A growing awareness of the role of religion in peacemaking and peacebuilding has encouraged interfaith dialogue (IFD), particularly since 2001, and intentional dialogues have taken place around the world, including in the Middle East. This book endeavors to shed light on IFD by closely examining the work of many individual actors and organizations in a strategic and diverse region: the Middle East.

Contrary to the stereotype that the Middle East has always experienced unremitting religious fighting and war, for many centuries, religious actors have worked for peace and reconciliation in various parts of the region. Despite wars and ethnic tensions, peaceful interfaith interaction has always been a part of the social and cultural fabric of the different religious groups coexisting there. In the Arab cultural discourse of Egypt, Jordan, Lebanon, Palestine, and other societies, stories are shared about cooperation among Christians, Muslims, and Jews throughout various periods of history.

This research recognizes such narratives and acknowledges the history of interfaith relations in the region. Regrettably, these stories and illustrations of interfaith peace work have been marginalized and often neglected, especially recently. Instead, religious and sectarian differences have been highlighted and often utilized to divide communities.

This study intends to investigate specific IFD efforts in five selected societies in the region. As the first study of its kind, it actively examines the nature of the conditions and challenges facing IFD participants in these contexts. Most of the previous research that has been done in this field has either focused on one society or on one religious group. We attempt to draw a clearer picture of the types, nature, and conditions of IFD activities in five religiously heterogeneous societies: Egypt, Jordan, Lebanon, Israel, and Palestine. Even though all these cases demonstrate realities of religious diversity, they differ in terms of their ethnic and sectarian divisions, their level of violence and conflict, and the degree of openness or space for interfaith peace work that each political regime or society provides. We do not intend this book to be used as a primary historical resource for the reader interested in the political history or interfaith relations in any of the countries included in this study. While we do attempt to present a condensed historical context for the IFD activities in each case study, we acknowledge that we are only painting a broad overview of the conflict in each setting. Our intention is to refocus the discourse on the role of interfaith dialogue in each of these societies.

In our efforts to compare IFD in these five settings, we composed a standard list of questions to guide the local researchers in each community. The local researchers were asked to provide a brief introduction about the interviewees and their organization, an exploration of the assumptions and theories that guided IFD work (models), identification of the processes and issues of interfaith interaction, examples and criteria of IFD, challenges and obstacles IFD faced, and needs or recommendations to improve the interfaith field in the specific community.

Many challenges emerged in the process of data collection, and even designating and selecting the local researchers proved more difficult than we had anticipated. The tension and the actual eruption of the war in Iraq constituted a major obstacle for the field research in all five societies. The field researchers encountered a disappointing stream of rejections from potential interviewees. For the first few months of the research, until June 2003, it was extremely difficult to conduct any interviews, and the main response from interfaith organizers was "this is not a good time to discuss interfaith relations and peace." Such responses illustrate the crucial impact that political events and contextual factors often have on the ability of the interfaith actors to operate or even freely and comfortably express their views on issues of religion and peace. In the volatile political reality of these five societies on the eve of the

Iraq war, interfaith actors and their communities shared the uncertainty and insecurity evoked by the possible consequences of the U.S. invasion of Iraq.

In the Palestinian context, the continuation of the Palestinian Intifada and the Israeli military activities throughout the Occupied Territories added to the difficulties and challenges of scheduling interviews and even attending certain meetings in areas such as Nablus and Gaza. In addition, many political changes took place during the field research, including the continuing siege of Arafat's compound, the assassination of several prominent Palestinian leaders from Hamas and other factions, the death of Arafat, the election of the new Palestinian government and Prime Minister Mahmoud Abbas, and the victory of Hamas in Palestinian elections. Such factors often were cited by the Palestinian interviewees, who would ask, "Can religious peacebuilding really help under these circumstances?"

In the context of Egypt and Jordan, local researchers reported with extreme caution that the discussion of interfaith relations might be perceived as a threat to national security. In some cases, special framing of the questions and the subject of interfaith relations had to be worked out before any interviewee would agree to meet with the researchers. In Egypt, the security forces constantly monitor such research and interfaith interactions between Copts and Muslims due to the sensitivity of the subject and its implications for Egypt's national security and foreign relations.

It is essential to remind the reader that this is not a comprehensive or exhaustive study of all the interfaith activities or intrafaith organizations in these communities, but rather a snapshot of the kinds of activities prominently occurring in each context. In each country, we tried to reach out to most of the active individual actors and organizations in the area of IFD. However, due to the small number of actors involved in IFD in each country, we relied on the snowball methodology to compile a list of interviewees. In other words, we identified a few well-known actors in each community; then, based on their recommendations, we identified additional potential interviewees. On average, we have managed to formally and informally interview at least twenty-five (in the case of Israel and Palestine, the number of formal interviewees exceeded forty-five) interfaith peace actors in each of these communities. The interviewees in each community are diverse, and each has at least five years of experience in this area.

Data from all the interviews were transcribed and translated from Arabic, French, or Hebrew into English. Data from each case were classified and analyzed according to general themes that had emerged from the literature review and had been identified by the authors as key concepts for all the cases. A content analysis of the data was completed according to themes, general patterns, and responses in each category, as opposed to individual words, sentences, or paragraphs. Despite the agreement of most interviewees to publish their opinion and their consent to record their statements, in reporting the findings, the authors attempted to preserve some degree of anonymity for most interviewees due to the sensitivity of the subject and political context. Thus, names of most interviewees were omitted from the text; however, the identities of some public figures and organizers are disclosed.

Chapter 2 comprises our literature review of existing research in interfaith dialogue and reviews some basic concepts and approaches in IFD that we see as central. The chapter aims to present the major approaches in interfaith dialogue as captured by various scholars and practitioners. In chapter 3, we begin the detailed description and analysis of each of the IFD cases, beginning with the conflicted area of Israel-Palestine. This chapter examines the interfaith field from the perspective of at least forty-five individuals who were interviewed by various local researchers as well as by one of the authors, Mohammed Abu-Nimer. In the fourth chapter, the work of the various Lebanese interfaith organizations is critically presented and examined based on informal structured interviews by Amal Khoury, who conducted all the interviews for this chapter. The fifth chapter focuses on interfaith activities in Egypt, based on interviews completed by Mohammed Mossad and his research assistant from Cairo University. The description of the interfaith organizations and the synthesis of the chapters were completed by Emily Welty, who conducted the research on the secondary archival sources on interfaith in Egypt. Our last case, in chapter 6, on IFD in Jordan, is based on interviews completed by a Jordanian journalist, Rana Husseini, who also provided some of the archival data on the subject.

The seventh chapter is our attempt to examine the five cases comparatively and present some of the shared lessons and general trends that emerged from this study. This final chapter is a comparative analysis of the common patterns and unique developments that characterize each set of interfaith peacebuilding activities in the different countries or societies. The last chapter presents a process model for IFD based on the intercultural sensitivity model used by Milton Bennet and Mitch Hammer. Our aim is to share the model as a potential guide for interfaith professionals who seek to design a more systematic approach to interfaith peacebuilding.

The final offering of the book is a selected list of resources describing the various interfaith organizations and initiatives operating in these five societies. Obviously this list is not exhaustive, but it demonstrates the scope of activities occurring in each region and it certainly includes many of the major actors in this emerging field.

Our hope is that this study contributes significantly to the emerging field of research around interfaith dialogue as a resource for peacemaking. We believe that those involved professionally in the field of dialogue will benefit from a focused look at interfaith dialogue in the Middle Eastern context, and that academics will use this as a resource to supplement their understanding of the many ways in which religion plays a role in civil society and peacebuilding in the region. As interest in dialogue grows, we hope that this book will be a step toward furthering the field of interreligious understanding.

2

INTERFAITH DIALOGUE

Basic Concepts and Approaches

D ialogue is a powerful method of conflict resolution and peacemaking because of its ability to draw on people's most cherished beliefs. Religion is a boundary marker for identity and presents people with a system of laws, narratives, and language with which to express their deepest beliefs. Genuine dialogue can create bridges between isolated and estranged people, and the power of this bridging process is more potent than a truce born out of violence. As writers and researchers, we espouse religious pluralism and tolerance. We believe, as eloquently stated by Richard John Neuhaus, that "the will of God is that we are tolerant with those who disagree with us regarding the will of God" (Neuhaus 1985, 43). Even as we recognize the important differences in the world religions, we also affirm the potential of religious traditions to overcome fragmentation and violent conflict, and see that the resources that religion possesses are a contribution to peacemaking efforts.

This is a study of faith-based diplomacy—that is, using religion as a lens through which to view and analyze international conflict. Contrary to the popular assertions that religion is a source of conflict, scholars in this area choose to see it also as a source for peace and conflict resolution. Abdul Aziz Said has called religious/spiritual dialogue a primary place for the development of "transnational consciousness" and an "emerging global spiritual ethic" (Said 2002, 6–7). In examining Muslim-Christian dialogue in Ghana, Hizkias Assefa (2001, 184) observed, "Exploring the religious and spiritual dimension allowed the process to move beyond the competitive and legalistic discussion and get to the bottom of the problem." Abu-Nimer, Said, and Prelis (2001, 342) have concluded that "religion is an underutilized and powerful tool to assist in resolving many of the intractable ethnic conflicts." While many politicians (and scholars of international relations) feel that religion must stay out of international politics, intellectuals in this area of faith and diplomacy recognize religion as a legitimate form of cultural and social narrative that must be taken into account in the world of conflict and peacemaking.

Interfaith dialogue (IFD), a form of Track Two diplomacy,[1] may have an important part to play in peacemaking and reconciliation in the Middle East. Recognition of IFD as an integral part of peacemaking work is based on the assumption that fostering deeper relationships between people on opposite sides of a conflict is a critical part of the resolution of conflict. Failed Track One peace processes such as the Oslo Accords periodically lack support from public citizens and ignore the significance of religion in the region. Politics in Israel-Palestine (or in the Middle East in general) are often influenced by religious forces, values, and beliefs. To impose a secular peace plan on holy places is to ignore the millions of residents there who are motivated largely by religion. Despite this, IFD, as a process, will not single-handedly solve the major conflicts in the world today. However, it is one of many important tools and contributing factors for resolution because it reduces the amount of dehumanization and ignorance on both sides of the conflict, as well as providing symbols of hope.

CONCEPTUALIZING DIALOGUE

Broadly defined, dialogue is a safe process of interaction to verbally or non-verbally exchange ideas, thoughts, questions, information, and impressions between people from different backgrounds (race, class, gender, culture, religion, and so on). Dialogue requires not only mutual sharing and exchange, but also mutual listening and consideration of the other's view. Dialogue clarifies misunderstandings and illuminates areas of both convergence and divergence. Dialogue is not preaching or explaining or debate; it maps the transformation of people from postures of intolerance or passive tolerance to attitudes of deep understanding and respect of the other. Typically, dialogue and debate are conceptually blurred, but they are distinct phenomena. The Jewish-Palestinian Living Room Dialogue Group of San Mateo, California, highlights the importance of distinguishing dialogue from debate (Jewish-Palestinian Dialogue Group 1997, 6). The group helpfully notes the drastic differences between dialogue and debate in the following way:

Dialogue:	Debate:
To inquire and to learn	To tell, sell, persuade
To unfold shared meaning	To gain agreement on one meaning
To integrate multiple perspectives	To evaluate and select the best
To uncover and examine assumptions	To justify/defend assumptions

Drawing these distinctions illustrates that the driving purpose behind dialogue is collective and subjective understanding, while the impetus behind debate is an inherently more competitive and individualistic approach to winning or convincing the other. Though dialogue between neighbors on opposing sides of a conflict may be both revolutionary and helpful, the dialogues examined here take place in a more organized and official fashion. While interracial, interethnic, or other boundary-crossing forms of dialogue can be transformative, the purpose of this research is to elucidate the idiosyncrasies and broad trends strictly within IFD.

What makes IFD distinctively different from other resolution-based forms of dialogue? IFD contributes toward conflict resolution because it draws on peacebuilding processes that, in themselves, have religious connotations. One example is the concept of reconciliation, a major theme in the context of IFD. Reconciliation usually involves processes of confession, repentance, mercy, and forgiveness. These processes are inherently religious concepts rather than secular concepts (Sampson 1997, 276). Drawing on religious resources as the basis for dialogue allows participants to draw upon some of their deepest motivations, beliefs, and fears: "Religion is one of the deepest motive forces of human action. Our religious convictions, attitudes, sensitivities and prejudices do influence to a great extent our approach to the questions of the day" (Arinze 1986, 58).

In the context of many conflicts, religion is a convenient rallying point for those who want to explore bridging differences. In most societies, religion continues to have influence and integrity in people's eyes. Cynthia Sampson (1997, 275) writes, "In societies in which the government is widely viewed as illegitimate, or centralized authority has broken down altogether, organized religion may be the only institution retaining some measure of credibility, trust and moral authority among the population at large."

Bringing religion into the dialogue allows participants to draw upon a deeper, more transcendent part of their being and recognize similarities in those on the other side of the religious divide. Even in times of violence and conflict, religious believers from different faiths often find that they have more in common with one another than they have with nonreligious people even from their own ethnic/cultural/racial background. However, while IFD can provide structure and framework to work for peace across faith lines, such opportunity is often neglected or marginalized by many secular politicians or nongovernmental organizations (NGOs).

DIALOGUE IN A MIDDLE EASTERN CONTEXT

The unique demands of the region make it important to address particular phenomena that are accentuated in Middle Eastern societies. The Middle East holds the distinction of being home to all three Abrahamic traditions. With this distinction also comes a complicated and painful history. The impetus for interfaith dialogue in the Middle East is even greater when one considers the significant impact that conflict in this region has on considerable portions of the Jewish, Christian, and Muslim communities in other parts of the world.

In terms of historical issues, IFD in this region must contend with issues such as the Crusades, the Holocaust, neocolonialism, the creation of the state of Israel, and the ongoing Israeli-Palestinian conflict. The collective memory of the people of this land is long and stained with numerous seemingly intractable conflicts. The Middle East (especially the five societies in this study: Egypt, Lebanon, Israel, Palestine, and Jordan) is deeply affected by religious identities and meanings, and its conflicts require reconciliation processes that recognize that religiousness. A comprehensive peace based solely on secular values, actors, and frameworks will not be sustainable; peace must involve the religious believers and resonate with their faith.

Particularly within Israel/Palestine, specific recognition of the pains and tragedies of the past is needed. Marc Gopin (2000, 172) writes that "the Holocaust and European persecution is at the heart of the entire style of Israeli interaction. They are also, surprisingly, at the core of intra-Jewish religious/secular conflict in Israel, in addition to being a principal factor in the persistence of at least half the Israeli population's mistrust of Arabs that goes beyond the understandable fear of terrorism." Even though the Palestinians were not responsible for the Holocaust or European persecution, acknowledgment of the Jewish people's experience of these events often paves the way for greater trust and understanding among people. Similarly, Palestinians need acknowledgment of their inherent basic rights in the land of Palestine (to which the right to Jerusalem is central) and self-determination as a crucial part of any genuine reconciliation process. In the case of Lebanon, recognition and manifestation of the religio-ethnic identity of many groups are crucial to the development and stability of their society. In Egypt, the religious status and affairs of the Copts are central to the intercultural fabric of the Egyptian society.

The Abrahamic faiths of the Middle East share a historical and cultural background. Their narratives have been shaped by a common geography. Kenneth Thomas (2001, 340) writes, "The forms of family life, society, economy, nomadic life, government, agriculture, animal husbandry and societal customs described in the Bible are Middle Eastern and are known to all three religious traditions. Particularly the moral codes, legal forms, and stern ethics of desert societies reflect the context within which all three religions originated. There is far more similarity and commonality between these three religions with their common cultural background than any of them have with Far Eastern cultures and religions." Thus, for better or worse, the Abrahamic faiths within the context of the Middle East are the perfect place to carefully examine IFD.

From a wider perspective, religious movements have been playing a significant role in countries such as Egypt, Israel, Jordan, Lebanon, and Palestine. In each of these societies religious movements have been central forces of political opposition. Engaging such forces in interfaith conversation or narrative can be a major avenue to promoting basic tolerance of the other. (Tolerance is the mere acceptance of the other's right to exist.) It also may contribute to religious pluralism (defined in this study as accepting the other's right to exist without passing any value judgment of superiority or exclusivity, and allocating resources to further such attitudes).

INTERFAITH DIALOGUE: AN EMERGING FIELD OF PRACTICE

Formal, organized IFD is a relatively recent phenomenon. Until the twentieth century, people of different faiths largely lived in different areas and did not come into intensive contact with one another (Watt 1991, 142–43). Increased mobility typically brought increased tensions between different religions. Today IFD is a by-product of increased political, cultural, and economic globalization. M. Darrol Bryant (1998, 58) notes, "Dialogue between people of different faiths, in an environment of mutual respect, is a process that has emerged only in the second half of our century. There have been isolated moments of dialogue between Muslims and Christians over the centuries, but it is only in our century that we can speak of a movement of interfaith dialogue that aims at understanding between the different traditions of faith."

Abrahamic dialogue is a relatively recent development in IFD. In a recent Western European context, the need for interfaith dialogue was greatly affected by the Second World War and the Holocaust. The first few years of dialogue between Christians and Jews were based on general concepts of brotherhood. We can talk to each other, share common concerns, be friends. Gradually, we began to talk of religious matters, primarily the commonalities between our two faiths. A major turning point in the dialogue movement came in the 1960s, with introduction of Nostra Aetate (the Second Vatican Council's 1965 Declaration of the Relationship of the Church to Non-Christian Religions) by Pope John Paul XXIII.

Another significant step in IFD was the founding of the World Conference on Religion and Peace (WCRP), established in 1968 as a symbol of goodwill among Buddhists, Christians, Jews, Muslims, and Hindus. This organization has sought to be a forum in which religious believers can undertake initiatives for peace in the name of their religion. However, this group is less interested in a dialogue consisting of discussions than in one consisting of action taken together. Cardinal Arinze (2002, 101) writes, "WCRP is proof, if any were needed, that it is possible for believers in the major religions in the world to come together to do something to promote justice and peace, without necessarily discussing their particular religious beliefs and practices."

Since the 1970s there have been many interfaith initiatives (such as conferences, workshops, journeys, and joint religious celebrations), which have led scholars and activists to identify effective frameworks and approaches to interfaith dialogue. Research in this area has grown tremendously in the past two decades.

ATTITUDES TOWARD, AND MODELS OF, IFD

In examining the existing models of IFD operating in the field today, it is important to understand the range of attitudes that people bring to the study and practice of religion. These attitudes directly affect the approach people will take toward IFD in general. We find it useful to examine attitudes about religion, both one's own and others', in four basic categories: exclusivism, syncretism, pluralism, and transformation. These four basic approaches to religious experience represent a spectrum of the approaches typically found in an

IFD. Within any given dialogue, a variety of attitudes emerges. By more closely examining each of the attitudes, we can better understand the different tones of dialogue each attitude encourages.

Exclusivism

The exclusivist believes that only his or her religion is fundamentally and universally true, while the others are either wrong or misled. This attitude is among the least conducive to dialogue. The existence of other faiths might even be acknowledged by the exclusivist, but only one's own religion has a grasp of the truth. An exclusivist will engage in a form of dialogue that is not dialogue at all, but rather an attempt to convert the other to one's own true religion. Sadly, books or pamphlets published under the guise of IFD are often actually exclusivist tracts of propaganda for proselytizing. Take, for example, a small booklet by H.M. Baagill entitled *Christian Muslim Dialogue.* This booklet in no way attempts mutual understanding between Christianity and Islam—in fact, the "dialogue" that is constructed does not even include two actual people. Rather, it is a script in which the Muslim attempts to educate the Christian about the errors in Christianity. In the final scripted conversation between the Muslim and Christian, the Christian converts to Islam:

> *Muslim:* Islam is based on reason and is a pure teaching of all Prophets of Allah, not contaminated with paganism and superstition.
>
> *Christian:* That is what I am looking for.
>
> *Muslim:* Why don't you consider the Shahadah, first in English, then in Arabic? Let me help you pronounce it . . . (Baagill 1984, 33).

Similarly, Christian publications or missionaries have operated among Muslims and attempted to convert them through forums comparing Islam and Christianity, or through aid and development.

This is not dialogue but rather a feeble attempt at conversion that assumes that if the other only knew more about one's own faith, then he or she would quickly convert. Such proselytizing efforts to convince others of the validity of one's own faith have also been termed "doctrinal assertive dialogues." (Kolvenbach et al. 1999) Both Christians and Muslims have engaged in such efforts for many centuries in different parts of the world.

Exclusivism used to be the primary attitude of mainline Christian churches toward other faiths. Fortunately, this is slowly changing. "In the contemporary theological world, the exclusivist position no longer holds sway, as it did under the influence of Barth and Kraemer earlier in the twentieth century. Many churches, Protestant and Catholic, and many academic theologians have rejected exclusivism. . . . But the exclusivist position cannot be dismissed as easily as some of its critics would like. For one thing, it remains the official position of most evangelical denominations" (McCarthy 1998, 77). One of the most common misconceptions about exclusivism is that exclusivists reject

IFD. In fact, quite the opposite is often true: exclusivists often embrace the chance to "dialogue" with the religious other, as it affords them a potential opportunity to win converts.

This attitude toward evangelism and exclusivism is most commonly associated with Christianity, but it can be found in other faiths as well. Fundamental sects in all three Abrahamic faiths have tended to embrace exclusivism as a way to "define and defend personal and communal identity in a social and political context in which such identity is lost or threatened" (McCarthy 1998, 83). Kate McCarthy notes, "To the extent that they share Christianity's monotheism and its unitary conception of truth, Judaism and Islam articulate exclusive claims comparable to those in Christianity. . . . But confidence in the unique and normative status of their own God and God's revelation to them has not resulted in full-blown exclusivist theology for the majority of Jews and Muslims" (80). McCarthy attributes the difference in the amount of exclusivism in the three faiths to historical circumstance. "Judaism's minority status and relative lack of political power throughout history have certainly inhibited its tendency to develop an outward-looking exclusivism" (80). For Islam, being the third religion to be embraced in the Middle East, it has theologically acknowledged Christianity and Judaism as religions and prophets of truth.

Despite the deserved criticism of exclusivism, it must also be noted that exclusivists often bring a valuable grounding presence to IFD. The advantage of exclusivists is their deep knowledge of their own faith. "The great strength of the exclusivist approach to religious difference is precisely its profound commitment to its own vision. As critics of pluralist theologies have noted, it is often those with the most absolutist theologies who bring the most substantive resources to the dialogue table" (McCarthy 1998, 100).

Syncretism

At the opposite end of the spectrum from exclusivism is syncretism. Syncretism is an attempt to merge two or more faiths into a single, unified faith. However, scholars of IFD agree that religious uniformity is not the goal of IFD and that differences should not be negated in favor of agreement. Dialogue is not a movement toward syncretism or conversion, but is a building of relationships. "There can be no talk of syncretism here, for syncretism means amalgamating various elements of different religions into some kind of a (con)fused whole without concern for the integrity of the religions involved—which is not the case with authentic dialogue" (Swidler 1998, 29). Syncretism is not an attitude that fosters deep exchange of ideas or recognition of religious differences. Some dialoguers, when discovering the similarities between different religious groups, have begun mixing different religious rituals and symbols. In other cases, some dialoguers have adopted "spiritual practices" that have been borrowed from certain religious groups. As a result, many such interactions are perceived by outsiders as if the dialogue were an attempt to create a new religion.

Pluralism

Pluralism is a highly touted buzzword in Western culture. It is used to convey a variety of meanings, ranging from simple religious diversity to a laissez-faire noninterference in the religious affairs of others. For the purpose of our study, the pluralist is defined as one who seeks to move beyond an exclusivist perspective on religion by affirming the inherent worth of all religions. However, the pluralist does not go as far as the syncretist and does not try to adopt more than one religion as his or her own. The pluralist model concentrates on the similarities within the religions represented in dialogue—a sort of "I'm okay, you're okay" approach to dialogue. Great emphasis is given to the parallel themes and myths. Participants operating with a pluralist attitude toward IFD go beyond polite listening and observation of other traditions to recognizing the validity of the other's faith. There is no effort to convert others or convince them of the superiority of one's own faith. Pluralism may be accurately described as a kind of lowest common denominator of ethical principles from all the religions (McCarthy 1998, 105). Pluralists can also point to the religious differences when comparing their faith with the other. They also withhold their absolute judgment and accept the right of other faith groups to share the public space.

While pluralism is highly valued in Western society, it may not be the most appropriate model for IFD in the Middle Eastern context. The pluralist model has been criticized for ignoring or refusing to deeply engage some of the most difficult issues in dialogue, especially when it is equated with passive forms of tolerance. For example, Barnes (2001, 138) writes, "Certainly a religious world in which truth claims and the significance of difference are buried under a theology of mutual noninterference seems decidedly uninteresting." This model assumes "that every human tradition has in itself all the elements for further growth and development; in a word, it assumes the self-sufficiency of every tradition and seems to deny the need or convenience of mutual learning or the need to walk outside the walls of one particular human tradition. . . . It flatters every one of us to hear that we possess *in nuce* all we need for a full human and religious maturity, but it splits the human family into watertight compartments. . . . It allows growth but not mutation" (Panikkar 1999, 8). In an increasingly globalized world marked by an evolution of both ideas and religion, this sort of strictly cognitive model seems lacking.

Exclusivists may be criticized for their overemphasis on the validity of one particular faith, but pluralists receive criticism for lack of emphasis or depth in any one tradition. Various scholars note that "the most interesting conversation partners are often those who have entered most deeply into the particularities of their own traditions, and thus to base dialogue or interfaith collaboration exclusively on a pluralistic understanding of reality is to cheat dialogue of some of its richest resources" (McCarthy 1998, 104).

Most of the criticism of pluralism is based on the assumption and perceptions that pluralist dialoguers are universalists in their approach to their own and the other's faith. Thus they often lack the knowledge and emphasis on their own particular religious values and avoid dealing with the inherent exclusivist claims in many religions. Another group of scholars equates pluralist religious attitudes with "absolute relativists," who refuse to pass any moral or ethical judgment when interacting with the other. In either case, religious dialoguers in such groups are viewed by exclusivists as unrepresentative of their own faith.

While the pluralist model can be useful in the emphasis on tolerance and acceptance of religious difference, many scholars argue that dialogue must leave behind the theology of pluralism and concentrate on a postmodern mode of dialogue. Such a postmodern dialogue requires a theology *of* dialogue rather than a theology *for* dialogue (Barnes 2001, 135). This postmodern mode of dialogue brings us to our final religious attitude: transformation.

Transformative Dialogue

Many veterans of IFD may not fit into the categories of exclusivism, syncretism, or pluralism—for them the dialogue itself has become a form of religious expression. Scholars have suggested that the primary distinction between IFD and other identity-based dialogues is that the interfaith dialogue becomes a religious experience in itself. Michael Anthony Barnes (2001, 139) writes, "Dialogue . . . is not a contribution to or a reflection on religious experience; it is religious experience. This praxis is the most theologically promising aspect of the wider engagement with the postmodern condition." The most successful forms of IFD reach beyond a merely cognitive, academic understanding of difference as participants begin to experience a sense of interdependence with people of faith. Sharing faith experiences allows for the enrichment, as well as the challenging, of participants' personal faiths. There is a sense, as one writer puts it, of "mutual interpenetration without the loss of the proper peculiarities of each religiousness" (Panikkar 1999, 9).

Transformative dialogue recognizes the increasing interdependence of a globalized world in a way that other models do not. Being a person of faith, of any faith, creates a powerful link to the larger community across the globe, to which religion acts as a governing principle. To dialogue through religious identity is to see the world through a particular lens, to believe in particular governing principles that are the same regardless of which faith a person practices. "It looks as if we are today all intertwined, and that without these particular religious links, my own religion would be incomprehensible for me and even impossible" (Panikkar 1999, 9). Without a conception of what it means to not be a Hindu or a Jew, one cannot conceive of what it means to be included in either of these groups. We are, in the end, defined as much by what we are not as we are defined by what we are.

Participants with a transformative attitude toward dialogue seek to honor the differences in faith at the same time as they recognize similarities. "Believers do not want to be accused (especially in an age of 'civilizational conflict' and growing nervousness about American 'empire') of imposing their religious or philosophical worldviews on others. But at the same time, no one wants to experience censorship or otherwise find oneself forced by conventions of liberalism to 'translate' one's voice into a secular tongue" (Brink 2003, 14). The balance is a delicate one, but one given continual attention within the transformative dialogue.

One expectation of transformative IFD is that participants will, in some way, behave differently after the dialogue. The participants in the dialogue are "converted" to a new version of their own faiths. As differing ideas about the nature of religious expression are exchanged, a new kind of shared truth emerges. This does not require a complete transformation of personality, but participants should leave the dialogue slightly altered—better informed or more compassionate towards the other party. Transformative dialogue goes beyond mere tolerance of the other by inviting participants into a deeper form of openness to one another.

The above description of transformative dialogue can also take place in a secular context. However, the unique feature of the interfaith setting is the fact that participants are motivated as well as engaged in the process, with their religious identity as their primary point of reference.

IFD PROCESS AND CONTENT: COGNITIVE VERSUS AFFECTIVE

Another significant way to classify IFD is by the subject matter that it seeks to address. Dialogue can be widely classified into one of two categories: cognitive or affective (Hanson, 1992). Cognitive dialogue primarily compares religious traditions, seeking to learn more about other faiths and the nature of religion as a whole. Affective dialogue centers on building relationships and concentrates on participants' sharing stories.

Cognitive models center on information exchange. Each participant or each faith shares basic facts about their religion in an attempt to dispel misconceptions. Emphasis is placed on a more historical or academic approach to information. Cognitive dialogue is often conducted by scholars and academics. Such dialogues prefer to stay solely in the realm of religion and limit the topics to questions and discussions of spirituality and religious practice. Cognitive dialogue has also been called doctrinal scientific dialogue, as its primary goal is to objectively examine and compare religious doctrine (Kolvenbach et al. 1999).

The theory behind cognitive dialogue is that each faith group must first have correct information about other religions for there to be peace. The assumption in such a process of interfaith meeting is that when religious beliefs and their meaning are understood through information exchange, participants can formulate their perceptions and behaviors toward the others based on more objective grounds. Cognitive dialogue does not necessarily see individual stories as irrelevant, but it places a higher priority on the exchange of "factual" information. "There is no pure dialectical dialogue. When two persons enter into dialogue, in spite of all attempts to keep the 'personal' to a bare minimum, it emerges all along. We never have an encounter of pure ideas" (Panikkar 1999, 30). Cognitive dialogue therefore does not dismiss the personal stories of participants, but emphasizes the exchange of theological information, seeing it as a route to peacemaking. Addressing the need for information exchange, Cardinal Arinze (2002, 68) writes, "To be sure, goodwill is needed among the followers of the various religions. But this is not enough. If caricatures and incorrect ideas of the other religions exist, practical steps should be taken to right the situation. A planned study of the other religion is needed if relationships are not to stagnate at the superficial level of generalizations and clichés."

Affective dialogue encourages participants to share personal stories and compare narratives that often go beyond religion. These dialogues leave the field wide open and allow discussion of politics or conflict as well. The goal in affective dialogue varies. Some participants may hope to deepen their own spiritual lives and value the opportunity for self-discovery that dialogue offers. In comparing cognitive and affective dialogue, Panikkar (1999, xviii) writes, "All this is very complex, but intrareligious dialogue transcends the purely sociological and historical levels. . . . It is, in a word, a constitutive element of Man, who is a knot in a net of relationships, that is, a person—not an isolated individual, conscious atom, or mere number—within an undifferentiated democratic complex. It is our human nature that beckons to discover within ourselves the whole human world and also the entire reality."

Affective dialogue reaches beyond information exchange to help participants find the other within themselves. While comparing theological similarities and differences may be important, affective dialogue believes that participants must reach further. "The dialogical dialogue challenges us on a much deeper level than the dialectical one. . . . With the dialectical dialogue we can only reach the 'it is' aspect of the real and cannot be in full communication with other subjects and their most intimate convictions. With the dialectical dialogue, we may discuss religious doctrines once we have clarified the context, but we need the dialogical dialogue to discuss beliefs as those conscious attitudes we have in face of the ultimate issues of our existence and life" (Panikkar 1999, 38).

Cognitive models of dialogue alone are limiting, because they do not address wider cultural, economic, and political phenomena. The cognitive model does not adequately acknowledge that participants have multifaceted identities that extend beyond their membership in a particular faith. The nature of the dialogue will be continually challenged and shaped by factors outside the dialogue itself. "Our future relations will be determined not just by impressive statements at international dialogue conferences. Our future will, to a very large degree, be determined by secular developments, perhaps couched in somewhat religious language" (Bijlefeld 2001, 168).

The format of personal storytelling is one way for participants to balance the affective and cognitive models of dialogue. Storytelling encourages participants to express their feelings, thoughts, and beliefs from a personal point of view and allows past hurts to be gradually revealed. IFD as a tool for reconciliation works best when participants are allowed to voice their confusion, sense of victimization, or interest through the vehicle of storytelling. Storytelling respects the fact that dialogue is not a linear process and helps to accent the depth of the different traditions. The clash of nonnegotiable beliefs may be lessened when presented in the context of one person's story. Joseph Liechty (2002, 92–96) uses the term "mitigation" to describe a way of dealing with nonnegotiable beliefs that avoids offense without ignoring important differences. Storytelling is one form of mitigation.

Storytelling allows participants to articulate the values and concepts that lie behind the particular religious figures or religious narratives that they most revere. Instead of a debate over the role of Isaac versus Ishmael, participants are able to reflect on how they personally engage their faith tradition. When the dialogue is framed in terms of common values, such as truth, justice, and peace, the differences in historical narrative or theological interpretation seem less divisive. Abu-Nimer (2002, 20–21) addresses this concept with the term "secondary language": "Secondary language helps participants discover their similarities and creates an atmosphere of trust that encourages meaningful interaction. Secondary language gets participants moving toward the process of exploring religious differences as well as political positions."

THEOLOGICAL ABRAHAMIC DIALOGUE

Theologically based dialogue, a common form of cognitive dialogue, offers participants the chance to highlight religious similarities and differences in the faiths represented in the dialogue session. Often a sacred text from each religion is examined as a way of instigating conversation about commonalities or points of contention. Theologically based dialogue is a common form of Abrahamic dialogue, as all three share an identity as "people of the book"—a reference to the fact that all three faiths respect scriptures and sacred texts as primary sources of inspiration and devotion. In fact, many of the scriptures are even shared, such as the Torah/Taurat, Psalms/Zabur, and Gospels/Injil (Kateregga and Shenk 1980, 25–26). Theologically based dialogue provides an opening for participants to learn more about other faiths by questioning and interacting with others through the process of learning diverse religious scriptural interpretations. This model has a number of strengths, one being that it often provides the most fertile starting point for heavy discussions that draw upon participants' most cherished beliefs. Also, knowledge of the shared ideas and interpretations brings confidence and trust to the dialogue.

The most profound concept shared by Muslims, Christians, and Jews is a belief in ethical monotheism and the worship of one Creator. This God has been called by different names and worshipped in different ways throughout history, but Yahweh/God/Allah remains at the very heart of all three traditions. Though most followers of these faiths do not formally recognize or utilize the language of the other faiths (that is, most Christians do not call God by the name of Yahweh or Allah), almost all members of the Abrahamic faiths share similar beliefs regarding the qualities of the divine: creative, merciful, just, omnipotent, omniscient, and eternal.

In light of their commitments to ethical monotheism, Jews, Christians, and Muslims strongly renounce idolatry. Speaking at a conference of the U.S. Interreligious Committee for Peace in the Middle East, one rabbi said, "We share . . . the negation of idolatry. If there is any one thing we most share as communities, it is the deep negation of idolatry. We can ask, what is the idolatry of the Middle East? It's the idolatry of power, of greed, and of everyone claiming that he has the whole truth in his pocket" (Halbertal 1990, 12).

Jews, Muslims, and Christians share an identity as fellow pilgrims on a path—a path that all three faiths understand to be profoundly rooted in concepts of truth and peace. Adherents of the Abrahamic faiths believe that right conduct is essential and that sacred texts hold instructions about how to live an ethical, just life that is pleasing to God. Jews, Christians, and Muslims share the belief that God wants them to live a life full of respect for justice, peace, and human relationships. All three believe in the validity of revelation as a sign from God and struggle to maintain unity in spite of splits in their populations (Reform/Orthodox, Shiite/Sunni, Protestant/Catholic).

The Abrahamic faiths also share common frameworks and a belief that their faith is rooted in a historical tradition. This history gave birth to creeds, worship practices, prayer, and mysticism in all three faiths. These religious acts, though expressed differently in each tradition, are central tenets of life for the believer and are based around a common philosophy of devotion. Community is an important element in worship and reverence.

Given the common texts, it is not surprising that the three religions revere common religious figures. At the heart of all three traditions is the figure of Abraham. Bruce Feiler has written a book, exploring the figure of Abraham in the Abrahamic faiths, called *Abraham: A Journey to the Heart of Three Faiths*. This book has prompted discussion groups across the country in the form of "Abrahamic salons," which are a rudimentary form of IFD. Other prominent figures acknowledged by all three faiths are Adam, Lot, Jacob, Jonah, Moses, David, Elijah, Zachariah, Ezekial, Noah, Jesus, Joseph, Isaac, Ishmael, Aaron, and Job.

One of the stumbling blocks of theological dialogues is that even as an interfaith group explores commonalities, it must be wary of assuming that everyone in the group understands a seemingly similar concept in the same way. What appears to be a commonality on the surface may be a difference in reality. Even though the three faiths share many theological beliefs, frameworks, and understandings, some of these similarities hold within them the paradox of deeper differences. All may agree that God acts directly in the stories of human beings, but the way those stories are told and understood may vary greatly.

One of the areas in which this stumbling block is most apparent is with regard to the figure of Jesus. Jews either reject the figure of Jesus altogether or acknowledge a historical figure but do not see him as a prophet or deity. Muslims and Christians both revere Jesus, but that does not mean that they have shared understandings. Christians believe that Jesus was one part of a triune God and was both human and divine. For Christians, Jesus' death on the cross and later resurrection was atonement for the sins of humanity. Muslims do not believe that Jesus actually died on the cross or that his death could offer atonement. Atonement is not a necessity in Islam because there is no concept of original sin. Each person is responsible to God only for the sins they personally commit. Muslims believe someone who resembled Jesus was crucified, but that the actual Jesus ascended to heaven. For Muslims, Jesus was a human prophet, not divine, and, as such, the concept of the Trinity is confusing and meaningless. Both Jews and Muslims see the construction of the Trinity as a barrier in Christian monotheism (for more, see Bennett 2001).

Another significant point of departure is the role and person of the prophet Mohammed. Many Jews and Christians do not acknowledge the figure of the prophet Mohammed at all in their theological framework. The lack of reciprocity in this nonrecognition of Mohammed is troubling to Muslims, who freely accept Jewish prophets as well as Jesus as profoundly significant religious figures. "If Islam can bring within its fold not only Jesus, but many other prophets, the Muslims wonder why the Christians cannot accept Prophet Mohammed as a true Prophet who brought the same message from the same divine source" (Ali 1998, 45).

Another stumbling block in theologically based dialogue is that the different Abrahamic faiths have different expectations about each other's texts. Christians assume that Jews will be familiar with the entire Old Testament. Jews resent the term "Old Testament" and see the Pentateuch as the primary textual source. Muslims often have little knowledge of the Bible and expect it to be like the Quran—a direct record of what God revealed to prophets, not an eclectic collection of letters, history, and poems (Thomas 2001, 339). Pannikar (1999, 113) writes, "Paradoxically, quotations from the Holy Scriptures are not suited to interreligious discourse. We should not take our own premises as the basis for others."

Ultimately, IFD based on theology or texts may be a valuable part of the interfaith experience. However, approaches to dialogue that take into account larger moral and ethical questions rather than focusing solely on theology may be more pragmatic and useful for creating greater understanding and tolerance. David Scott (1995, 153) notes that "in a more profound sense, if we view religion as ultimately instrumental rather than definitional in conceptual terms, then it is precisely instrumental/transformational areas of practice and conduct that need to be developed, whereas doctrine may in spiritual terms no longer be the actual central issue anyway." Dialogue for peacemaking must address larger issues than the mere theological. "It is a dialogue of persons, not a reading of texts. Persons can answer back in a way which texts may not. Moreover, they may do so in unexpected and unpredictable ways; the relationship established between people is rarely, if ever, symmetrical. The tradition of hermeneutical thinking in Western philosophy, for which reading a text is the model of interpretation of the 'other,' tends to forget this" (Barnes 2001, 149). To contribute toward significant peacemaking, dialogue must reach beyond each faith's sacred stories into the stories, triumphs, and tragedies of the participants themselves.

THE ISSUE OF POLITICS IN IFD

One of the most difficult aspects of conducting dialogue in a region marked by conflict is deciding to what extent politics can be or should be addressed in the dialogue setting. David Smock (2002, 9) writes, "The justice issues that lie behind conflict must be central to dialogue. Dialogue that contributes to peace must confront the political issues that divide the communities. . . . Rarely is conflict between two religious groups simply a matter of theological difference or religious misunderstanding. Politics and power and military aggression are usually deeply intertwined with religious difference." While IFD is powerful and potentially transformative, participants are always aware that dialogue alone will not solve enormous and complex political crises. As our five case studies demonstrate, the issue of politics almost always simmers just beneath the surface of any dialogue. Some dialogue facilitators try to mute this topic by establishing ground rules that steer participants away from raising contentious political issues. The impact of the political reality on the day-to-day lives of the participants and their political orientations are often deliberately excluded from the meetings or agenda. Other facilitators allow for the discussion of politics, provided that it occurs within the context of personal storytelling. The Middle East has been characterized by a history of the deep, organic mixing of politics and religion. Throughout history, the religious identities of Jews, Muslims, and Christians in the Middle East have been politically employed both to justify wars and to promote tolerance.[2] To continuously ask participants to talk about religion and completely ignore their own sociopolitical realities seems counterproductive in terms of promoting political changes to address violence and achieve justice.

While politics is the most contentious issue to arise in the interfaith dialogue context, avoiding such issues—especially global ones—is not always possible or entirely desirable. In Jordan, for example, politics has been used in the context of IFD to issue a common statement or position on an international issue, such as the Palestinian question, the status of Jerusalem, the September 11 attacks, or the war in Iraq. Such statements aim to broadcast a political solidarity among the participants, regardless of their religious affiliation. Focusing on a common cause removes the discussion from the personal-individual level to the more general and thus releases the stress that can accompany interfaith encounters. Similar patterns were identified in other interfaith discussions in the Arab context (Lebanon, Egypt, and intrafaith Palestinian groups).

CONFESSION AND FORGIVENESS THROUGH IFD

Jews, Christians, and Muslims believe in a God that is both just and forgiving. This belief is the foundation for another form of affective dialogue: the confession/forgiveness approach. The first phase in this model is the confession phase, which invites participants to share personal losses and tragedies from the conflict as well as acknowledge their personal responsibility for conflict. The second phase, forgiveness, requires a gesture of pardon from the wronged party. For those who see dialogue as a tool for fostering reconciliation in divided societies, both confession and forgiveness are necessary.

Confession

For a reconciliation to be born out of dialogue, it is crucial that issues of justice be addressed. Much painful history has passed between the Abrahamic traditions, and words like "Holocaust," "Crusade," or "Jihad" still fill the air with anxiety and tension. For parties to be rehumanized, the history of prejudice and pain must be acknowledged. "Apology is the acknowledgment of one's misdeeds and the expression of sorrow to one's victim" (Cox and Philpott 2003, 35). For forgiveness and healing to take place, many followers of the Abrahamic faith believe there must be some sort of repentance, that is, admission of guilt (which for many Muslims is a form of justice, too). This does not mean that interfaith participants should personally and directly apologize for acts that they did not personally participate in (that is, one cannot expect a Muslim to apologize for all suicide bombers, or a Christian to apologize for the Crusades). But participants can confess that they have not tried hard enough to reach out to the other or have blamed the other unjustly. Also, for members of the majority or dominant faith groups, it means acknowledging that individually they might have benefited from the power system and structure that emerged as a result of the past oppression and victimization of the other faith groups.

According to this approach to reconciliation, participants must accept moral responsibility for their own individual and collective actions in the past and recognize the hurt that their ancestors in faith may have caused others. An ethic of self-criticism must be fostered within the dialogue group. This self-criticism helps to produce more openness and honesty. Participants will not feel obligated to doggedly defend their faith if others are also self-critical. Cardinal Arinze (2002, 84–85) writes, "Acceptance of fault where it exists, willingness to engage in self-criticism, asking and giving pardon, and willingness to seek reconciliation are virtues badly needed for true and lasting peace."

The confession/forgiveness model occasionally presents difficult questions regarding self-criticism and power. Some scholars question whether being self-critical is only a necessity for those in power and whether such criticism, even internally generated, may make weaker communities feel even more under siege.[3] Often religious or community leaders avoid interfaith encounters precisely because they fear having to undertake a course of self-criticism that could be detrimental to their religious or political career goals. However, other scholars feel that self-criticism builds trust and openness because it involves a greater degree of vulnerability and risk. David Steele (2002, 81) writes, "If participants can acknowledge one another's pain, then they can also be helped to see that someone should be held responsible for inflicting the pain. In a two-sided conflict, for example, when the pain is experienced by people in the other group, then those responsible are likely to be from one's own group."

Forgiveness

For many centuries, the Abrahamic faiths have held oversimplified images of one another that must be replaced with new understanding and communication. Stereotypes and misconceptions must fall away so that visions of a shared future can emerge. Each side must let go of distrust and old prejudices so that both might move into a vulnerable new vision of interdependence. The impact of an act of forgiveness may be immeasurable. Joseph Montville suggests that acknowledgment may be the most crucial part of healing for victims of atrocities (Dyck 2001, 478).

Forgiveness occurs when individuals of both faiths are able to acknowledge and heal individual and collective wounds. Cox and Philpott (2003, 35) write, " . . . forgiveness is the victim's foregoing of all claims to anger, resentment, and payment against the other." Forgiveness does not mean that the wounds of the past have disappeared. It means that the past has been acknowledged and that the participants do not need to dwell in it. As such, forgiveness is not about forgetting. For the families who have lost loved ones, the past will never be forgotten. But the wounds of the past must be addressed, to prevent them from developing into crippling obsessions with revenge over time. Forgiveness requires honest storytelling and a willingness to change old ways of being.

Different faiths may have very different understandings about what forgiveness means. "To be sure, differences abound among and within faith traditions about the meaning of reconciliation and about the relative roles of punishment, forgiveness, apology, atonement, and the practice of these concepts. . . . Still, reconciliation is important in each tradition. It pervades Judaism, in which atonement, central to the Torah, infuses halakhah, the Jewish law, wherein punishment, repentance, and restitution are all arrayed towards restoration. Christianity extends the logic of atonement to God's mercy towards sinners on the cross. In Islam, the Quran's repeated references to Allah's mercy and injunctions to forgiveness imply a restorative logic" (Cox and Philpott 2003, 34). Discussing this concept and its implications may be an important step for interfaith dialogue groups to take together.

The confession approach may be especially appropriate and necessary in intractable and deep-rooted settings such as the Israeli-Palestinian conflict. The two groups need to mourn together all that has been lost—family members, security, peace of mind, property. Marc Gopin (2000, 173) writes, "The losses of one hundred years, for each group, represent an important time span, which generally includes the memories that people have directly from parents and grandparents. It is these memories that must be addressed. . . . It would be powerful indeed if groups of Arabs and Jews . . . would begin, in detail, to mourn what was lost. They must begin to visit the dead together, to bury them together in symbolic ways, to memorialize lost lives and lost homes."

The model of confession and forgiveness works in part due to the nature of conflict and trauma in human psychology. Susan Thistlethwaite (2002) notes, "One of the things trauma does, and terrorist attacks and suicide bombings are designed to [do, is to] produce collective trauma, to make those traumatized draw in upon themselves." Even those who may not directly witness a particular event may share in the collective trauma of the event's aftermath. Thistlethwaite goes on to explain how acknowledgment may address such trauma: "As peace activists, we must study carefully the research done on trauma and on the ways people recover from trauma."

Adopting interfaith processes that lead to acknowledgment, forgiveness, and reconciliation is certainly one of the emerging transformational approaches of peacebuilding.

RITUALS AND IFD

In interreligious settings, rituals are powerful modes of communication and interaction. Values, symbols, and entire meaning systems are often codified in series of rituals. Lisa Schirch (2001) has identified the power of rituals and their potential function and usage in peacebuilding activities. Concepts of justice, forgiveness, and solidarity become physically manifest in the form of rituals. Some scholars have suggested that holding a dialogue is, in and of itself, a ritual. "Dialogue is not about religious experience, it is religious experience. The entry into and the experience of dialogue has about it something of the nature of ritual" (Barnes 2001, 150).

Ritual may involve participating respectfully in one another's spiritual traditions. Such participation in the faith life of the other must be done sincerely and not in a spirit of syncretism. Not all religious rituals are appropriate for an interfaith setting. Some participants may find certain rituals uncomfortable, while other rituals may not invite the participation of all, especially when they are exclusive or introduced without much explanation of their religious meaning and significance. Great care and preparation should be taken beforehand to avoid such awkward encounters. (For more details on how ritual can be misunderstood and contribute to misconception, see Abu-Nimer 2002).

Using common prayer as a ritual has potential benefits as well as pitfalls. In theory, addressing prayers to a common God can be an overwhelmingly powerful experience. Ideally, in the Abrahamic circles, joint prayer is assumed to help individuals and groups to focus on their similarities and connections, to discover the realities that bind them together as brothers and sisters of the same family. Joint prayer allows members of the three faith groups, instead of being torn by conflicts and divisions, to step away from arguing about their beliefs and instead focus on the common need to practice their religions.

However, in practice, communal prayer may be more delicate. Even if all the participants are members of Abrahamic faiths and practice a monotheistic religion, choices about content of shared prayers can still present difficult dilemmas. Cardinal Arinze (2002, 97) remarks, "Even presuming that the participants all hold to strict monotheism and pray to the same God, there still remain the problems of the content of the prayer and especially of the real danger of scandal that would be caused by the appearance or danger of relativism or syncretism, whether real or merely apparent." A common way to avoid such dangers seems to be to avoid interfaith prayer and instead opt for a shared silence in which participants may choose to pray in whatever manner they are most comfortable. This allows differences to be respected rather than denied. Another approach adopted by many interfaith groups has been to allow or create the space for each faith to pray using its own particular language, symbols, and rituals without imposing on others in the group to join in.

Communal ritual grieving may be especially powerful in places that have been torn by conflict. Rabbi Marc Gopin (2000) suggests the Jewish practice of *aveilus* as a model. "Aveilus is the ritual process of expressing the death of a loved one. That loved one is a part of oneself, one's history, one's very being. . . . Aveilus is the ability to acknowledge loss unabashedly, to watch the lost thing or person buried in the ground, especially to engage in burial yourself and to feel the full horror of it. . . . The experience of aveilus means that one is moved by the community and one's relationship to God toward a slow and steady recovery from the loss." This practice could be modified and used as a powerful ritual of both loss and healing.

The dialogue group may choose to create and perform its own rituals of unity and celebration. Elements may be borrowed from various traditions to create a "third culture" (Abu-Nimer 2002) that is comfortable for all faiths in a dialogue. When words fail, rituals can often be the bridge of understanding between the gulfs of hurt or confusion that may arise in IFD. Ritual provides a special identity to the group and offers a way of building relationships. Lisa Schirch (2001, 154) writes, "Rituals are special contexts conducive to the symbolic transformation of identity and the reframing of conflict toward sustainable, coexisting relationships." Ritual can be a way of recognizing, encouraging, and celebrating the transformation that may occur in the context of a dialogue.

INTERFAITH DIALOGUE FOR ACTION AND ADVOCACY

As with other dialogue groups (ethnic, cultural, or racial), one criticism of IFD is that it does not accomplish anything tangible. For this reason, the action and advocacy model emerges, which focuses on undertaking a common project with those of another faith. This model may be the newest development in the IFD movement. "What is new at this point in the modern history of interreligious dialogue is not pluralism itself or even the awareness of it, but the degree to which interfaith exchanges are linked with the global effort to address problems of human suffering and injustice" (McCarthy 1998, 98).

An Institute of Peace summary of Abrahamic dialogue efforts discovered "a number of participants were concerned that an overemphasis on talking would diminish the importance of undertaking joint activities together. It was believed that engaging in activities and projects with one another was a more reliable manner in which to build trust and mutual understanding than could be achieved solely through discussion or debate" (USIP 2002, 1). Charles Kimball (1991, 74) concurs, suggesting that dialogue may be especially successful when participants work together to address common social concerns, such as drug problems in the community or prison work. Cardinal Arinze (2002, 74) writes, "It is a positive step for peace when people of differing religions undertake joint projects. The more people work together, the better they will accept one another."

One of the strengths of the action model is that it may provide a potent starting point for groups that have a difficult time communicating with one another and may provide a means of balancing power relations. Abu-Nimer (2002) notes both of these potential results: "In addition to empowering the religious minority, a collaboration such as a concrete development project allows members to interact safely and default to an action or a task when their ideological or theological differences are at an impasse. Also, the successful outcome of any concrete project will contribute to the development of minority communities and will provide minority participants with much-needed credibility and support for their efforts to engage in or attend an interfaith dialogue forum."

Used alone, the action/advocacy model is not a form of dialogue. However, it can be quite effective when coupled with actual interfaith conversations. Kolvenbach and others (1999) identify action as one of seven prototypes of dialogue. They identify "practical dialogue," in which participants strive to carry out a common action or project, as one of the most basic forms of dialogue, from which all other dialogue should proceed. Marc Gopin (2002, 44) writes, "It is critical that religious dialogue be an act as well as a verbal communication. That act must be honorable. The act of dialogue must

0719580

consider and anticipate what constitutes civility and dignity for all the cultures in question."

In the early 1990s, the Social Summit in Copenhagen and the United Nations Conference on Population and Development in Cairo were opportunities for Muslims and Christians in particular to utilize the advocacy model through Christian and Muslim NGOs. In the April 2000 Pontifical Council for Interreligious Dialogue survey, Michael Fitzgerald (2000, 5) writes, "The problems of this world—drought, disease, poverty, the displacement of persons—do not respect any religious divide. People of all religions, including Muslims and Christians, are equally affected. There are vast fields here open for Christian-Muslim cooperation. There are other domains, too, where Christians and Muslims are joining together, but where more could be done for defense of life, care for drug addicts, care of the handicapped, concern for the aged and dying."

The greatest strength in the action/advocacy model may be that it allows members of different religions to transcend the conflict of religion to address larger social concerns. In addressing such concerns, the universality of the human experience is highlighted.

The above attempts to conceptualize the processes of interfaith interaction fall short of explaining the actual process experienced by a person who participates in a long-term and intensive awareness-raising dialogical process that can result in a new framing of the individual's own cognitive approaches and feelings about the faith of the other. Currently, the field of interfaith studies lacks serious and comprehensive examination or identification of the concrete developmental stages experienced by interfaith participants. What happens to the awareness (attitudes and behaviors) of a participant who is changed by the experience of interfaith dialogue?

In intercultural communication, such a developmental process of stages has been developed and tested in various settings. Its validity and applicability across cultural situations has been confirmed by many empirical studies. The model offers the most comprehensive view of the possible developmental stages for a person to transform from an ethnocentric into an ethnorelative perspective. The following section explores and discusses the possibilities for adopting such a developmental model into interfaith dialogue groups and into the interreligious peacebuilding processes.

TOWARD AN IFD MODEL: FROM A RELIGIOCENTRIC TO A RELIGIORELATIVIST PERSPECTIVE[4]

Frequently, attempts at conceptualizing interfaith activities fail to explain the psychological and cognitive shifts that occur as the result of effective IFD. This section proposes a model to categorize the type of attitudinal and perceptional changes that often result from interfaith peacebuilding interventions. Unfortunately, there are few models that explain developmentally how individuals and groups move from a perspective that focuses on the need to protect one's own religious identity to an orientation that recognizes differences between one's identity group and the other, yet supports cooperative interaction and relations. Further, there is a paucity of relevant theoretical models for guiding peacebuilding interventions aimed at different religious identity groups in conflict. Recently, however, Hammer, Bennett, and Wiseman (2003), based on Bennett's (1993) Developmental Model of Intercultural Sensitivity (DMIS), have proposed a modified model of intercultural competence development that has direct relevance to peacebuilding between religious identity groups in contexts of conflict. The DMIS, as a theoretical framework, incorporates religious identity development into the experience of cultural/religious differences.

The core assumption of this model of intercultural relations is that the complexity of one's experience of cultural difference determines one's capacity to engage more competently in intercultural interactions. By extension, the more complex one's experience of religious identity group differences, the greater one's ability to engage in more cooperative, peaceful interactions across religious lines. It is important to note that the development of intercultural competence and improved cross-religious group relations is not based on the "surrender" of one's own cultural or religious identity or practices. Rather, the development of such competence is focused on one's ability to understand the other in more complex ways.

The DMIS identifies specific cultural worldviews through which individuals and groups experience cultural/religious differences. Based on research conducted in the development of the Intercultural Development Inventory (a psychometrically valid and reliable measure of an individual's orientation toward cultural difference), Hammer and Bennett (1998) argue that one's religious/ cultural worldview orientations are considered "ethnocentric" (i.e., one's own culture is experienced as central to reality), "ethnorelative" (i.e., one's own cultural worldview is experienced in the context of other cultural perspectives), or "transitional" (i.e., one's worldview is developmentally "in transition" from more ethnocentric perspectives to more ethnorelative viewpoints).[5]

Applying this model to religious identities, we might distinguish between religiorelativism and religiocentrism. A religiorelative person is firm in his or her belief that others have the right to practice their religion, even if it contradicts his or her own set of religious beliefs. A person with such an orientation is less likely to engage in violence or discriminatory actions against others. In contrast, a religiocentric person views his or her religious viewpoint as an absolute truth and therefore is likely to deny other religions' "truth," leaving no room for the validity of other religious practices. A person with such a worldview is more likely to dehumanize, exclude, and discriminate against other religious groups and individuals. Often, as a result of negative and destructive exposure to conflict and war, religiocentric beliefs are exacerbated and may be translated into violence against the enemy. There are conflict-resolution and peacebuilding activities that can assist peace workers in such settings to help religiocentric persons transform their beliefs into religiorelative ones. To address religious exclusion and religiocentrism, two possible frameworks exist: the interreligious encounter and interfaith activities.

The following discussion attempts to capture the dynamics and process of change that take place when a religiocentric person is exposed to and challenged with a different set of beliefs and religions. The process that will be described is adapted mainly to the Israeli-Palestinian conflict; however, such processes have been observed in intercultural and interracial relations in the United States and elsewhere.[6]

FROM RELIGIOCENTRIC TO RELIGIORELATIVE: A MODEL FOR RELIGIOUS TRANSFORMATION

A person with a religiocentric perspective has several reactions to the "other religion." However, such a view's core characteristic is the inability to recognize, respect, or accept the validity of the other religious beliefs as "truth" in any sense. In the religiocentric framework, there are two common worldviews.

Denial/Defense (DD) Orientation

The DD worldview simplifies and polarizes cultural/religious differences. This orientation ranges from a tendency toward disinterest and avoidance of difference (denial) to a tendency toward an "us versus them" paradigm, in which one's own group is viewed as superior. Individuals who deny other religions tend to live and die in their own narrow and closed religious communities. These individuals experience other religions as less complex and "real" than their own. This tendency can arise either because of physical separation or because of social, political, or religious arrangements that prohibit contact with other religions. For example, in the war zone areas of Mindanao in the Philippines, some Christian and Muslim communities forbid their children from entering each other's holy sites or engaging even in simple inquiry about the other's religion.[7] Although such socialization processes are extremely functional in protecting against religious conversion, they contribute to an extreme form of religiocentrism. Similarly, in Lebanon, the sectarian divisions between communities have functioned for many generations as a barrier to learning in-depth about the others.

The DD worldview under conflict conditions can push groups and individuals to attempt violent elimination of the other religions, or simply to isolate themselves from the others. In an interfaith setting in Mindanao, a Muslim youth shared with the group the dilemma she faced when she began working in a Catholic Christian institute for dialogue: she was unable to look at Christ on the cross. Every day, when she passed the crucifix, she turned her face away. Gradually, through conversation with her religious elders and colleagues, she accepted that she would not lose her Islamic identity by looking at the crucifix.[8]

Denial of the other's religious identity can be manifested through policies or institutions. In Israel, examples of institutionalized denial include the post-1948 removal of Muslim religious sites (such as cemeteries and mosques), governmental policies and rules segregating Muslims and Christians from Jews in residential areas, and the de facto policy arrangements in place to preserve the Jewish nature of the state (Arabs are not allowed to purchase or use state land). In Egypt, many Christian Copts hide the Christian cross or a similar symbol somewhere on their person, or tattoo it on the insides of their arms or wrists as an exclusive identification mark that asserts unique religious identity, yet is, in most cases, invisible to outsiders.

For those who refuse to see the value of differences that exist in other religions, participation in IFD may provide information that allows them to safely see the similarities between their faith and another faith. IFD is especially effective if employed within a safe and open learning environment by a teacher who is trusted by both religious communities. Under these conditions, religiocentric Muslims can discover that there are Jews who actually tolerate Islam and admire the concept of justice in Islam, and religiocentric Jews can discover, via conversations with other Jews, that Christian presence in the Holy Land will not reduce the holiness and the Jewishness of the place. The primary objectives at this stage of IFD are to expose the participants to the values, norms, and rituals of the other in safe and nonthreatening ways, and to raise awareness of the fact that other religions have valid religious beliefs and rituals that are both similar to and different from one's own.

To pave the way for constructive contact with the other, intra-Muslim, intra-Jewish, and intra-Christian forums and conversations can address ways to relate to the other groups in Israel and Palestine, and programs can be particularly targeted to religious circles that deny the existence of the other in exclusivist ways.

The DD orientation may also focus on "defense" against others, in which differences are recognized but are polarized in terms of good and bad, right or wrong. This defense emphasis within the DD orientation can be seen, for example, in situations where the believers are aware of the other religious differences in beliefs, rituals, and practices, but develop either a superior or inferior set of reactions. Manifestations of this attitude include sentiments like "We, the Jews, are the chosen people," "Islam is the only complete religion," and "There is no salvation outside the Church." All these statements reflect the perspective that one's own faith is superior and that, therefore, one's own religious group deserves special privileges and benefits.

Another ethnocentric worldview is that of reversal. In reversal, an individual (or group) experiences a conversion, such that he or she reverses the "us" and "them" polarization and considers the other religion superior. This reversal orientation is uncritical toward the newly adopted religious viewpoint and overly critical toward the original religious affiliation. Conversion, it should be noted, often is undertaken from a religiorelative stance. However, when religious conversion is undertaken in such a way that converts relate to their new faith as a superior way and belittle their previous faith, the individual remains within a religiocentric mind-set. For example, a Muslim convert in Mindanao was participating in a Christian-Muslim IFD group and began describing the advantages of the Islamic faith over the Christian faith, citing unresolved and contradictory theological issues in Christianity.

Since the primary source of religiocentrism is the belief that one's own religion is better, more complete, or more authentic than the others, IFD can broaden the worldview. Some helpful frameworks for establishing such broader awareness might include an exploration of stories from the Bible and Quran (such as those of Abraham, Joseph, and Mary), or focus on practices and values that exist in all three traditions (such as fasting, sacrificing, and justice). For a person stuck in a DD framework, discovering commonalities among the three Abrahamic traditions may reduce both the tendency to exclude the other and the possibility of dehumanizing the other based on religious superiority.

The "Transition" Phase: Minimization

Minimization is a worldview that highlights cultural commonality and universal values through an emphasis on similarity (assuming that people from other cultures are basically "like us") and/or universalism (applying one's own values and beliefs to other cultures in ways that do not take into consideration the cultural context of the other). Minimization permits cooperative relations to exist between divergent communities to the extent that commonalities exist between members. However, minimization alone cannot accommodate cultural differences when those differences are important.

Minimization functions as a transitional orientation that acts as a bridge to a more ethnorelativist experience of differences. However, because this phase is transitional, it can prove unstable as a worldview if conflict conditions escalate into more polarized circumstances. Under these conditions, individuals who are in minimization may return to a DD worldview as a coping strategy for dealing with differences that are perceived to threaten one's own community.

Minimization as a transitional phase reaction is characterized by a realization of the differences and contradictions in beliefs and rituals between one's own faith and the other, and by a conscious or subconscious choice to ignore them in interfaith interaction. In the Abrahamic interfaith setting, minimization is most recognized by the tendency to focus on the similarities (including harmony, love, and peace) and to avoid confronting the core differences in theological or hermeneutical approaches to conflicting issues, such as Jewish-Muslim-Christian relations in different historical contexts. Dialogue participants who hold this transitional perspective tend to ignore their own religious differences by highlighting the abstract, transcendent commonalities expressed in classic statements like "We are all the children of God," "We are all the children of Abraham," or "We are Brothers and Sisters, members of the same family."

In such interfaith interactions, a major obstacle is that often those who issue such statements have not yet recognized the equal rights of the other and do not view the other religion as an equal spiritual path. In addition, when such individuals are confronted with a fourth religious tradition that does not necessarily reside in the Middle East (such as Buddhism or Hinduism), they tend to default into their superior or defensive mode of interaction with other religions. In an IFD group in Jerusalem, several members refused to accept the Buddhists and Hindus into the group, arguing that "dialoguing with such groups provides them with legitimacy in the Holy Land."[9]

Minimization was the most prevalent stage for participants in IFD in the five societies examined by this research. Most of the interviewees had adopted this mind-set and felt comfortable operating in it, especially if they were members of the majority religious group. In Jordan, Egypt, and Palestine, interviewees emphasized the need to focus on similarities when dealing with Christians. Most Israeli Jewish interviewees also adopted similar patterns in their interfaith perspective.

For individuals who insist on emphasizing only religious similarities, the starting points are their own belief systems. They begin from their own beliefs and seek the same beliefs among others—for example, the belief in one God —remaining blind to the different nuances of the supposedly identical belief, and unaware of their blindness. In the minimization phase, one's own faith is the measure of all others, and the inherent contradictions between faiths are brushed aside.

To raise the awareness of such individuals and help them to recognize the validity of religious differences and develop an appreciation for the vast range of religious beliefs, IFD activities should be designed to focus on exploring the different meanings behind similar practices and on unbridgeable gaps between various faiths. Such a shift might require, for example, a Muslim or Jew to understand the concept of the Holy Trinity from a Christian perspective and be able to respect it as a theological principle. For a Christian or a Jew, a shift in awareness might mean respecting Islamic belief in the Quran as the word of God and in the Prophet Mohammad as the messenger who transmitted and recited the word of God. For Christians and Muslims, a shift in awareness might mean respecting the particular understanding within Judaism of the "return of the Messiah" and the centrality of the land of Israel to the faith. Interreligious encounters and conferences focusing on an in-depth examination of religious differences are a possible first-step framework to achieve such awareness. For instance, at a conference sponsored by the Interreligious Coordinating Council in Jerusalem, participants focused on the concept of martyrdom in the Abrahamic religions and explored the meaning of Islamic Jihad as compared to martyrdom within other religions.[10]

An Acceptance/Adaptation (AA) Worldview

In contrast to religiocentrism, religiorelativism establishes minimal ground for peaceful coexistence by making violence against other religious practices and beliefs unthinkable. On an institutional level, acceptance of differences could be regarded as the foundation for the Ottoman Empire "millet" system, which granted non-Muslim minorities an autonomous religious status (Masters 2001), or the historical period in Muslim Spain in which the three Abrahamic traditions peacefully coexisted. In fact, in many Arab communities, there is a typical statement regarding the historical religiorelative coexistence between Christian and Muslims: *Lakum dinakum wa lee dini* ("You have your own religion and I have my own"). An AA worldview is able to comprehend and accommodate complex cultural and religious differences and is therefore religiorelative. The religiorelative worldview can range from acceptance (the ability to recognize and respect patterns of difference between one's own and other cultural or religious communities) to adaptation (the ability to alter perception and behavior to appropriately suit different religious contexts). Adaptation involves an ability to cognitively frame-shift (take on the perspective of the other) and behaviorally code-shift (intentionally change behavior in response to cultural/religious context). The religiorelative believer does not pass a negative judgment on other religious beliefs or practices, but recognizes the different religious and spiritual values, norms, rituals, and behaviors; understands their meaning; and accepts them as they are in their religious and cultural context.

The acceptance mode provides interfaith dialoguers with at least a minimal level of tolerance of differences. A focus on acceptance in the AA worldview might take the form of a Muslim believer who does not argue against or attempt to negate the Christian belief that Christ was crucified and does not belittle the kosher practice in Judaism, but accepts such beliefs as valid and understands their spiritual reasoning, consequences, and historical context. In the AA worldview, no negative judgment is passed on people who believe differently. For example, a Jew accepts the Muslim belief of *Isra' wal Mi'raj,* or the Miracle of Transcendence, in which Prophet Mohammed ascended heavenward in one night from Mecca to the Al Aqsa mosque in Jerusalem. Acceptance means recognizing that the belief is valid for Muslims and understanding its consequences in terms of the Muslim *ummah's* relations to Jerusalem and the Holy Land.

An emphasis on adaptation within an AA orientation occurs in two primary ways: cognitive frame-shifting and behavioral code-shifting. Religious frame-shifting occurs when the believer is actually ready to experience (even just temporarily) another spiritual path and is able to understand (even for a brief period) the other's religious meaning, context, and points of reference. An example of an adaptational reaction is a Muslim who agrees to participate in a prayer with Christians or Jews in their houses of prayer and is willing to spiritually experience Christians' or Jews' unique ways of connecting to God.

Religious adaptation is categorized by behavioral code-shifting, in which one person develops two religious frames of reference. Spirituality can be experienced and lived through two religious paths. The person can operate in both religions and understand, accept, and internalize the religious meanings and codes in both of them. For example, at one of the interfaith workshops at the Summer Peacebuilding Institute (SPI) at Eastern Mennonite University in 1998, a woman expressed both her Catholic religious identity and her upbringing among Muslims. She attends Friday prayers and fasts Ramadan with Muslims; she goes to church on Sunday and celebrates Christmas with Catholics. Children of interreligious marriages often experience such a pluralist approach to their religious identities, something that is also experienced by Jewish-Buddhist spiritual groups that have been emerging in the United States.

It is important to point out that adaptation as a tendency within an AA worldview represents the capability to shift perspective and behavior appropriately to cultural and/or religious context. It is not a perspective that is grounded in an individual surrender of religious belief or practice. Adaptation as a developmental orientation may not be essential to achieving stable and lasting peaceful relations. Rather, the sine qua non is perhaps acceptance— the recognition that the other's religious identity, beliefs, and practices are as complex and viable as one's own. From this worldview, both commonalities and differences are evident and can be appropriately accommodated within a multicultural social milieu.

Criticisms of the adaptation perspective are raised by those both within and outside the dialogue community. Adaptation raises the fear of conversion and the loss of one's perceived authentic religious identity. This resistance is reflected in statements such as "I do not need or want to become a Muslim to work for interreligious peace," "If developing religious pluralism becomes our goal as an interfaith group, our communities will ostracize us," and "The religious pluralist revokes the fear of conversion and interfaith groups often struggle to overcome the communities' fear of religious conversion."[11] In the Palestinian-Israeli conflict, such a possibility has been often rejected by participants, especially Muslims, who argued that being a religious pluralist might be possible for Jews and Christians in the West, due to their Judeo-Christian links, but that the political, historical, and cultural history of Christians, Jews, and Muslims in the Middle East prevents such a possibility. As one interviewee put it, "By raising such a possibility here I suffer grave consequences in my community and will not be able to work for peace."[12]

Some interfaith dialoguers reject the possibility of experiencing the other's religion and argue that there are certain rituals, values, and norms in one religion that—if experienced by a person from another religion—can violate one's own faith. For example, if an observant Jew were to violate kosher by taking part in a Christian ritual, or if a Muslim were to empathize with Christians by eating pork one time or drinking alcohol, these actions would probably be violations of their faith. Although certain areas of Abrahamic faith might be problematic for others to participate in, there is an abundance of other areas within the traditions which, if explored in IFD, might allow some level of cognitive frame-shifting. Examples include prayer, fasting, and sacred sacrifice. If one is able to join the other in his or her own practices, this sends a powerful message not only of acceptance, but also of a deep recognition and appreciation of the other's faith. Such messages are effective in preventing dehumanization, violence, and exclusion.

In IFD, or in any activity held within the broader context of a conflict in which conversion is a fear, these empathetic practices can easily be perceived as an attempt to convert the other or as a sign of conversion. Such perceptions, if spread in the community, can constitute a major obstacle for religious peace workers who participate in such joint rituals.

The Integration Worldview

A final worldview posited within the DMIS theory is that of integration. This worldview may well be unique to certain individuals whose environment is unusually bicultural or bireligious. Two aspects of integration are encapsulated marginality and constructive marginality. In both cases there is an element of marginalization of the individual from any culture which he or she adopts; however, in constructive marginality the person is able to reach out and connect from within the cultural context.[13]

An integration worldview is manifested by a spiritual person who has no affiliation with a specific religion or faith, but feels comfortable practicing many rituals and embraces beliefs from various religions. The New Age spiritual movement in the United States probably is the best example. Such persons are often excluded, isolated, and alienated by the traditional faith groups in IFD trainings. Other faith groups feel threatened by them because they are unable to categorize such participants in one traditional or defined faith group. As stated by a woman who attended an interfaith evening in the Washington National Cathedral, "I often feel that I do not belong to any existing faith group and would like to participate in all the rituals offered in the interfaith setting. However, neither the Christians nor the Jews [n]or the Muslims accept me."[14]

An integrative approach to interreligious differences is often opposed by the majority of followers of the Abrahamic traditions, dismissed as inauthentic and viewed as a phenomenon that can endanger the very existence of any interfaith group in the Middle East. This is primarily due to the clear boundaries drawn in such faith communities and the need to categorize people into clear religious or ethnic categories such as Israeli or Arab. There are those in interfaith groups who oppose the integration of several spiritual practices and who view a person with multiple religious or spiritual orientations as superficially practicing the religious rituals without comprehending or realizing the depth of the faiths.[15]

RELIGIORELATIVISM AND INTERFAITH PEACE WORK

Understanding the range of reactions to religious differences can be a helpful guide for IFD and peace work activities by providing an interreligious awareness model that calls for moving participants in IFD from the religiocentric perspective into the religiorelative perspective. The major theoretical assumption behind this strategy is that religiocentric beliefs cause believers to be receptive to violence against other religions, and allow political and religious leaders to easily manipulate their followers by mobilizing their religious fears and insecurities about their faith. Another assumption is that the heightened awareness and understanding of the other's religious beliefs and rituals, and recognition of their right to exist and be part of the society, eventually may prevent escalation and promote nonviolent negotiation of how each group ought to utilize the public space to express their faith.

Regardless of whether people operate from a DD or a reversal perspective, those operating from a religiocentric perspective do not appreciate or legitimize other methods of belief or worship. Religious adherents (both individuals and groups) in this mode seek ways to ensure the superiority or their beliefs. Thus, exclusionary policies, physical removal, or quick reactions to rumors regarding the evil intentions of other religions abound where religiocentrism prevails. For example, if a Jewish settler believes that the land of Israel was given only to Jews and that non-Jews have no right to it and should be second-class citizens, that settler is more prone to commit violence than is a religious Jew who believes that controlling the land is not the most important priority of Judaism and that Muslims and Christians have an equal right to it. Similar rationales operate in the case of Muslim religiocentric or religiorelative believers. The religiocentric believer denies Jews their religious claims in the land of Israel, based on certain interpretations of Islamic teachings and history, and calls for the expulsion of Jews from the land (not only the Occupied Territories, but also all of historic Palestine). The religiorelative believer recognizes the right of Muslims, Jews, and Christians to the same piece of Holy Land and draws arguments from different Islamic religious interpretations.

Through certain IFD and interfaith activities, religiocentric attitudes may transform into religiorelativist ones. These activities might include visits to holy sites or joint rituals to commemorate certain events related to the three traditions, such as Abraham, Jerusalem, or fasting. However, development of religious pluralism is a deep change in religious identity and only occurs over many years of spiritual exploration and experience. In working for IFD or interreligious peacebuilding, this model implies that individuals who adopt an interreligious pluralist perspective are less likely to engage in violence and extremism. Creating space for pluralist religious orientations in each community is essential for building a genuine culture of peace, openness, and tolerance.[16]

Rejection of the cognitive frame-shifting and behavioral code-shifting elements of an AA worldview in IFD by many participants raises a question as to the purpose and limits of IFD among the Abrahamic faiths. Can Abrahamic IFD nurture deep appreciation of other religions if participants are unwilling to jointly experience each other's rituals? Are those dialoguers who have developed a spiritual consciousness and are ready to temporarily experience other faiths more tolerant and able to develop stronger relationships with the other, especially during periods of conflict and violence? These questions are important to explore in order to improve existing interfaith models and tools. Further, what is the role of culturally or religiously "marginal" individuals (those who hold an integration worldview) within IFD? Should they remain marginalized because they do not locate their identity within one religious tradition?

The above proposed interfaith process continues to be tested through various workshops and professional meetings, and it is offered here as a framework to guide practitioners and activists in their efforts to engage in interfaith encounters. Nevertheless, further research is needed to systematically confirm its effectiveness in such settings.

BEST PRACTICES FOR IFD

IFD requires individuals to lower their own defenses and meet as equals in a process of giving and receiving information. There must be an atmosphere of openness and equality. The following ground rules are suggested for making IFD as effective as possible.

Speak for Yourself

To achieve this atmosphere, participants must recognize that their opinions are not necessarily the views of their entire faith tradition and must be willing to share their opinions in the context of their own life story. Within the context of dialogue, participants often feel called on to speak on behalf of their entire religious tradition. This poses complex and painful dilemmas. It is nearly impossible to speak of "the" Christian, Jewish, or Muslim position on any issue. "Dialogue conventionally means that the participants take up and speak in the name of a position that has been more or less defined in advance. . . . Neither side can claim to represent *the* Muslims or *the* Christians but the meetings are gatherings of particular Muslims or particular Christians who want to communicate with each other" (Waardenburg 2000, 301, 303). As individuals, dialogue participants cannot be abstracted from their social, political, and economic contexts. The diversity that exists within traditions can be best preserved if participants acknowledge that they can only define themselves and speak for what they personally believe. Involvement in a dialogue is most effective if participants do not presume to speak for a whole tradition.

Recognize Complexity of Religious Traditions

One key element in fostering greater understanding between faiths is to have a sense of the breadth of the faith tradition. There is no one Islam, no single form of Christianity. Each faith should be aware of the complexities and varieties of the other faiths. Addressing the issue of religious identity in Israel, Ron Kronish (1997) writes, "We live in separate worlds in Israel. Jews and

Arabs tend to live in distinct communities with their own ways of life. Yet there is a large degree of pluralism within each group. Jews can be religious, secular or traditional; Ashkenazi or Sephardi; sabras or immigrants. And Arabs can also be religious, secular, or traditional; they can be Christians, Muslims, or Druze; they are Israeli citizens and yet at the same time part of the Palestinian people." Participants in IFD must be aware of such diversity within each religion to appreciate the complexity of worldviews that a seemingly homogenous group brings to the table. One way to foster this awareness is by having participants from across the faith spectrum participate. One cannot responsibly hold a Christian-Jewish dialogue with only Reform Jews and Catholics, for example. In Israel, the presence of ultra-Orthodox Jews in the dialogue group would be a great asset, as they are a powerful presence and typically underrepresented within dialogue circles.

Unireligious Caucuses First

Some scholars have suggested that religious traditions should primarily seek dialogues with themselves instead of engaging in IFD (Goddard 1995), while others have noted that unireligious caucuses are an important precursor to interfaith meetings (Cilliers, 2002; Abu-Nimer 2002). A unireligious meeting helps to provide support to participants, strengthening them for the challenge of dialogue. IFD is most effective when participants stand firmly in their own faith while remaining self-critical and open to new perspectives. An Institute of Peace study of IFD revealed that a common problem is "implicit assumptions rooted in prejudices are brought to the table which, unacknowledged by those holding them, inhibit potential progress as participants are forced to respond to these unstated expectations and are not listened to on their own terms" (USIP 2002, 3). However, the same study also demonstrated that "learning about the other before interreligious meetings take place, conducting intrareligious sessions prior to meeting, and agreeing on terminologies from the outset would help to create the necessary safe space and sensitivity to engage mutual concerns and fears" (USIP 2002, 3).

No Apologetics

By agreeing to engage in IFD, participants commit to a process that may feel risky to them. However, the dialogue process requires that participants not vigorously defend their own religion. Similarly, participants must undertake a realistic rather than idealistic view of their faith. Speaking to this, Bishop Krister Stendahl (1990, 19) said, "It is always important to compare equal to equal. If you compare your own tradition in its ideal form with the actual manifestations of the other, you will always win. And even if we have stopped using that method consciously, we do it unconsciously." There may also be a tendency in IFD to form a common bond as believers and to jointly denigrate unbelievers. This is not a productive vein of discussion for groups. "The attitude proposing a common front for religion or against unbelief may be understandable, but it is not a religious attitude—not according to the present degree of religious consciousness" (Panikkar 1999, 62).

Resist Watering Down Beliefs to Find Commonality

Often as an interfaith group experiences conflict and tension, it may resort to finding joint values as a means of ignoring the conflict. Rather than address the tension and anxiety among participants, a facilitator may try to persuade the group to produce some sort of joint statement. If this is done, the document will be so abstract and vague that it will likely only add to the group's sense of futility. Writing from his experience with drafting the Universal Declaration of Human Rights, Paul Brink (2003, 18) observes, "This can be a tempting choice in situations of diversity; we might call it 'the politics of abstraction,' an attempt to create an abstract justification that is independent of any and all religious views, and that asks participants to confine their deliberations to those terms." Such an act of watering down faiths to reach agreement is the antithesis of genuine IFD.

Power

In dialogues where the different faiths are also adversaries, the potential for clashes resulting from differences in power is even greater. Conducting a dialogue between the Abrahamic faiths during such a volatile time in history will require careful balancing of power dynamics. In any reconciliation effort, a power differential exists between different groups. "The dialogue of persons is no more a dialogue of equals than the dialogue of the interpreter and the text, but at least in the former the other has a voice. The dissonance of power relations and the lack of common concepts, if not of a common language, make the experience of dialogue disturbing" (Barnes 2001, 150). This power differential must be addressed beyond just trying to have an equal number of participants from each faith. For example, even if equal numbers of Jews and Muslims participate in a dialogue in Israel, the Jews will be the majority group in terms of power because they are a numerical majority in Israel and hold a preponderance of political, social, and economic power. This dynamic may drive the dialogue in certain directions, as the Muslims, due to their economic and social deprivation, have more at stake and more to lose from the dialogue experience.

Minority groups do not want to participate merely for the educational benefit and instruction of the majority group. Participants from different communities may consequently have very different expectations for the fruitfulness of the dialogue. Amy Hubbard (2001, 281) notes, "Majority participants are more likely to approach dialogue with an interest in communicating with minority participants. Minority participants are more likely to expect political action to come out of their dialogue efforts."

Marc Gopin (2002, 43) writes, "Simply stated, adversary groups often come out of circumstances in which one group has more military, economic, political and/or demographic power than the other group. But the asymmetry also may express itself in the nature of the encounter, its language, structure and cultural ethos." Dialogues in places of conflict often involve more complex dynamics between groups than merely a difference in religion. These other characteristics (such as race or economics) will also affect the power dynamics within the group.

Communication differences also preclude the equality of participants in dialogue. "Despite well meaning intentions, there exist competing cultural, religious and historical approaches and styles of communication that strongly influence the ability of participants to understand and be understood" (USIP 2002, 3). These differences in communication styles may be difficult to correct, but their acknowledgment may provide a degree of clarity to the dialogue.

Language may also play a part in majority/minority dynamics in the group. In many dialogue settings, all participants may not share a common first language. "We are obligated to respect other parties as equal participants in the process; accordingly we cannot require other participants to borrow a language not their own to make their arguments" (Brink 2003, 19). This problem is largely avoided in Lebanon, Jordan, and Egypt, but may present particular difficulties in Israel/Palestine. Language contains cultural and religious assumptions not fully expressed in translation. For example, Arabic plays a significant role in Islam as a vehicle of the sacred Quran. Certain Muslim concepts thus may not be fully comprehended by non-Arabic speakers.

The selection of participants in IFD cannot fully overcome power differentials, but it may make substantial progress toward equalization. All parties to the dialogue should come prepared with the same information regarding the dialogue. Also, participants with similar religious histories should be recruited. It would be unfair to hold a dialogue in which one faith was represented by secular participants while the other faith was represented by active followers of the faith. Robert Eisen (2002, 5) explores this issue with regard to the complexity of modern Jewish identity: "First, Jews who are committed more to history and culture than religion may not easily communicate with religious individuals in the Christian and Muslim communities. They may also not earn the respect of the latter, either."

This may present a particular problem in Israel, where Jewish participants are far more likely to be secular progressives than religiously observant followers. Eisen (2002, 5) writes, "Israeli Jews must find a way to speak to Muslims whose religious beliefs dictate that Jerusalem is a holy city and that the Temple Mount is sacred to Muslims, and this will be much more difficult for Israeli Jews who may be ambivalent about their own religion or may even have contempt for religiosity of any kind."

The imbalance of power can be partially corrected by careful attention to the location, timing, participant selection, and other dynamics of the dialogue design. One Denver group developed a few guidelines to manage the majority/minority relationship—keeping the group small, striving for equal representation from the faith groups, balancing the gender membership, and rotating the meeting place (Smith 1998, 254). Keeping the group small enables everyone's voice to be heard more frequently and allows participants to come to know one another on a deeper level. Rotating the meeting among places that are familiar to different participants enables the location to play a more neutral role in the power dynamics. Groups have often found that meeting in one another's homes adds an additional element of hospitality and trust to the dialogue.

Suspend Role and Status

Within the dialogue setting, all participants should be considered to have equal status and importance. When a "local celebrity" such as a powerful government figure, professor, or other distinguished person participates in a dialogue, their opinions are often given more credence and emphasis than other voices. This natural tendency should be avoided, as it further complicates the power dynamics of the dialogue. Often the easiest way to avoid this situation is to choose participants of relatively equal status in the community.

Establish Ground Rules

The dialogue group itself should establish some basic ground rules for the meetings. These rules should include a commitment to the group over a period of time, a willingness to keep listening even when it becomes difficult to do so, and a way to make all participants feel safe.

This general review of some of the existing interfaith research and literature is aimed at examining the major current theoretical frameworks in the study on interfaith dialogue. It also illustrates the need to further explore these theoretical frameworks or propositions in the field. There have been very few attempts to conceptualize the process of perceptional and behavioral changes experienced by participants in IFD processes. Thus we have limited understanding of the effective conditions that can lead to such transformation of religious perceptions and beliefs toward the other. However, we certainly have plentiful data and theories on how religious beliefs can lead to violence and exclusion. This book attempts to fill in the gaps in the literature by exploring, cataloguing, illustrating, and analyzing the existing state of IFD in the particular context of the Middle East. We hope that the following chapters, which analyze the various ways in which interfaith groups manage to work and intervene in five Middle Eastern societies, contribute to the development of both the theory and practice of interfaith peacebuilding and dialogue.

3

INTERFAITH DIALOGUE AND PEACEBUILDING IN ISRAEL AND PALESTINE

RELIGIOUS IDENTITY AND VIOLENCE

Most religious traditions offer resources for peacemaking as well as resources that can be interpreted to justify violence and exclusion. Scholars who discuss this ambivalence in religion have clearly identified the destructive role that religious leaders and followers have played in many conflict areas (Appleby 1998; Gopin 2000; Kasimow and Byron 1991; Kimball 2002; Johnston and Sampson 1994). In the field of conflict and conflict resolution, studies and research have generally either neglected the role of religion or focused solely on its destructive aspects. This chapter seeks to explore the constructive role that interfaith groups played in the case of Israel and Palestine.

As in other divided societies, the Israeli-Palestinian conflict is complex, deep-rooted, and involves a clash of multiple individual and collective identities; its sources and causes cannot be defined by one single set of economic, social, political, or religious factors. Although religion continues to play a significant role in the conflict's dynamics, and features in any interactions between Israelis and Palestinians, many analysts and scholars reject the classic assumption that the Israeli-Palestinian conflict can be classified as a religious conflict, and see the conflict as mainly about issues of self-determination and resources.

But even if we accept this assumption and ignore the religious nature of the Jewish state and Palestinian society, it is clear that religious identities (symbols, rituals, values, and so on) have crucially affected the perceptions and behaviors of even those Israelis and Palestinians who do not define themselves as religious or observant. Obviously, to ignore the role of religion in any conflict, but especially in the Middle East, and to presume that the conflict between Israelis and Palestinians is purely secular, would be a superficial understanding of the conflict. Religion in this region of the world has never been distinct from politics; the centrality of religious affiliation to Jews and Arabs is clearly captured by an Arab IFD facilitator: "Interfaith relations is a natural part of our lives. . . . We can not live without asking what the other religion is. It is part of our daily lives."[1]

The history of the Arab-Jewish conflict abounds with examples of religious beliefs and rituals being used to justify violent and forceful policies and reactions. However, such use of religion is not unique to the Israeli-Palestinian conflict. In India, Hindus and Muslims have fought over religious sites for centuries. In Sri Lanka, Hindus and Buddhists have also been engaged in a conflict over self-determination for the Tamil Sri Lankans; both parties have used religion as a dividing force.

In the Israeli-Palestinian context, manipulation of religious identities and beliefs intensified as early as the mid-1800s with the emergence of Zionist ideology. Hertzel and other founders of Zionism used Judaism to legitimize their demands for a homeland for European Jews[2] in historic Palestine (Mezvinsky 1988). For the Zionist movement, the Jews' right to the land stems from three major sources: (1) religious linkages—the belief that God promised the land of Israel to the Jews, (2) historical political continuity between the ancient Jews who lived on the land and today's Zionists, and (3) security—there is no other refuge where the Jews of the world can be safe from religious and ethnic persecution by other nations.

By 1948, in addition to mobilizing religious symbols, rituals, and sacred texts to justify national claims, the Zionist movement had established a strong link between the nature of the Jewish state and Judaism. However, later, religion was institutionally separated from the various governance structures of the state of Israel.

Supporters of the Palestinian national movement base their claims for the land of Palestine on three similar sources:

1. Religion—Palestinian Christians have lived on this land from the time of Christ, and they see themselves as followers of his original message. Islam entered Palestine and Jerusalem as early as CE 638, and Jerusalem is the third-holiest site for Muslims.
2. History—Today's Palestinians view themselves as a continuation of the historical Muslims and Christians who have lived on the land for the past 1,400 years.
3. Security—Palestine is the only refuge for the Palestinian national movement due to (or in the context of) the historical persecution of Palestinians by other Arab and non-Arab regimes. "There is no other place to go," many Palestinian leaders frequently state.

As early as the 1930s, Palestinian national leaders, such as Sheikh Izz Al din Al Qassam and Haj Amin Al Hussieni, have employed Islamic religious identity to rally popular support for the resistance movement to gain freedom from Zionist and British colonialism (Abu-Amr 1994). The Christian Palestinian religious leadership has vigorously opposed the occupation of the Palestinian territories and has played an active role in the resistance to the occupation, especially in cities such as Jerusalem, Bethlehem, Beit Sahour, and Beit Jala.

Since the beginning of the first Palestinian Intifada in 1987, the increased influence of extremist religious groups in both societies was evident. On the Palestinian side, Hamas and Islamic Jihad's influence increased tremendously (Hroub 2000). This was paralleled by the increased influence and role of Israeli Jewish religious parties in Israeli society (Arian and Shamir 1999).[3] The religious factor has gained even more power since the Al Aqsa Intifada in September 2000; the Israeli-Palestinian conflict is increasingly framed and presented as a zero-sum survival matter and a religious, identity-based conflict.[4]

RELIGIOUS IDENTITY AND PEACE

It is unrealistic to deny the significant negative role that religious identities have played in the creation, escalation, and outcomes of the Israeli-Palestinian conflict, at least throughout the last century. Despite the negative role of religion in the conflict, there is an apparent secularization of the peace process. The religious aspects of the conflict—Jewish, Muslim, and Christian—have been ignored by politicians and decision makers in all formal and informal negotiations, including the latest initiative of the "Road Map for Peace."[5] This deliberate neglect of the possible positive role that religious identity or affiliation can play in prenegotiation, negotiation, and postagreement processes has been a strong motivating factor for the Palestinians and Israelis who have become active in interfaith peacebuilding.

Religious leaders who have attempted to claim a role in this peace process have insisted that "There will be no peace between Muslims and Jews here without religious people's intervention."[6] Rabbi Jeremy Milgrom stated, "Religion is not only concerned with the theological. Religion is a connecting and disconnecting point. Jews and Arabs have cultural and religious stereotypes. With the passage of time, I have come to understand that religion can contribute in positive ways; it has the potential to remove the intolerance and misunderstanding."[7]

Israeli and Palestinian leaders have signed many agreements and accords, but none make reference to the religious dimension of the conflict. This was true even in the negotiations for access to Rachel's Tomb in Bethlehem and Joseph's Grave in Nablus (or Muslim and Christian sites inside Israel). By failing to integrate the religious dimensions of the conflict, these political agreements and processes have alienated significant segments of both Palestinian and Israeli societies. (Abu-Nimer 2002; Gopin 2000; Landau 2003). Rabbi Michael Melchior (who served as deputy minister under Barak between 1998 and 2000) expressed his frustration regarding this issue: "Since the peace effort has been led by secularists, peace itself has become identified in Israel with [the] secular left; religiously committed people feel threatened by it. They may not be against peace or compromise, but they see this effort linked to increased secularism."[8] The incorporation of religious dimensions in the Israeli-Palestinian peace process can provide the legitimacy lacking among the grassroots for agreements crafted by the elites, especially with regard to religiously sensitive issues (the future of Jerusalem, access to holy sites in Israel and Palestine, and the status of Temple Mount/Haram Al Sharif).

If interreligious peace initiatives are to be launched or adopted, there are certain necessary realizations that must be made among religious leaders and activists. First, there should be awareness that religion can play a constructive role in conflict dynamics, not only a destructive one. Second, religious leaders and activists should not hold on to religiocentric worldviews that permit the exclusion of other religions, but should develop a religiorelative perspective in relation to other religions. Third, instead of being a force that calls for the separation of political peace processes from religion, IFD and encounter groups should view themselves as part of the process of political change. Such conditions can be created and facilitated only by religious peacemakers.

There have always been Muslims, Christians, and Jews who insisted on presenting their religion in an inclusive, humane, and peaceful manner—individuals with the courage to meet with members from other religions and share religious symbols, rituals, and beliefs in hope, human connection, and desire for peace. This chapter focuses on the work of these individuals who struggle to bring a peaceful religious perspective into the violent dynamic of the Palestinian-Israeli conflict. We look at their goals, assumptions, and motivations in working in this field; review some of their major activities; explore their perceptions of their own success and impact; identify the major obstacles and challenges facing these IFD participants and organizers in the violent reality of Israel/Palestine; and, finally, propose some suggestions and recommendations for the advancement of the interfaith field in Israel and Palestine.

Whose Story Is This?

This study was launched to capture the state of the interfaith field among both Jews and Arabs in Israel and among Palestinians in the Occupied Territories. During the course of gathering the data for this study (February 2003–June 2004), there was an escalation of violence in Israel, Palestine, and the region (with the Iraq war). The Israeli military continued its operations in the Occupied Territories, which resulted in the killing of more than three thousand Palestinians and the injury of more than ten thousand more. Assassinations of top political leaders of groups such as Islamic Hamas and Jihad groups, curfews, and closures continued. On the other side, more suicide bombers carried out operations in Israel, killing hundreds of Israelis. Furthermore, Jewish settlements continued to be under constant attack by Palestinian militia groups.[9]

Such reciprocal violence affected the relationship between Arabs and Jews in Israel, where 82 percent of the inhabitants are Jews and 18 percent Arabs. (Among Arabs, 70 percent are Muslims, 20 percent Christians, and 10 percent Druze). Rising tensions have led to social, cultural, and political separation of

Arabs and Jews and thus to less contact between them (Abu-Nimer 2004). Such separation has increased significantly since the Al-Aqsa Intifada.

Due to the political and security situation, major interfaith activities between Israeli Jews and Palestinians from the Occupied Territories were minimal; the main activities involved Arabs and Jews from Israel. However, these, too, have significantly decreased in number, according to the majority of our interviewees. The political and security context affected the gathering of data, as it limited accessibility to interfaith participants and leaders. It became more difficult for us to organize interviews and visit certain Palestinian areas. (During that period, for example, Gaza was inaccessible to the local researchers.) Moreover, on several occasions, certain religious figures would decline interviews, stating, "It is not a proper time to discuss peace and interfaith."[10]

Despite these difficult circumstances, local researchers—hired from Jerusalem and with the ability to travel and access both Israeli and Palestinian territories—managed to interview thirty-four active participants and heads of interfaith organizations: ten Palestinian active community leaders and NGO personnel in interfaith relations (five Muslims and five Christians); fourteen Arabs from Israel (five Christians, eight Muslims, and one Druze); eight Jewish leaders active in interfaith organizations; and two Christian foreign-born interfaith leaders. Due to the small number of people and organizations involved in IFD, the snowball method of identifying NGO and community leaders and active participants was highly effective and allowed the researchers to cover more than 70 percent of the organizations (see appendix B for the list of interfaith organizations interviewed). The interviewees were mainly leaders and active participants who have been in the field for at least three years and have participated in numerous IFD meetings.

All the participants were asked to respond to a semistructured list of questions, and their responses were tape-recorded in Arabic and Hebrew and transcribed into documents for analysis. In addition, the researchers observed several interfaith activities in Jerusalem, Majd Al Kurum, and Tiberias. An average of forty to fifty people participated in each of these events. Finally, two training workshops in IFD were conducted in Israel by Mohammed Abu-Nimer, as part of our efforts to gain insight and learn more about the nature of interfaith relations in Israel. Responses from the interviews and other data sources were analyzed and classified into categories, from which certain thematic patterns emerged. This process of analysis further permitted the distinction between the Arab and Jewish responses and uncovered differences and similarities based on religious affiliation and minority-majority status.

MOTIVATIONS AND GOALS FOR BECOMING INVOLVED IN IFD

Despite the wide range of goals motivating the participation in IFD meetings, it is possible to generalize that the majority of participants are motivated by the horrible reality of war, violence, and dehumanization that have characterized

Arab-Jewish relations. Jewish, Muslim, and Christian participants are deeply driven by the need to inject a positive change into this reality. Motivated by the need to bring social and political change to the context, Rabbi Milgrom stated his belief in interfaith work: "I believe that every person has to pursue peace to reduce animosity. If most of the Israelis do that, they can contribute to [peace]. Similar to the soldiers who serve in the army to increase security, I think that religious persons can contribute to security by reducing insecurity among people. Every one gains from the added security. In addition, I have curiosity about other cultures. No need to leave the country for that, a few miles will do."[11]

In addition to changing the reality and getting to know the other, many participants are motivated by the need to present their national identity and concerns. A Muslim woman active in a women's IFD group in Jerusalem captured this motivation among many participants:

> My national identity was clear always to me. I felt lots of hatred for Jews through TV and media etc., because of the political events. I suddenly found myself in a cycle of hatred. I hated everything. I even stopped enjoying life. I could not see my Jewish friends. I could not deal with them. I needed to change my pessimistic [views] and had to forgive and continue in life. . . . It took me months. I began working on myself regardless of the political situation. I wanted to return to my happy mode and enjoy life. How can I forgive the enemy/aggressor against me? It took me months, and when I got to this place of forgiveness I wanted to continue and see if I can apply this to other people and groups. Can we forgive and get to our happiness on the national level? Can we forgive each other? It is not an easy or short time. . . . During this period I was looking for women, to share with them these feelings.[12]

Another common motivation is to find alternatives to protests and demonstrations, about which participants are already disillusioned. Interfaith activities provide a personal context where participants can sit and talk together, rather than the impersonal setting of a political protest.

A central motivation for Muslim participants is the need to correct the negative images of Islam among Jews, and even among Christians. Such a need became even more urgent in the post–September 11 context. Even Muslim participants who were not religious or aware of their spiritual identity found themselves adopting a defensive position and wanting to clarify the meaning of basic Islamic beliefs and practices. Projecting a positive image of Islam was a consistent motivation among Muslim and even some Christian interfaith participants. One woman saw an important role for herself in breaking the stereotypes some Jews hold about Muslim women wearing hijab (veil): "This image [Muslim women wearing hijab] I can pass to the other. Personal example is many time[s] better than any thing else. Even being happy and participat[ing] in the society sends a positive message, too."[13] An imam in Majd Al Kurum confirms this motive: "We want to encourage interfaith relationships to prove to the world that Islam is not an aggressive religion; [although] if it is attacked, it will defend itself."[14] A leader of the Muslim Sufi community further points to the importance of dispelling the myth that Islam was spread through violence and instead spreading a genuine knowledge of the religion.[15]

The Christian-Muslim dynamic is similar to the Jewish-Muslim one in that both reflect a minority-majority configuration. Christian participants in interfaith groups are motivated by their need to educate the Muslim majority about their status as a Christian minority within the Arab and Muslim world, their theological differences with Islam, and the desire to enlist Muslim support for stronger religious pluralism in the Palestinian community: "As a minority, Christians are calling for dialogue and reaching out to Muslims because we feel threatened. This is one of the goals of Christian-Muslim dialogue. This is the goal, it is social, not religious. It is also political, to preserve the self, so we do not disappear. We are shrinking fast; we were 10 percent, now barely 2 percent. This is typical minority thinking. I have met Muslims in other countries who feel the same way."[16] However, what is interesting is that despite the deep-seated fears among Christian Palestinians as a "double minority," only two Christian interviewees addressed this concern directly.

The participants in interfaith meetings ranged from those who were highly religious to those who rediscovered their religious and spiritual identity through these conversations. A Palestinian Muslim woman explained the discovery of her Muslim identity through IFD and her need to clarify the image of Muslim women: "I changed; I thought, I am far from religion, as on the outside I am not religious. But then I realized that I know [about religion] and have opinions and different perspectives [than those who present Islam]. The other was in need for the information which I knew; he was entitled to meet a different type of a Muslim person, with different attitudes. I was also anxious to give the other [Jews and Christians] this information; to teach them about Islam and about the diversity that exists in Islam."[17]

In a conflict situation, there are very few safe public places in which to meet the other. Interfaith meetings provide such space. According to Rabbi Milgrom, many Jews who attend interfaith meetings are motivated by "the lack of information and lack of knowledge. People are seeking opportunities to fulfill the lack of knowledge. . . . Our reality is one of separation and ignorance of the other. We do not know each other. So people meet to know the others." Curiosity about the other's religion is a motivating factor for participants in such activities.

In addition to getting to know the other, interfaith interaction also empowers participants by bringing them closer to their own faith. One interviewee said he was motivated by "Curiosity; wanting to know other religions. Also I love my faith and feel that the more I know the other faiths, the stronger I become in my own faith."[18]

Fear of conversion is a factor that inhibits interaction. Fear of being proselytized often prevents people from interacting or even inquiring about the other's religion. Children are socialized to avoid any inquiry about other faith groups. An Arab from Israel, active in Women's Interfaith Encounter, describes this reality of separation: "We live in total separation in Jerusalem; we live beside each other, yet bypassing each other. It is similar to the situation in the north. My Jewish coworker refuses to know anything about Christianity and prevents her children from learning about other religions, fearing they might convert to Christianity or another branch of Judaism."[19]

Israeli Jewish participants often cite the history of persecution and victimhood as the primary reason for taking part in IFD. The memory of the experience of the Holocaust is a major motivating factor for this group. A Muslim organizer from Yesodot[20] explained this motivation among some Jewish participants, using an Arab proverb: "'The person who has been stunned by a snake bite is afraid of the movement of a rope.' Historically, innocent people were killed just because they are Jews. Persecuted, [some become more radical and violent] but others, if they are human, Holocaust survivors, they decide to work on taking pain away from Palestinians."[21]

A number of interviewees, both Arabs and Jews, also identified building a better future for the young generation and women as a strong motivator for participation. An organizer of Women's Interfaith Encounter stated her unique perspective on the motivation of the women who participate in her IFD group:

> The people who are now doing interfaith work, I sincerely believe, are laying the groundwork for eventually when we get beyond war, when we will have to find ways to bring faiths together. The point of what we are doing is to strengthen the feminine energies, which are reconciliation, tolerance, forgiveness, inclusion, and cooperation. So we recognize that there are feminine energies in everybody, just like there are masculine energies in everybody. But the problem we see in the Middle East is that it's the masculine behaviors and energies that dominate and keep us locked in eternal warfare. So we are trying to strengthen the feminine energies, and we are starting first of all with the women, because the women are so disempowered here that it's impossible for feminine energies to become empowered. So we are trying to empower women within religion and we are starting with the most basic thing—studying our texts and simply seeing the truth of our religions. . . . We know we are not going to come to blows, we are not going to take out knives, and we are not going to kill each other. We are going to do whatever we are going to do from a place of love and openness. So this is a feminine way of working together, this is like the underlying philosophy of what we are doing.[22]

Looking at the responses of Jews and Arabs to the question of motivation, it is important to note that while the majority of Arab participants mentioned that they were driven by politics, the majority of Jewish participants claimed that politics should not be part of the goals of IFD. Rather, according to the latter, the focus should be on the basic human transcendent similarities; that we are all God's children. According to a veteran of Israeli-Palestinian IFD meetings, "The goal is humanistic, and Abrahamic traditions are very similar, with very little differences. All are children of God and worship and love the same God, who loves all of us and wants us to love each other, too. This is as simple as it gets. We live in the same country and land, but we live separated and in enclaves of religious communities. No one wants to get to know the other, a clear sign of disconnection and separation. We are trying to show that we are all the same creation and we are equal. . . . All religions have the same message: to correct people's wrongdoing and bring them to the correct path."[23]

Historically in Israel, interfaith meetings and discussions have been used as apolitical tools to co-opt and normalize relations with Arabs, especially during the 1950s and 1960s, when the traditional religious Arab leadership represented the various communities. A veteran of interfaith relations related a story about the efforts to settle a piece of land in the Galilee (Arabeh and Sakhnin) in the early 1950s, which reflects to some extent the genesis of inter-ethnic and interfaith dialogue in Israel. The Karen Kaimet (an agency that purchased and controlled the land in historic Israel/Palestine) brought religious settlers to launch a new settlement on disputed land near these two Arab villages. The settlement was to revive a lost Jewish town from the Roman period, although the selected site was not archeologically proven to have been the lost Roman town. Nevertheless, Joseph Emanual and others began interfaith meetings with residents of the Arab villages, who "did not like the settlement in the middle of their land, but they were very nice, helped and worked all the time."[24]

IFD is also perceived as a forum for the process of rehumanization and prejudice reduction. All participants identified rehumanization of the other as an important goal—to break the negative collective images of all people on the "other side" through interpersonal relationship building. For example, a Palestinian Christian woman stated: "The goal is simply to create relationships, not necessary friendships, but to break the enemy image from the news. This is not portrayed as a political goal by many; they do not negotiate or decide on solutions, but everyone knows that we differ on who should control Jerusalem. These are side conversations. Breaking stereotypes is the central goal."[25] The work of the Jerusalem Interfaith Women's meeting reflects the objective of rehumanization in a context of fear and separation, according to a Palestinian Christian woman participant: "We live completely separated from each other, close but divided. Jewish women are scared and fearful of coming to visit us, it took long time to overcome that. I get also scared if I am lost in the western part of the city. We met in Tantur—a neutral place. I still attend because I want to show the true face of Palestinians. They are afraid of us and do not trust us; we thought that they live better than us and had an easier life, [both] these were two stereotypes that we discovered."[26]

A Christian priest from Al-Liqa'—the only Christian-Muslim organization that focuses on internal interfaith work among Palestinians—identified the desired goal of IFD:

> The goal of interfaith is not preaching or conversion. I do not dialogue with the Muslim to guide him to my religion. But we dialogue to get to know each other better, because as a Christian in my popular culture or tradition, I have stereotypes

about Muslims and Jews. For example, as a kid I was told, "The Jewish rabbi sells shoes" [*khakhami yahudi dawa'r sarami*] and "Mohammed stole the eggs" [*Muhammad sarka al beid*]. These are told and exchanged among Christians. We live together while we have these stereotypes. We like to get rid of these preconceived notions. . . . We acknowledge the otherness and differences, and live with each other. With no problems I say there is something for the future; a step forward. It is a living. We both do our best to avoid the other and not cause a problem. But I am talking about genuine living together in the future. I live in a square and you live in a square, you interact with me and you enrich me and I enrich you. Not only to get to know each other, not to coexist, but to witness something different.[27]

Indeed, interfaith meetings are effective in breaking some of the initial stereotypes often held by participants about the other faiths, as a Palestinian Christian woman participant confirms:

First I was very careful and cautious, but now I am frank and even too direct and sometimes insulting and rude. We were fearful of the Mossad or hurting their feelings. Maybe things I say can become liability or used against me. I am first Palestinian and then a Muslim or Christian woman. Our national identity is more important to us. After the meetings I stopped feeling weak or the need to look for help from Arabs or Jews; I realize how strong I became as a result of these meetings. I can save myself. I am preparing the ground for my children.[28]

IFD from an Israeli Jewish perspective, according to the director of the Interfaith Encounter Association (IEA), responds to a central problem in Arab-Jewish relations, which is that most Jews have never met Arabs.

There [are] a lot of stereotypes and preconceived notions and fears. There is no separation between Arabs in Israel and Palestinians in the territories and no separation between most of the Palestinian population, which is nice, and the small minority of terrorists. Also, Arabs do not have chance to meet in depth with Jews: each one stands on his own; there is high degree of individualization. The encounter helps people know each other, interact, and build trust and mutual understanding and respect. We assume that dealing with religious issues from a religious perspective is more helpful than dealing with issues from a political perspective.[29]

This objective of rehumanizing the other is most prevalent in the women's interfaith groups: "We do not only meet but also call each other on the phone and visit each other's homes. This deepens the understanding, breaks preconceived notions, and gives a feeling of humanizing the other. For many Jews, Arabs have no figure; but if we meet, then they become a person."[30]

THE NATURE AND STRUCTURE OF INTERFAITH ACTIVITIES

The dominant structure of interfaith activities has been focused on cognitive learning of new information in the form of interpretations of religious texts and rituals. This information is delivered either by selected groups' participants or by specialists on a specific subject who are invited as guest speakers. (This format has been prevelant among groups such as Women's Interfaith Encounter, IEA, Interreligious Coordinating Council in Israel [ICCI], interreligious meetings in Hartman Institute, and Yesodot.) A typical structure of these two-to-three-hour meetings begins with interpersonal and group activities to get acquainted, break the ice, and build personal relationships. This is usually followed by thirty to forty minutes of speakers or participants who prepare and present information on any given theme identified by the organizers or other participants. Next is thirty to forty minutes with mixed small groups to deepen the conversation, and the activity ends with joint or separate prayer. The assumption is that people learn more through the discussion, and the encounter becomes deeper and more positive, when participants discover the humanity in each other.[31] Themes and questions include the meaning of Isra'e Mi'araj (the Prophet Mohammed's night journey to Jerusalem and ascension to heaven), Sukkot, Christmas, jihad, sacrifices in Abrahamic traditions, marriage rituals and conditions, women's status in the Quran, New Testament and Hebrew Scriptures, purity, and so on.

A second format of IFD is to hold theological conversations between religious clergy and theologians. The focus of such meetings is the discovery of differences and similarities in theological interpretations of religious texts. The Hartman Institute has adopted such a theological approach in its activities. These exchanges are highly intellectual and involve elite religious scholars and clergy.[32] Each of the participants delivers a presentation on an agreed-upon theme, and the remaining participants react to the thesis of the presentation.[33] A great deal of theological learning and discovery takes place in such settings; however, as suggested by its critics, this format is disconnected from both current real-life events and from followers of these three faith groups on the ground.

The third interfaith format or structure has been associated with the *sulha,* or reconciliation, meetings, in which large numbers of people attend one or two days of public ceremonies involving music, dance, religious chanting, prayers, and speeches from clergy. The *sulha* meetings were carried out in the Galilee, Jerusalem, and several other locations.[34] Hundreds of local villagers, Israeli Jews, and international guests have attended these gatherings, which aim to bring people together and cultivate their spiritual energy and effort to create a wider network and movement for religious peace.

Such activities have attracted the type of participant who is trying to discover and experience spirituality outside the mainstream faith traditions, as well as a nonobservant audience, who is attracted by the social and cultural characteristics of the event. Lack of individualized process, continuity, and follow-up are major criticisms of this structure, yet it offers an opportunity to reach out to large numbers of average people in these three faith traditions.

PROCESSES IN INTERFAITH MEETINGS

The processes, approaches, and activities of interfaith meetings in Israel and Palestine can be classified according to three major continua: (1) religiocentric versus religiorelative (objectives and framework), (2) political conflict versus harmony (nature of the content), and (3) action and outcomes versus educational process (results). Obviously there are no organizations or approaches that can be classified as falling at only one end of these continua, yet there are certain tendencies in each organization—in terms of how they frame and introduce their interfaith activities, goals, and outcomes—which favor one side of the continua or the other.

Religiocentric Approach

The first type of process in IFD concerns a distinction between passive tolerance and genuine religious appreciation. At one end of the continuum, participants focus on the articulation of a religiocentric perspective, in which each derives his or her own feeling of superiority from his or her own faith tradition. Yet, they carefully leave room for other faiths to be practiced and represented without any direct or conscious attempt to convert others.

A religiocentric Muslim community leader from Israel explains why he began practicing Sufism at age forty:

> I took Sufism as a path after I read the Bible and reached Ben Noun's story before entering Jericho and how his God told him to kill all the inhabitants as they are filthy unbelievers. I realized this is not for me. I took the New Testament and loved the teaching of peace and mercy, but could not solve the Holy Trinity contradiction. How can I believe that there are three entities in one? When I returned to the Quran and read it with new lenses to learn, I realized why Islam is the perfect religion. Peace is perfection and safety, and that is why the saying: "Religion for God is Islam." When we say "peace be upon you" with genuine faith, it means safety and security; no one will harm you.[35]

It is clear that such belief leaves little room for being undermined by theological dialogue with other faiths, but the belief that one's faith is the perfect one may also leave little room for a deep appreciation of other faiths.

Another difficulty with religiocentric conversation is the assumptions that participants often make about the other faith groups. One participant in interfaith dialogue observed this common pitfall in this way: "In IFD groups in Italy, Christians recognize that God has been revealed in different forms many times during history. Thus God was revealed to Mohammad. This is not the same here: Jews in Israel here will not recognize that God was revealed to others. They hide their feelings when they meet with us, but essentially they refuse to share such recognition."[36]

The space of interfaith tolerance shrinks when the predominant theme is theological debate on the nature of "truth" and who holds it, as stated by a Muslim community leader active in IFD:

Islam does not speak against all [forms] of Judaism or Christianity. . . . However, we should talk about Jews who did not follow the teaching of the Bible and those Christians who believe in the Holy Trinity. That is deviation from the truth. . . . [Despite these theological differences,] But on earth we should work together to build communities and live equally and not fight. God will arbitrate or determine at the end [judgment day] who is right or wrong theologically. What is dialogue if I cannot talk about these issues?[37]

Religiocentric assumptions reduce IFD to a stage for displaying one's contentment with chosen beliefs and practices, and limit opportunities for questioning one's own faith, practices, or beliefs. Thus, IFD becomes a way to demarcate different faith traditions more rigidly and to serve as a preventive mechanism against conversion. The following statement, from a Muslim sheikh, illustrates a fundamental dilemma that faces dialoguers in terms of explaining and hearing the meaning of a faith without undermining the other or being undermined: "Meeting the other and knowing him is my goal. The nature of interfaith dialogue should be complementary not contradictory or confrontational. Dialogue between a Muslim and Christian would not mean that the Christian has to accept that Christ was not crucified. That would be the end of his Christian faith and the Muslim cannot accept crucifixion."[38]

Pushed by this paradox, the reality of ethnic discrimination and oppression, and lack of knowledge of the other cultural groups, participants on the community level therefore tend to focus their interfaith conversations mainly on "earthly" or day-to-day issues, with some basic information about specific and selected religious practices. Thus the main distinction between participants in IFD and those who attend secular dialogues and coexistence activities becomes the self-declared religious affiliation; the content of the discussions might actually be quite similar.

Politics versus the Harmony Model

The second continuum has to do with the degree to which political topics enter overtly into dialogue. The majority of interfaith encounters in Israel and Palestine are designed to help participants learn about the other's faith practices and the personal and collective meanings of those practices. The impact of the political reality on the day-to-day lives of the participants and the participants' political orientations are often deliberately excluded from the meetings or agenda. Political issues or conversations about resolving the conflict are absent and explicitly avoided. The three major interfaith organizations (IEA, ICCI, and Yakar Center for Torah, Tradition and Creativity) have each declared their approach to be purposely apolitical. According to a Christian priest and veteran of interfaith dialogue, "The Council for Interreligious Understanding decided not to deal with politics. The focus was on what religion tells us about our lives and ourselves. But for Arabs everything is politics; it does not matter what the issues are, all comes back to politics. Then Jews had to respond [to the political views presented by the Arabs]."[39]

A major cause of frustration among Arab IFD participants has been the tendency of Jewish participants and organizers to exclude serious discussions of contextual conditions. In fact, this refusal to deal with the question of power and the impact of the current political structure often leads to further suspicion, causing Palestinians to be wary of the intentions and motivations of the organizers and stay away. The head of Shari'a Court in Israel captures this distrust:

> For example, when Mufti Al Azhar and chief rabbi meet, it is only symbolic, and they avoid talking about real problems. Even when youth from Ramallah meet with Israeli youth, it is a waste of time when they do not talk about the killing of children but only focus or highlight the beautiful, explain a few verses from the Quran or Bible to each other, and avoid demanding rights and talking about religious political issues. (This is different from the activities of Rabbis for Human Rights, who came to Safad, an Arab City in the Galilee whose Arab residents became refugees in 1948, to discuss the use of the former mosque as an art gallery; in Beir Sabi' the mosque became a dumping area for the city's garbage, and in Qisarya the mosque was used as a bar.) My experience with Jewish religious leaders is frustrating and I have reached the conclusion that this discourse does not help, they represent the powerful side and they are the oppressors, too (even in the interfaith dialogue). Before the Intifada, I worked with a religious interfaith organization; after the head of the organization issued a flyer supporting the occupation and the abuse of human rights in the Intifada. So why waste our time and work with nifaq (inauthentic facades, lies). Thus I do not like to participate in these meetings, but some Muslims participate to portray a positive image of Islam and try to explain why Islam is accused always with violence.[40]

The avoidance of politics is often implemented through restrictions at three levels:

1. No formal political party association of those who participate, something that is accepted by all Arabs and Jews who participate in these interfaith groups.
2. No engagement in any political action, especially demonstrations or other forms of political advocacy, during the meetings. Muslim and Christian participants often disagree and would prefer to include this type of activity, but Jewish participants reject political action as inappropriate in IFD, arguing that there are other venues for political engagement.
3. No political conversation about the conflict during the interfaith meetings. This is the most difficult condition for the participants, especially the Arabs.

The director of ICCI captured the general tendency to avoid political conversations in interfaith settings when he explicitly delinked political change from interfaith educational missions in the following statement:

> I am not trying to solve any conflict. Yossi Belein, Abu Ala' and others are working day and night and have written the Geneva Accord. Our role as civil society

educators and religious figures is a "people-to-people" approach. We bring people to learn how to live together. Politics affect our work; we had joint projects with the bishop in Bethlehem but stopped all activities, as it became dangerous to travel there. Our assumption is that we are not politicians. It is a waste of time to try and talk about how to resolve the conflict. We will get to the Geneva Accord. So we decided to use the time in one project called "Ideals" and focus on land and its meaning, etc. We discussed many painful issues and shared our perceptions, but within a context of understanding and reconciliation.[41]

Jewish participants and coordinators of the various interfaith programs consistently complained that Arabs (especially Muslims) wanted to systematically steer the interfaith conversation toward political issues. These efforts would be resisted with insistence on humanistic, or "pure," religious conversation. The dynamic was captured by the Jewish coordinator of the Women's Interfaith Encounter group in Jerusalem: "Everything is political. I have sat in dialogues where we had no agenda other than to talk about the situation together. So of course it is political all the time. These are endless discussions that go on and on and on and, I mean, I just get tired of them."[42]

The majority of Arabs and Jews (regardless of their religious affiliation) in interfaith settings struggle with the dilemma of how to address the political reality of occupation and violence without severing their personal and organizational activities. The overwhelming majority of Jews want to avoid any political discussion, whereas the overwhelming majority of Arabs want to convince and show Jewish participants the cost of occupation in the territories and the discrimination against Arabs in Israel. This divergence can be extremely frustrating and tiring.

> I am tired of even going over and over people's suffering . . . only hearing people talk about what they are personally suffering from, and I talk about what I am personally suffering from. Unless we can get beyond that, it is just an endless competition. You talking about the problem you are having by being locked in your house and me getting a chance to talk about how my son is still recovering from his bomb-inflicted injury is a never-ending competition on suffering, which I hate.[43]

Most Palestinians (Muslims and Christians) accept the need to avoid the blaming and victimhood exchanges in the interfaith encounter, yet they object to confining the conversation to nonpolitical issues. They insist on conveying their political views and rights and demand political action from Jewish participants. A Palestinian interfaith community leader expressed his views on this issue: "Jews in these dialogues did not want to discuss these problems and do not want genuine peace. They want us to do celebrations, dance, and learn Hebrew songs. This will not bring peace to Jews or Muslims. We should say the truth and the things that the other does not like; these are the basis of peace. Not inviting Jews for mujadra cooking, teaching them our songs, or learning from them the Biblical or Talmudic songs."[44]

Jabour Jabour, another veteran of dialogue and interfaith relations, described these events as "Interfaith—Hollywood and Disney style." He spoke passionately about priorities: "The religious issue is secondary in this context; the Jews are going to take my land, not my religion. Religious discussions are good to remove ignorance. But why there is no declaration against the land confiscation!"[45]

Eventually Jewish coordinators of these interfaith programs become the force or gatekeeper of the apolitical model and disallow any political comments or actions. For example, an Arab woman who attended an IFD meeting could not share her fliers announcing a protest against the Separation Wall; a Palestinian participant who showed a film about the suffering of Palestinians under the occupation was scolded by the coordinator, and the film was interrupted by other Jewish participants because they thought it was too political.[46] A Jewish woman who attended that meeting described the event:

> Nothing [was] said [in the publicity] about people coming and bringing videos for you to confront the reality of what the Israeli army is doing. I understand everybody's point of view in this, and how threatened everybody got. One woman [a Jewish participant] got terribly threatened, I mean she had to sit there and have this thrown in her face when this isn't what she came for. She probably came to escape that and talk to others as a human being. And instead she is being told that she is not a human being; that she is the Israeli army that is oppressing us. A Palestinian organizer got out of his mind: he [had] risked his life, it took him five hours to get here and this woman is telling him he is a terrorist. He got so upset that he just started screaming and a Jewish organizer had to physically restrain him and shut him out of the room. The Jewish organizer was also very upset because he felt betrayed.[47]

While one regional interfaith meeting was taking place in Amman, a double suicide bombing happened in Israel. The participants did not mention it at all for the next three days. For some of the participants, there is a strong degree of disconnection between the political reality and their interfaith experience. As one Jewish coordinator said, "When we do not deal with politics we do not deal with other related issues like suicide bombings. During the same meeting, a reaction operation in Gaza and [the] September 11 attacks took place; those passed and we did not relate to them at all. They did not affect our work."[48]

For Palestinians who attend these interfaith meetings, or any other joint activities with Israelis, not talking about the occupation and its collective and personal impact feels almost like a betrayal of their national identity and community. There is no justification for their participation if they are unable to address these issues. In fact, this is the primary and meaningful contribution to their community's collective need for liberation that they can carry back to justify their participation in such activities in a time of war. The Jewish coordinator of the Women's Interfaith Encounter group in Jerusalem expressed her views regarding the issue of politics in IFD:

So I think that when we are dealing with Palestinians who truly are suffering enormously every day in their situation, they feel that to not talk about this is almost a betrayal. Whereas the Jews who are suffering in their own way from the bombings and from the terrorism that is coming from these same towns, feel like talking with these people is almost traitorous; but they want to do it. They don't want to be threatened by having to explain or justify the actions of the Israeli government or the Israeli army. They want to be able to talk to people as human beings, because they also do not want to have to talk about what Hamas is doing in their towns. The Jews start from this point of view of do not threaten us with all of this stuff about why are we doing this because then we are going to go nowhere. And the Palestinians come saying—okay, we won't—even though they really want to. But of course it comes up in different ways.[49]

Whether to preserve the status quo, escape internal guilt, or avoid competing over who is more victimized, most Jewish participants (and some Arab participants, too) reject discussing political issues in IFD groups. Their insistence on separating religious identity from political or national identity in a conflict context produces pressure on the minority and gives them a less powerful role in dialogue. A Jewish coordinator of the Women's Interfaith Encounter group in Jerusalem stated,

We Jews are defensive because we know our army is doing terrible things and our police are doing terrible things within our own country. We know that. Arabs are having terrible things happen to them, in Israel, in Jerusalem and in Palestine. . . . My point of view is the only way we are going to change it is at a personal level—one to one, person to person. And that is the work that we are doing with Women's Interfaith. I'm learning to understand these women, to love them, to accept them and they are learning to understand and to accept me. They do not see me as an Israeli soldier with a gun. I don't see them as a terrorist with a bomb around their waist, and we can be together, and from that I feel that things can start to radiate out.[50]

However, not all Jewish participants reject the topic of politics in dialogue. Jeremy Milgrom is an example of a religious peace worker who believes in political involvement:

We want people to know the needs of the other, learn more about them, motivate them to do things, and understand the occupation and oppression reality, especially those who work in Jewish frames to policy. Palestinian participants can explain to their side that there are Jews who oppose it and act to change it, and to prevent the indifference among Palestinians and Israelis. It is not possible to talk about religion without relating to the reality of occupation and discrimination. If we neglect this, it will limit the outcomes and results because the true obstacle between people will not be removed. There is a metaphor that people in the encounter who refuse to acknowledge or confront the political reality are similar to a person sitting on a chair that is pressing on the foot of the other person. How can we ignore that the chair is on the foot, causing pain, and continue to talk about work, music, culture, food, religion. How can we neglect the pain and suffering of the other and talk about theology?[51]

Events on the ground constitute a major challenge to the supporters of the apolitical interfaith model because suicide bombings or major military operations in the West Bank and Gaza often interrupt the interfaith meetings, participants drop out, and some interfaith groups stopped meeting. As a Palestinian woman interfaith coordinator confirms, "First we strictly made sure that religion is the only theme in the encounter, but soon realized that we cannot with the current situation, for example when 'problems in Jenin' occurred we were forced to cancel the meeting. We met after and decided to continue because of the situation."[52]

For the minority participants, religion is not separate from politics or social life. One Arab participant expressed this perspective: "In our meetings, Jewish participants refused to accept that religion affects other aspects of life, so we do not deviate from the discussion of religion and rituals, we speak about weddings, how each religion prepares the bride and groom for it. But do we live on the moon? We talk about these things despite [the violence that] takes place around us."[53] In supporting political themes in the interfaith meeting, a Christian bishop compares the Arab-Jewish relations with European Christian-Jewish relations:

> You cannot take politics out of dialogue, we are not in the seventh century or fifteenth, we are under occupation and I am dialoguing with my occupier. You have to enter into politics, otherwise it is unsuccessful dialogue. Our dialogue agenda in Palestine is different than Europeans': we never killed or persecuted Jews, like Europeans who killed them because of their religion, whether in inquisitions or [during the] Third Reich in Germany. We are not anti-Semitic. We killed each other for political reasons. We tell them that in dialogue.[54]

The tension of avoiding political issues holds the group hostage; it often does not move or establish genuine trust or relationship, because "the elephant in the room" syndrome persists until the issue is tackled in one way or another. In an interfaith training in Israel, a Druze woman stated, "After two years in this program, this is the first time we are able to talk about politics. We were scared of politics." Another woman claimed: "As a member of the minority I would like to talk briefly and concretely about the issues . . . after addressing political issues, I learned a lot and think it is worth talking about difficult things."[55]

Avoidance of the political and historical contexts of interfaith relations can also be attributed to the fact that many IFD activities have been launched by Jews and Christians born and raised outside the country, rather than by Jews and Arabs born and raised in Israel. The nature of Christian-Jewish relations outside Israel is different from inside Israel, where issues of occupation and self-determination dominate. Jews and Christians outside the Middle East may be asking for apology and expressing sorrow. As Rabbi Milgrom put it, "They want to prove they are fine." But although Jewish-Christian encounters outside Israel involve confronting a history of anti-Semitism, they are not encounters between occupiers and occupied.

An apolitical approach to IFD is mostly based on celebratory/ritualistic sets of activities. (Several of these initiatives were imported by Jewish immigrant activists.) Some described them as activities for fun (or *kaif*). In a critique of these activities, several interfaith participants agreed that this approach (celebratory and fun-oriented) does not fit in the Israeli-Palestinian context because Israeli Jews and Arabs expect the encounter to be difficult and painful, and they view it with suspicion. There is a difference between the animosity of past generations and the animosity of today, claimed one. "We cannot say today that our ancestors did this to each other, and we are friends today. It is impossible to say that to Palestinians today, as there is still pain. It is difficult or impossible to say we are friends today and nothing remains from the suffering. We cannot say that today. It is impossible not to think of Hebron in 1929 and 1948."[56] Encounters based on these assumptions and goals do not take into account the conflict, pain, and suffering experienced by both the Israeli and Palestinian communities.

The *sulha* events are an example of the apolitical "fun" approach. A Jewish rabbi IFD veteran criticized these initiatives as nonsense. "Whoever believed that is really naive…they wanted to fix everything in two days. They called it *sulha*. They disconnected from reality. There is this need and desire, but we cannot do it this way. We cannot do reconciliation this way. We need to do activities to prepare for reconciliation. It will not end in two days of celebrations. We do things to end the conflict."[57]

Hisham Najjar, from Bethlehem, attended several interfaith meetings before he decided to stay away from IFD. He criticized the apolitical model: "Most of these interfaith meetings have become cultural meetings, not necessarily theological or about belief systems. They chat about their food, music, the way they pray and live, etc. They avoid dealing with controversial issues in the Jewish faith, such as the view of the other, for example: how Jewish scripture of 2,000 years views the other as animals, etc. Why can't we deal with that?"[58]

Within the context of apolitical interfaith encounter, there is a tendency to emphasize harmony and similarity, which follows from the depoliticization of IFD. The harmony approach bases itself primarily on seeking similarities and positive connectors between the different religious groups or individuals. Thus, it focuses on universal values as expressed in a religious discourse or narrative. Despite the continuous complaints against this model and the frustration of Palestinian participants with these types of meetings, Palestinians continue to attend, using them as a platform to press for more exploration of political concerns.

In dismissing the assumption that religion is the cause of the problem rather than politics, the Palestinian coordinator of an interfaith project in the Hartman Institute recommends a focus on theological differences and contradictions:

> It is ridiculous to think that if all the religious differences are removed, there will be peace. . . . The problem is political. They bring religion in to gain publicity,

money, or from some other self-interested motive. The interfaith dialogue discussions in PASSIA [a Palestinian center that hosted a series of interfaith meetings] are a waste of time and superficial. Jews, Muslims, and Christians avoiding the real issues and declaring that there are no problems between them. This is fake. The real interfaith dialogue is in Hartman Institute, in which we examine the text and the scripture, with philosophers who want to know the relationship to God. How do Christians experience God differently than Muslims? How can a Christian see God and feel his presence, while I, as a Muslim, cannot? We live in two worlds far apart from each other theologically and spiritually; how can I understand that? These are the types of questions that interfaith dialogue needs to focus on. . . . Our purpose is to learn what humans think/say/feel about God. Understanding the dilemma of how a Christian can see God through Christ and as a Muslim, I cannot experience that. We need to ask "Why?" and "How?" and examine the intellectual, philosophical aspects of the Holy Trinity. We must dare to tackle these questions in our interfaith encounters, instead of trying to be nice and polite towards each other.[59]

In intra-Palestinian IFD, emphasis on harmony is not confined to Israeli and Palestinian interactions. It appears as well when Palestinian Christians and Muslims highlight the need for a focus on common ground to make their national unity central and to aid the struggle for their shared goals of equal rights in Israel and for the Palestinian state. The major aim of intra-Palestinian IFD is to create a common base for understanding and coexistence, and especially to create recognition that, as one put it, "we have the same national political cause."[60] The harmony emphasis appears in the slogan *Wihdat Al Masir* (Unity of Fate), as termed by several Palestinian Christians and Muslims. One Palestinian added, "Dialogue over the constitution of Palestine also brings awareness to Christians and Muslims who suffer from the same occupation and have the same fate."[61] For many Christians and Muslims, the Palestinian interfaith context becomes a forum for national cohesion and an instrument to emphasize their national unity in the face of occupation. Musa Daweish from Bethlehem confirms this Palestinian approach to interfaith:

Arab unity is our slogan. . . . The only way to resolve our problems is through Arab solidarity and unity, regardless what you name it. Now after 100 years, Arab unity is the key to resolution. Arab national unity requires subunities of Palestinian nationalism and religious unity. National unity is the only way to resolve the Palestinian problems.[62]

A Palestinian Christian priest who has participated in many interfaith groups concurs:

Muslim-Christian relations have an element of creativity, because we are not asking from what religion a person is but what he/she can do; whether he/she can fulfill his/her duties for nation and homeland. The slogan for Muslim-Christian meetings has been always "Religion belongs to God, but homeland is for all."[63]

Palestinian Christians' concerns in the Holy Land are generally framed within a national unity discourse. Thus, their appeal to European and American Christians for help is clearly framed by their national identity, as opposed to fear of Muslim repression or persecution, as is often portrayed by Israelis and certain Western Christian groups. Christians often serve an outreach role for Palestinian Muslims who cannot otherwise communicate their message to Christians in the United States and elsewhere. The use of Christian affiliation to tell the Palestinian story of victimhood and demand assistance from the outside world is a historical role played by Christian political and religious leaders, who are largely ignored and invisible among Europeans and Americans.

But the emphasis on this process within the Palestinian community has become a stale narrative. The reliance on the same discourse prevents participants from dealing with real-life issues:

> We need to penetrate new frontiers. We are repeating the same things. For example, we do the same thing in our annual conference. We repeat the same narrative: "Christians participated in the national Palestinian struggle" and "Christians participated in the Arab world national movement and are an integral part of the anticolonial movement." We need new stories and new directions to expand. . . . We have heard the same story for many years about the past. To make new achievements, we need to be close to reality. . . . Christians come and say "They attacked me because I am Christian." A Muslim complained, "the crosses are fifty meters high." That means there are problems in reality. Confronting these is the real encounter. . . . The genuine encounter is to confront this reality. . . . In the Bible there is a verse: "When you know the *Haq* [truthfulness, or the truth], that will liberate you."[64] ["You shall know the truth, and the truth shall set you free."]

In intra-Palestinian IFD that follows the harmony framework, even the basic stereotypes that exist between Muslims and Christians are not explored. In fact, all Palestinian interviewees admit that there are no appropriate channels or spaces to deal with such themes. But there is a need to begin delving into the dynamics of Christian-Muslim relations, in both Israel and Palestine, especially in schools and community gatherings. A Palestinian bishop, Muneeb Yunan, has been encouraging Christians to address the topic and attend to the relationship:

> We are the same national group, why should we be lower or higher? This is the type of dialogue we have with Muslims: What type of Islamic state should there be in Palestine? Some Christians are hesitant and fearful that dialogue with Islamic sheikhs might produce problems and conflict. But, on the contrary, we are reaching good understanding and exploring deeper relationship with them. In Palestine you cannot separate Muslims from Christians. We also should talk about the problems of intermarriage, why can't Christian boys marry Muslim women? Why can't a Christian man marry a Muslim woman in the church with Christian vows? We have to talk about these earthly things too, in honesty. We cannot prevent boys and girls from loving each other . . . but maybe we can discuss the way to do that and the consequences of eloping. . . . Arafat and Muslim religious leaders

refuse to address or discuss this issue. We need to confront religious fanaticism and radicalism. . . . They say, "We do not want to cause *fitna*" [internal quarrel or strife]. But we cannot continue denying religious extremism and fanaticism.[65]

A similar concern was voiced by a Muslim scholar who identified the need for intra-Muslim dialogue and space for various Muslim groups and voices to exchange views and positions regarding their relationships with other faith groups. The majority of efforts and resources are devoted to interfaith meetings, while Muslim intrafaith meetings are not recognized yet as a primary need.

Theoretically, the foundation for the interfaith harmony model stems from the minimization and transcendence of differences. It prefers to focus on basic human similarities such as the needs for respect, love, and dignity. Such emphasis on this secondary language (as opposed to primary or particular language used by each religious tradition) is reflected in another classic example of the harmony model in a creative book published by Ghantus Ghantus, an Arab educator from the Galilee.[66] In his description of the book, Ghantus Ghantus focuses on patience as a common religious quality:

> I proved that the three religions motivate the person to be patient. I proved that patience brings understanding love [*mahabat*]. Things can be restored to their order. The holy books push us to work according to these messages, to work for the benefit of the people and our people. . . . It [religion] is positive, it is sweet water. Religion is a stream of water, many do not see it and many others see it but do not drink from it. . . . Religion brings good motivation. . . . It calls people to *khayer* [doing good]. Prophets are educated men and have messages to solve human problems and conflicts through faith and good treatment. Love each other, make concessions, not to support [oppression]. Support your brother if he is with a *haq* [just or right cause], but not if he is oppressive, as religion does not support this. Religion states that we should stand against oppression and prevent the negative.[67]

Such emphasis on similarities and harmony is prevalent in regional and local interfaith meetings. For example, in his speech in Amman, a prominent Druze sheikh emphasized commonalities and harmonious human relations. He also portrayed a perfect, positive image of his own religion, without any critique or self-examination.[68]

Another form of minimization and idealization of religion is based on the assumption that all religious teachings are similar in their call for peace and harmony. Such an analysis is offered by Musa Darweish and confirms this assumption: "If all religious people in all three religions interpreted truthfully their religion, then peace will be a reality, because no single religion calls for hatred, oppression, and fighting, but for brotherhood and friendship. Islam, for example, states, 'we created you tribes and nations to be acquainted.' Also Judaism has teachings to treat others nicely and gently. However, contrary to the true teachings of religions, religious leaders are giving *fatwa* to kill and fight. Ovadia Yosef, a chief rabbi in Israel, describes Arabs as insects that need to be smashed. This is not mentioned in any Biblical text."[69]

In this minimization of religious differences, participants often overemphasize similarities, despite their fear and distrust of other faith groups. This fear and distrust often, nonetheless, find their way into the conversation, and appear in the midst of our interviews with those who embrace the harmony model. For example, a Muslim participant said, "God recognizes the three religions; our fathers are Adam, Mohammed, and Christ, etcetera. The Christians are similar to us, despite their saying that *Isa is ibn Allah* ("Christ is the son of God"). I say that God gave to every religion the same; the difference is in traditions and rules. I do not drink alcohol or eat pork, but Christians do. Druze are more difficult to understand because of the nature of their beliefs. I feel that we are the same as humans, but we make things more complicated. I do not trust to eat in a Christian house because they might put pork for me. . . . They are humans like me and if I understand them as humans, then I will have less fear to get closer. We are all humans."[70]

In the harmony model, religious and theological differences are dismissed as insignificant or not a serious block in Arab-Jewish interaction. However, beneath this often lies a deep and strong preference of one's own faith, as stated by a Muslim IFD leader:

> Interfaith dialogue is not far from social and economic dialogue or calling for rights. On the contrary, it is as essential to Islam as equality. As the Prophet said, "no Arab is better than a foreigner except in faith." Dialogue in Islam is strongly founded; as believers we have full belief in dialogue. We present our faith to Jews and Christians as it is: we are not ashamed of the Quran and we show them how beautiful it is. It is a perfect holy book.[71]

In this context of harmony, Arabs and Jews in many cases idealize the period of Islam's hegemony in Spain and cite it as an ideal period reflecting harmony and peace among Jews and Muslims. There is no doubt that the Islamic empire in Spain, in comparison to European kingdoms at the time, provided more pluralist and tolerant institutions for religious minorities (including Judaism). Overemphasizing the period in interfaith interactions to justify pursuit of the harmony model, combined with ignoring differences and the political reality of violence, become an obstacle for achieving genuine understanding and meaningful dialogue.

Linking Theology with Action

The third process model has to do with linking IFD to action and outcomes. As illustrated above, the harmony and apolitical interfaith model dominates Israeli-Palestinian interfaith exchanges. However, there are a few activists and theologians who call for an alternative type of IFD based on a liberation theology model. Such dialogue is aimed at advocacy and a critical examination of reality to contribute to a resolution of the root causes of the conflict, instead of approaches that de facto provide opportunities to tolerate or live with the occupation or discrimination.[72]

In addition, the liberation theology model allows a path to collective and individual action in interfaith groups. It connects the interfaith field with other Israeli and Palestinian social movements working directly to remove the occupation, a dimension that has been absent from the majority of interfaith organizations and their directors' goals. The need for linkages to social or political movements in Palestine and Israel was also emphasized as a criterion of success by a few interviewees (four Arabs and Jews). Walid Salem, director of Panorama, a Palestinian community development NGO, stressed that there should be a link between these interfaith organizations and initiatives and the wider human rights and democracy organizations, even if the majority are secular nonreligious groups.[73]

Rabbi Jeremy Milgrom offered several examples of this model by examining the work of the organization Rabbis for Human Rights. Naeem Ateek from Sabeel (a Palestinian organization in Jerusalem) has also organized several interfaith activities based on nonviolent resistance to the occupation. These types of faith-based peace and justice activities operate on totally different assumptions than those within the apolitical and harmony IFD model. Participants in such meetings have taken a clear stand against occupation and violence deployed on both sides. In addition, the majority of participants have developed a level of political awareness that motivated them to adopt political actions as a form of advocacy for human rights and peacebuilding.

THE INSTRUMENTALITY OF RELIGION: SEPARATING RELIGION FROM NATIONALISM

When examining the various motivations, goals, and models of IFD, a clear distinction emerges between using a religious approach to deepen one's faith and to understand other faiths, versus using religious beliefs as an instrument to reduce violence and preach for political coexistence. The analysis that follows shows how all three of the process models described above point to a clash—not of theologies, but of views on the relationship of religion and nationalism, or religion and political justice. That religious identity is distinct from national identity is not taken for granted by all participants. For others, the distinction is obliterated because the responsibility to work for political justice is intrinsic to religion. In this view, political equality as a value originates in religion.

The need to separate the discussion and exploration of religious beliefs from national and political dynamics is rooted in a Western political philosophy of secular liberalism that separates religion from politics. It associates religion with the private rather than collective public sphere. The classic example is the expressed "separation of church and state" written into the United States' Constitution. When examining IFD models as they appear in Israel and Palestine, it becomes clear that individual and apolitical dialogical processes respond to the needs of those participants who affiliate with or are accustomed to such Western values.

Within the current political structure, in which Arabs view themselves as collectively oppressed and discriminated against, asymmetric power dynamics are perpetuated by an individualized approach to dialogue and peace. Thus, when the majority model of apolitical, individual, and purely spiritual approaches dominates IFD, the cultural and political power paradoxes become a source of constant tension among participants, and they reduce the legitimacy of the entire interfaith field in the eyes of the minority. The interfaith meeting is perceived as another forum serving majority political and cultural domination. Such a perspective was clearly reflected in most Arab and some Jewish participants' statements quoted throughout this chapter.

This tension within IFD appears as well in other Arab-Jewish encounter groups in Israel. Many preach coexistence and work toward cultural understanding, with little attention to the political and conflictual realities and no ideology of social and political change (Abu-Nimer 1999). Linking politics and IFD is a measure of legitimacy for Palestinian participants, as can be seen in the statement of a Muslim Sufi leader and founder of several interfaith programs:

> The successful meeting is based on the truth not on the belief of the Jewish state [the land belonging to Jews only]. I reject that [belief] and support a state for all its citizens. I am before you [present on the land before the Israeli Jews] here and was not imported from Mexico. I am part of the rocks in Marj Ibn Amer [reference to the plains of lower Galilee], I was molded here. No one can separate me from it. I say these things without fear, because it is God's word of truth.[74]

The strong linkage between national identity and interfaith encounter for Palestinians has to do with the different identity priorities of dominant and minority cultures. Women's Interfaith Encounter's experience classically illustrated this when they ventured to create a joint Web site: "We created a linkage on the website to portray our identity—how Palestinian national identity is the source for Palestinian women while for the Israeli women, their family identity comes first."[75]

Deepening religious understanding is not the primary goal for some Jewish participants. Rather, it is an instrument to increase a feeling of coexistence with Arabs without addressing the discrimination Arabs face in Israel. "We brought together 200 people for the first time in Khan Yunis. They never met each other before. It was a start, but two weeks later the Intifada began [so we could not continue with the project]. We have visited many places and brought many people together to break the misperceptions and build understanding. We have some religious aspects, but our encounter is mainly human. We build relationships and break the dehumanization processes."[76] A Jewish veteran of interfaith encounters stated her perception of the need to preserve the separation between politics and religion because of her belief that, when the two are mixed, violence and debates emerge: "We should not mix politics with dialogue. In politics people accuse each other and interfaith dialogue is about learning and getting to know each other. Politics and religion are two totally separate and different things."[77]

On the other hand, for many Arabs, IFD is just a platform from which to break stereotypes about Islam, educate Jews about discrimination against Arabs, and state their historical right to the land. A Muslim interfaith leader described offers of reassurance along with his nationalist message:

> The Quran says, "When in control, the Muslim forgave [*ida malak afa*]." See how beautiful these teachings? The Islamic text always emphasizes mercy and forgiveness of others. We say to Jews, why be afraid of Islam if we both are humans? Our objective is to bring back the Israeli society into a civil human society, not a military one. [Israel] should not confiscate land. God is Great—Why take his land after having it for thousands of years for someone coming from Russia? Our work is aimed at this [to communicate this message] through dialogue with the other.[78]

Utilizing the interfaith setting as a forum mainly for interpersonal relations is perceived by Arab participants as a form of denial of reality. An Arab woman from Israel confirms this:

> A person who thinks that [the conflict] is only religious is cheating himself/herself. When you discuss politics, left-wing women say that they do not want to be put in the corner so they become defensive; I can understand that. But the right-wing women come with the belief that they do not have a political identity. They want others to get to know them as humans, as religious persons. This is immaturity.[79]

Because they believe that Jews tend to ignore their plight, Palestinian participants view the articulation of their political rights through IFD as the national duty of every Palestinian who attends. This notion was best expressed by an Arab Sufi Muslim leader:

> The majority and Jews initiate dialogue because they are the majority and want stability; they do not want the minority to be violent. Yet Muslims are not a minority; we are a majority in the world. . . . We are more numerous than the Chinese, Americans, or Europeans. Thus it is a matter of internal perceptions. We—Muslims—are stronger and morally higher. Jewish dialoguers manage to "buy" some Muslim leaders [that is, those who refuse to express Palestinian national rights, and support Jewish Israeli interests in exchange for certain personal benefits], but these are a minority and they are traitors, any nation has traitors. They are lower than human, like animals.[80]

These two sets of intentions clash when both realities are brought into the IFD setting. Jewish participants, especially organizers, often assume the role of process guard and prevent such deviations from the "agreed upon" rules.

Those sentiments of rage and frustration among Palestinians who took part in IFD during the Intifada were summarized by a Palestinian Christian priest who attended many interfaith meetings: "A person who believes in reconciled humanity cannot tolerate this situation: interfaith dialogue was more an abnormal and stressful situation. It did not change anything, it was more like 'dialogue and kill us.' I could not do that anymore."[81]

In addition, the paradox of nationalism and religion in the interfaith encounter is reflected in the contrasting criteria for success employed by participants. For example, when Muslim IFD participants evaluated their encounters with Christians, they used understanding and finding ways to coexist and learn about the other as measures. Yet when evaluating their encounters with Jews, their main concern was whether the occupation was discussed, which prevented deeper understanding of the other's faith. Measures of success are discussed in greater depth in the next section. To conclude this discussion of preferences on the separation of nationalism/political engagement and faith/religion, it seems clear once more that to separate IFD from the reality of the conflict and to focus solely on theological questions goes against the needs of the underdog or minority.

SUCCESS AND ACCOMPLISHMENTS

As in other areas of peacebuilding, in IFD, defining success is crucial for sustaining participants and organizers as well as for engaging a wider circle of people who learn about or observe that success. Thus, it is crucial for interfaith participants and organizers to be able to clearly articulate their indicators of success and compare them with their ongoing expectations. One of the typical sources of frustration among dialogue participants is the gap between their declared and hidden expectations and their assessment of actual outcomes. Such is the case among the majority of Arab participants (as well as the general public), who measure success according to whether IFD accomplishes the following: (1) leads to macro or micro political change; (2) motivates individuals and groups to change their behavior and take concrete actions to change political reality; and (3) increases awareness among Jews regarding discriminatory policies, the reality of occupation, and the rights of Arabs to the land.

For many Muslims there are concrete urgent issues IFD should address. The head of the Islamic Shari'a Court in Israel summarized these concerns and proposed them as criteria for measuring the success of IFD:

When the Knesset began its campaign against Islamic mosques, the rabbis did not help us. We [Muslim judges] tried to ask for help to intervene to stop demolition. There is a gap between dialogue and actions:

- Imams only receive 2,800 Israeli New Shekels as salary, which is below the poverty line salary.
- It is permitted to teach Islamic religion only one hour in schools.
- Religious studies are not recognized as part of matriculation exams.
- Islamic private schools, unlike Christian and Jewish ones, do not operate freely.

Why doesn't religious dialogue work on these issues that stand in the middle? Only recently was the Islamic Shari'a court in Israel separated from the ministry of religion: it was under the Jewish domination and control for so many decades. Dialogue should be based on equality and symmetry to serve humanity; it should not be based on superiority.[82]

Despite having a variety of motives, hopes, and criteria of success, most Arab participants settle for confining their criteria of success to stereotype and prejudice reduction, and limit their expectations of IFD's impact to individual change in attitudes and perceptions. For example, a Muslim Sufi active in IFD declares,

> Interfaith groups are different in their approaches; our perspective is that protest is not necessarily effective and does not do any good. Our motto is "plant a tree rather than curse those who uproot a tree; do not curse darkness, instead light a candle." Nothing will disappear or change if we curse in protest. Through my connection with others, I can have an effect. How much can a protest affect [the political situation]? Take the example of the protest against increasing Arab towns' budgets: how many days have we put tents in front of the ministry and how much was the impact? More important than protests (which have a cumulative effect) is to sit in front of a person who has preconceived notions and stereotypes and try to change these notions and stereotypes. Getting rid of those through dialoguing with the other is more important and effective than trying to get rid of them through protest.[83]

As we have discussed at length above, IFD settings, designs, and implementation in Israel and Palestine are largely defined as apolitical and deliberately avoid addressing any aspect of political structures or themes. As a result, the main measurements of success and accomplishment are applied at the individual rather than the collective level of interaction, and focus on interpersonal relationship building through rehumanization processes as well as on prejudice- and stereotype-reduction activities. A powerful example was shared by an Arab woman: "Success is getting rid of the paranoia of the Mossad being everywhere and behind all eyes, ears, and tongues. This is an internal change due to the trust of the Jewish side. When dialogue breaks all stereotypes it is successful."[84]

Learning About and Understanding Other Faiths

Interfaith encounters, like any other dialogue processes, aim primarily to deepen one's understanding and knowledge of the other. The assumption underlying such processes is that ignorance is humanity's enemy. Understanding the other's faith (including rituals, values, and practices) functions as the primary tool or vehicle to achieve that knowledge. By focusing specifically on similarities and exploring some differences in faith practices and beliefs in a highly tense and violent reality, participants experience a sense of accomplishment and success.

All Jewish participants and coordinators identified such learning as the primary criteria of success in the interfaith setting. A Jewish participant described her views of a successful interfaith encounter: "Success is to stay with the group and learn new things like, for example, discussing women's purity and the Jewish rituals to achieve such purity and cleanness in a certain period. Such a concept was surprising to Muslim women, they were surprised; even some Jewish women did not know that. Muslim women suggested that similar practices could be implemented in Ramadan when men and women do not have sexual relations."[85]

IFD for understanding might add to the simple exploration of the other's faith rituals and the study and comparison of sacred texts. The director of ICCI articulated this interest:

> An example of a successful group is one that met for eighteen months and studied the texts, both religious and other forms of narratives. An hour was allocated to the study of the text and half hour for discussion. In addition to this, activities included presenting papers, finding meanings and energy, learning new things, and having a less angry discussion. The meaning of land in religious traditions was also explored. Most of the work focused on the text instead of the free-flowing conversations. We try to have a product at the end, but this is not always successful.[86]

Another successful example is the interfaith meetings organized by PASSIA (Palestinian Academic Society for the Study of International Affairs), a Palestinian research center in Jerusalem. The Jerusalem project began in 1996 with the blessing of the Palestinian Authority, and it involved highly visible religious scholars and leaders (Christians, Muslims, and Jews). Discussions in PASSIA explore the shared and unique meaning of Jerusalem in the three faith groups and the ways in which Jerusalem can be shared. The Arab Christian-Muslim dialogue group (centered in Beirut, Lebanon) emerged from this series of meetings and was expanded to include Christians and Muslims from the Arab world. This type of group was adopted by Al Azhar as well as the Middle East Council of Churches. The Muslim-Christian-Jewish dialogue also produced results through the participation of Israeli negotiators on Jerusalem, especially Rabbi Melchior, who participated in the dialogue regarding Jerusalem and benefited from the reports and research produced by the group. Negotiators also used the group's reports and research in the Camp David negotiations.[87]

Rehumanizing the Other

Forming interpersonal and genuine human relationships with people from other faith groups was cited as a primary criterion of success by many participants, especially the Jewish members. In the Jerusalem Women's Interfaith Encounter, the story is told that Muslim and Christian Palestinian women were organizing food and medicine for the Palestinians struggling to endure the siege of Jenin. When they heard that a Jewish participant had lost her nephew, who was serving in the Israeli army during the fighting in Jenin, they went to visit her. The Jewish coordinator of the group described the woman's reaction: "After the death of my nephew, I thought about everything, I did not know how to continue living. After the women visited me, it was obvious that I will continue."[88]

These courageous moves taken by people from the community break the boundaries erected by the continuous dehumanization processes. A Palestinian Christian from Israel and an IFD participant confirmed her solidarity with this Israeli Jewish woman: "As a Christian believer I try to implement this [forgiveness] in all my life. When Jenin events took place, a nephew of one Jewish participant was killed, I forgot I am Palestinian and that Jews entered Jenin and I went to visit her. I wanted to share her pain, and I rejected my Palestinian and her Israeli identity. She was very touched and affected by my visit. I encouraged her to return to the meetings. . . . following this we decided to visit each other in our houses."[89]

This act of humanizing the other is deeply satisfying to participants. The Jewish coordinator of the Women's Interfaith Encounter group in Jerusalem provided additional examples of caring expressed among participants:

> That we were already at a level of being human was enough to be able to do that. Another success for me is that every time there is a *pigua* [bombing], there is a Christian Palestinian woman who lives in Jerusalem who will call me just to make sure how everyone is, how everyone is doing. When it was Christmastime, my daughter, who is in the group, said, "I want to see Christmas," something we don't have. So as I was calling all of the Christian women to wish them a Merry Christmas, if any of them said anything, I said, you know, we would love to see a Christmas tree. So we went to several homes in East Jerusalem to visit their Christmas, to be part of their Christmas celebration. At Sukkot time, I invited all of the women to come to my sukkah. And women who have never come to my neighborhood, who have never been in a sukkah, all of the sudden were participating in that.[90]

Events like this, in which Muslims and Christians attend a Jewish religious ritual, are indeed rare in the context of the conflict. The interfaith group provides a unique opportunity for mutual exploration of the meaning of the religious rituals of the other.

The process of rehumanization has powerful transformative impacts that affect many individuals who participate in the encounter. Instances of such individual transformation are often cited as indicators of success. A Sufi imam from Majd Alkurum (an Arab village in Israel) provided some examples: "For instance, some people who lost family members were willing to donate human organs to others, even to their enemies; bereaved parents who are willing to meet their victimizers, etc. That is the peak of forgiveness."[91]

Reducing fears and overcoming stereotypes is another success of IFD, especially when the group continues to meet on a regular basis. A Jewish IFD coordinator described her own transformation as a result of contact with a Palestinian woman:

To me, the success this showed is that our planning or coordinating group had been able to develop that level of confidence in each other that their women would come and sit in the same room with a stranger that they might be very afraid of. The first night I spent with [an Arab participant] was when we went to Berlin together for an interfaith conference. In the middle of the night, while we are lying there talking, sharing the same bed, she said to me, "You know if my friends knew that I was doing this, sharing a bed with a Jew, they would say to me, aren't you afraid she is going to knife you in the middle of the night?" And I said, "You [Palestinians] are the guys with the knife, we [Jews] don't do that." It is like this kind of thing to me is enormously successful, that the women are able to just trust. Even though it goes against their fears, and what their communities are telling them.[92]

The above statement reflects a basic degree of mistrust and fear even among women who attend IFD events. These emotions are not necessarily derived from or rooted in religious differences, but are shaped primarily by the dynamics of the conflict. IFD functions as a relatively safe space in which such fears and suspicions are explored.

Success Is Just Meeting at All

Under the harsh conditions of the Al Aqsa Intifada, success for most Jewish participants was identified as simply being able to meet Palestinians from the Occupied Territories or even from Israel. Suicide bombings, curfews, and the constant escalation and militarization of the Intifada have significantly reduced the possibilities of meeting people from other faiths, in any setting. Most of the post-Oslo Israeli-Palestinian joint projects collapsed or were put on hold (including many IFD meetings). Thus, meeting the other became a success in itself, regardless of the actual accomplishments of the encounters.

An Israeli Jewish veteran of IFD confirmed that this is what many participants believe to be criteria for success: "Success is the mere fact that we continue to meet and are not destroyed by the external conditions, bombings, etc. We used to start all over again after every bombing or violence wave, but now we keep in touch and have cell phones, and it is much easier to go on despite the escalation."[93] Under the pressure of the violent conflict and dynamics, every interfaith meeting becomes a success in the eyes of its organizers. It is a step forward. Seeking human connections despite religious differences keeps alive the hope for a different future. An Arab Muslim woman from the Galilee remarked "[Success is when] we reach this place in which Jews, Hindus, Muslims, Christians or Sikhs are all treated as human brothers [and] I will work for their interest like they do. This will be a better and more enjoyable world to live in."[94]

Success in intra-Palestinian IFD (between Muslims and Christians) is also found in the mere fact of its existence: being able to carry it out, produce some publications, and utilize it to draw attention to the need to remove the occupation and to a common enemy. Musa Darweish from Bethlehem described success for Palestinians in IFD: "In Al-Liqa [a Christian-Muslim center for interfaith relations created in the 1980s; the name means "encounter"], success lies in the fact that they meet and discuss problems of occupation and denounce oppression. It is also reflected when participants oppose some ways of religious fanatic expression on both sides."[95]

Spreading the Message of Interfaith Peace

Carrying out more programs and conducting more activities, even without specific evidence that such activities are contributing to a wider understanding or change in people's action or behavior, is still considered an indicator of success among several organizations and coordinators.

> In Yesodot [interfaith organization] we felt complete success that there are programs that grew out of us. We did not remain in dialogue ourselves, but we have "children of our programs," such as the emergence of the Jaffa school encounter. In addition to more participants, there was also expansion to the outside: we were in Bosnia and Germany. Activities also go beyond the meeting. Three active interfaith participants are doing a weekly radio program, there are visits among families, etc. We broke the barriers of Jews to visit Arab villages. [Even after thousands were killed], we managed to break the image and barriers. They placed the Jewish participants in a dilemma of seeing that we are not savages. [The Jewish participants] admitted the discrimination, but said, "we did not know." There was an understanding of the other.[96]

Again, success for many Arab participants is measured by removing negative perceptions among Jewish participants regarding Islam and Arabs in general, even when the tool is reading scripture.

> The Abraham Path is a Sufi way to read the Sufi text with Jews and Arabs, to show the Sufi image and text as peaceful and tolerant. There is great attraction [on the part of] educated and intellectual Jews [to learning] to know Sufism. Thank God we managed to show the Sufi text in [a way] which [had] the Jews [say], "We see the enormous philosophical traditions as well as the cultural scientific aspect of the Islamic tradition."[97]

Reaching out beyond the "the preaching to the choir" syndrome is perceived as a criterion for success among all participants. In fact, the inability to reach out to wider Jewish, Muslim, or Christian communities was consistently mentioned by those who criticize the role of IFD in the Israeli-Palestinian context. A Palestinian woman IFD participant from Bethlehem criticized interfaith work: "Peace workers and dialogue do not have [a] community base or grassroots followers or constituencies; they also lack impact on the policy or high-level leadership."[98] An Israeli Jewish director of the IEA group described his group's efforts to reach beyond the usual circle:

> Success is to get to people who are not professional dialoguers or addicted dialoguers. We get to settlers and [the] poor population and marginalized groups. We

encourage people to be honest and bring their religious differences, even if they believe that Jews are the chosen people or that all people should be Muslims. . . . There are three interfaith organizations in Jerusalem who work with the same 300 people, what value do we have [through] such meetings?[99]

However, the paradox of reaching a wider community is connected with the ability of the organizers to portray their interfaith meetings as apolitical and aimed at facilitating mainly individual relationships and spiritual explorations. The power of this "safe approach" (avoiding political discussions and focusing on religious explorations) is that interfaith conversations can reach Jewish participants with center or right-wing political ideologies. This type of interfaith conversation has even made a historical appearance in a Jewish yeshiva.[100]

The need for interfaith groups to reach out to the wider community also exists within the Palestinian community, as stated by a Christian priest:

There should be some efforts to bring the encounter outcomes to the street. The Al-Liqa Center had an initiative that stopped because of the Intifada. We brought sheikhs and priests from Beit Jala and Bethlehem and started a conversation. There were fifteen of them. . . . Even though there is only half a mile between the church in Bethlehem and the Omar mosque, they have never met before. We need to create spaces and stages where they can meet each other; stages that can be seen from the street. . . . For example if I, a priest, sit beside the imam or sheikh on a TV program, this will send a message to the people. We need to increase these spaces not in fake way, but genuinely. Or we can go to schools and talk to students; these actions will help in developing the culture of dialogue.[101]

A popular example of success in Israel, which was repeatedly defined as the initiative that has reached furthest beyond the usual interfaith audience, is the joint Arab-Jewish delegation to Auschwitz. A Christian Arab priest, Emile Shoufani from Nazareth, joined by many Arab community representatives, initiated a trip to learn about the Holocaust and the suffering of the Jewish people as an act of compassion and an expression of sympathy with the pain and victimhood of the Jews. The delegation received extensive coverage in the Israeli Jewish media and was recognized by several government officials. Many Jewish IFD participants acknowledged the impact of the initiative among their acquaintances on the Israeli side.

Despite the media coverage and the delegates' intention of acknowledging Jewish victimhood as an act of compassion that might lead to Jewish acknowledgment of Palestinian victimhood, there were critical voices among Arabs (Muslims and Christians). The criticism focused on several arguments. First, it accused the initiative of supporting Jewish Israeli political right-wing parties that often link Jewish victimhood and persecution with the need for tighter security measures against the Palestinians. Second, it held that the initiative was manipulated and utilized by political forces in Israel to continue denying the rights of Palestinians to self-determination because of this historical injustice committed against Jews. Third, it accused the initiative of denying Palestinian victimhood by comparing it to the Holocaust. Fourth, it said that the initiative was not followed up with any symmetrical actions or statements by Israel recognizing the current Palestinian victimhood.

Regardless of the above criticism, the initiative is an example of a confidence-building measure that breaks stereotypes by surprising the other. A Jewish woman from Haifa shared her views of the assumptions and goals of the unique interfaith initiative as aimed at knowing the Israeli [Jewish] side of the identity: "As a citizen of the state, [he] needs to know the meaning and history of the majority and connect with it. . . . The group consisted of 250 individuals of diverse religious [Christians, Muslims, Jews, Druze, Bedouin, and half-Jews], ideological [diverse political opinions], and social backgrounds [from the north and south, etc.]. It was not difficult to understand why it made us closer to each other: we cried, hugged, and wept together about the other. No matter who was in front of me, Arab or Jew, we all changed. Something inside me changed, like Shoufani expected."[102]

IFD can empower participants when carried out on the grassroots level. Women participating in such groups have gained an important and rare opportunity to discuss their perceptions and understandings of their own faith, a space that does not exist in any of the three Abrahamic faith or religious institutions in Israel and Palestine. For a woman, it is twice as challenging to find opportunities to study religion and be recognized as an authority in her faith. The Jewish coordinator of Women's Interfaith Encounter confirmed that "many women who are not that religious become very empowered [by] . . . studying their own religion and finding out things that they are not usually that familiar with." Women experience double discrimination: on one hand, in civil society, as victims of violence, often deprived of their basic rights, and on the other hand, in religion, where they experience discrimination when it comes to interpreting and discussing faith matters.

INTERFAITH DIALOGUE AS AN INSTRUMENT FOR CONCRETE ACTIONS

Despite the frustration with the lack of impact on the macropolitical level, members of interfaith groups, especially Arabs, are eager to find examples of concrete individual actions to remedy injustice that emerge from IFD. Success in most of the meetings has been individualized or defined on a personal level, without reference to behavior change. The director of ICCI repeatedly emphasized that "people learned a lot and built friendships, but did not translate this to action. . . . This is one of the problems of dialogue, it is for people who like to talk and not do. . . . We hope to integrate this action dialogue into our future plans, not only remain on the level of personal interest and learning."[103] The above realization, as stated by the director of the largest interfaith organization in Israel, reflects the beginning of a change among Jewish organizers of interfaith meetings. However, such change has not yet been translated into the program or project reality. A Palestinian woman interfaith participant stated her wishes on this score:

> I wanted the Jewish women to feel our pain too and be able to do something about it. When an Arab woman [speaks] about her difficulty in going to the interior ministry [to] deal with her papers and identity card issues, Jewish women should go and support her. That would be genuine dialogue. For example, Jewish participants [could] assist an Arab woman by writing a letter to the ministry in Hebrew asking for help in pursuing an education, career, etc.[104]

The quest for concrete action is repeatedly raised by Palestinian participants as a measurement for success: "Encounters do not achieve their goals; they do not do any actions. Show me your action before your words or statements."[105]

This type of intervention by Jewish participants on behalf of Palestinians remains dependent on the individual's capacity and willingness to assist in specific situations. Certainly, in terms of capacity, Jewish participants have familiarity with the Israeli political and security system. For example, when a security service officer in the Ministry of Education insisted on firing a Christian Palestinian teacher, after accusing him of spreading radical national views, his interfaith colleagues intervened on his behalf and after many months and letters, the ministry backed away from its decision.[106] Other joint activities have resulted from IFD, such as visits to each other's houses; participation in each other's celebrations (such as bar mitzvahs and baptisms); development of religious guided tours; meetings among bishops, imams, and rabbis; visits to synagogues; and so on.

Mobilizing interfaith networks for help in solving community and individual problems has an even greater function among intra-Palestinian interfaith participants (Christians, Muslims, and Druze). Priests and bishops can especially be of help, because the Israeli military is more careful in dealing with them, due to their linkages with the foreign Christian churches and the international community. One example is when a bishop was called to rescue a woman who was facing losing her pregnancy because of delays at a checkpoint.[107] Many of the interfaith leaders are active in settling community disputes according to the Arab *sulha* tradition. In fact, in these settings of traditional dispute resolution, the arbitrators and mediators have interreligious tolerance and coexistence among Palestinians as their primary message.[108]

Intervening to dispel fears of conversion or misunderstanding in interfaith settings is also a concrete action that interfaith religious leaders have assumed. For example, Bishop Moneeb Yunan traveled to Hebron after being called by Muslim interfaith colleagues who informed him of a rumor that a Christian teacher at a hospital for blind children had been accused of converting Muslim children to Christianity.

Concrete actions are also defined as individuals taking responsibility by initiating activities that challenge their own faith groups. Rabbi David Rosen, a veteran of interfaith relations, responded to the question of interfaith and political action: "I am not sure what you mean by politics, but when a flooding took place in Mozambique, we sent two Palestinians and two Israeli doctors. On [the] Passover holiday I decided to give away bread to poor Arabs. Religious Jews could not believe I would do that. Rabbi Eliahu [in Jerusalem] declared on the radio that Jews should not give anything to Arabs because they are the enemy. [For me] the question is how to convert the enemy into the beloved one."[109] Linking interfaith encounters to the "street" or grassroots public level, instead of limiting it to the elite or to the intellectual theological approaches that currently dominate the interfaith field in Israel/Palestine, is also an indicator of success, cited by Muslims, Christians, and Jews.

Taking a political stand against certain violent events or policies is the most difficult and challenging measure of success, yet it is cited as the most desired and pressing action by many Palestinians who attend interfaith encounters. They give the following examples: Jewish participants' acknowledgment of the massacre of Palestinians in Jenin; Jewish rabbis' denunciation of *Hadar Dam* (permission to spill blood or kill); condemnation of the killing of Muslims in the Hebron mosque; engaging in political protest against occupation; denouncing the killing of Arab or Jewish children; and actions among Palestinians to confront fanaticism or prejudice and stereotypes, such as the example of Jeries Khoury, a Christian Arab priest, who traveled to Hebron to confront an imam who justified the killing of Christians.[110]

In his criticism of IFD's limited impact and lack of linkage to political action, Rabbi Jeremy Milgrom articulated the limitations of IFD seminars in the harsh reality of the occupation: "When I was young I was very optimistic, but now as I got older and more veteran, I do not go to encounters with such high expectations. My work is more that of human rights work, into which I bring volunteers. The situation is very difficult and I bring people to the reality and show them the real picture so that they realize that they need to do something. That encounter is not made for Bedouins to know their Jewish visitor's family and personal life, but for that visitor to enter and leave with a better realization of the Bedouin situation. These are successful meetings because they give me the feeling that it is possible to do something, and hence [I have] a desire to continue and work with it."[111]

In examining the above examples of success and achievements identified by IFD participants, it is clear that despite specific concrete actions, Jewish and Palestinian interfaith participants and coordinators still need to go beyond "preaching to the choir" by reaching out more to their respective communities and generating ways for influencing policy or decision-making actors. None of the interfaith organizations covered in this research have conducted a systematic evaluation of their impact on policy or on general public perception; these objectives are not part of the organizations' agenda or priorities. However, if we employ criteria having to do with deepening understanding, learning about the other faith, and rehumanizing the other, all interfaith participants eagerly provide proof of success, in the form of stories of attitude change and shifts in perception on the individual level. In some cases, deep personal transformation also has occurred.

OBSTACLES AND CHALLENGES IN IFD

In Israel and Palestine, interfaith encounters and interreligious peacebuilding is an emerging small field compared to the well-established and well-funded secular Arab-Jewish peace and dialogue initiatives. Since the 1950s, there have been projects and individuals who worked for peaceful relations among Arabs and Jews. It was only in the late 1980s, however, that interfaith organizations were launched, and today there are about fifteen different organizations whose work is founded on an interfaith or religious framework. As with any emerging social change movement, the interfaith field, still at its inception, has a limited number of participants. Often the same participants are moving from one activity to the next.

IFD is an integral part of a larger network of organizations that educate for interethnic and intercultural peace between Arabs and Jews in Israel. These Arab-Jewish coexistence organizations have developed over the last three decades and have emerged as a special NGO sector (Abu-Nimer 1999, 2004). On the Palestinian side, there are a few equivalent organizations working for Israeli-Palestinian peace (among them only two interfaith organizations), but they are often smaller operations that rely on their Israeli counterpart for joint funding (Baskin and Dajani 2006).[112]

Given that the few projects and organizations that address interfaith relations are based in Israel, it is inaccurate or premature to identify them as an independent or even developed Palestinian-Israeli interfaith field. Israeli interfaith organizations mainly operate inside Israel and occasionally manage to engage Palestinians from the Occupied Territories, especially in the Jerusalem area. Palestinian interfaith groups in the Occupied Territories or inside Israel hardly exist (we identified only two fully operating entities), and most of the participants attend the meetings in an individual or personal capacitiy. However, it should be noted that the Palestinian-Israeli interfaith activities are perceived as extremely marginal, and due to the political reality of occupation and security threats, there are very few.[113] But the Arab-Jewish coexistence work in Israel (Israeli Jews working with Arabs from Israel) is more developed, and there are more organizations and activities focused on such work.

The challenge or crisis within IFD in Israel and Palestine is reflected in the nature of its leadership and participants and in how it is perceived by both its immediate constituencies and the general public. An Arab Christian woman, like other active members, was critical of the quality of guest speakers and of the fact that they were predominantly Jewish. "The majority of the people in interfaith are Jews; there are very few Muslims and Christians. Even though the speakers represent the three religions, Jewish speakers are usually better organized and more convincing. The Christian speaker sometimes is fine, but the Muslim speaker is often poorly selected or not prepared."[114] Similar observations are made by others regarding the qualifications of invited experts who serve in these different projects, especially when dealing with theological and educational issues.[115] The inability of interfaith organizations to attract qualified Muslim figures or participants who are publicly, politically, and socially recognized can be attributed to the apolitical nature of its process models, which do not appeal to these figures. In addition, the interfaith Jewish organizers' conscious and deliberate decision to mainly focus on purely theological or celebratory activities pushes away Muslim and Christian Palestinian leaders who enjoy wide public recognition and individuals who have focused their energies on the daily suffering of Palestinians in the Occupied Territories or Israel. Thus, for many Palestinians, if they participate in such joint events they would be accused of supporting "normalization" with the Israeli occupation.

In Israel, the internal security service (Shabak) is another threatening factor for Muslim and Christian participants. The fear that their political statements can be skewed or communicated to the security service dictates a certain level of participation. When Abdul Salam Manasra gave a lecture on the meaning of jihad in Islam in the Triangle Arab area, he was summoned by Israeli security, threatened, and warned. This type of warning illustrates the continuation of a control mechanism imposed on Arabs inside Israel to prevent their national or religious identity expressions (Abu-Nimer 1999; Lustick 1980). Other factors that contribute to the limited ability to reach out to Muslim leaders with academic and religious qualifications relate to the individualistic, Western nature of such dialogical models imported from a European or American cultural context. The format and processes of the encounter are based on informal and interactive processes. In addition, the models assume that each individual can represent himself or herself, regardless of religious or national collective identities.

The issue of representation and ability to affect public discourse is a primary criticism of the interfaith field. Ghantus Ghantus captured this criticism: "These organizations just have conversations or writings that have no effect after fifteen minutes. . . . We need to select representative people. . . . These conversations are only a pure waste. If there is dialogue, it should be between states so it has the support of some formal institutions. Persons should be responsible: they should represent some sections of the community and have responsibility for every word. . . . Not only people like me who can represent only themselves."[116]

Sustainability and the Impact of the Political Context on Interfaith Dynamics

In peacebuilding and other forms of social and political intervention, sustainability is the major challenge participants and organizers face in their efforts to bring short- and long-term change (Abu-Nimer 2003). IFD is not an exception; the inability of the organizers and participants to sustain their contacts over a long period of time, especially with the frequent eruption of political violence, was cited as a primary source of frustration and disappointment affecting the degree of effectiveness of the projects. One major obstacle is logistics: permission to move, entry to territories, geographical problems, distance between people's homes, and so on. As stated by Rabbi Jeremy Milgrom, "many Israeli Arabs do not feel that they are members of the state, even in Jerusalem neighborhoods."[117] Palestinians, banned from traveling outside the territories, are not the only ones with travel restrictions. Israeli participants are also reluctant to visit Palestinians in the Occupied Territories, fearing for their safety. In many cases the army can prevent them from entering. This reality significantly limits the available space for joint meetings and narrows the possibility for Jerusalem-based interfaith encounters and Jewish-Arab meetings in Israel.

The primary obstacle for IFD is the escalation of violence and the volatile political situation. Interfaith groups have struggled to keep the reality of the conflict outside of their meeting doors. On occasions, such as during the massacre in Jenin and the killing of Israelis in Jerusalem bombings, participants' motivation is affected. They begin to question why the dialogues should continue.

Palestinian participants are constantly frustrated by the continuous violence and victimhood of their communities and have found it extremely hard to sustain their faith in IFD. A Palestinian Christian priest who is a veteran of interfaith dialogue captured this feeling:

> I have been in encounters or dialogical relations with Jews for fifteen years, but last year I stopped [it] all. Because of the political situation, I felt that we are not in a real dialogue, but a fake one. . . . We talked about Abraham and saw fifty kids killed at the same time. Same on the Jewish side, people are killed. The political obstacle is the largest obstacle in Palestine. The question [of whether dialogue can] help the political situation or not is an academic one. I believe that it might and that we should meet. But at some point I had my doubts and could not sleep; it all felt like lies and fake. I could not see Palestinians killed every day while I still go to the dialogue encounters and [we] smile [at] each other.[118]

The outbreak of the Al Aqsa Intifada brought a full stop to all joint activities between Palestinians and Israelis. For many Palestinians in the Occupied Territories, the primary obstacle to engaging in joint activity with Israelis continues to be "fear of normalization of the occupation." After June 2001, and despite the reversal of the Palestinian Authority's decree that prevented all NGOs from cooperating with Israeli NGOs in late 2000, Palestinian-Israeli joint initiatives continue to be viewed as an undesirable act of acquiescence. Among Palestinians in the Occupied Territories, the reality of the occupation and the Al Aqsa Intifada increased the level of resistance to any form of joint work with Israelis. Several Palestinians voiced their concerns and resistance regarding their participation in IFD: "We cannot participate in these encounters with Jews because of the occupation's attacks on our people. There are internal forces that affect these decisions too. This type of encounter does not fit our reality now, it will create internal tensions that we do not need."[119]

The escalated tensions and violence brought by the Al Aqsa Intifada crept into many of the IFD projects. In several projects, Palestinian and Israeli participants abandoned their initial commitment to continue their encounters. Various explanations are provided by the organizers and participants regarding the destructive impact of the political context on their encounters. Those who prefer to avoid political and conflict-related themes in IFD identified political debates as the primary reason for breakdown of the encounters. Elana Rozenman explained,

> I just saw so many things break down and especially with this last Intifada. I had people who were in dialogues for twelve years in Beit Sahour and Abu Tor and it all fell apart. . . . When this whole Intifada broke out they couldn't sustain themselves because all they did was get together, scream, and yell about what each side was doing to the other; pretty soon nobody wanted to get together. The Palestinians and Arabs based their refusal to meet with Jews and Israelis on the incursions into Jenin and other occurrences. Jews refused to continue meeting because of the bombings, which [led] to a number of deaths, especially children's. You know, its like when push came to shove it didn't hold together. So first of all my feeling is—I don't want to use the word "bored"—I get sick of dialogue, even.[120]

For others, especially Arab participants, the reality of the occupation and political events made it impossible for them emotionally and politically to participate in IFD as the violence escalated. "For example, in the aftermath of Jenin and its events—the killing of innocent people, the destruction of homes, etc.—Arabs did not go to dialogue. Some Arabs stopped participating without any notice. I personally could not go; I had so much pain that I could not do that. I have a cousin in Jenin, he is sixty years old. We are refugees; everyone of us had relatives. We are Palestinian people. We cannot give up on our people and origins."[121]

In addition to the obstacle of normalization, Jews, Muslims, and Christians in interfaith circles face the challenge of recruiting new members and attracting people to their activities. A Muslim Sufi leader from the north of Israel articulates this difficulty by indicating the context of oppression:

> The problem is not among Arabs—they are persecuted. In the dialogue, the Arab is looking to say what is bothering him; he is *Sahib haq* [a person with a right]. The problem is among Jews, religious Jews. First Jews say that they do not sit with Arabs. . . . I know that they feel pain when there is a suicide bombing, I understand that, but get out of the territories. However, sometimes we face some Muslims who say that they do not want to sit with Jews who are persecuting our people in Jenin and the West Bank. The Israeli military has been an oppressor and carried out atrocities in the Occupied Territories. Yes, I say, but come with me and let us tell them that.[122]

Asymmetric Management and Funding of Interfaith Programs

All the organizers and participants we spoke with mentioned the lack of funding and resources to support their initiatives. The majority of funds are channeled through American Jewish agencies and donors who have become aware of the role of faith in supporting peace and coexistence. Such awareness increased even more after September 11, 2001. However, lack of funding was dismissed by many organizers and participants as an impediment to the expansion of IFD. The hindering factors that were more often mentioned were quality of participants and their ability and willingness to take risks, adequate process models, and lack of support from political leadership.

The unequal distribution of resources in interfaith organizations was also cited as an obstacle that demoralizes active coordinators and participants. The majority of Muslims and Christians interviewed expressed their discontent with the fact that all funds are managed by Israeli Jewish coordinators and directors. This raised the suspicion that the interfaith field has become a form of earning a living, and casts Arab participation as merely an instrument by which to raise funds for interfaith activities. All Arab interviewees were aware of the asymmetric distribution of funds and attributed financial interest as an important factor motivating Jewish coordinators.

Lack of financial transparency, inadequate distribution of funds, and lack of compensation to coordinators or program organizers are cited as sources of tension among members of the same organization, as well as a factor in the lack of widespread participation in the program. Several Arab Muslim participants and IFD leaders expressed their frustration with this issue of personal gain and interest in IFD. One said, "Many of these institutes are founded to steal money. You can find people in them who hate peace like they hate pork, but they benefit and want to show up for the conferences."[123] Another added simply, "Some people attend these meetings for financial motivation and social visibility; some of these institutions seek Arab names for decoration. So I left them."[124] A Sufi leader supported this view:

> In this wave of interfaith dialogue, there always will be parasites who will ride for free. In every party there are free riders; we do not fight them. May God grant them success. We know that there are some organizations who only serve their political or economic interests. They claim that they are for dialogue. . . . they have created illusionary organizations, fake, or manufactured [entities]. These people who try to create illusionary dialogue through illusionary organizations, even people use our names without our knowledge. . . . I say one thing, the correct will remain. We know human nature always looks for the sources and their eyes are on the money. History is the most beautiful filter: they will go through the filter because they are not genuine. If they work against the truth or reality they will not remain.[125]

The small number of participants and organizers in IFD contributes to the relatively quick spread of stories about funding and management. A female Palestinian interfaith coordinator described this dynamic: "[IFD] is excellent. If we change the people who exploit [it] as business we might have even better interfaith. People do not know what is inside these organizations. You are living [at] the expense of other people. They did not understand that. . . . People do not know the secret."[126] The same perception and frustration was echoed by the director of PASSIA: "Successful dialogue is not to produce a book or report and do fundraising. . . . Today most of the interaction is like business. It is not genuine dialogue that emerges from inside or out of true interest, it is a business relationship."[127]

The perception of discrepancy among Arab and Jewish organizers and participants regarding financial issues is related to the fact that the Jewish heads of the organizations rely on the funds for economic survival—as a source of employment—while Arabs either volunteer or receive partial and symbolic compensations. Without the non-Jewish coordinators or organizers, inter-faith events would not take place. It is true that financial compensation is mainly controlled by Jewish coordinators, who often write the grant propos-als and manage the donor relationship. Thus, to outside observers it seems that organizers have mainly financial motivations. A Palestinian Muslim wo-man stated, "I do not want to generalize, but generally they write the grant, secure their salaries, and put a small amount to weekend workshops."[128]

The lack of trust in the financial management of the programs has pro-duced a great deal of skepticism among leading participants in these programs. This statement is from a woman who has spent many days and months of her time in IFD: "To be honest, it is a cover, in which the Israeli people show off what good things they are doing. . . . The objective is not that 'I want you as [another] human,' but [rather] to get money."[129] Another Palestinian woman expressed her frustration: "I was frustrated and disappointed when they invited me to an interfaith meeting to talk about Jesus. I discovered that the Muslim and Jewish coordinators are there to raise funds and write a nice report to Europeans."[130]

There is a mixture of factors that explain the asymmetric relations within interfaith organizations and the domination (or overrepresentation in leader-ship) of Jewish participants and coordinators. An imam and IFD veteran was asked why Jews are the founders of IFD organizations. His answer may shed some light on such perceptions among some Arab participants:

1. They [Jews] want to live in peace to save their children and their economic privileges.
2. They are not discriminated against like us [Arabs].
3. If an Arab launches an organization, the security services come and investigate and there might be some problems, but not if a Jew does that.
4. Jews pay more attention to their children, education, and life conditions because they have only one or two children and they are always trying to pro-vide to these children more and more, while the Arabs have on average nine children and cannot afford to respond to all their needs.

5. Jews pay more attention to and respect for improving and learning about human life. They need to live in a secure home because their children are funded and supported by the government and opportunities are open for them more than [for] Arabs.[131]

The above list of limitations also reflects how certain Arab participants in Israel view the dominant majority culture and their values and lifestyle. It is clear that there is a sense of cultural superiority attributed to the majority.

Language Barriers

All the encounters between Israelis and Palestinians from the Occupied Territories (including East Jerusalem) face the challenge of using English as a common language for dialogue. Few Israeli Jews master Arabic, and few Palestinians are comfortable speaking in Hebrew. Thus, English becomes a necessary skill for IFD, which automatically limits the profile of interfaith participants to a well-educated and often economically privileged few.

Interfaith meetings between Arabs and Jews in Israel use Hebrew, which increases asymmetry, providing Jewish participants with additional privilege over Arabs. Among Arabs and Jews in Israel, use of Hebrew does not necessarily limit the interaction to economically and educationally privileged participants. Hebrew is widely spoken among the Arab minority in Israel, which allows for a more diverse profile of participants in such meetings. However, it does mean that Arabs are forced to express their spiritual and religious identity and needs in a foreign language associated with oppression and prejudice. Arab participants are quick to point out their mastery of the Hebrew language as evidence of their willingness to reach out to the majority, citing Jewish members' inability or unwillingness to learn Arabic as indicative of arrogance, superiority, or indifference.

Preaching to the Converted

The most frequently cited obstacle, however, was that the entire emerging interfaith field is confined to a small number of people from all sides. IFD cannot reach large numbers of people, nor does it reach those at the extreme political right in these communities. This realization has frustrated both participants and organizers, and was repeatedly pointed out by critics.

> How can we move the dialogue to the street and translate it into people learning to tolerate Christians and Muslims; that is the challenge—not the books, lectures, or debates. It does not matter if you believe in Mohammed as the last Prophet or confirm the message of Christianity. The point is that as a Muslim you can recognize Christianity as valid and as a Christian, you recognize the same of Islam. How can we communicate that to the Palestinian street?[132]

Preaching to the choir in this context does not necessarily mean that participants are in full agreement on the political and theological issues. On the contrary, they often have significant differences regarding perceptions of historical events, dynamics, and preferred outcomes for the Arab-Jewish conflict. But participants of these meetings share the willingness to speak with the other, recognize the other's rights and existence, and assume a certain level of trust. Thus, IFD does not include Muslims, Christians, and Jews who refuse to meet, reject the other's right to live in that land, or totally distrust the other.

Another challenge related to IFD's target audience is the challenge of bringing IFD to groups and organizations that work with youth from the three faith communities. The overwhelming majority of the activities are aimed at adults and professionals; youth are excluded or neglected.

Different Expectations and Needs

A major obstacle in the implementation of IFD has been the contrast in the participants' and organizers' expectations, especially regarding IFD's political or apolitical purpose. A Jewish interfaith organizer identified the divergent needs among participants when he stated, "Jews always want [IFD] without politics and Arabs want it with politics. It is not going to be effective if we do not deal with politics. For example, can we talk about the Or Commission? How can we suppress the political and peace conversations? We are assuming that peace belongs to the politicians and not the people."[133]

The disparity in the needs among participants and organizers is also reflected in the overemphasis of some organizations on academic and intellectual exchanges, which results in the exclusion of participants who are concerned with daily-life matters. Another IFD veteran confirms this: "The interfaith meetings focused mainly on academicians and clergy, but average people are not as interested in the religious aspect; they are interested in their daily lives. We hardly managed to get Arabs, [and they] did not return after the first meeting."[134]

Localized IFD Models

The format, structures, and assumptions of interfaith activities (including lecturing and overemphasizing analysis and study of the scriptures) are perceived to be imported approaches. The nonacademics and nontheologians feel alienated from these forms of interaction. In fact, some interviewees ventured even further, depicting the very concept of IFD as a foreign approach that needed to be localized in the Israeli-Palestinian context. A Palestinian Christian priest commented in this regard, "Dialogue and tolerance is a Western model of interaction. It is a Western import. How can we localize it like the Rwandese or South African conflict-resolution indigenous mechanisms? Interreligious relations were born in the Open Society, not in the Galilee."[135] Several other Jewish and Christian organizers expressed their belief that Middle Eastern cultural norms and values do not support the concept of dialogue.

However, some individuals reached back in history to the Muslim period in Spain to provide a precedent of interfaith tolerance and harmony. Furthermore, all the interviewees portrayed their traditions as supportive of peace, justice, tolerance, and respect of other religions. A partial explanation of this paradox is that IFD's techniques and funding are perceived as Western imports, even as its concepts and values remain an integral part of Middle Eastern culture. Nevertheless, these interviewees believed that IFD and tolerance represent foreign values, practices, and methods in an Arab Middle Eastern cultural context. This view is echoed by orientalist authors and scholars, who reject IFD as "colonialist views" or "internalized oppression" (see Said 1979).

Public Perceptions of the Interfaith Field

There is a great deal of criticism and suspicion regarding the impact, intentions, and sincerity of the organizers of interfaith meetings, especially within the Palestinian community, both those who participate in IFD and those who do not. For example, some critics voice the belief that many of the participants have ulterior motives. Hisham Najar, an IFD insider, believes that, "For some people this is an opportunity for vacation and relaxation."[136] Further suspicion is raised when IFD programs receive funds and support from the Israeli government, as many did in the past. According to at least one source, "Funding is an obstacle, but you do not need much. The government supported our activities. Finding people with sincere commitment is the major obstacle."[137]

Another cloud of suspicion collects around the intentions of those IFD programs that invest considerable resources in their publications and produce glossy quarterly or annual reports. Such forms of documentation and marketing of organizational activities were perceived as ways to manufacture inaccurate images of the reality of coexistence and harmony among the faith groups. Their main purpose is to solicit funds for IFD, which is, in fact, marginalized and lacks wide public representation. One interviewee commented on the gap, "The glossy paper and rosy reports on accomplishments are not necessarily what takes place in reality."[138]

Strong Sense of Religiocentrism

Beliefs such as "my own religion is perfect" and "the others are 'infidels,' 'incorrect,' or have deviated from the original Abrahamic massage" were also identified as an obstacle in reaching a wider circle of people in the various faith communities. This kind of a sense of superiority is shared by people of the three faith groups and not exclusive to one group only. A Palestinian Muslim who has participated in the Hartman IFD group over five years describes his experience in interfaith conversations with some Jewish participants:

> Another obstacle is the nature of the conversation with many Jews about Judaism. It always leads to politics, because of the Jews' belief that they are always persecuted and victims. Thus, talking to a Jew about these issues always seems against peace. A second difficulty stems from the Jews' inability to recognize that God revealed himself to other than Jews in different historical periods. . . . The Jews'

belief in the return to Israel is tied with politics. Their religion is tied to politics, ours is not. However, they tied our religion to politics.[139]

A similar realization regarding the religiocentricity among Muslims was described by other participants. Hraimi from Bethlehem said,

The main obstacle is the accusation of infidelity, even between Muslims [and] Christians. The Muslim religious clergy refuses to see that there is a diverse Islam. Some refuse to dialogue with others, even Christians, unless it is mandated by the ministry of religion or education, as a mandatory dialogue for diversity. We have that problem of believing in "one Islam." The unwillingness to understand the other and [the tendency to] think of one's own religion as the perfect one is a problem. For example, Islam is the ideal "just" religion, some believe. Yes it might be very specific about justice, yet there is a difference between Islam and Muslims. There is a gap, because Islam left many things open for the individual to decide. . . . Among Muslim scholars in the Gulf area and especially Saudia Arabia, there is resistance and rejection of dialogue because it is perceived as a foreign agenda imposed by the Vatican in 1965.[140]

Strong religiocentric beliefs are deeply ingrained among the three faith groups, to the extent that some interfaith participants argued against any exploration of theological differences, preferring to focus on the political. Saliba Taweel, from Bethlehem, even called for a boycott of such ineffective encounters:

Interfaith meetings cannot affect the political situation. We have fundamental and theological differences that cannot be resolved. Muslims think they are the best nation brought by God; Christians were told by Christ that they "are the children of God"; and Jews think they are the best and the chosen people. These are historical and theological differences that cannot be bridged; therefore we need to separate these differences from the political discussion.[141]

Similarly, Hisham Najar stated,

As a Muslim who believe in *daawa* [calling people to convert to Islam] and belief [*aqida*] these meetings will not necessarily be receptive to my message. I [would] not conduct these meetings if I had the funds. If information is the purpose, then there is the Internet, or books. The Quran is translated into many languages. As for knowing the other side, I can do that without meeting in such [a] context.[142]

The above criticism reflects a lack of understanding and appreciation of the dialogue process, which can lead to a powerful shift in individuals' perceptions and even behaviors. Also, it reduces the process of change to a mechanical and mainly cognitive process, when, in fact, human and face-to-face interaction has proven to be the most powerful aspect of interethnic encounters. The possibility of rehumanizing the enemy is greatly enhanced by face-to-face interaction, as opposed to reading a book about the other.

Lack of Professional Preparations and Proper Representation

Most participants provided concrete complaints about a pattern of inadequate preparation in IFD, especially with regard to the selection of Palestinian Muslim or Druze participants, who tend to be the hardest to attract. Organizers continue to contact participants at the last minute.[143] A strong opposition to this tendency was expressed by a Palestinian Muslim scholar who criticized the structure of a meeting he attended:

> Effective interfaith encounters cannot be based on participants who are unable to articulate their historical, social, political, and religious concerns. . . . If [IFD] is about genuine dialogue, then why [was] the agenda prepared by Jews and the papers and themes determined by Jews and some Christians? Even among Christians, the representatives were poorly selected and they did not conduct themselves like, for example, the Jewish woman, who was well prepared and came from a respected and well-recognized branch of Judaism and knew her culture and history.[144]

The issue of problematic representation is related to the fact that there are still relatively few people involved in this field. Arab women are especially few, and those who get involved quickly are assigned an onerous representational status (that is, are unfairly thought to speak for all Muslim women). In addition, most of the interfaith leaders among Muslims in Israel and the Occupied Territories are associated with Sufi sheikhs who have spearheaded Arab representation in the various interfaith organizations. This limited representation from among the majority of Muslims reinforces perceptions of IFD as serving (or being controlled by) Israeli Jewish interests. An Arab Muslim woman coordinator of Women's Interfaith Encounter spoke to the absence of Arab participants in these programs:

> I can tell you that there are some Jews who are nice and friendly. They have nice ideas, sit together alone to plan the activity. They work on an idea, sew it and design it, etc. After that, they look for an Arab to work with them, register the name, and beg for money through grants. [These are] the lowest groups [in terms of how active the Arabs are in the organization]. Other [Israeli Jews or organizations] design and think there is no Arab around to work with, but then they find a token Arab. These [Jewish organizers] want to create change, but the organizers did not listen to the Arab needs and [do] not know what bothers the Arabs in Israel or outside. They built their own objectives and looked for a token Arab. . . . This is a better version. [They are] not intentional in ignoring [the] Arab role in their organization.[145]

It is not clear whether Jewish coordinators deliberately recruit from a certain category—Palestinians who generally tend to be less challenging or assertive of their national and religious rights—or whether Palestinian individuals who would be more qualified opt out because they do not see the usefulness or benefits of participation. Regardless, the outcome is that, in general, only Muslim and Christian participants with certain profiles take part in

these events, namely those who are politically marginalized, willing to separate religion from politics, view interfaith meetings as a framework to achieve
other gains (monetary, public recognition inside Israel). These Arab participants
do not represent the views of the majority of Palestinians. Even active IFD
participants identify this as a major problem. Poor selection of Palestinian
participants often reflects the power dynamics and relationships in the interfaith groups themselves, and is due to the nature of the activities (dialogue
without action or political agenda, and so on). Interfaith forums are not known
for their engaging activities or as being a particularly mobilizing force. Politically
or socially influential and widely recognized individuals who legitimately represent their communities do not attend.

Hisham Najar listed the qualities that effective Muslim participants
should have, in his view:

> Confident and able to articulate their religion and culture, know their religion,
> and are able to discuss it in depth with others, are able to [understand] the dynam-
> ics of the encounters and its facilitation and process, so they are not lost in the
> interaction, and are able to confront in honesty the other and [not] respond pas-
> sively to Jewish domination.[146]

Similar questions about participant selection arise concerning instances of
nonobservant Muslims representing Islam. In most cases, credibility is attributed based on observance. For example, at a conference, three women from
Abu Gosh, a village in the vicinity of Jerusalem, were met with resistance
from certain Muslim male participants who questioned their legitimacy as
representatives because they were not praying on a regular basis, and yet had
been chosen to represent Islam and women. Najar continues his criticism:

> Interfaith meetings failed because of the nature of the participants who attended
> or were selected. They were not balanced. The Muslims could not talk about
> Islam like the Jews could talk about Judaism. Their background was very simple;
> they did not have the capacity to articulate Islam or anything else. You wonder
> why they were selected.[147]

A similar criticism was voiced by Yousef Hraimi: "Muslims who participate in
interfaith are not as responsible and some of them do not practice their faith.
That affects the authenticity of the participation and [others'] internal and
external perceptions [of them].[148]

The above is a typical criticism, especially in cases where IFD is ostensibly
a meeting of cultures. Hisham Najar remembered when "a woman who has
lived all her life among Jews and [was] closer to Jewish society than the Muslim
one, [was] still brought to represent Islam. The woman spoke Arabic, but her
heart was with Israelis. She did not abide by any Islamic rules regarding dress
codes or even male-female interactions. In my view, she was not a Muslim."[149]

Perceptions are crucial in determining the impact of IFD on Palestinian
and Israeli society. If personal reputation obscures and invalidates IFD, it can-

not fulfill its transformational purpose. One interviewee described this obstacle: "The dialogue field is suffering from personification of the issue [when institutionalization would be preferable]. People attach themes to persons. Thus, Naim Ateek is known for something, and Mahdi Abdul Hadi and Sari Nusseiba are known for something else, and people do not hear new ideas."[150] The risk is that certain themes are attributed to personalities and thus dismissed. Organizations may be created because the mosque, church, or synagogue could not absorb them. They end up marginalized and unable to have influence because they are too far outside these institutions.

CONCLUSION

For centuries, religious identities (values, practices, and sacred sites) have been invoked in the conflict between Muslims, Christians, and Jews in Israel/Palestine and the larger region. There are many examples of leaders and followers using their religious beliefs to establish superiority or exclusion. By the same token, the same historical and current contexts offer examples of people and leaders who employed their faith traditions (values and practices) to promote tolerance and peaceful relations between the three groups. Based on the findings of this study, it is obvious that, regardless of the period, peaceful and pluralist religious approaches to Arab-Jewish conflict are necessary to engage significant portions of Arabs and Jews in this conflict. Secular peace processes are not sufficient to transform or settle this conflict.

The emerging interfaith field in Israel and Palestine is growing rapidly and attracting more participants from both sides of the conflict. Yet it remains in crucial need of professional development, monitoring, and evaluation of its impact and approaches. Its association with Israeli government officials or semiofficial organizers has contributed to its image as serving the Israeli Jewish political and religious agenda. How can Muslims, Christians, and Jews in this field create an autonomous field of operation that equally serves the interests and needs of the three communities? This is the major challenge facing interfaith organizations. Responding to this question requires organizers and participants to closely examine issues related to organizational management, funding, transparency, and inclusion in the further development of this field.

IFD in Israel and Palestine aims to play a constructive role in rehumanizing the images of the various groups involved in this conflict. The interfaith meetings aim to accomplish change by reducing stereotypes and prejudice on the individual level through sharing basic values and practices among faith traditions, and creating interpersonal friendships and relationships. By avoiding political discussion, association, and action, Jewish organizers and participants manage to focus the meetings on either theological and intellectual discussions or on the cultural practices of religious traditions. For Arab (Christian and Muslim) participants, this harmony/apolitical model is a source of constant frustration and alienation. Finding the "holy" balance between a theological conversation that relates to the current reality and producing concrete outcomes affecting conditions on the ground has been the major challenge for the emerging field of IFD.

RECOMMENDATIONS

To implement such a balanced interfaith approach to the conflict, it is essential for organizers of these meetings to examine several domains. Here are a few proposals:

1. Reexamine the criteria in selecting participants, instead of focusing on clergy or intellectuals who have interest in religion, and rather than accepting anyone at all, without any selective procedures.
2. Insist on genuine partnership in coordinating and organizing the interfaith programs among Muslim, Christian, Druze, and Jewish participants and organizers (including distribution of organizational resources). Such standards will counter both the perception and the reality that the overwhelming majority of the organizations are run and managed by Israeli Jews.
3. Seek wider publicity for activities, participants, and desired outcomes. Palestinian leaders (Muslim and Christian) are willing to participate in events that are designed to respond to their communities' needs and interests. Activities can be designed to attract Israeli Jewish leaders, too. Interfaith and intrafaith activities can be devised in ways that engage wider participation from both communities.
4. Invest in the preparation of participants and leaders. Intrafaith activities are essential as a preparation and selection phase for interfaith meetings. More time and resources are needed for this stage.
5. Attach a concrete and practical expression to interfaith programs. Change in perception and celebration of religious diversity and similarities are acceptable objectives, yet for many on the grassroots level (and even for those on the elite level), a concrete economic or social development outcome illustrates more commitment to social and political change. Interfaith actions aimed at resisting injustice demonstrate a deeper level of dedication to peacebuilding and change.
6. Consider ongoing intrafaith meetings as an integral part of interfaith projects. Long-term commitment to IFD ensures deeper knowledge of the other faiths and sustainable relationships across religious divides.
7. Conduct systematic evaluation and monitoring of programs. Models and intervention design can be further developed only through reflective practices and evaluation and monitoring of success. Interfaith organizations need to conduct regular evaluation and identify ineffective processes.
8. Finally, despite the urgency and stress imposed by the Arab-Jewish conflict, which burdens IFD's agenda and outcomes, it is essential for each faith group to initiate its own intrafaith meetings. Such forums can provide a

valuable space for safe and constructive education for religious tolerance. Muslims, Jews, and Christians desperately need these forums for exploring their intracommunity affairs and needs.

The interfaith field in Israel and Palestine is still in its infancy. In their interviews, activists listed many needs and creative suggestions for its development. The following are some of their recommendations to enhance the development of the field.

Introducing Interfaith into the Educational System

There is a need to integrate the interfaith approach of studying scriptures into the schools and academic institutions. It is important to teach religions pluralistically in schools. Currently, children from the three faith traditions complete high school without necessarily having learned anything about the other faiths. On the academic and theological level, several participants indicated that they have a dream of a joint academic college: a religious school for Muslims, Christians, and Jews. It is necessary to bring Islamic studies to every Jewish rabbinical school and Jewish studies to Muslim schools. This recommendation is linked to a wider need for the institutionalization of interfaith pluralist education in the ministries of education or religion (in both Israel and Palestine). There is a need to promote such change at the level of the official policies of the political leadership. One way to pursue this issue is by paying further attention to the inclusion or linking of policymakers with the various interfaith activities launched by the different organizations.

Funding, Professional Development, and Capacity Building

Most IFD organizations are not equipped with the skills to identify funding sources or mobilize and manage the funds in symmetrical ways. Thus, capacity building, especially with regard to funding and NGO management, would benefit interfaith organizations. All interfaith organizations and participants have indicated their need for professional facilitators and further development of their understanding of the IFD processes and dynamics. For example, there has never been special training or professional support for participants, facilitators, or directors of these organizations.

Seminars and specialized training could contribute to the development of the interfaith field and allow it to benefit from the experience of other interfaith peacebuilding work from other conflict zone areas such as South Africa, Northern Ireland, or the United States.

Intrafaith Groups

Interfaith organizations have to tackle intrafaith issues and facilitate more forums to address issues pertaining to intracommunity problems and differences. Muslim-Muslim, Christian-Christian, and Jewish-Jewish dialogue groups are needed to widen the circle of conversation and reach out to a larger audience. These intrafaith meetings can also function as preparation for meeting members of the other faiths. They also provide a shared space for people from the same faith or national group, such as Christians and Muslims, to allow the different voices within them to emerge. Most of the existing institutions have neglected these internal issues. Several interfaith participants voiced the need for nonclergy initiatives to address intrafaith issues. The domination by the clergy deprives "average" people of participating or articulating their own faith interpretations.

4

INTERFAITH DIALOGUE IN LEBANON

A Cornerstone for Healing and Overcoming Sectarian Divides

INTRODUCTION

Interethnic and interfaith dialogue is absolutely necessary in a small and diverse country like Lebanon, which has nineteen officially recognized sects, especially when the citizenry has been involved in violent conflict for more than a decade. Civil war in Lebanon, which began in 1975, shattered the relatively peaceful web of coexistence between people from different religions that had been enjoyed for more than a century. Some historians do note that despite this seemingly peaceful coexistence, conflict between the different communities was always present, as was apparent in the Mount Lebanon clashes during the 1800s.

Nevertheless, until 1975, many Middle Eastern and Western analysts considered Lebanon a model of coexistence, with a uniquely diverse confessional political structure that does not recognize any official state religion, but maintains a balance of power between communities by assigning political and administrative positions according to each sect's proportion of the population (Sayah 1998, 9). This formula of coexistence in Lebanon was first conceptualized in the 1926 Constitution, elaborated on in the 1943 National Pact, and later reemphasized in the 1989 Taef Agreement that officially ended fifteen years of civil war.[1]

Some intellectuals and activists believe that IFD has been a permanent reality in the Lebanese context and is reflected in such historic initiatives as the 1943 National Pact—a nonformal agreement about the distribution of power between Christians and Muslims (Al-Mawla 1998, 6). A Maronite Christian IFD expert notes that "Christian-Muslim dialogue in Lebanon started a long time ago, since the rise of Islam."[2] It was a dialogue of everyday life among people living together on one territory; it did not discuss differences in an atmosphere where freedom of religion and belief was the order of the day. He goes on to note that "The current frameworks and meaning of dialogue only developed after independence, when relations between people from different religions and sects were institutionalized through administrative procedures to manage differences in the public arena."[3]

After the civil war, such dialogue reemerged as a pressing necessity to safeguard the experience of coexistence as previously enjoyed by the Lebanese (Ghazzal 1992, 3); it has "evolved as an important way to reassert and solidify coexistence (or common living)" (Ghazzal 2002). According to some authors, the aim of dialogue in Lebanon today is to help the country move past the civil war that led to the social, political, economic, and national collapse of the country. "Ultimately, the objective of dialogue is to lead to national reconciliation by means of reinstating common living and coexistence in the pluralist, multireligious nation, and build a peaceful country for the emerging generation" (Al-Mawla 2003a, 11).

Historical Background on Interfaith Relations in Lebanon

Lebanese society is often cited as an example of religious diversity that thrived for many centuries. Relations between Christians and Muslims were not, however, totally free of tension and violent skirmishes as the two communities resorted to attempts to dominate politically and to propagandize to build a base of popular support (Al-Mawla 2002, 1). Diversity also characterized the intracommunity structures and views. Both Muslims and Christians are far from being homogenous or cohesive communities; each religion is made up of a number of sects or denominations, which "leads to cleavages not only on interconfessional, but also on intraconfessional levels" (Messarra 1998, 7). The relationship between and within these two communities, at times peaceful and at others conflictual, has affected and still affects the history of the country, especially since the political system is confessionally structured.

To understand the needs, possibilities, and challenges for IFD in Lebanon, it is important to look at the history even before the Republic of Lebanon—as it is known today—came into existence. Lebanon's multireligious, multisectarian character dates back to premodern or ancient history. Throughout the ages, Lebanon provided a refuge for different communities and minorities who came to settle after fleeing persecution in neighboring countries. Jews, Christians, and Muslims all lived "side by side, displaying each its peculiar ethnic, social, and cultural characteristics" (Hitti, 1957, 7). This "mosaic social structure" is what has characterized Lebanon from the onset and benefited its state and society as "it made possible the establishment of a free, pluralistic society that enjoyed political openness and economic prosperity" (Zisser 2002, 244).

Lebanon was a cradle for the three monotheistic religions in the region—Judaism, Christianity, and Islam. Jews in Lebanon enjoyed political, social, and economic rights equal to those of Christians and Muslims. However, with the creation of the state of Israel in 1948, the subsequent Arab-Israeli wars, and the Israeli invasion of Lebanon, Jews immigrated to Europe, South

America, the United States, and Israel. There are no accurate statistics on the number of Jews still present in Lebanon; however, the number is estimated at fewer than 300.[4] This chapter will thus focus mainly on the Christians and Muslims (including Druze), as they are the only two communities that are active in IFD in Lebanon.

Muslims and Christians have lived together for more than thirteen hundred years. However, religious and sectarian relations and balances were highly influenced and defined by the waves of invasions, conquests, and mandates throughout Lebanon's history (Winslow 1996). Even before the creation of modern Lebanon in 1920, religion and sectarianism played an important role in the political and social affairs of the country. Throughout the centuries, the different communities engaged in battles regarding issues of land ownership, political power distribution, and foreign allegiances, to name a few. So even though Christians and Muslims lived together, their coexistence was not always peaceful. In addition to these economic and political issues, the cultural and social differences between the communities promoted communal and sectarian allegiances rather than citizenship loyalty.

Issues of identity and loyalty have been a driving force in intercommunal relations in Lebanon. Christians, mostly from the Maronite sect and who were in the country centuries before the Muslims arrived, do not consider themselves Arab and believe that they are descendents of Phoenicians (Wessels 1995, 105). Yet, these Christians consider themselves an integral part and important contributors to the area's cultural development. Rather than opting to live a "ghetto existence" after the Muslims settled in the country, they continued to work for and believe in a society with Muslims (Wessels 1995, 119).

Identifying with the West, the Maronites welcomed the Crusaders and offered them military assistance (Wessels 1995, 105). Such a position, however, negatively affected the Maronite community after the Crusaders' withdrawal: while they were the most privileged group until then, the Maronites lost their privileged position with the Mamluks, who discriminated against them and other minorities—including Islamic minorities like the Druze—and forced some to flee.

Conflict in Lebanon was not clearly defined as one between different communities, but also as one between sectarian groups. Although most of the conflicts took a religious overtone, they were in reality struggles for power and positions. Druze-Maronites relations, for example, were characterized by amity, and until the 1840s, "the warfare in the mountain had been of intermittent intestine variety, with Druze fighting against Druze, and Christian against Christian. . . . The alignment was feudal and partisan rather than religious and denominational" (Hitti 1957, 433). The fighting was not only between different communities; some fighting also took place within the same community: factions or sectarian groups struggled for power and position. However, from 1840 to 1860, the conflicts and struggles of the nineteenth century, which "in reality were socioeconomic in nature, were projected into and experienced as religious conflicts" (Wessels 1995, 108). During that period, the Maronite clergy played a role in events between the peasantry and nobility as well as between Maronites and Druze. This period was characterized by massacres between the two communities; those atrocities remained in the memory of the two groups at the onset of the 1975 Lebanese civil war and continue to define their relationship today.

With the outbreak of violence, the Ottomans resorted to dividing the mountain into two districts (Double Kaymakamate)—one Druze and one Christian—with the hope of limiting the warfare. However, this political division, which would later be the basis of the 1926 Constitution and the 1943 National Pact, rather than diminishing tensions, widened and aggravated religious cleavages. One problem was the fact that each of the districts had a mixed population, and people within the district would engage in brawls. Another problem was that the arrangement was based on religious representation, and the minorities in the mixed areas felt underrepresented. Such an arrangement, however difficult, brought ten years of peace to Lebanon. However, its limitations soon caught up, and the different communities were engaged in violent conflict in 1860. In 1861, the system was reorganized and Mount Lebanon fell under the Mutassarifiyya system—a more elaborate system that provided for representation on a sectarian basis. Thus, the current sectarian system in Lebanon existed for nearly a century before the creation of the Lebanese Republic. The interreligious relations in Lebanon were thus defined by the country's history as a safe haven for different communities and yet a place where each community enjoyed its political, social, and cultural uniqueness.

The Ottoman Empire disintegrated during World War I and left the area to be divided among the European powers. In 1920, the French mandate over Lebanon began. Greater Lebanon was established by joining regions that were heavily populated by Muslims. The Maronite and Christian communities, which had enjoyed majority status until then, diminished with the growth in the Muslim population, even though they remained a slim majority. The plurality that characterized Lebanon grew and the country became one of minorities, where no majority rules. Such a system remains at the basis of the Lebanese state. However, one major problem with the creation of the Lebanese state/Greater Lebanon was getting different communities to identify as citizens rather than as members of a religious confession—a problem that is still considered a weakness of the Lebanese system.

Starting in the 1930s, Lebanese began to realize that there were sufficient grounds for cooperation between the different Muslim and Christian communities. This led to an oral agreement—the National Pact—which was a compromise between the communities on Lebanon's identity (neither Arab nor Western) as well as on the division of responsibilities and political/administrative positions among the sects. This pact was the starting point of the segregation of the Lebanese political system (Wessels 1995, 114), or what is now known as confessionalism. Such a system further encouraged the communal, rather than citizenship, feeling.

Due to the sensitivity of the sectarian proportional balance and representation, demographical data in Lebanon are politicized. Accurate data on the percentages of each sect and religion in the country, therefore, do not exist. The fear of destabilizing the political system and exacerbating the civil war dynamics has prevented the implementation of an official census in Lebanon since 1932. That last census shows a Christian majority, which is used to justify the unequal balance of power in favor of Christians. However, through the years, the 1932 balance has drastically shifted toward the Muslims, who are now said to make up 70 percent of the total population, although there is no official census to support such a statement.

The Lebanese political system is based on the principle of religious representation, wherein all nineteen recognized sects are assigned positions in the system. But as we have said, there is no official state religion. This "representational" system has existed in Lebanon since independence in 1943 and was agreed upon in the National Pact. In this formula, and up until the Taef Agreement, which ended the civil war in 1990, Christians enjoyed more political power than Muslims, maintaining a 6:5 proportional representation in the government, the parliament, and in public administration. This unequal representational system, as well as the static formula that failed to reflect the changing demographic reality of the country, have been the primary reasons cited in the various theories attempting to explain the breakdown of Lebanon in 1975. The Taef Agreement corrected the balance and instated equal representation in political and administrative positions; the ratio became 6:6. The balance of power was also equalized: the powers and prerogatives of the Muslim Sunni prime minister were increased, and those of the Christian Maronite president were decreased. In the decades before the Taef Agreement, the president had enjoyed more powers than the prime minister.

In the negotiations leading to the end of the civil war, there was an explicit effort to set everything on an equal basis. For example, the Muslim and Christian religious holidays are officially and equally recognized as national holidays. Another symbolic sign of Lebanon as a multireligious country is the absence of application "of any particular religious laws to the civil legislation," a norm compatible with the absence of an official state religion (Sayah 1998, 9).

Historically and officially, religious and cultural plurality, as well as the idea of "unity in diversity" in a democratic free, open, and tolerant system, were protected and embodied by all national documents: the 1926 Constitution, the 1943 National Pact, and the 1989 Constitution. These documents have further confirmed political confessionalism, within which the various religious communities in the country coexisted. However, misapplication of these agreements led to the civil war, and important national values were sidelined. This was further sustained by the regional-international context, which played an important role in accentuating the civil war. The fifteen years of normalized violence did not lead to any military advancement by one side over the other, but they have pushed everyone to put energy into demoralizing the "other" (Messarra 1998, 9–10).

As religious affiliation began to be deployed and exploited for the advancement of political interests, coexistence on the political level collapsed. However, this political and institutional collapse did not manifest itself on all levels: people's daily relationships among the many different communities continued. This coexistence was reflected in the numerous peace campaigns and movements during the war, including the human chain that connected the two sides of the capital on August 20, 1987; the march of the handicapped through Lebanon in October 1987; the thousands of Lebanese citizens who crossed from East and West Beirut across the demarcation line to assemble together in front of the parliament; and the defiance of the museum demarcation line by General Workers Syndicate demonstrators in November 1987. The main objective of these demonstrations was to show the willingness of the Lebanese people to coexist in national unity and reject sectarian division.

Those joint movements brought together Christians and Muslims from the different Lebanese regions to contradict the claims that the Lebanese civil war was mainly a religious or sectarian war. Different factors—social, economic, and political—played a more significant role in creating and perpetuating the destructive war. Nevertheless, one cannot ignore the impact of religion on this conflict, especially its role in initiating and exacerbating the conflict. "Religious identity was mobilized into destructive participation," as scholar Jorgen Nielson wrote, and the country was divided into two camps: Christian and Muslim. The fighting was not restricted to religious camps, but also took place within religious groups. That was enough to earn the religious or sectarian conflict label. Nevertheless, the importance and functionality of the religious factor in comparison to other factors is still debated among analysts, politicians, and religious leaders. Father Salim Ghazzal (1995, 1), an active participant in IFD, explains that "despite the fact that conflicts, persecutions, and theological debates between Muslims and Christians have taken place throughout history, these wars were not engendered for religious reasons but by political motives." Abbas El-Halabi, also an active participant in dialogue, notes that the Muslim-Christian duality was only one ingredient of a bigger problem (Initiatives of Change 2003).

A REALITY OF POST–CIVIL WAR DIVISIONS

As noted, the Taef Agreement was signed as an attempt to balance the division of power between the different religious communities and consequently solve the national crisis in the country. However, fifteen years later and even after the signing of the new constitution, most Lebanese agree that the crisis is still deeply entrenched. Lebanese are greatly divided on how their crisis should be interpreted and solved, and so tension persists despite the numerous political and national efforts to end sectarianism. While some Lebanese call for federalism and cantonization as the best solution, others put emphasis on the Lebanese history of coexistence and common living as upheld by the National Pact and the Taef Agreement. The supporters of the latter view believe that this should be done by "promoting communities of mixed populations and developing a vibrant economy that will encourage members of various confessions to associate with one another" (Havemann 2002, 61–62).

The importance of promoting such association between the different communities stems from the increased divisions in the country—especially after the war—into several districts "where each citizen is constrained to geographical limits within which to live" (Messarra 1998, 21). This exacerbated the situation and made it more difficult for people to interact. The imposed division (through demarcation lines) has made communication between people from different religions more difficult and has narrowed the space for interaction.

These geographical barriers are not the only division between the different communities. The educational system in Lebanon also reflects the country's confessional system and contributes to the segregation of communities. Lebanese, like others who live in divided societies, do not have one national unifying collective memory. Each community has its own, which obstructs the creation of one common history. The result is that contrasting views of history are being taught in different schools. Depending on the school's location and sectarian affiliation, the history of a particular community is emphasized to the detriment of other versions. History books, rather than bringing people together in national unity, have "served only to mirror and defend the confessional affiliations and political outlooks of their authors" (Havemann 2002, 52). History in Lebanon is another means by which the "self" and "other" dichotomy is emphasized. As Axel Havemann asserts (2002, 54), "the failure to understand and view both the past and the present in a complex and unbiased fashion" is the reason behind the continued existence of contradictory versions of the same historical events.

The educational system presents other challenges to unity through divergent religious education and civic formation. Religious clergy, intellectuals, and scholars have been working to assemble unified education material to be taught in schools around the country. Moreover, they are trying to introduce an educational program on peace and reconciliation, as well as one on development—both are considered necessary to rebuilding postconflict societies. Focusing on the educational system is crucial, because schools aim to be places for meeting, discovery, and mutual enrichment. These dynamics are often easier to accomplish with youth, who are more tolerant and open to such interaction. For this reason, reform of the educational system has been a primary focus of attention since the 1990s, the Taef Agreement, and the end of the civil war. Numerous attempts at "achieving national unification of the different confessional views" by creating and adopting new and uniform textbooks that overcome or integrate "confessional, communal, and primordial concerns" have been taking place, especially since the end of the war in 1991 (Havemann 2002, 59).

Even though a new history book has resulted from such initiatives, the extent of its use in schools around the nation, both public and private, is not clear. Perhaps more widespread was the publication by the Cultural Foundation Institute, sponsored by Prime Minister Hariri, of two volumes on Lebanon's history and heritage. These volumes included contributions from prominent figures drawn from all confessions. Another notable event was the organization of a conference in Beirut, attended by historians of the Lebanese University, members of the government, and representatives of the Sunni Al-Makassed Society. The discussions focused on a national view of history and on the importance of finding common historical experiences. The prevalence of ideological differences was most noticeable during the discussion. Another important initiative brought together members of the country's six major confessions with the aim of preparing a textbook on national history. These meetings did not produce any concrete results or achievements, since they occurred only sporadically. Rather, they highlighted the difficulty of such an endeavor and showed that the "historical memory and experiences of the different communities cannot be easily minimized or forgotten" (Havemann 2002, 59).

The segregation resulting from the war made communities isolated, self-sufficient, and independent; very little mixing and intermingling took place. This was reflected not only in schools, but also in universities, hospitals, clinics, scouts, youth organizations, and so on. As a result of the war, these institutions emerged with a certain confessional or sectarian color and contributed to the forces of segregation, rather than to their normal task of uniting people.

Efforts at IFD in a country where different religious communities coexist is not a new phenomenon; for Lebanese, interacting with the other faith groups is a part of daily life. However, the reaction to official, structured IFD efforts has varied among the religious communities. According to Saoud Al-Mawla (1998), a Muslim scholar and IFD activist, Christians were more supportive of such dialogue, which "until the last decade was a Christian initiative, especially supported and directed by churches." Muslims in general were distrustful of such dialogue, and it was not until the 1990s that the first Islamic initiative in this field emerged, with the creation of an Islamic commission for dialogue in Lebanon. This effort was undertaken by Muslim intellectuals and religious leaders who saw the necessity of active Muslim involvement in international conferences and participation in the works of the Synod for Lebanon, described below. This Muslim initiative for IFD culminated in the Lebanese Islamic Summit and later the National Committee for Dialogue, and was based on the belief that Lebanese from different communities and sects share a common life.

It is clear that there are different and mixed perceptions of dialogue in Lebanon. Carole Dagher (2000, xv) notes that despite the increased importance and occurrence of dialogue throughout the years, many Lebanese are still cynical about the real possibility and the value of dialogue, dubbing it "mutual deceit" or "reciprocal trickery," as well as "no more than ink on paper." Dialogue has been mostly viewed as a tool by which those who participate in it seek to advance their own interests, rather than to sincerely use it as a forum in which differences can be sorted out and trust can be built.

INTERFAITH INITIATIVES AND ORGANIZATIONS

IFD initiatives in Lebanon have increased tremendously throughout the last decade with a proliferation of organizations, committees, and groups dealing with the issue. IFD initiatives were thus diversified and included efforts by churches and Muslim religious leaders on the one hand, and secularist intellectuals and NGOs on the other. They also include initiatives by both local and international organizations as well as by academic institutions. Even though Christian-Muslim dialogue has been a reality and an aspect of daily life since the country's creation, such dialogue only started officially in 1965, with the organization of international and local conferences. However, these meetings, until the end of the civil war, were very sporadic and participation in them was very limited. One Shiite Muslim interfaith activist explains, "While these numerous, sporadic, and informal dialogue meetings took place in the country for many decades, the institutionalization of IFD in Lebanon can officially be dated to 1992, when more structured, institutional, and intentional efforts began."[5] A defining moment for IFD came with the first postwar "spiritual summit," convened in Bkerke, the Maronite religious headquarters, in 1993, which brought together all Christian and Muslim religious authorities. This summit, the first of its kind, established the the National Committee for Christian-Muslim Dialogue, which is still today the most important committee for Lebanese IFD.

The Lebanese government does not directly or officially sponsor any interfaith activities or initiatives. However, it does indirectly promote interreligious understanding by supporting the efforts of the National Committee for Christian-Muslim Dialogue, the only group that officially represents the leaders of the different religious and sectarian communities in the country.

A Lebanese Christian IFD expert and National Committee member describes the gradual strengthening of IFD: "Dialogue in Lebanon started out as shy, fearful, and hesitant due to the situation of internal wars and violence. Numerous conferences and symposia were held on Christian-Muslim relations, but it was not until the 1990s that such initiatives became organized or institutionalized."[6] For security and logistical reasons, the first meetings took place outside Lebanon and brought together Lebanese from different ages, backgrounds, sects, careers, and regions. The discussions focused mainly on the experience of coexistence and coalescence, national reconciliation, elimination of fears, abolition of stereotypes, and building a common future for Lebanon. Dialogue was open, uncontrolled, and without prior imposed planning and programs. Since 1984, such meetings had been held in Cyprus. It was not until

1987 that it was possible to meet in Lebanon. The venue chosen for the first meeting in Lebanon was the Taanayel Covenant in the Bekaa area.[7] Some progress was achieved. According to a Muslim IFD expert, "The successes in consistently holding such meetings throughout the years contributed to the progress of the Christian-Muslim dialogue in Lebanon and the Arab world."[8]

Even in a country like Lebanon, where coexistence is the norm and where communities have lived side by side for centuries, promoting IFD was a sensitive issue during the war, when people identified primarily with their religious or sectarian community and felt that any participation in such initiatives was considered a betrayal to their own group. For this reason, most of the activities that took place then were held outside Lebanon and were not very regular. After a long period of erratic interfaith work, Christian-Muslim dialogue developed an official momentum and expanded to a higher degree of clarity and transparency, especially with the formation of the National Committee for Christian-Muslim Dialogue (also known as the Islamic-Christian National Dialogue Committee) in 1993 (Center for Christian-Muslim Studies 1996a, 65–70) The National Committee was the result of the aforementioned first postwar "spiritual summit" convened in Bkerke, the Maronite Patriarchate. The meeting, which brought together all religious leaders in Lebanon, took place following the Israeli aggression and was a venue through which a unified joint statement condemning the attack was issued. The National Committee for Christian-Muslim Dialogue was established as a permanent committee in which the main Lebanese communities would be represented at a formal level by delegates/representatives appointed by the religious authorities. The seven members of the National Committee serve on equal footing, with no one presiding. As one interviewee put it, "You don't want to have someone of one sect or confession presiding over others from different sects."[9] Another important characteristic of representation on the National Committee is that in order to serve as representative of one religion, the nominated member must be accepted by all other religious leaders.[10]

As mentioned above, the Lebanese government is not directly involved and does not sponsor IFD initiatives. While some IFD committees have emerged and were sponsored by a religious leader, the National Committee for Christian-Muslim Dialogue is the only initiative that was supported officially by all of Lebanon's religious leaders and by the government. However, the field of IFD is not restricted to this committee, and other initiatives—organizational and individual, academic and practical—emerged in Lebanon throughout the years. The initiatives include meetings, lectures, symposiums, workshops, camps, training, and publications.

OTHER UNAFFILIATED IFD ACTIVITIES

IFD efforts in Lebanon are reflected in study groups, conferences, workshops, lectures, and symposiums, among other kinds of work. They have existed for years and have been organized by local, regional, and international efforts. In addition to those efforts held in Lebanon, a number of Lebanese also attend meetings abroad, in places such as Italy, Ghana, Spain, Egypt, Tunisia, China, Libya, Switzerland, Sri Lanka, Nigeria, and Malta.

Another extremely important element of IFD is the publication of books. There are numerous books, journal articles, newspaper articles, and research papers on the topic of Christian-Muslim dialogue that demonstrate how dialogue is conceived in Lebanon, as well as in other parts of the world. In addition to their impact on future Christian-Muslim relations, they are a good documentation of the evolution of the interfaith field throughout the decades. Such initiatives also bring Muslim and Christian intellectuals' papers together in the same volumes and discuss the same issues from different points of view. One such book, entitled *Christian-Muslim Relations: An Authoritative Reading of History, the Present, and the Future,* was published by the Center for Strategic Research and Documentation in Beirut. The contributors to this volume were four Muslims and four Christians who presented their communities and beliefs as they wish the other would see and understand them. The main idea behind the book is that for dialogue to be serious, the frames of thought have to be broadened. Other books, such as Ayatollah Mohammed Husayn Fadlallah's *Horizons of Islamo-Christian Dialogue,* hold a kind of IFD by contrasting religions themselves through the thoughts and words of religious leaders.

Another book, entitled *Between Sand and Spirit; How Lebanese Religious or Spiritual Communities Evaluate the 'Other,'* is a compilation of a series of lectures that took place in the 1980s. The lecturers, official representatives from all spiritual Lebanese communities, were invited by the Youth Group of Saint Mary Orthodox Church to give lectures on how each one sees the other from within his own religious discourse or background. It examines questions of how we deal with the other, how we evaluate the other and classify the other as an enemy or a friend. The lectures, which took place at the Greek Orthodox Church in Ras Beirut, were attended by university students (Tabshouri 1992). Lectures that introduce the perspectives of the different communities in relationship to one another are important, but capturing a record of these and other activities in book form is perhaps equally important. UNESCO also published a book entitled *Coexistence in Islam and Christianity* to try to overcome stereotypes and encourage the pursuit of knowledge of the other (UNESCO–Lebanese National Commission 2002, 5).

There is another common practice among organizations active in IFD: the sponsorship of summer camps that bring together Lebanese youth from different communities—sometimes also youth from other countries—to live together for days or weeks to get to know each other; play together; share in social, developmental, and cultural activities; and participate in lectures and seminars. One such study-and-work camp, jointly organized by Middle East Council of Churches (MECC) and the Arab Working Group on Muslim-

Christian Dialogue (AWGMCD), took place in Hamana, Lebanon. It provided a controlled environment of coexistence where Christian and Muslim youth worked together in public service and social development, undertaking projects such as reforestation or refurbishing a hospital. While this practical work took place during the mornings, the youth also participated later in the day in discussion groups and listened to lectures on a variety of issues such as citizenship, democracy, education, human rights, coexistence, media, and change, among others. The lecturers were intellectuals, scholars, and religious leaders active in dialogue (Ajouz 1999, 31).

Another camp that brought together young people from Lebanon, Syria, Jordan, Egypt, and the Netherlands took place between August 24 and 31, 2000, at Hamlin Hospital, also in Hamana. The camp, named Coexistence and Belongingness, included visits to displaced people in Mount Lebanon, learning about programs to help the displaced, renovation of the hospital, and discussions of various topics relating to coexistence and deepening Muslim-Christian cooperation. The participants called the camp a success, and they voiced their hope that such camps would become more common and accessible to a wider portion of society (Khoury 2000, 21). The large number of youth camps that take place in Lebanon are a clear indication of the importance of bringing young people, who are naturally curious and often more open to difference, together for dialogue to help abolish stereotypes and understand the other (El-Halabi 2002, 100). In August 2002, the MECC, in cooperation with the AWGMCD, hosted more than forty young men and women from the different sects in Lebanon, Syria, Egypt, Jordan, France, Britain, Holland, and Norway. They met together for seven days in the Lebanese Najda Sha'biya Hospital in Mrouj and held discussions focused mainly on the impact of September 11 on shared living. The participants also did some volunteer development activities in the nearby villages (MECC 2002b, 46).

Given the recent civil conflict, many in Lebanon feel the need to bring Christians and Muslims from the new generation together to promote coexistence and respect for differences. Camps have taken place all over the country. The Camp for Youth of the Unified Lebanon in Batroun brought together 120 participants to discuss issues such as higher education, electoral law, and corruption. Caritas-Lebanon also sponsored a five-day leisure camp for the kids of Bekaa with the cooperation of the National Education Scout, in which the children participated in environmental and social activities. The Virgin's Knights in Jezzine also organized a six-day cultural, religious, and leisure camp for the region's children. It was attended by 185 boys and girls. The Committee for Church Collaboration for Development and Relief, of the MECC, organized a camp in Akkar under the title "Talk to Me so that You Know Me." Sixty young men and women participated in this camp from different international regions.

One Sunni activist in dialogue has a new idea for a summer camp: "To have a tent divided into two rooms—the same tent divided into two—one part will be a church and another will be a mosque; the youth will pray under the same roof and see each other pray, each in his own way. The tent is not to convince each other of one's own way, but to respect and understand the other."[11] He is hoping to implement this idea in an upcoming camp.

In the majority of these activities, whether workshops, meetings, academic sessions, or camps, the focus is on daily life issues and socioeconomic needs, which are of importance to every participant and which affect each one's perception of the other as well as the dynamics of their interactions. Even though faith, religion, and theology are not central themes of most of these meetings, those factors are the criteria for choosing participants. It is important that the composition of the group reflect that of the nation. Because faith and religion do play a role in shaping the individual's views, traditions, and thinking, they thus affect the dynamics of dialogue. Because of Lebanon's traumatic experience with divisive civil war, many dialogue activities deliberately stress the commonalities among people in a pluralistic society, and emphasize the importance of accepting difference and using it constructively.

GOALS, ASSUMPTIONS, AND TYPES OF INTERFAITH ORGANIZATIONS

The goals and assumptions of IFD have shifted significantly over the years. When such programs started, their objective was to bring people from different religions and backgrounds into the same room to simply coexist and discuss issues of concern. If people from opposing camps consented to meet, the dialogue was considered a success. Now, the criteria for success have expanded. While IFD still serves as a forum (in the words one Druze interviewee used in his interview with us, "The goal from such [interfaith] activities is to make available a common space for people to meet") there is now an expectation that interpersonal understanding will result. According to Samir Frangieh (2003), "The goal of interfaith dialogue work is to help people overcome their crises by the recovery of healthy relations between the different Lebanese communities." A Christian active participant in dialogue considers the purpose of IFD to be simply to get to know each other. He notes that the groups and individuals engaged in dialogue transcend their confessional boundaries and work together to accomplish this aim (Chahine 2000, 4–5). Such mutual understanding between Christians and Muslims is now the point of most IFD activities. Better understanding through dialogue and the development of a shared set of concepts and vocabulary have contributed to greater rapprochement between the two communities in the wider society.

> Sessions that last more than a day and bring participants to live together are of great importance, for such shared living enforces friendships between the participants

and leads to better understanding and knowing the other in all aspects of his or her life. Thus the stereotypes which are learned through family and television and which pose the most important obstacle to meeting and dialogue are eliminated.[12]

In addition to overcoming stereotypes, knowing the other, and fortifying coexistence, another important goal of dialogue is to end the fundamentalism and extremism that result from ignorance of the other. "Such fundamentalism and extremism, found in homes, schools, public spaces, and media, are real obstacles to coexistence. . . . Dialogue is the way by which it could be eliminated and peaceful relations could be promoted" (Ghazzal 2002). IFD has the potential to provide this because it is a space where sensitive issues are discussed and different thoughts are presented (Donahue 1996, 6–7). True dialogue takes a willingness to learn and listen, not just to tell and be heard. It cannot be undertaken with the aim of scoring points against the other, but rather with the intention to focus on concepts that might bring groups closer together (Donahue 1996, 8). This point is reiterated by Bishop Khodr, the Greek Orthodox Bishop of Mount Lebanon and an authority on dialogue, who warns the "aim of dialogue is not to pierce through the defenses of the other" (Donahue 1996, 10). The difference is between an intention to dominate versus an intention to discover the other. According to Donahue (1996), IFD is not even about making concessions or avoiding sensitive points (6–7), but rather is a concern with discovering what might bring groups closer (8) These goals for dialogue focus on the individual and community levels. Some activists see the potential for change beyond these spheres and hope to see IFD ultimately shifting the political system from confessional to democracy-based (Ghazzal 2002).

In Lebanon, IFD is based on the assumption that pluralism can be a useful resource for all Lebanese to respect one another's differences. For centuries, pluralism and diversity have characterized Lebanon, and preserving them is necessary for the survival of the country (Ghazzal 2002). Coexistence in such plurality is possible and has existed for centuries. As many see it, there is no inherent conflict between Christianity and Islam. In fact, the two agree on many important "basic issues relating to the human, his rights, and his pride" (Al-Sammak 2003a, 11). Differences between Christians and Muslims "do not stem from disputes about religious doctrine, but from long-standing disputes of history and power sharing, disputes that affect day-to-day political decisions" (Al-Sammak 2002, 134).

Al-Mawla (2001, 5) sees IFD as in some ways the lifeblood of Lebanon, a national necessity "to safeguard and renew the Lebanese formula," as a religious and moral duty, given that Lebanon will not exist or have meaning without both its Christian and Muslim populations. He presents IFD as an "adventure" occurring in history, in which the outcomes are subject to human conditions and not always predictable. But he feels—along with many other Lebanese —that IFD is an important adventure to embark on (Al-Mawla 2001, 5; MECC 2002a, 42).

Major Interfaith Organizations in Lebanon

Interfaith activities and organizations in Lebanon, as we see, are numerous and diversified. Christian and Muslim religious leaders and intellectuals have been actively involved in interreligious dialogue initiatives since the 1960s. Even though such work was sporadic, with few meetings abroad (for example, Cyprus) and in Lebanon, such activities became more organized and regular in the 1990s, after the end of the fifteen-year civil war.

One of the most important efforts, the Synod for Lebanon, was called for by Pope John Paul II in 1991. The aim of the Synod was to start a period of deep thinking that would allow for moral renewal in the Catholic sects in Lebanon in order for them to reconstruct their nation. A preliminary document was prepared in which the issues and problems important to the Catholic Church in Lebanon were presented. Discussions of this document lasted for two years and included religious and sectarian intellectuals. The result was an agenda for the Synod Committee's three-week meeting in Rome in 1995, which included representatives of all religions and sects in the country (Bakradouni 1997, 7). The meeting focused on the concept of unity in plurality, which was thought not only relevant to regulating relations between the different Christian denominations, but also to building relations between Muslims and Christians. It also emphasized Lebanon's multireligious identity as a model for coexistence and interaction among religions (Bakradouni 1997, 9). The Synod for Lebanon urged Lebanese Christians and Muslims to collaborate together in all areas to build a common future (Sayah 1998, 10). This collaboration was reflected in the Muslim participation in the preparation of the Synod and in the national scope of its document. However, despite the Muslim participation in the Synod, the effort was predominantly a Christian one that brought Christians together to think about ways to live with and dialogue with Muslims.

The Episcopal Committee for Christian-Muslim Dialogue, another important Christian religious initiative, was formed by a committee of Catholic religious leaders in Lebanon. Its main aim was to reduce the tensions between communities and to encourage dialogue and coexistence, as encouraged by Vatican II (Ghazzal 1995, 8). Vatican II, according to Bishop Mounjid Al-Hachim, was a turning point in the relations between religions. It led to deep changes in mind-sets as well as to reforms and renewals in the Catholic Church and within Christian groups. The main message of Vatican II was that churches should start taking the subject of Muslim-Christian relations seriously and should put all their efforts into education about dialogue: in the family and church, in groups and universities, and at all levels (UNESCO 2002, 86).

The Episcopal Committee works in close cooperation with other papal committees, the National Committee for Christian-Muslim Dialogue, dialogue institutions around the world, universities, schools, institutes, organizations, and political parties. It seeks to openly approach the differences in the points of view between Christians and Muslims, promote dialogue between the different communities around everyday life issues, teach each side about the other side's faith, advance the understanding and acceptance of the other, and apply the decisions of the Synod for Lebanon. The Episcopal Committee further aims to propagate the culture of dialogue in families, schools, universities, and civil society institutions through educational, cultural, and media programs. Theological dialogue also occupies an important place in the Episcopal Committee's work. According to author Father Salim Ghazzal (n.d., 12–13), deepening knowledge of the Bible, theology, and religion is indispensable to effective dialogue.

In addition to these Christian initiatives, some important Muslim IFD initiatives and forums emerged. The first Muslim committee for dialogue, the Lebanese Islamic Committee for Dialogue (LICD), was formed in 1990 by the leaders of different Muslim sects. Its aim was to create a Muslim counterpart that would partner with the World Council of Churches and other Christian forces engaged in dialogue. It played a very important role in the preparation of the Synod declaration, as well as in the National Committee for Christian-Muslim Dialogue.[13]

Another forum, the Lebanese Encounter for Dialogue (LED), has a mixed membership of Christians, Muslims, and secularists. It was founded by a group of intellectuals and does not have any ties with religious authorities. Its activities are intellectual and cultural, and it functions in collaboration with various centers and leagues. When religious men—and it is important to note that primarily men take part in and organize IFD initiatives in Lebanon—participate in the activities, they do so in an unofficial capacity (Donahue 1996, 22).

A more structured and formal interfaith group, the National Committee for Christian-Muslim Dialogue,[14] was formed in 1993 and continues its activities currently. Although religious in nature—that is, it is made up of representatives from all the different sects and endorsed by the religious leadership—the National Committee was formed by intellectuals. It starts with the notion that "the value of Lebanon rests on the plurality of its society and confessions and that there are many common spaces between Christianity and Islam that should be widened, while the spaces of existing differences should be narrowed."[15] The group feels that coexistence between the different religious denominations is a pattern of life and the country's destiny and mission to the world. Seeking to "renew the forms of national solidarity and cooperation" (Center for Christian-Muslim Studies 1996a, 70–71) the main task of the National Committee was to prepare a working paper for dialogue (Donahue 1996, 21). In this historic joint document, approved and signed by the religious leaders in 1995, the aims of the National Committee were presented. The most important were to "preempt any imbalance which might endanger the Christian-Muslim co-living in the country; to prevent events of sectarian nature abroad which [affect] the unity of Lebanese; to emphasize civic spirit rather than sectarian fanaticism; and to rewrite the history of a unified

Lebanon" (Center for Christian-Muslim Studies 1996a, 12). The working paper was presented to the president of the republic, the prime minister, and the speaker of the House for their information. It was the first attempt to elaborate a common vision of national problems and a common value system through dialogue (Al-Mawla 1998, 8).

The National Committee's objectives are promoted through emphasis on virtues such as tolerance, mutual respect, and coexistence. To meet these aims, the National Committee meets regularly to discuss national, political, social, and religious issues. It also organizes seminars and conferences, releases policy statements to the media on issues of concern to Muslims and Christians (Al-Sammak 2002, 134), facilitates exchanges between the religious leaders from the different communities, establishes contacts with existing organizations involved in Muslim-Christian dialogue, promotes local dialogue, organizes IFD public events, researches the common causes and values among the religions, and facilitates interreligious cooperation in different areas, especially education (National Committee for Muslim-Christian Dialogue n.d., 3–4).

However, due to the National Committee's dependence on voluntary service and personal contributions from its members, its work has been slow. Lack of resources, both human and monetary, has limited the scope and number of its activities (Donahue 1996, 21; National Committee for Muslim-Christian Dialogue n.d., 4). The National Committee would be able to function at a higher level if more funds were available for an official office with paid staff. Nevertheless, it is pursuing its mandate, which is to promote a Muslim-Christian dialogue to rebuild "common living in Lebanon on the basis of unity in plurality." Its work is based on the belief that it is through dialogue that traumas of the past can be surmounted and that stereotypes can be eliminated (National Committee for Muslim-Christian Dialogue n.d., 3). The main issues raised and discussed in the National Committee's dialogues, which take place in an honest and open environment, relate to international events (such as the war in Iraq and the question of Palestine). By discussing these problems, the National Committee looks to consolidate the internal front on issues that affect internal solidarity (*An-Nahar* 2003, 5).

The World Council of Churches (WCC) is also involved in IFD (Donahue 1996, 2). Based in Geneva, it includes more than 300 churches and sects. The dialogue committee, which emerged in 1971, has its permanent headquarters in Geneva and is divided into two offices—one dealing with relationships with Islam and the other with Judaism. The office that deals with relationship with Muslims has sponsored and organized meetings, lectures, and conferences in a number of countries worldwide. The WCC works in conjunction with local partners (churches, NGOs, universities, intellectuals) and initiatives. According to one source, in the last ten years, the Muslim-Christian dialogue, under the auspices of the WCC, "overcame the old conception and focus on interreligious theological debate, where each side tries to prove its religious truth in contrast with the other, to become more a dialogue based on mutual respect, understanding, and recognition of the differences as both a condition of human existence and a manifestation of divine wisdom" (Saif 2000, 1).

Indeed, a dialogue can be constructive without the abandonment of religious conviction on either side. A constructive dialogue is one in which participants are secure, confident, and trustful enough to "argue their competing understandings and interpretations of their own religious resources, in response to the challenging issues brought up in the dialogue" (Saif 2000, 2). Successful dialogue relies on one's ability to open up spiritually to other beliefs. According to a program executive at the WCC, interreligious education rests on knowing one's faith very well, learning about the faith of others by listening to them, knowing the skills of conflict resolution, analyzing history and memory, analyzing situations where religions are used for political reasons, and understanding the richness of pluralism and the importance of reconciliation.[16] In the case of Lebanon, it is important to listen to history from the different communities' points of view, to differentiate between national and confessional identity, to encourage the culture of peace, and so on. The WCC also suffers from funding problems, which is why the participants are limited in number, chosen by the partner organizations, and do not include the grassroots.[17]

According to a Christian veteran of IFD, the initiative by which dialogue between the Lebanese officially started was the Lebanese Meeting for Dialogue (also known as the Lebanese Forum for Dialogue), which is a partnership of the WCC with the MECC. As early as 1975–76, meetings were organized with the aim of bringing together Lebanese youth from different regions and religions to workshops in Cyprus. Such a setting provided a chance for Lebanese from different backgrounds to meet together, something that was not possible in Lebanon during the civil war.[18] As he told us,

> The motivation to conduct such workshops and meetings stems from [the] personal experience of knowing Lebanon, with its vibrant plurality before the war broke out, and wanting to preserve the bond between people from different religious communities. . . . Dialogue is not about theology, even though it might include some. Most dialogue deals with issues of citizenship and politics.[19]

This particular partnership brought Lebanese researchers, professors, and other professionals from different backgrounds, representing a variety of cultural and political perspectives, to a Muslim-Christian dialogue meeting in Montreux, Switzerland, between June 16 and 20, 2001. Holding the meeting outside Lebanon was considered necessary for security reasons as well as for convenience—that is, for being far away from the daily diversions and work in Beirut. The participants decided to start an organization for dialogue to meet regularly and monitor the developments in the relations between Muslims and Christians, to promote Lebanese consensus on issues of national sovereignty and coexistence, and to promote religious culture through education. The participants also issued statements supporting the Lebanese resistance, condemning Israeli occupation, and supporting the Palestinian Intifada ("Lebanese Muslims and Christians Establish 'Caucus on Dialogue'" 2001, 27).

A follow-up meeting was held in Laqlouq, Lebanon, on August 25, 2001, after which the organization of a Lebanese Caucus on Dialogue was announced. The aim of this caucus is to strengthen national solidarity, increase public participation in dialogue, prevent differences from turning into absolute religious and sectarian divisions, and deepen the foundations for dialogue on issues that are important to Lebanese ("Lebanese Muslims and Christians" 2001, 27).

Following these two meetings, a third one was held in Beiteddine, Lebanon, on September 30, 2001, in which the participants applauded the second Palestinian Intifada and condemned as criminal the September 11 attacks on the United States. Twenty-eight participants (twenty-six men and two women) asserted that progress must be achieved in dialogue on the national level. The main objectives of such discussions, they said, should be "to avert the threat of sectarian division from whatever source it might come and to strengthen the foundations of Lebanon's national consensus with respect to the following issues: national sovereignty, complete liberation, coexistence, protection of civil liberties" ("The Lebanese Forum for Dialogue" 2001, 14).

Another example of the vibrancy of dialogue in Lebanon is the Middle East Council of Churches (MECC). Starting from the premise that religion cannot be anything but a source of love and peace, the MECC's main aim, in the area of Muslim-Christian dialogue, is to "look for ways to deepen cooperation between peoples of different religions, cultures, and ethnicities so that the experiences we witnessed do not repeat themselves" (Jarjour 2002, 1). According to its director, the MECC started in 1975 as a program that brings Muslims and Christians together to assist people who have been affected by the war.[20] The MECC has made Christian-Muslim dialogue its top priority. (UNESCO 2002, 222–23). The numerous meetings and workshops that it sponsors and organizes are a sign of its operational commitment to deepen integration and understanding between the different religious communities.

The emphasis in the MECC is on a dialogue of life, not on ideology or dogma. Father Riad Jarjour (2002, 7–9) believes that dialogue is necessary for the following reasons: it allows people to begin to think in terms of common living; it treats the roots of sectarian tensions "by forbidding the use of religious differences to support or incite political conflicts"; it helps Lebanese from different religions take a common stand on regional and international issues and stops them from exacerbating conflict in the society; and it abolishes the dominant dualities, such as East/West. Dialogue is thus founded on respect for the other, on knowing the others as humans and as they want to be known. The ultimate goal is coexistence and equality between citizens.[21] These goals are what personally motivated this Christian interfaith organizer to get involved in IFD, as he has lived and interacted with Muslims most of his life and considers such coexistence to be the norm. His experience in South Lebanon, the predominantly Muslim area where he was stationed as a priest, has pushed him to pursue his master's degree in Islamic studies and to send out the call that each citizen should make the effort to learn about and understand the religion of others.

The Arab Working Group on Muslim-Christian Dialogue (AWGMCD) is a group of thinkers, scholars, and religious leaders. It was created in 1995 by seventeen men who are motivated by their personal convictions (that is, not representative of any political group or force). The group is sponsored by the MECC and with its help organizes numerous local, regional, and international projects (UNESCO 2002, 225). The AWGMCD decided to expand and enhance the scope of its work, as well as the number of participants in its conferences. Its most important accomplishment thus far has been the pact, or accord, of dialogue and unified living, which occurred six years after the creation of the group and was endorsed by the meeting in Cairo in 2001. This document, entitled *Dialogue and Coexistence: An Arab Muslim-Christian Covenant,* is the result of almost two years of meetings and discussions between the members of the group, who come from Lebanon, Syria, Egypt, Jordan, Sudan, Palestine, and the United Arab Emirates.[22] The accord calls for reinstating and solidifying national unity and encouraging dialogue between Christian and Muslim citizens. It also confirms the importance of treating the root causes of religious and sectarian tensions (which are mostly political, economic, social, and cultural conditions), as well as differentiating between religiosity and fundamentalism. It defines dialogue as a "dialogue of life," or one that happens through intellectual discussion and common action programs, and it declares, "we stand together in the face of social, education, cultural and moral dangers (Arab Working Group 2002, 20). The accord calls for frank communication and open, honest discussion of issues, and further confirms that dialogue should not be limited to a closed circle of Muslim-Christian elites, but should be more broadly available to a wider, popular mass (Al-Sammak 2003b, 11). The AWGMCD considers this covenant "a guide or a foundation for programs or practical plans which will apply them in the real world of living together and in various communicational, formational, cultural and social contexts" (Arab Working Group 2002, 15).

The AWGMCD organizes a series of activities—conferences, seminars, specific studies, and meetings, both regional and international—through which it deals with various aspects of Muslim-Christian relations. One of the objectives in these conferences and seminars is to affirm a united Muslim-Christian stance on certain causes. As one founder of the AWGMCD told us,

> The Arab Working Group does not get involved in theology. Theological differences can be discussed in other settings. The Arab Working Group's work is national: we discuss ways in which we can solidify our national life and common living, how we can understand and solve our differences, etc. All this takes place without using faith at all—each one can stay on his or her religion. . . . The par-

ticipants in these conferences and meetings belong to a certain intellectual level, as it is better to have some sort of balance in the discussions."[23]

The ideas from the meetings are then propagated through the media, lectures, youth camps, and so on.[24]

Since its creation, AWGMCD has been very active, organizing large conferences both in Lebanon and abroad and bringing together hundreds of intellectuals and religious leaders. Among those initiatives was a conference entitled "Muslims and Christians: Together for Jerusalem," which took place in Beirut in 1996 and was attended by 120 religious and intellectual authorities from sixteen Arab countries. The participants issued a statement in which they declared their unified position on Jerusalem and the rights of Palestinians. Such statements of solidarity on an issue like Palestine and Jerusalem are a central approach to interfaith work among Christians and Muslims in the region and can be seen as a strategy to rally the two communities in a unified way. Through such statements, participants in dialogue emphasize a discourse of national unity, without really exploring internal problems. The AWGMCD aims to show that there is no real conflict between Christians and Muslims.

In 1998, AWGMCD organized another conference in Beirut: "The Abrahamic Tradition and Christian-Muslim Dialogue." Its main aim was to emphasize the commonalities between people on the basis of faith rather than primarily on the basis of national interests. It rejected any kind of differentiation between people based on race or sect. This conference was not limited to Arab participants and was attended by around forty religious figures and academics from Syria, Jordan, Egypt, the United Arab Emirates, Lebanon, France, Italy, Switzerland, the UK, and the United States (Arab Working Group 2002, 11). In 1999, a meeting was held in Cairo, Egypt, to discuss "the relations between Christians and Muslims in the Arab world as well as issues of citizenship, civil society and development based on justice, dignity, and equality." The participants approved of the cooperation between Muslim and Christian youth in Lebanon who liberated the occupied village of Arnoun in South Lebanon ("Muslim-Christian Working Group" 1999, 24). In April 2000, another meeting was called in Beirut in collaboration with the MECC. It was entitled "Coexistence and Religious Tensions in Some Arab Countries," and it dealt with the negative impacts of religious tensions in countries such as Sudan, Egypt, and Lebanon (Arab Working Group 2002, 14–15). Discussions tackled the questions of the role of religion in public life, religion and extremism, and the issue of power, among others.

In 2002, a symposium was held in Cairo: "Muslims and Christians Facing Present Challenges Together." The aim of the meetings—which were attended by religious leaders, scholars, thinkers, and media people from Egypt, Sudan, Jordan, Bahrain, Syria, Lebanon, and Palestine—was to show that the essence of Christianity and Islam are the same and that each can contribute fruitfully to dialogue.

In 2003, two new initiatives were launched. One, in Beirut, dealt with the issue of religious fundamentalism, and another, in Paris, discussed the relations between East and West. Existing conflicts and differences were traced to political factors, not religious or cultural ones. The AWGMCD, in collaboration with the Justice, Peace, and Human Rights program at the MECC, also organized numerous conferences touching on such issues as citizenship, democracy and human rights, and American law concerning religious persecution.

In addition to these conferences, AWGMCD sponsors annual summer camps to help transfer the culture of dialogue to the public through the youth of various Arab countries (Al-Sammak 2003b, 11). According to most interviewees, these camps have created an environment that allows young people to discover the benefits of living together. During a period of twenty to twenty-five days, the participants are involved in various activities, such as volunteer development work (cleaning a village, planting trees, and so on), discussions, seminars, and lectures (Arab Working Group 2002). Participation is by invitation only; youth are chosen from the members of the AWGMCD in collaboration with community leaders.

The World Student Christian Foundation (WSCF) and the World Conference on Religion and Peace (WCRP) are two other organizations that work on IFD. One interfaith participant told us that although the WCRP does not have an office in Lebanon, it coordinates its work with the National Committee for Christian-Muslim Dialogue and the AWGMCD.[25] It has a community of practitioners and friends from the different faith traditions—about sixty young people—and creates informal interreligious councils in coordination with other dialogue groups in Lebanon.[26] The group also sponsors other projects and activities that bring people of different religions and faiths together. Examples include a multifaith blood donation for the Palestinian Intifada, joint sports day, joint day of prayer, and youth camps.[27] All the organization's work is based on the belief that religion should be part of a positive process of change and not a reason for conflict.

The Lebanese Conflict Resolution Network (LCRN), a nonprofit organization established in Lebanon, coordinates and advances the field of peace and conflict resolution in Lebanon through initiating conflict-resolution training workshops in and between various Lebanese communities. The LCRN, whose members come from all faiths, first started "in 1996 as a project initiated with the joint efforts of Lebanese NGOs and academic activists, with the support of international organizations and experts." Throughout the years, LCRN's trainers and experts have organized "various educational, training, consultancy and intervention activities for a wide array [of Lebanese nonprofits and] business organizations." In 1999, its activities expanded to other countries, such as Syria, Jordan, Montenegro, and Armenia. Such activities are carried out in close cooperation with NGOs and academic centers in the countries concerned (LCRN n.d.).

The work of LCRN in the area of IFD involves helping resolve conflicts between different communities through an array of activities. LCRN's interfaith projects first began in 1998, and one of the most important projects it has implemented in this regard is the reconciliation project between Druze and Christians in the mountainous Shouf-an area, which witnessed intense sectarian conflict during the war. Deep social wounds, still fresh in the region, are at the center of the internal displacement problem in Lebanon.[28] Even though some refugees are beginning to return to the area, it is clear that relatedness among communities is weak. One representative from LCRN told us that "interventions of this type usually target youth and include skills at communication, trust building, and cooperation projects. The aim is to reestablish harmony, coexistence, and [heartfelt] reconciliation between these youths, and hopefully the communities at large in the long term." These youths should feel involved in such projects and given the chance to decide what projects they need; it is important to "empower them to take ownership of the process."[29]

Interfaith organizations and efforts are not restricted to a specific area of the country. Not only in Beirut, but also in North Lebanon, Mount Lebanon, and South Lebanon, IFD is strong. In the South, such activities started even before the outbreak of the civil war and still continue today after the cessation of hostilities. Interfaith work was motivated by living in a mixed environment, where both Christians and Muslims have lived together for years, interrupted by instances of fighting and massacres. One notable project was the creation of a social center, Garden of Peace, in Sidon in 1987. Bishop Salim Ghazzal, an activist in IFD, played a significant role in creating this social center, in collaboration with a number of Christian and Muslim social and humanitarian associations. The center was intended as both an educational and recreational program and brings children and youth together from different communities. The Garden of Peace is divided into a section for social aid, another for physically and mentally handicapped people, and a section for children. It sponsors a number of programs, including one-week formation sessions for trainers and supervisors and twelve-day free sessions for children between the ages of six and fifteen. These sessions highlight the importance of daily relations and interactions to the construction of peace (Ghazzal 1995, 4).

Another important center, established in the South in 1990, was the Circle for Development and Dialogue (CDD). It was made possible by the efforts of Bishop Salim Ghazzal and a group of intellectual Muslims and Christians, and was intended as an active social center, mainly serving South Lebanon. It brings together Christian and Muslim professionals, scholars, and intellectuals between the ages of twenty-five and fifty with the aim of reestablishing coexistence between the communities by providing a space for exchanging views and debating issues (Ghazzal 1992, 12). In addition to its activities in interfaith relations and dialogue, CDD also sponsors projects that support development and raise the standard of living, such as a senior citizens' club, monetary loans, and helping refugees and displaced persons (Ghazzal 2000). In addition to their developmental aims, these projects further relations between people of different communities who come together to implement them. The CDD depends on Lebanese and foreign sponsors to cover its expenses (Abboud et al. 1995, 98).

The CDD also sponsors cultural and social activities on a more intellectual level, including lectures, conferences, reunions, meetings, symposiums, and colloquia (Ghazzal 1995, 6–7). One of the important projects of the center, for example, is the technical school, where ex-militia come to learn a vocation to reintegrate more easily into society and support themselves after the war (Ghazzal 1995, 5). Other projects include a library specializing in issues of dialogue, a sports club, and a youth club for different activities. According to its brochure, the CDD is involved in a "dialogue of life," not ideology; it is a process aimed at accepting the other.

In addition to these activities, the CDD coordinates activities and events with other organizations in South Lebanon, as well as with UNICEF. One result of this cooperation was a program for peace education, where children live together in a camplike setting (Ghazzal 2000). CDD encourages such camps and has organized several summer camps and training workshops throughout the years. These bring together children and trainers from different regions and confessions—about 600 trainers and more than 20,000 children (Abboud et al. 1995, 91). They provide the opportunity for the campers to play, dance, and sing together (Ghazzal 1992, 11). These activities provide a space for children and youth from different communities to get to know each other during everyday activities. It is Ghazzal's belief (1992, 12) that events like this, which most of the time pass unnoticed, are the ones that actually contribute to cementing the unity between people from different communities.

The Initiatives of Change (IC), formerly known as Moral Rearmament (MR), also plays an important role in IFD in Lebanon. An informal, international network of people from all faiths, with a less academic bent than some groups, the IC has a basic ideology of personal transformation, that is, people should change their own lives before trying to change the world. IC seeks spiritual truth, which is expressed in nonreligious language. The IC does not have a formal membership and is largely financed by contributions from people who believe that this spirit and practice are needed (Initiatives of Change n.d.) The IC held a number of meetings in the Deir al-Jabal Covenant and the Covenant of Jesuit Fathers in Taanayel, Lebanon. Even though these meetings were very fruitful, the most important project that the IC launched in Lebanon was one that gathered ex-militia from different communities for the purpose of reconciliation. The IC is, according to one of its active participants, a spiritually based movement.[30] However, he points to the fact that most of those who experienced a basic transformation were people who did not profess spiritual tendencies or faith. The changes that occur, however, are difficult to measure or evaluate, as they are internal. IC in Lebanon has at least thirty members in its core group, but many more supporters and friends.[31]

The IC's project in Lebanon was launched with the objective of reconciling Lebanese communities through inviting four specific ex-militia members (two Christians and two Muslims), who fought each other throughout the war years, to come together, reconcile, and forgive one another. The first event in this project was to invite them to Britain for a six-day visit in April 2002 to share their experiences and perspectives with 300 people at a public meeting in the Westminster Cathedral Hall in London. The most important lesson that emerged from their stories is that one has to reconcile with oneself and the past and change from within to be able to reconcile with others and change the world. This group was composed of Asaad Shaftari, an engineer and ex-senior officer in a Christian militia during the war; Muheiddine Shehab, the notary public of Ras Beirut and ex-commander of a Muslim militia; Hicham Chehab, a journalist and an ex-member of a Muslim militia; and Ramez Salame, a lawyer and an ex-member of a Christian militia. What is important to note is that before they got together in Britain and spoke on "Breaking the Chain of Hate," each one individually experienced an internal change and tried to reconcile with himself and his past. Shaftari has made a public apology to those who were his victims during the war; Shehab has acknowledged the evil acts he committed; Chehab refused to shoot civilians and walked away from the militia; and Salame also left the militia and tried to reestablish links with Muslims during the war (Initiatives of Change 2003).

During their visit to Britain, the four spoke in detail about their experiences and what made them change. Hicham Chehab recalls that the day he was unable to shoot an old woman who looked like his grandmother walking down the street was the day he realized that "others" are also human beings and left the militia. Shaftari, inspired by his love for his son and his hope that the child will live a better life and have a hopeful future, published a letter of apology in the press and took responsibility for his wrongdoing during the war. He saw this as an attempt to repair whatever could be repaired in order to build a better future for the next generation. The IC's reconciliation project was not limited to the Britain trip; the four talked to groups throughout Lebanon, particularly in colleges and universities, where the men hoped to persuade the next generation not to repeat their mistakes. They also participated in international conferences and visits in Caux, Australia, and Washington, D.C.

The primary aim of the project was to promote among as many people as possible the idea that religion can be part of a solution rather than a problem, as demonstrated in these passionate individual stories (Initiatives of Change 2003). Specifically in Lebanon, their aim was to defuse the culture of hate in the country, which was entrenched as a result of years of civil war. The group has put together a documentary entitled *For the Love of Tomorrow,* which depicts the Muslim-Christian aspects of the conflict and shows how each one of these ex-soldiers came to the realization that they needed to reconcile with the past, to realize that the "other" is also a human being, and to build constructive relations with him (Initiatives of Change 2003). This movie is a powerful tool by which IC transmits its message.

These ex-militia members were also involved in interfaith activities with other groups and worked at other levels to promote dialogue and understanding between the different communities in Lebanon. Hicham Chehab, for example, proposed the establishment of an organization, the Center for Reconciliation and Democracy. The purpose of this center, with headquarters in Mashgara, Western Bekaa, is to build bridges between the Christian and Muslim communities that live there and to promote peacebuilding initiatives. The Center for Reconciliation and Democracy offers conflict-resolution courses, language classes, computer skills, and so on, and targets university students and young community leaders. Other activities will include forums, conferences, and service projects in the local communities (Chehab 2003a).

One Muslim interfaith participant explains how his interest in IFD is not a new phenomenon but was prompted by his brother's death in the 1980s. This tragic event triggered an interest in Christian studies, an attempt to understand the beliefs of those he was fighting and who were responsible for his brother's death. After the war, he founded a local committee, the Ras Beirut Association, which held mixed gatherings for the purpose of reconciliation through Christian-Muslim dialogue.[32] In the early 1990s, he wrote in a leading newspaper about the need for dialogue and mutual understanding; he also published a letter of apology in 2002. Through his work, he emphasizes the importance of going beyond coexistence to create citizens with allegiance to the state and not the sect. "Living peacefully together is not enough to consolidate relations between people from different communities and leaves them vulnerable [to] the slightest instability. Interaction is what opens [the] way to strong relations that will withstand all tests and disagreements."[33] Although he promotes understanding between the two faiths and believes in the importance of knowing and discovering deeply the others' religion, he adopts a secular approach in his interfaith work.[34]

The list of IFD organizations does not end there. In addition to these religious, social, developmental, spiritual, and nongovernmental efforts, educational centers, schools, and universities also play an important role in IFD in Lebanon. One initiative worth mentioning is the first of its kind: no meeting had previously taken place between a Muslim religious center and a Christian religious one in Lebanon. It was held in Harissa, between students from the Imam al-Ouzai School for Islamic Studies and those from the Saint Paul Center for Theology and Philosophy. The students participated in a symposium that emphasized the importance and necessity of dialogue, meeting, and cooperation between communities.[35]

Academic centers and university institutes have increased in number throughout the years and have been the most active actors in this field, organizing activities such as conferences, lectures, and seminars, as well as offering academic degrees in the field of religious studies and dialogue. One key institute is the Saint Joseph University's Institute for Islamo-Christian Studies (IEIC). This center, at the heart of a university run by Catholic priests, was created in 1977 and provides an informal meeting space for Muslim and Christian students. The IEIC's main objective is to promote "the knowledge of Islam and Christianity by Christians and Muslims in a spirit of mutual respect and according to academic methods" (Institute of Muslim-Christian Studies n.d.; 2003–2004). The IEIC's activities continued throughout the civil war and in 2000, the institute became attached to the School of Religious Sciences at the university. The institute offers a two-year program leading to a certificate in Islamic-Christian studies and research. The curriculum includes basic studies in and introduction to Christianity and Islam for the purpose of teaching students about one another's religions; advanced courses on both religions, on methodology, and on literature; as well as specialized courses on theological and philosophical principles of Christian-Muslim dialogue, contemporary religious thinking, and the Bible and the Quran (Institute of Muslim-Christian Studies n.d.; 2003–2004).

Just as the IEIC welcomes students from both faith traditions, it also hosts a diverse faculty, and classes are given by both Muslim and Christian scholars. The lecturers are chosen to give students a solid and comprehensive knowledge of the subject matter; in some cases, the same course is cotaught by a Christian and a Muslim to provide students with different views on the same topic, to maintain objectivity, and to encourage students to accept differences. According to the director of the institute, students who join the program "in general have some kind of openness."[36] This openness is necessary, as there are frequently sensitive issues that lead to heated debates and discussions.

In addition to this important academic component, the IEIC also organizes and sponsors a number of conferences, seminars, and workshops on Christian-Muslim relations. The activities that take place are decided upon by the members of the IEIC, who meet once a week to discuss the agenda. Examples of such activities include a three-day seminar on "Religious Fact in Lebanon: Problematic and Approaches"; a series of lectures by Abbas El-Halabi entitled "A Cultural Approach to the Druze Society in Lebanon," intended to familiarize students with the Druze community's history, social organization, cultures, traditions, and their political role in the country; and a conference by Father Louis Boisset about the future of Islamo-Christian dialogue and its possible evolution. Even though some of these events deal specifically with the Lebanese case, there are numerous events that talk about the field of interreligious relations in general. "The objective is to benefit as many people as possible, regardless of their country of origin. This is especially important when considering that, in addition to the Lebanese majority, there are a few Sudanese and Algerian students enrolled in the program."[37] The conferences are sponsored by the IEIC and hosted either at the institute or at a venue convenient to the participants. Usually thirty to forty participants openly discuss a theme of interest to the group and in line with its needs. In addition to discussions, participants take part in exercises on dialogue and cooperation. Despite the limited number of participants, these meetings are documented in books to disseminate the culture of dialogue to a wider audience and to show that dialogue is possible. It is important to note that in all these conferences and meetings, the participants are there in their own individual capacity and not serving as representatives of their communities or groups. Furthermore, according to one Christian organizer and active participant, "The dynamic of the meeting reflects the background of the participants and whether they come from a region that has experienced coexistence and religious plurality or not."[38] Membership in the IEIC is free, and the university provides the institute with offices as well as an administrative assistant.

The IEIC also sponsors informal biweekly meetings between Lebanese Christian and Muslim students. Although these encounters are not covered by the media, the proceedings and results are published by the IEIC. The first volume in the series of such interactions, entitled *Challenges to Mutual Understanding: Muslim and Christian Students Face to Face,* presents the events and results of the 1995 academic session, which focused on the exigencies of common living between Christians and Muslims in the light of the living experience in Lebanon.

The session's aim was to bring about true acquaintance and reciprocal understanding between the students and to specify and clarify the necessary conditions to improved coexistence. The format of the discussions was based on participants sharing lived experiences and discussing real-life problems, with special emphasis on those relating to Christian-Muslim coexistence (*Challenges to Mutual Understanding* 2002, 5). The aim is not to exchange ideological teachings or learn about the other's faith starting from theoretical ideology, but to discover the faith in lived reality, in the context of the other's humanity (*Challenges to Mutual Understanding* 2002, 6–7). The topics discussed in such sessions vary and are chosen by the participants. They include stereotyping, freedom, coexistence, and the problem of generalization, among others. Although sessions are limited to a few participants due to limited resources, it is hoped that such a dynamic group will diffuse this culture of dialogue into the larger society (*Challenges to Mutual Understanding* 2002, 36).

Expanding on its program, the IEIC launched the Islamic-Christian Dialogue Committee in 2002. The committee has a Web site (Hiwar.net) and provides a space for youth from all the Christian and Muslim communities to dialogue in a climate of mutual respect.[39] In addition to face-to-face meetings, dialogue takes place through e-mail, where interested individuals share their experiences of living with people of other faiths as well as the challenges and opportunities such experiences provide. All e-mails go through the webmaster, who posts them on the Web page in the hope of eliciting responses from readers. In addition to the cyber-dialogue, the Islamic-Christian Dialogue Committee holds monthly meetings, discussions, and cross-country trips. Its Web site, Hiwar.net, provides an online version of the *Islamo-Christian Chronicle,* the bulletin of the IEIC.

In addition to these many activities, the IEIC publishes studies on Christian-Muslim dialogue with the hope that these publications, along with the meetings, lectures, and seminars, will consolidate, deepen, and extend the culture of dialogue. One of the IEIC's most consequential books was a compilation called *Christian-Muslim Declarations Issued between 1954 and 1992.* The book, a collection of the declarations resulting from worldwide meetings on the Middle East, reflects the importance of the field of IFD and the scope of the efforts deployed for its sake (Sayah 1998, 6). The IEIC also sponsors a series of books entitled *Lebanon Today: Culture and Religion,* which raises key questions about the diversity and complexity of Lebanese society. It presents different approaches to IFD and disputes common stereotypes and misconceptions about IFD.

Another important series published by the IEIC, *Notebooks on Dialogue,* specifically deals with IFD in Lebanon. The series is a collection of volumes by activists in the field in which each author shares a compilation of the speeches and lectures he (or she) has given in meetings, conferences, and workshops throughout the years. Two volumes have been published so far. The first volume in the series is Abbas El-Halabi's book, *On Dialogue, Reconciliation, and Civil Peace,* in which the author introduces dialogue as a necessary tool for building cohesive relationships among people. El-Halabi's thesis is that there is a causal relationship between dialogue, reconciliation, and civil peace. He emphasizes and explains the role of dialogue in national unity and the importance of including youth (Zeineddine 2003, 17). Throughout the book, El-Halabi illustrates how Lebanon, due to its violent and bloody past, is a difficult country to rebuild and reconcile, but that through patience and persistence it is nevertheless possible to do so (Al-Mawla 2003a, 11; El-Halabi 2002).

The second book in the same series, *Justice in Coalescence,* by Saoud Al-Mawla, was published in 2003. According to the author, the true value of dialogue rests in truth, justice, friendship, and knowing the other. The aim of dialogue is to ultimately reach comprehensive national reconciliation and civic peace through reconciling with self and the other; building internal and national civic peace inside the individual and the group; and seeking peace, security, and stability for everyone (Al-Mawla 2003b, 9). While repeatedly confirming the importance of dialogue as a principle in Islam and a religious duty, Al-Mawla finds the practice of dialogue in Lebanon wanting, observing that participants do not really engage in dialogue but rather posture in support of dialogue and exchange pretentious statements confirming its importance. Dialogue has been treated as a scorecard or a ticket to fame (Al-Mawla 2003b, 116–18) and an instrument for obtaining power and asserting rank or leadership roles (2003b, 175). He observes that Lebanese still do not seek to know, recognize, or accept one another, and he attributes the lack to a failure of courage.

The Al-Makassed Higher Institute of Islamic Studies was established in 1981 amidst intense civil strife. The main aim of the Al-Makassed Higher Institute was to "promote a better understanding of Islam and to prepare modern scholars who are capable of meeting the challenges of modern times with an open mind, a respect for others, and determination to overcome the obstacles which stand in the way of the development of a healthy civil society in Lebanon" (Al-Makassed Web site). The Al-Makassed Higher Institute is a center for Islamo-Christian dialogue and provides a space for cultural exchange, exchange of ideas, and freedom of expression. It is an academic institution offering under-graduate, graduate, and postgraduate degrees as well as nondegree programs in Islamic studies; the program is flexible according to students' academic back-grounds. Courses include Quranic studies, tradition, historiography, Islamic jurisprudence, mysticism, Islamic philosophy, Arab language, modern Muslim thought, Islamic education, Christianity, methodology, English, and Eastern languages (Al-Makassed Web site). The institute has academic links to nu-merous centers and universities, such as Al-Azhar University and Saint Joseph University. It is seeking to build similar partnerships with Antonine Univer-sity and the University of Balamand. The purpose of these cooperative links is to provide students with exposure to a broader array of viewpoints, lecturers, and professors and to give students firsthand knowledge of the views and be-liefs of the other. In addition to its academic program, the institute organizes numerous cultural activities and lectures. In 1998, it established a special cen-ter to promote Muslim-Christian dialogue and documentation.

The Center for Christian-Muslim Studies in the Human Sciences Depart-ment at the University of Balamand is another important academic center in the IFD field in Lebanon. It was founded in 1995 and is directed by a com-mittee of dialogue specialists. It has a steering committee, which sets its guide-lines on a yearly basis, and an executive secretary, who makes the necessary contacts, organizes lectures and seminars, and carries out the center's publica-tions and documentation work. In addition to organizing conferences, semi-nars, research, and lectures, the center offers a master's degree in Christian-Muslim studies. Academically, the center hopes to expand to incorporate more areas of concern and offer a Ph.D. program. This plan, however—which in-cludes creating a library, hiring full-time professors, and offering scholarships —will depend on the availability of funds and grants from donors.

The Center for Christian-Muslim Studies also publishes numerous works on issues relating to Christian-Muslim relations[40] and conducts an ongoing proj-ect archiving everything that deals with the issue in newspapers and other publi-cations. The variety of activities and programs sponsored and organized by the center reflects its approach to the subject of IFD and intergroup relations: in addition to academic research, tracking the daily interactions between Christians and Muslims is highly valued. Connecting the theoretical academic discussion to practical shared living is the best way to comprehensively understand the dy-namics of such relations (Center for Christian-Muslim Studies 1996a, 47).

The center's academic program is one of its strengths. It consists of a two-year master's program in Christian-Muslim studies, with a course list that includes methodology and research, history of Near Eastern religions, inter-religious relations, introduction to Christianity, introduction to Islam, and elective courses chosen according to the subject of a student's thesis. The program is open to anyone with a bachelor's degree, especially in theology, Islamic studies, or humanities (University of Balamand Web site). Faculty and students come from the different religious sects, which creates a truly diverse shared living environment. In 2000–01, twelve students were enrolled in this program (University of Balamand n.d.). Although the employment options for graduates are potentially somewhat limited, the main priority of the program is to benefit Lebanese society by bringing together students from different communities.

Since its establishment in 1995, the Center for Christian-Muslim Studies has been very active and has sponsored numerous lectures and symposia that brought Christian and Muslim scholars, both from within Lebanon and abroad, to discuss important issues concerning Christian-Muslim relations. In 1995–96, its activities included a series of lectures on Christian perceptions of Islam and Islamic perceptions of Christianity, an encounter dialogue between Dr. Mahmoud Ayoub and Archbishop George Khodr on theological dialogue, a summer session bringing students together on "Religion and the World in Christianity and Islam," and the launching of a documentation project on all the issues related to Christian-Muslim relations in Lebanon and the Arab world. In 1997, the second summer study session for students focused on "Mutual Views and Changing Relations between Christian and Muslims." In cooperation with the WCC, a parallel colloquium on the same topic took place, attended by thirty Christian-Muslim studies specialists. Also featured was a consultation on cooperation in the field of Christian-Muslim studies, attended by specialists who are currently working in centers for the study of Christianity and Islam throughout the world.

In 1998, a summer study session for students tackled the subject of "The Language of Christian-Muslim Dialogue." In 1999, a fourth summer study session for students was held on "Religion, Globalization, and Diversity." These yearly summer study sessions are one of the most important activities organized by the center. They bring approximately thirty students to live together for a ten-day period, creating an opportunity for an encounter between Lebanese students interested in the subject as well as awareness among them of the vitality of IFD. The center's hope is for such dialogue to become commonplace in daily life (University of Balamand Web site). As in activities sponsored by other centers and institutes, participation is by invitation from religious and civic leaders and intellectuals; according to the center's director, the center does "not accept [just] anyone."[41] Because of the residential aspect of the sessions, they bridge theory and practice: by interacting together throughout the duration, "a dialogue of life" develops among participants in addition to the structured intellectual dialogue. Participants do not deal with theology in the sense of discussing religious texts; neither the Quran nor the Bible appears in the curriculum.

The summer sessions owe their continuation through the years to their popularity among participants, whose evaluation forms have been remarkably positive. One important project that is still in the early phase of development is a plan to bring all those who participated in the numerous sessions together for a one-day follow-up on what they have done since they took part in the session.

Al-Ishrak Intellectual and Cultural Association/Transcendental Theosophy Institute: Theoretical and Practical is an academic, educational, and cultural organization launched in 1995. An Islamic organization, it works on coordinating work and organizing activities with other organizations, centers, and individuals—both Muslim and Christian—that share the same humanistic vision and outlook. It also offers a degree in Islamic studies, with classes in logic, methodology, epistemology, ontology, theosophy, the science of origin, practical and theoretical studies, practical ethics, and a number of electives (Al-Ishrak Intellectual and Cultural Association n.d.). Even though the institute is mostly attended by Muslim students, it is open to Christians for study, participation in workshops or training, and attendance at cultural meetings in which dialogue, sectarianism, and other issues are discussed.[42] In addition to its academic program, the association sponsors activities, such as dialogue sessions, acquaintance meetings, intellectual seminars, lectures, symposiums, conferences, and educational trips (Al-Ishrak Intellectual and Cultural Association n.d.) In addition to sponsoring such activities, the association participates in the activities of other associations and institutions, both Muslim and Christian, such as Father Gregoire Haddad's Social Movement and Moral Rearmament. The association has also participated in activities with Saint Joseph University's IEIC. The two centers are working together on a project that would encourage the exchange of teachers and students between them. Furthermore, the association publishes articles and papers on the issue of dialogue and relationships across boundaries of religious difference.[43]

According to the general supervisor of Al-Ishrak, the association has a unique sincerity in its aim to promote open-minded respect for differences. The underlying motives that typically drive dialogue efforts—desire for privilege and fame, for example—are absent in the association, he says, and this accounts for its low profile in the media. In a country that faces so many local, regional and international pressures militating against coexistence, dialogue, as the association sees it, is not merely a means to an end, but an end in itself. "Dialogue is a humanitarian objective in a plural country like Lebanon," he continues, and affirms IFD as almost an ineluctable process: "Coexistence in Lebanon is well grounded in daily life as well as in the law, and those who wish to sabotage it face difficulties in their endeavor."[44]

MODELS OF INTERFAITH WORK

Different models of interfaith work take place in Lebanon and are adopted by the different organizations active in this field. One important approach is the *dialogue of life,* which cultivates unity in the interfaith meetings (Takieddine 2002, 11). A dialogue of life is one between people and communities rather than between religious leaders or clergy (Dagher 2000, 55); it is one about the daily life experiences, the issues that concern Lebanese of all ages, communities, and backgrounds, and not about religious beliefs, faiths, or religious texts. It is a dialogue of daily conditions and circumstances and concerns what takes place in the many aspects of daily life (Ghazzal n.d., 3–4). The model discourages evangelizing/preaching and trying to convince the other to change his or her religion. According to a Catholic bishop, it is rather "to discover things together; how to live with each other and work together."[45] Our research and interviews on interfaith dialogue in Lebanon have revealed a special focus on this model in the planning and execution of interfaith projects.

The *unity dialogue* is another important model that is reflected in interfaith work in Lebanon. Here, discussions about local internal conflicts and differences are put aside in favor of focusing on the solidarity and unity of Muslims and Christians in the face of shared problems locally, regionally, or internationally. One Sunni journalist and activist in dialogue gives the example of how, in a Christian-Muslim conference in Cairo, all participants condemned the attacks on the United States and agreed to work together to enhance Christian-Muslim understanding in the post–September 11 environment. As mentioned above, other issues that have evoked a unified stand include the war in Iraq and the Palestinian question. This unity model is very fashionable in Lebanon; almost all discussions and dialogue deal with external problems that are of concern to Lebanese from both religions. These issues are used as a way to reassert the unified position of the Lebanese, regardless of religious difference. Such a united image is assertively promoted locally, regionally, and internationally.

Ritualistic and ceremonial interfaith dialogue is also common in Lebanon. Religious leaders participate in each other's religious celebrations, laypeople help each other organize religious festivities and events, and joint prayer sessions are held. One example of such cooperation occurs in Wadi Johanam, a village in Nabatiyeh, where Muslims help Christians in their preparation for a yearly religious celebration that takes place in the village (*Challenges to Mutual Understanding* 2002, 21). Another example is a project undertaken by the World Conference on Religion and Peace (WCRP), in cooperation with Fokolari, in which Christians serve needy Muslims food during Ramadan.[46]

The *advocacy approach,* which can be described as dialogue through action—linking IFD and development—has been systematically adopted by Lebanese interfaith groups, too. The widely accepted assumption is that through development projects, people from both communities can get to know each other while working together toward a common goal. An example of such approach is a tree-planting project in Mount Lebanon, which brought together youth from the Christian and Druze communities in an area that had witnessed massacres and displacement throughout the war years.[47] Reconstruction projects are symbolically appropriate as interfaith activities. In a war or postwar context, there is a physical and social need for development projects that restructure and rehabilitate cities and villages. Through such practical activities, individuals indirectly dialogue and rebuild their relationships.[48]

CHALLENGES AND OBSTACLES

Confronting the Monster of War

The years of civil war and the postwar situation present the most challenges to dialogue and to peaceful Christian-Muslim coexistence. The civil war experience, the role of religious affiliations, and the traumas incurred during the violence have presented major obstacles to launching and conducting effective IFD. Other obstacles to such dialogue are "the continued foreign presence in Lebanon; the unresolved displacement of Lebanese citizens by war; and the precarious position of Christians in Lebanese political life since the signing of the Taef Agreement" (Ellis 2002, 125). During the war, there were confessional interfaith massacres in numerous areas of Lebanon. Such events endangered coexistence and led to religious cleavages and the separation of communities that once lived together side by side. An atmosphere prevailed that perpetuated ignorance, fear of the other, increased stereotyping, and dehumanization. Faced with this segregation, IFD supporters and activists longed for a comprehensive plan that would eliminate these obstacles on all levels: religious, political, social, cultural, and within the media's discourse (Jarjour 2002, 3).

Segregation intensifies ignorance of the other and makes the task of dialogue even more difficult. One Muslim activist tells how during a lecture he gave at the Keserwan Covenant with a bishop, "a young university student in her twenties told me that it was the first time that she speaks to a Muslim."[49] So far, efforts at promoting coexistence and dialogue have not transcended these barriers nor entirely countered deeply embedded social messages. People acquire stereotypes from family, school, religious institutions, and the media (Ghazzal 1989, 4). Such forms of socialization are of utmost importance in the Lebanese context, where children learn about the other from their parents and sectarian agents. The parents' level of cultural religious awareness and the behavior they model (whether they befriend people from other religions) shape children's perceptions of these issues.

Agreeing on the Nature, Framing, and Efficacy of the Dialogue Process

The inability to agree on a proper designation for the process of dialogue presents an obstacle. Rashid Al-Kadi, for example, objects to its being called Muslim-Christian dialogue. According to him, the conflict is not between two religions, as both Christianity and Islam share the same values. The conflict is between competing understandings and visions of the Lebanese problem. These views are different not only between Muslims and Christians, but within these two communities as well. The dialogue, he says, should be called "dialogue for a new system for a renewed Lebanon" (El-Kadi 2003, 9). Calling the process Christian-Muslim dialogue might limit interreligious cooperation, or it might emphasize the differences between people from different religions and bring them into the meeting as separate entities. Furthermore, such a designation might isolate people who do not feel comfortable talking about or debating religion and discourage the participation of those who are not religious.

Political Manipulation of IFD

One of the most important challenges to IFD is the exploitation of religion for political purposes and interests—an exploitation that continues to exist despite the government's informal support and encouragement of dialogue. Political sectarianism is the main characteristic of the Lebanese system, and politicians and religious leaders have a vested interest in the status quo because it is a cheap way to maintain political power. This makes it almost impossible to abolish. But the politicization of religion has a negative social impact on human relationships and it muddies the waters of IFD. As we have seen in the comments of a number of activists, IFD is predominantly used in Lebanon as a "feuding ground over power, public posts, and private profits" (Dagher 2000, 55).

Political sectarianism manifests in a number of ways. One example was the rejection of then-President Hrawi's proposed civil marriage legislation in 1998. The fact that the proposed legislation resulted in controversy was a confirmation of the influence of religious leaders and the sensitivity of religious issues in politics. Today, civil marriages are still not performed in Lebanon, although they are recognized by the state when done abroad in countries like Cyprus or France. According to a Muslim organizer and activist in IFD, political issues themselves negatively affect dialogue; the different points of view and political positions are expressed in a way that harm Christian-Muslim relations and misuse such relations.[50] Political leaders and parties advance their causes and issues in an "us versus them" discourse, tending to mobilize their followers by basing their rhetoric on conflict and differences between the communities. Any incident in the country can fire up sectarian tensions. A Shiite organizer and activist notes that the interference of politics in dialogue paralyzes the process and prevents efficient dialogue.[51] When political issues emerge in a dialogue encounter, discussions often can turn into heated debates that highlight differences rather than commonalities and put an end to a process by which participants can get to know each other, accept each other's differences, and respect each other's views.

Scarcity of Resources

The problem of funding is a very acute and important obstacle facing IFD in Lebanon; it stands in the way of numerous exceptional, creative, and beneficial projects. Some feel that much can be done even within current limits. According to the director of the Center for Christian-Muslim Studies, "funding is important but projects that are within the available budget could still be organized."[52] Many IFD initiatives cannot accommodate a large number of people due to budgetary constraints, although the need to keep the dialogue and sharing of ideas as efficient as possible is another limitation. But it seems that lack of funding does significantly restrict the number and scope of the activities that could be done.[53]

Media's Role

Another major obstacle to dialogue is media propaganda. Presenting the Lebanese conflict as a Muslim-Christian one, the media fails to reflect the complex reality of the situation (Ghazzal 1989, 2). Proliferation of television and radio stations along communal and sectarian lines has intensified the problem. Each station advances the interests of the group it represents, and thus, rather than calling for dialogue and understanding between the different communities, the media is inciting conflict by emphasizing differences. With the end of the civil war, many feel that the media should address themselves to a larger public, not only a specific community (Messarra 1998, 15), to advance common values and reveal similarities.

That media fill this role is all the more important because shared spaces where both groups can interact are decreasing; communities live separately, go to different schools, and so on. Civil society institutions are weak and Lebanon has an increasingly limited mutual culture. The feeling of being threatened by the other community is strong (Takieddine 2002, 11).

Nature and Audience of IFD

According to one participant in IFD, the limitations of interfaith projects are that they are constrained to cerebral exercises and "are ritualistic rather than practical actions."[54] Dialogue in Lebanon is limited to a small circle of people: religious leaders, politicians, researchers, scholars, and activists in civil society organizations (Jarjour 2002, 1). One of the most significant challenges is how to transfer the Christian-Muslim dialogue from the elites and intellectuals to the masses and to a wider segment of society (Jarjour 2002, 1). Carole Dagher (2000, 55) notes that "dialogue confined to restricted intellectual and academic circles is an impediment."

The major problem in this regard is the extent to which these participants are representatives of particular communities and have leverage within them. In other words, "are they able to commit their communities and the decision makers" to such dialogue or any concrete policy that results from it? Even if it only occurs between a few people, dialogue is still beneficial, as it brings people closer together and opens the way for mutual understanding. The benefit of dialogue increases, however, when the audience widens. According to a Christian veteran of IFD, "the problem is that much of what goes on in terms of dialogue does not trickle down to young people, to the masses. The network of people that works on interfaith dialogue is of 100–200 people that have become friends [and] developed their own language, but have not been able to reach out to a wider audience."[55]

Another structural problem in dialogue in Lebanon is that participation in such activities and efforts is not open to everyone; participants are usually recommended and chosen by the organizers in consultation with community leaders. The fact that the process is not an open, random selection process limits the participation to a small circle of elites or well-connected people.[56]

Measuring Interfaith Impact

Like other forms of social change interventions, it is difficult to evaluate the individual and social results of IFD. Results cannot be measured in the short term; "Interfaith dialogue is not quantifiable and its effects are noticed in the long term."[57] As one Muslim participant and activist puts it, "the seeds of dialogue are being planted, but the fruits do not grow directly."[58] Attitudinal and behavioral changes that occur inside the individual are difficult to measure.[59]

Despite these limitations, interviewees from all organizations involved in interfaith activities mentioned the importance of evaluation and impact assessment. Good evaluation is key to improving IFD efforts. The most common method of evaluation cited was administration of questionnaires to participants to assess their level of satisfaction with the activity, the changes they experienced, their overall reaction to the meeting and dialogue, and what recommendations for improvement they might have. Other interviewees have mentioned another form of evaluation or impact assessment, which is based on observing the changes in behavior of participants: how these individuals come to these encounters, how they behave during the activity, and how they leave.

Despite the lip service that organizers and participants have paid to assessment, they can point to but few tangible changes associated with their interfaith work. The many conferences, meetings, forums, symposiums, camps, and so on, on dialogue in Lebanon since the 1990s have actually shown an absence (or a minor level) of self-criticism or methodological revision. "Tens and even hundreds of dialogue experiences are done in Lebanon without anyone drawing any lessons in order to deepen their content and aims" (Institute of Muslim-Christian Studies n.d.). Lack of evaluation and follow-up limit the potential of learning from mistakes, and redundancy results; the same issues are discussed time and time again (Al-Mawla 2003b, 9–11). The opportunity to compile experiences, share expertise, and test ideas is lost. This explains the limited amount of information published on certain meetings and sessions, which makes it impossible to get an accurate picture of the state of dialogue in Lebanon, even after ten years of struggle and activism (Al-Mawla 2003b, 25 and 116–18).

Government Detachment

The lack of cooperation between civil society and the government negatively impacts IFD in Lebanon. The government has been absent from IFD work and instead has focused on the reconstruction of buildings and rehabilitation of roads and basic services (Al-Mawla 2003c, 18). Arguably, such physical reconstruction is not complete without the reconstruction and rehabilitation of the human minds and spirits—the work of IFD. The fact that dialogue is not a government priority is an obstacle, as government recognition and support usually brings legitimacy to the process.[60] This lack of coordination and connection between the different meeting places and different organizations and efforts gives dialogue meetings their seasonal and disconnected character. In addition to lack of coordination, there is no contact between the different forces or groups that work on dialogue, and publicity is uneven across organizations, with some going almost entirely unnoticed.[61] It also leads to duplicated efforts and lack of synchronization.[62]

Lack of Career Opportunities

According to the director of the Institute for Islamo-Christian Studies (IEIC), one of the limitations of the program at IEIC, which affects every academic program in the field of Christian-Muslim studies and dialogue, is the lack of job opportunities for graduates. Even though Christian-Muslim dialogue is emerging as an important field, it is limited to those who are well off economically or those who come to the program fueled by idle curiosity while in pursuit of other degrees. IFD programs are not expensive, but they also do not open the door to viable livelihoods.[63]

Global Polarization in the Post–September 11 Reality

Opinions differ on the impact of 9/11 on IFD. Some activists feel that it negatively affected coexistence and posed a challenge to IFD throughout the world in general, and in pluralistic societies like Lebanon in particular. Dr. Saoud Al-Mawla and others believe that the attack has made it much harder for efforts at dialogue to move forward, as it necessitated a shift of focus toward explaining and defending Islam ("Impact of the September 11 Events on Coexistence" 2002, 22; Scudder 2001, 4–11). Others, such as Mohammed Al-Sammak, believe that the Christian-Muslim relationship has not changed in Lebanon after September 11 and that steps are being taken to limit the impact of external incidents: many conferences and dialogues took place after September 11 to deal with the possible impact on coexistence (Scudder 2001, 4–5).

SUCCESS STORIES AND ACCOMPLISHMENTS

Despite the numerous obstacles that face IFD in Lebanon, dialogue activities have persisted. As interviewees have mentioned, obstacles are common in this type of work, especially in a deeply divided, war-torn country like Lebanon. However, all these challenges can and should be overcome through persistence. Building a culture of dialogue is long-term work, and the impact of each effort is felt indirectly. Luckily, there are numerous success stories in IFD to provide encouragement to activists.

According to the interviewees, all dialogue is successful in that it brings together people from different communities to discuss issues, get to know and understand each other, and respect and understand differences. Simply bringing people from different communities to discuss an array of issues and share views is a great accomplishment after a long civil war that divided communities and isolated them from each other. A review of Lebanese IFD literature and discussions with activists in the field reveal that there are numerous success stories. A few of these perhaps bear mentioning in detail.

The success of IFD can be measured by the strength of friendships that emerge between the participants, some of which last for years. A Catholic bishop tells the story of one young man who, years after his participation a summer camp, painstakingly tracked down all those who had participated with him to invite them to his wedding. He asked each one, Muslim and Christian, to accompany him and his family to the bride's house—a richly meaningful tradition in the village. Such small occurrences are important in a confessionally dominant environment like Lebanon and portray the importance of providing shared spaces in a divided society. IFD is one of the only providers of such shared spaces, if not the only one.[64]

Even the early interfaith encounters in Cyprus proved successful. Despite the fact that they took place outside Lebanon because of the security situation, they had impact inside Lebanon. For example, the participants would look out for one another's safety when traveling. An individual's safety in any territory was "guaranteed by having friends of another religion accompany them" (Messarra 1998, 11). This was important in a time when the situation was unstable and it was dangerous for people to cross demarcation lines that divided the country into confessional areas. It was a powerful contradiction to the confessional reality on the ground, in which help and friendship across sectarian lines was unheard of.

A Christian priest remembers the Cyprus meetings and how Muslims and Christians came to the meetings as distrustful strangers. The division in the country was such that Muslims used to leave Lebanon through the airport, while the Christians, unable to cross the green line to the airport, used the seaport—an indication of the extent of segregation. He remembers how, at the end of the workshop, the participants made a commitment to each other to help out any one of them who was arrested, stopped at a checkpoint, and so on. After one of those meetings, Christians decided to go back with Muslims through the airport, and some Muslims decided to travel with the Christians through the seaport.[65]

These meetings were also successful in transforming the perspectives of the participants. The priest recalls a conversation he had at the end of the session with one of the participants, a Christian militia member who had never met a Muslim person before. He was complimenting the participant's suntan when the latter answered, "This is not the only change in me; I have another change that is taking place in my heart and mind."[66]

A Druze activist in dialogue talks about a successful project that organized visits between different schools, for example, between Christian schools in Jounieh and Muslim schools in Beirut. Students from one school were brought to spend a day in class at a different school. Schools in Lebanon tend to lack religious diversity. The exchange attempted to bridge this divide. Although the experiment was full of problems, it was a success overall. In addition to bringing students together, organizers decided to bring the parents together as well. Thus, both students and their parents began to eat Sunday lunches together. The participants were excited and responsive.[67]

Success can also be recognized by measuring a reduction in stereotyping behavior. A Muslim trainee participated in the training of Lebanese and Arab public and private school teachers in active educational techniques (a workshop intended to test the *Handbook Teaching and Resource Material in Conflict Resolution, Education for Human Rights, Peace and Democracy*, which aims to educate students about conflict resolution, human rights, peace, and democracy). She spoke of how, throughout her life, the "imagery of Christians was reinforced negatively in her family and social environment." She explained that her opinions and behavior changed completely after she had lived with, interacted with, and befriended Christians. According to this woman, sheer lack of opportunity to come into simple contact with the other after fifteen years of war is the underlying cause of prejudice. Many similar examples were shared during the training workshop, and these testimonies brought participants even closer to one another (Osseiran 1995, 8).

Father Ghazzal recalls the technical school he helped establish to help ex-militia members reintegrate in society and find jobs in the postwar period. These sessions brought students who had fought on opposing fronts during the war together after years of bitter animosity. Students came to the first day of classes armed, distrustful, lacking self-confidence or faith in the process, and full of unruly energy. A process intended for building trust began with participants breaking chairs. But the dialogue proved very effective. The atmosphere became respectful and trusting, and students took responsibility for their actions by repairing the broken property (Ghazzal 1995, 5).

Dialogue also succeeds in making people listen to each other and to different points of view. One of the participants in the Institute for Islamo-Christian Studies' informal meeting between students noted that the dialogue meeting has helped him overcome his inability to listen to other people with whom he disagrees. While he used to aggressively respond to and attack a person who advanced an idea he did not like, he now chooses to listen and has the ability to be more open and accepting of differences (*Challenges to Mutual Understanding* 2002, 21).

Dialogue sessions have been successful in helping people realize that their prejudgments of the other did not match the other's realities, and that the generalizations they made about the other did not have any basis in truth. Such sessions made participants more accepting of criticism; they taught people to listen to each other so they could get to know and understand each other (*Challenges to Mutual Understanding* 2002, 41–43). Summer camps help youth change the way they think and look at reality after they have been living in isolation from each other with limited opportunity for interaction. Positive change is evident in the children between their arrival at camp and their departure. One child, distrusting the other campers, refused to leave the dormitory on the first day, fearing that his luggage would be stolen. The monitor talked to him and encouraged him to trust the others and reached a deal with the child to have him leave the room for some time, "to experiment" and see whether any of his things went missing. The deal was that he would be compensated for anything that was missing when he came back to the room. The experiment was successful; none of his possessions were stolen in his absence. This experiment helped break the ice; the child participated fully in camp activities and built numerous friendships with other campers. At the end of the camp, this same child refused to leave the center and asked to be enrolled for the second session (Iskandar 1991, 102–3).

It becomes clear from these stories that measuring success and accomplishments in interfaith activities in Lebanon is modestly limited to anecdotal evidence. The criteria for success in most of these activities have to do with trust, mutual understanding, and awareness of common values. Upon this foundation of trust, respect, friendship, and political and institutional change may be built. Interviewees have mentioned that dialogue activities have not led to changes on these levels yet. To build up relations after years of violence and isolation is a long process; it would be too ambitious to expect change at the macro level to emerge after so short a time.

CHANGES AND RECOMMENDATIONS

Coordination

Consolidation of dialogue efforts in Lebanon would be one important step toward strengthening IFD. There is such a proliferation of organizations and institutes that work in the field and organize conferences on IFD that exchange of professors, research papers, theses, information, publications, and bibliographical indexes would provide access to best practices, greater coherence of IFD theory, and greater opportunity for serendipitous collaborations. Another recommendation, made by the Center for Christian-Muslim Studies, is for the creation of a mailing list of all the activists and researchers in the field, which would activate communication between the participating centers, provide opportunity for exchanging and improving curricula and study programs, and open the possibility of creating an association of intellectuals and researchers in the field (University of Balamand Web site). Along similar lines, a database of the names, e-mails, and other contact information of the organizations and individuals active in the region would help to coordinate efforts.[68]

Tracking is one way to build a sense of consistency and continuity; funding is another. Organizers should not have to worry about whether the center will still exist in a year's time, about whether the director of the center or organization will change, or whether funding for planned activities will become unavailable.[69]

Mapping the Interfaith Field

Government institutions have a responsibility to help build a culture of peace and interfaith understanding. Despite the end of the war in a military sense, society is still divided socially. But there is no government policy concerning the creation of spaces where people from opposing communities can begin to interact.[70] In addition to the current focus on physical infrastructure, there should be more emphasis on rebuilding the human dimension and broadening the common spaces that have been reduced in the years of war (Initiatives of Change 2003).

Although there are an increasing number of IFD organizations, they cannot do the job alone. To have a successful culture of dialogue, all sectors of society must participate, and it is the state that should take the legal, financial, and moral responsibility for broad-based public dialogue projects. Civil society is also an important partner in such an endeavor; its religious, educational, and social organizations should be actively involved in promoting a culture of dialogue.

In addition to local initiatives, such a project requires the participation of regional and global organizations that are interested in IFD, civic peace, development, and justice (Jarjour 2002, 4). It is also very important for communities to be prepared for dialogue in order for it to be efficient—efforts will not yield any positive results if participants are not convinced of dialogue's importance and effectiveness.

Systematic and Consistent Interfaith Meeting

Dialogue also needs to occur more regularly to be more effective. It should be systematic and continuous; dialogue is a way of life, not a single event or project (Al-Mawla 2003b, 35). To facilitate this, according to a Christian activist, more volunteers to initiate and promote dialogue are needed.[71] People must be helped to overcome their fears and embrace serious and deep dialogue so that they are motivated to work on promoting a permanent stable dialogue in the political arena (Al-Mawla 2003b, 43). For dialogue to work, participants cannot be mandated to attend; they must come of their own volition.

Interreligious Education for Pluralism

Much remains to be done in the field of education. There is no educational policy that teaches coexistence, nor does the public curriculum include courses that deal with coexistence, reconciliation, nonviolence, or conflict resolution. In fact, a true public curriculum does not exist at all: there are no unified history and religion books taught in all schools. Hence, people can be easily and unknowingly manipulated. "We are working to make our degree recognized by the state and to have a place in the educational program—either at schools or universities. And it is preferable that this major—coexistence in Lebanon—be obligatory; it is neither civic education nor religious education."[72]

It is through the educational system that the values needed in society are planted and stereotypes are eliminated. Teaching students to respect others in their religions and ideologies should be part of the curriculum (*Challenges to Mutual Understanding* 2002, 113–14). There is an urgent need to revise the history and religious education textbooks that are used in schools (Kolvenbach et al. 1999, 70). Perhaps nothing is as important for interreligious understanding and coexistence as the ability to accept competing versions of history and let go of the need to impose one's own biased perspective to the exclusion of others (Kolvenbach et al. 1999, 71). Revising religious education is also of utmost importance. Rather than separating Muslim and Christian students in religious classes, during which time Christians listen to the bishop talking about Christianity and Muslims listen to the sheikh explaining Islam, students could be brought together to learn about each other's faiths and beliefs.

Although putting together a unified book for religious education that looks objectively and impartially at the different religions is an immense challenge, such a religious education is a necessity. This education is basic to cultivating good citizenship and teaches students to forgive rather than to identify with fanaticism (Massouh 2003, 184–86). One active participant in dialogue also believes that dividing students during religious classes is a way of telling them that they are different and cannot coexist, and that there is no value in learning about other faiths. According to him,

> The first solution was to ask the government to put an end to religious teaching in school—but this is of course not the best solution as it makes both Muslim and Christian students more vulnerable to religion as taught by extremist groups. A better solution would be for both Christians and Muslims to attend both lessons, in which they learn about the religions as well as the ethics and the commonalities between [their religions] in a unified religious book.[73]

A Christian organizer believes that what is needed is to make dialogue part of the educational system and to devise history and religion books that promote and support the idea of dialogue.[74]

Involve the People in IFD

For dialogue to be more efficient and to reach a wider audience, meetings between Christians and Muslims should not be restricted to a circle of specialists or community leaders (Ghazzal 1992, 2). Everyone should engage in dialogue, and the participants need not be scholars or theologians. Faith, hope, and interest in participating in dialogue should be the only requirements (Ghazzal 1992, 2). "It is important to have a 'culture of dialogue' spreading at the grassroots level in order to have results" (Dagher 2000, 54). The media can play an important role in this and should give more attention to IFD. There is a TV station in Lebanon that brings together religious leaders as well as laypeople from the communities to participate in discussion and debate. Such an initiative should be encouraged and supported so that the culture of dialogue transfers to a larger number of people.

Youth are an important demographic group for IFD, as they are often quite willing to get involved with others and learn to know them. The socialization of youth happens through such events such as IFD sessions, as well as through families, media, and schools. The war in Lebanon did not suddenly happen —it was prepared in the minds, in the houses, schools, and neighborhoods. It is these that require reform if true dialogue is to emerge (Ghazzal 1995, 2–3). Including all groups in society is of utmost importance. As well as youth, women should be involved in IFD as important social actors. Their role and unique leverage has been neglected by uneven representation in dialogue thus far.

Guidelines for Dialogue

There are a number of guidelines and best practices that should be kept in mind when planning IFD. First, it is important to realize that dialogue is a long process; it requires patience, time, and effort. Efforts should be sustained for as long as necessary to achieve the vital purposes of healing social cleavages, despite the temptation to give up. Mentalities do not change overnight (Ghazzal 1995, 8). Rebuilding the person takes many years of work and fervor (Ghazzal 1992, 13). For dialogue to succeed, a national will, civic education, and a comprehensive view of Lebanon are required. Such conditions are easier to meet as the country moves further away from the war. The more distanced citizens are from the fresh memory of the war, the clearer their visions and the stronger their spirit and willingness to engage in dialogue. The time factor is very important to keep in mind when engaging in dialogue, as it plays a "positive role in the rapprochement between the Lebanese, in understanding each other, and accepting the other with his differences" (El-Kadi 2003, 9).

Another important condition of success for dialogue, and something that is still mostly missing in Lebanon, is self-criticism (Jarjour 2002, 9). Ridwan al-Sayyid, a Sunni intellectual, notes that this lack of self-criticism blocks effective dialogue in the country (Donahue 1996, 9). The level and quality of self-evaluation and self-criticism among IFD practictioners in Lebanon should increase for the health of the field.

Third, dialogue must be authentic and relevant. It should deal with issues and problems of everyday life, issues to which participants can relate and that they have experienced. Ideological research or theoretical topics, whether or not they are touched upon in discussions, should not dominate the dialogue. Also, discussions should address sensitive topics rather than avoid them; it is through discussing these issues that rapprochement between participants takes place and tensions begin to ease (*Challenges to Mutual Understanding* 2002,

37–38). Discussing these issues gives dialogue an authentic quality. If conversations are overly diplomatic and courteous, issues that are at the root of real conflicts are ignored, and participants therefore become convinced that there is no conflict and thus no necessity for dialogue, or that dialogue is an exercise in bad faith.

Another crucial related guideline is that dialogue not be about convincing the other of the superiority of one's own religion. Participants need to be encouraged to avoid preaching or evangelizing, and discussions should assume an equality of religions (Ghazzal n.d., 4). According to a Christian organizer, dialogue should not be formulaic: a single-recipe-for-all-situations, one-size-fits-all formula. Its design should depend on the context in which it is being done; it should be responsive to the situation at hand and the needs of the participants.[75] Another activist believes this is occurring already: "The tasks of Christian-Muslim dialogue are repeatedly being reordered. This revision of tasks is determined by sense of urgency and desire to confront the shortcomings and failures of dialogue itself" (Waardenburg 2000, 71). Along these lines, it is important, according to a Christian priest, to have "creative local initiatives by both Muslims and Christians to maintain dialogue and coexistence," because people get tired of the same format.[76]

The fifth important guideline for best practices in IFD is that of depoliticization. It is important for those working in dialogue to understand the root causes of the political, social, and cultural crises that stand in the way of dialogue in the country, and to separate religion from politics so that religion is not exploited for political interests, as commonly takes place in Lebanon (Takieddine 2002, 11). On one hand, dialogue needs the official support and sponsorship of the government and the collaboration of politicians. However, on the other hand, dialogue should not be used as a political means and should not be funded by politicians or political tycoons: it should be funded by NGOs or neutral sources.[77]

CONCLUSION

Lebanon, as a model of intercommunal coexistence, has been viewed by many scholars, intellectuals, and political and religious leader as the hub from which Christian-Muslim dialogue should begin (Dagher 2000, 2). The plurality of Lebanese society makes it a natural starting point for IFD, as dialogue is a requirement for coexistence and common living (Dagher 2000, 5). Awareness of the importance of IFD grew tremendously at the end of the long civil war, and it was considered the means by which to restore relations between communities. However, awareness of its significance did not prevent it from stalling. Numerous challenges, most significantly the religiously divided political system, face IFD, and participants hasten to underscore the fact "that their dialogue [has] no official quality and they [have] no representative capacity" (Dagher 2000, 51).

Christian-Muslim dialogue should be encouraged and supported because it enjoys popular support, at least in principle. Even though the challenges are many—especially after a civil war that endangered coexistence, bred hatred, and severely damaged Muslim-Christian relations—"it seems that Christians and Muslims in Lebanon remain open to dialogue and the possibility of peaceful coexistence in a free republic" (Ellis 2002, 129). This is confirmed by the large number of IFD activities, as well as by a study conducted by the Institute for Educational Development in 1997, in which the majority of seventeen- to eighteen-year-old Christians and Muslims in Beirut did not register any objection to making friends from other religions (Ellis 2002, 129). The situation of dialogue in Lebanon in general is good and has improved over the years; people have started to accept the idea of debating or dialoguing with each other. Those who are active in dialogue should be careful that this does not become an ineffective fad for appearances instead of an effective tool for rebuilding human relations.[78]

In Lebanon, Muslim-Christian dialogue is a necessity and should not remain limited to theological seminars, intellectual debates, or theoretical luxuries. For IFD to have the appropriate level of impact and reach adequate numbers of people, it should become an integral part of the projects and programs of the state, political movements, and civil institutions, such as schools and even churches and mosques (Al-Mawla 1998, 6). According to Mohammad Al-Sammak (2002, 134), such dialogue is "the key to resolving the differences among these communities." Sayah (2002, 128) adds, "[IFD] is essential to removing the obstacles to peace in Lebanon."

Throughout the years, it has become apparent that there is no alternative to dialogue as a means of safeguarding, reasserting, and stabilizing coexistence. There is no doubt among those involved in dialogue that it is the right thing to do to salvage Lebanese plurality after fifteen years of a civil war that degenerated Lebanese society on all levels—social, political, economic, and pedagogical—and that resulted in hundreds of thousands of dead, injured, and handicapped. The provisions of documents such as the Taef Agreement are not enough to reinstate relations between religious communities in Lebanon. Such documents were created "to stop the war, the military action, and artillery, but [they] did not stop the hatred towards the other."[79] Eliminating the war mentality requires much more than just documents and agreements; it will take a more comprehensive and aggressive approach. The war is still reflected in the media, in sports (whenever Christian and Muslim teams meet on the field, they express their confessional hatred), and elsewhere. Dialogue is one important way by which such hatred is disarmed and the possibility of neighborly interaction between groups is opened.[80]

5

INTERFAITH DIALOGUE IN EGYPT

National Unity and Tolerance

This study serves both exploratory and analytical purposes. It is exploratory in that it creates a general picture of Muslim-Christian relationships in Egypt and maps out the variety of IFD activities conducted in the country. It is analytical in that it contextualizes these relationships historically, politically, and socioeconomically. Unlike approaches that reduce socioreligious problems to psychological explanations—such as hatred, fear, or intolerance —the approach presented in this chapter examines problems socioeconomically and culturally, in their anthropological sense. We argue that these "problems" are better understood as a very part of the modernization process in Egypt and as reflecting the contradictions of modernity in the particular form it has taken in Egypt. The current versions of these problems are nested in the context of globalization, with all its political, economic, and cultural implications.

The study is based on a series of interviews conducted in Egypt in the fall of 2003. The interviewees are Egyptian IFD activists, representatives of IFD organizations, and writers who are concerned with (or experts on) Muslim-Christian relationships in Egypt. It is also based on a review of books, papers, and documents on the topic of IFD in Egypt. Fifteen people were interviewed: three females and twelve males, nine Muslims and six Christians. The Christians were from different denominations: four Coptic Orthodox, one Roman Catholic, and one Evangelical.

What we could not attain directly through interviews was gleaned through the review of publications and Web sites from the forums and organizations not represented in the interviews, as well as books and articles of a number of writers, scholars, and researchers in the field. Although many people involved in IFD in Egypt refused to be interviewed or even to meet with us, we believe that the interviews we conducted drew from most of the dialogue forums in the country, and that most literature on the topic is covered here. However, we discovered that using printed materials such as books and articles could be problematic; we often found competing narratives about the reality of life in Egypt today. Often even the "facts" themselves varied widely, depending on the source and the way the information was intended to portray Egypt.

Interviews were either recorded on tape or by hand on paper, depending on the interviewee's preference. Interviewees frequently emphasized that the views expressed in the meetings were their own and that they represented no one but themselves. Even those with institutional affiliations felt more comfortable speaking only on their own behalf and not in the name of the organization or forum. Furthermore, it became apparent from the research that the term "interfaith dialogue" is very problematic and highly politicized in the Egyptian context.

The controversial nature of IFD in Egypt made research extremely difficult. Throughout, we struggled with numerous problems that arose due to the sensitive nature of the topic. Most of the people whom we interviewed wished to remain anonymous, fearing that the publication of their name would result in personal retribution from institutions or individuals who disagree with them. Numerous people refused to be interviewed at all, concerned not to have their name linked in any way with a book about IFD. To present the socioeconomic and cultural dynamics of Christian-Muslim relations in Egypt, the study is divided into three major parts: historical background, problematization of Muslim-Christian relationships, and interfaith dialogue in Egypt.

HISTORICAL BACKGROUND

Premodern History

Islam entered Egypt for the first time through the Arab conquest under the leadership of A'mr Ibn El-Aas from 639 to 642 CE. The Arabs used the word "Copt," derived from the Greek word "Aigyptos," to denote the entire indigenous population of Egypt, which was dominantly Christian at the time (Van Nispen 1997, 23). The beginning of contact between Arabs and Copts—Muslims and Christians—was very warm and peaceful. The new ruler, after defeating the Roman army and thus ending the persecution of the Copts by the Romans, invited the fleeing patriarch to come back and live in peace with his people (Kelada 1994; 1998). Three major factors dramatically changed the nature of Egypt in the four to five centuries following the conquest, transforming it into an Islamic country: the immigration of Arab tribes from Arabia to Egypt; the gradual but massive conversion of Copts to Islam; and the change in the language used in everyday life from Coptic to Arabic (Ibrahim 1994; 1998, 382; Labib 2000, 17). Studies indicate that it was probably during the Mameluke period (1250–1517) that the proportion of Copts to the population as a whole became generally fixed at its modern level: scarcely 8 percent (Van Nispen 1997, 23).[1]

Throughout the course of history, Muslim and Christian inhabitants of Egypt have shared extensive commonalities. In Christian Van Nispen's words (1997, 24), they "speak the same language, live in the same culture, practice more or less the same customs and traditions, and share the same feelings and relations." Interestingly, the prominent Coptic intellectual and judge, William Soliman Kelada, removes the line of division between Muslims and Christians and instead differentiates between "the rulers" and "the ruled." For him, the ruled are "the people of the land,"[2] whether Muslims or Christians. He wrote,

> There is a basic fact in the Egyptian history that is the sharp division between the rulers and the ruled. This division continued for hundreds and thousands of years. There is a horizontal sharp and decisive line dividing the Egyptian society into two sectors: the rulers who occupy the upper sector . . . and the ruled down the line; they are the people of the land with all their components (Kelada 1994, 28).

Kelada's ideological argument, though capturing an important perspective, neglects much of the sociopolitical reality of Egypt and the complexity and specificity of Muslim-Christian relationships through long centuries. Kelada frames the relationship between the two communities as one of "citizenship," a relationship that is grounded in the land, between people of the same land. This is, doubtless, a very modern framing, one involved in the nation-state concept. To understand the current Muslim-Christian relationship in Egypt, we need to trace it back to the foundation of the modern Egyptian state.

Muslims and Christians in the Modern State

It was during Mohamed Ali's reign (1805–48) that Egypt was transformed from an Islamic satellite state—part of the larger Ottoman Empire—into a modern nation-state, politically independent and nationally distinct. The creation of modern Egypt turned the "people of the land" into the "Egyptians," an identity that categorizes all citizens based on nationality, not religion. In his distinguished work, *The Muslims and Copts in the Framework of the National Society,* Tarik El Bishri wrote (1988, 12), "the Egyptian organization preceded the consciousness of Egyptianality." El Bishri extensively and eloquently demonstrated that modern Egypt was created through, first, the creation of a modern Egyptian army, and then, the creation of modern administration, education, and parliament.

An Egyptian army composed of the local people was created in 1822, not to wage jihad but to protect the nation-state. However, it was not until Khedive Said's 1855 decision to allow Christians to join the service that this army became representative of all communities in Egypt. With this decision, the *jizya* system, by which Copts were not asked to fight for the country, was overturned. The decision crowned a series of others that granted equal rights regardless of religious belief. Henceforth, Copts would be on equal footing with Muslims in educational missions, the administrative system, the parliament, and the army. In 1879, the National Party, the first political party in modern Egypt, was founded. It reflected the same spirit of nationalism and equality. The fifth article of the party's political program describes the party as follows:

The National Party is a national, not religious, party. It is composed of men belonging to diversity of beliefs and denominations. All Christians and Jews and whoever cultivates the land of Egypt and speaks its language can be included in the Party, as it does not look at the difference in beliefs and considers the all [members] brothers, with equal political and legal rights. It is especially considered by the Sheikhs of Azhar who address this Party and believe that the true Shari'a forbids animosity and considers people equal (El Bishri 1988, 46).

The movement from the traditional to the modern system, in the first half of the twentieth century, was rough. Elements of the inherited religious system and religious identity intermingled with those of the national system and Egyptian identity. The constant exploitation by Muslim and Christian political actors—namely the king, the British occupation, the political parties, and the religious political movements—made the transition even more difficult. The traditional religious institutions, such as Al Azhar and the Coptic Orthodox Church, were dragged onto the complicated sociopolitical stage. The implied tension, however, never erupted into extensive violence.

The second decade witnessed both the worst example of a national split and the best example of national unity. In March 1911, the Coptic Conference was held in Asiout to demand political rights for the Coptic minority. It was followed one month later by the Islamic Conference, held in Heliopolis, Cairo, in which the very basis and legitimacy of the Coptic demands were refuted. The two conferences, which have been used to symbolize the peak of the Egyptian Muslim-Christian problems, were followed by a healthy and vivid discussion of the national destiny. Eight years later, in 1919, the most prominent national and popular revolution against the occupation erupted with its two unforgettable slogans: "Religion for God, homeland for all" and "Long live the crescent and the cross!" Even today, the 1919 Revolution is used as the symbol of national unity.

One can get a glimpse of the national political debate around the Coptic question by reading the literature published in 1922 and 1923. At this time, the Constitution Committee was writing a constitution for Egypt. A Coptic member of the committee demanded that the parliamentary elections and the distribution of seats be confessional. Aziz Merhom, a Coptic writer and activist, objected to the proposal and argued that Copts were not a political entity. Mahmoud Azmi, a Muslim writer, contended that the religious minority must be represented in the parliament for the sake of national unity. He argued that Merhom's position was idealist and did not take reality into consideration. The reality, Azmi argued, is that people were still influenced by their religious affiliation while creating public policy. Azmi challenged Merhom's proposal of separating religion and public space by pointing out that declaring Islam as the state religion also violated such a separation. Merhom insisted on his position. He believed that the future would bring new stratification of the society and new classes and groups, and that the constitution must expedite the change, not block it.[3]

Political exploitation of the debate was obvious. King Fuad, whose ambition was to be the caliph of Muslims and stretch his rule to include the Islamic world, supported the creation of an Islamic state. He appealed to Al Azhar for support. The British, on the other hand, supported a confessional system in which the minorities in Egypt would be protected. Evangelical missionaries, who were actively working to convert Copts, immediately adopted "Coptic rights" as their agenda. The Coptic Orthodox Church rejected a confessional system and supported a national project in which Copts were not a political entity. The Wafd Party, the legal heir of the 1919 Revolution, was in favor of a secular national state, in which Islam was not the religion of the state and Copts were not represented through a confessional system.

Dualities shaped the sociopolitical life in Egypt in those fifty years: national independence versus political democracy, religious identity versus national identity, national independent church versus modern reformed church, traditional Azhar versus modern Azhar. These dualities influenced both the Egyptian bureaucracy and the Coptic Church. The bureaucratic relationships were not exclusively based on secular, modern regulations and laws. Traditional affiliations to communities and groups—the village, the family and, of course, religion—also played an important role in and influenced the workings of bureaucracy. Consequently, both Copts and Muslims complained about their rights not being adequately recognized in the administrative structure because of biases of each side.

The tension between religious and national identity also presented itself to the Coptic Church in the creation of El Maglis El Milli (the Communal Council), which was created in 1873. It consisted of Coptic laymen representatives who were elected to supervise the financial and administrative business of the church. From its creation until the July 1952 Revolution, the clergy and the council rarely worked in harmony. Their relationship throughout the years was shaped by bitter conflicts and inflamed competition for authority. While the clergy was in favor of a national independent church, with power maintained by the clergy, the council was in favor of a modern reformed church with power in the hands of the laymen. These conflicts influenced, and were manipulated by, the larger national political struggle.

July Revolution and State-Religion Relationship

In July 1952 the Free Officers staged a military coup, later referred to as the July Revolution, by which they ousted the king. In 1953 the monarchical regime was terminated and Egypt was converted into a republic. The Free Officers began political negotiations with the British that resulted in the departure of British troops in 1956. An ambitious new system adopted an Arab nationalist ideology with a socialist economic agenda. Leaders liquidated all political parties and political religious movements and tried to create a one-party political system through the Socialist Union. Overemphasizing national unity and national identity, the new system unified the court system and abrogated religious legal courts, communal councils, and nongovernmental Islamic and Christian endowments. It also stopped missionary work and put missionary schools under strict regulations. The confiscation of endowments, the collapse of the Coptic Communal Council, and the passing of Al Azhar reform laws made the participation of both Al Azhar and the Coptic Church in public life merely symbolic.

Summarizing the effects of the July Revolution on the Egyptian citizenship, Coptic writer and researcher Samir Morqus wrote that from 1952 to 1971, the political citizenship (in terms of political participation) retreated, while the social citizenship (in terms of social justice) improved because of the spread of free education and social services (Morqus 2000, 192–99). In fact, the July Revolution dramatically changed Egyptian society. Agrarian reform, the spread of free education, the industrial uprising, and the establishment of an egalitarian social system had a profound influence on the structure of the society and its classes. However, these reforms were conducted through an omnipotent state that recognized society as homogeneous. There was no discrimination based on ethnic or religious grounds, and all social and political diversity was downplayed. Civil society collapsed, and what remained of it played only a symbolic and insignificant role. A sharp line was drawn between the previous age—with all its ideologies, structures, and institutions—and the revolutionary age.

On the Coptic side, social reform had unfortunately some unexpectedly negative impacts. The nationalization of giant private properties excluding the Copts dramatically weakened the influential aristocratic Coptic class, "which had previously played an important role in political life; this also contributed to reducing the weight and role of the laity within the church itself. Some members of this upper class initiated the movement of emigration, which was a completely new phenomenon of the Copts (and for all native Egyptians) and which was to become so important from the 1970s onwards" (Van Nispen 1997, 27). Unexpectedly, the collapse of the Communal Council did not result in a conservative traditional church solely dominated by the clerical voice. Laity from lower middle and middle classes flowed back to the church during the 1950s and 1960s, leading to ecclesiastical renaissance of the Coptic Church.

> The newfound vigor included also the strengthening of theological instructions, especially with the foundation of evening courses in theology addressing university students, many of whom were to become parish priests or monks. This resulted in an important rejuvenation of the clergy (above all in the towns) and of monasticism, which was to become the principal pole of Coptic life, and hence of the episcopate. The nature of this renaissance involved a progressive strengthening of the ecclesiastical, indeed the clerical structure (Van Nispen 1997, 28).

In short, the church was rejuvenated but became strictly apolitical.

Economic Liberalization and the Political Role of Religion

The 1970s witnessed not only a new president, but also a second profound shift in Egyptian society. After waging a successful war against Israel, President Anwar Sadat dissolved the Socialist Union, created a multiparty political system, and introduced a new constitution. The more serious changes he made, however, were liberating the economy and encouraging private enterprise, as well as tolerating and even encouraging Islamic activism. The increasingly powerful Islamic movements aimed to compete against leftist opposition and called for a return to Shari'a and living in accordance with the "Islamic model." Such movements had negative effects on the Copts (Van Nispen 1997, 30). The call of these movements found increasing acceptance in Egyptian society. As one author predicted, "the influence of the Islamist movement will not be limited to the various Islamist groups. It will spread out through a growing Islamization of the general atmosphere of the country, even if the institutions of the state generally continue to function according to more secular models" (Van Nispen 1997, 30).

On the Christian side, the increasing clericization of the Coptic Church continued to develop the reign of Pope Shenouda III beginning in November 1971. The church began to play a greater political role and "the patriarch himself, Pope Shenouda, a very strong personality and one of the symbols of the Coptic renaissance, came increasingly to play a political role and to be seen not only as the representative, but as the real political leader of the Christians" (Van Nispen 1997, 30). Naturally that development was not welcomed by the state, which found in the church a challenging new political actor. Disputes, which became frequent between the president and the patriarch, reached a height in 1981, with the presidential decision to depose the patriarch. On a global level, especially in the United States, Copts in the diaspora began to advocate from abroad, taking the removal of the patriarch and the increase in terrorist attacks as the foundation for their claims of persecution.

The return of the patriarch and the quashing of terrorism during President Husni Mubarak's reign (1981–present) has not made the emigrant Copts' opposition less active. On the contrary, the opposition has often organized demonstrations when the president visits the United States and has paid for advertisements in American newspapers to denounce the systematic daily persecution, murder, forced conversion, and rape that Copts have experienced in Egypt. In 1997, the opposition took an even more active step, lobbying the United States Congress to issue the Freedom from Religious Persecution Act to "establish an Office of Religious Persecution Monitoring, to provide for the imposition of sanctions against countries engaged in a pattern of religious persecution, and for other purposes" (Ibrahim 1998, 14). The enactment of the law, with the annual follow-up visits by an American fact-finding mission committee that reports to Congress every year, is a source of major annoyance to the Egyptian state.

The situation became worse in the context of the American invasion of Iraq, the American sanctions against Sudan, and the Greater Middle East view of American President George W. Bush. The Coptic Church in Egypt has continuously and officially denounced all those claims and actions by the emigrant opposition, as well as the U.S. interference in the matter. It insists on a "national" discussion and solutions to any Coptic problem. In 2004, the congressional committee made its annual visit to Egypt, but the patriarch refused to meet with them. This development intensified the issue of Coptic problems. Coptic concerns today are met with suspicion and caution by the Egyptian government, as a politicalization of such problems might have potentially dramatic consequences for Egypt's national security.

PROBLEMATIZATION OF MUSLIM-CHRISTIAN RELATIONSHIPS

Coptic Problems

Sameh Fawzi, a Coptic researcher, discussed problems of Copts with more than thirty Egyptian intellectuals representing the whole political and cultural spectrum: Muslim and Christian, religious and secular, left and right. Analyzing the answers, Fawzi (1998, 62) concluded, "It is possible to put a common agenda, which represents the consensus of the intellectuals, from all currents, schools, and ideologies, of the Coptic problems." Fawzi notes that Egyptian Copts experience the following problems:

- Restrictive regulations on church construction
- Diminished Christian presence in media
- Ignoring Coptic history in educational curricula
- Appropriation of Coptic endowments
- Lack of an official population count of Copts
- Lack of access to high and vital governmental positions
- Constitutional recognition of Islam as the state religion, Shari'a as a source of law
- Lack of proper Coptic representation in the parliament
- Muslim terrorism against Copts

The problems listed above could be generally classified into three overlapping categories: political, administrative, and social. The political problems are those rooted in state policies and/or laws, such as the restrictions on building new churches or renovating old ones. The social problems are rooted in social traditions and cultures, such as the lack of a Christian presence in the media. The administrative problems, such as endowments and university appointments, are rooted in the practice and behavior of the administrative system of the state. The roots of these problems are not distinct: a state policy is driven by the culture of the society, just as the social culture is shaped by the state policy; the administrative area is an overlap between the political and the social areas.

The situation seems to have shifted during the last decade. The repair of churches was put on equal footing with that of mosques, and Coptic endowments were returned to church control. Chapters on Coptic history were added to the educational curricula, the media became more sensitive to Coptic issues, and the Christmas sermon is broadcast by the official TV station. Coptic characters and churches are more frequently shown on soap operas. A few Coptic ministers were appointed to the government, and a number of Coptic representatives serve in the parliament. Actions to eradicate terrorism are effectively being taken.

Social Problems

Despite these changes, problems persist. An important dimension to these problems, according to those interviewed for this study, is the social one. One major complaint was the lack of strong social relations between Muslim and Christian families. A Coptic mother commented that Muslim and Christian children prefer to have friends who share the same religion. It became clear from the interviews that sectarian feelings predominate and supersede those of national unity. The paradox, then, is that social cohesion is taken for granted and all blame centers on the government, while the latter attempts to solve the problem politically.

According to a Coptic interviewee, the problems have become so acute and deep that changing the Constitution, increasing the Coptic presence in the media, returning the endowments, or adding chapters to history books will no longer solve them. The main problem, according to him, is growing sectarianism: people live in faith-based, isolated communities where knowledge of the other is lacking and stereotypes about the other are created and nurtured.

According to many researchers, this "return" to religion or sectarianism was exacerbated by the 1967 Arab military defeat and the economic problems of the 1970s. Eric Davis argues (1984, 139), "the increasing contradiction between differential accumulation and decreasing legitimacy produces a crisis of authenticity." Islamists have declared the bankruptcy of "Western" ideologies, be they liberalism or secular socialism. This argument was also raised by Bryan S. Turner (2002, 28) who wrote, "With the failure of communism, Islamic fundamentalism becomes one of the few remaining political options in the Third World as a protest against secularization and consumerism." On the Christian side, there was a parallel return to the church (Habib 2001, 140). The end result was increasing religious fervor in civil society.

A Coptic author and researcher said, "Religion replaced the withdrawing state and collapsed civil society in providing social services. Muslims resort to mosques to seek social support and Christians to the churches. Children go to different summer camps, patients to different polyclinics."[4] Emphasizing this notion, Sameh Fawzi wrote (1998, 124),

> The society has received, since the mid 1970s, a sociopolitical crisis. The state withdrew from some social care fields, leaving people to their own and according

to the common logic of market. Had a strong civil society existed, social organizations would have replaced the State in offering social functions and would have secured the gradual withdrawal of the State. Nevertheless, in case there is a structurally weak civil society, bound with legal and bureaucratic restrictions, a simple citizen will have but to retreat to the traditional narrow loyalty to satisfy his/her necessary needs. The religious group is the first to be addressed. That was what happened and is happening now. Islamic institutions satisfy the needs of Muslims and Copts have but the Church to satisfy a greater part of their social needs.

Political Role of the Church

In this context, we must revisit the church and the central role it came to play. With the collapse of political participation and civil society in the 1950s and 1960s, the withdrawal of the state from provision of social services, and the rise of Islamic "revival" in the 1970s, the Coptic Church has come to play not only an important religious and social role, but a political one as well. Rafiq Habib said (2001, 133), "The Church attracted the [Coptic] people to make them one church group with mere religious interests and away from getting occupied with public concerns or social issues. Their belonging to the church became practiced on a daily basis. In this way, this institution absolutely dominated everyone. Later, in the 1970s, the church came to represent these people politically." Some interviewees complained that this development unfortunately resulted in isolating the Copts within the walls of the church. Two interviewees commented that after the clash between the patriarch and the president there was a new "deal" through which the church was guaranteed full freedom to conduct whatever social and religious activities it wanted, on condition that it not get involved in direct criticism of the state. In other words, the church has been supported by the state itself and political demands are directly negotiated between the state and the church.

This development is not welcomed by everyone. Many Muslims and Copts believe that it will only increase the isolation of Copts. Other Coptic researchers think that Copts are mistakenly considered a homogeneous group. Prominent Coptic intellectual Milad Hanna said (2001, 150–51),

> The Church was the only organization in which Copts find refuge after the abrogation of political parties, and societies. . . . When Sadat came to power and allowed the Brothers and Islamic Groups to work, Shenoda worked as well in an opposite direction. Copts became followers to the Pope who became their leader. No Coptic leadership gets out but through him. A minister or a parliament member will always be careful that the Church approves of him. The Church became the principal Coptic political institution, something that divided Egypt, because it turned it into religious institutions.

It seems as though the Coptic masses support the church to strengthen it in the eyes of the state and the increasingly Islamized society. It has become more apparent to secular Coptic intellectuals that they will be marginalized unless they decide to work through the church. Habib emphasizes this notion (2001, 134), noting,

> This opposition has its history that goes back to the beginning of the Communal Council and the endeavors of the seculars to have a role in the Church when Copts were playing a role as Egyptians in the political Egyptian field. What is happening now is quite different. The clergy is playing all roles in the Church and dominating the Copts in the public affairs. There are some objections but they are ineffective and interrupted . . . some words here and there. The real issue now is that whoever opposes the Church will feel that he is opposing a huge institution that has huge masses and consequently he is threatened to be rejected by them. There are many people who would get away from such an adventure.

An Islamic political activist and researcher complained that healthy Muslim-Christian interactions are frequently difficult because Copts unnecessarily behave as representatives of the church.[5] He said that even the Coptic candidate of the parliament, Munir Fakhri Abdul Nour, complained that Copts would not support him unless the church allowed them to do so.

A Coptic author and researcher added a new dimension by highlighting the bureaucratic nature of religious institutions:

> Institutionally, there are plenty of problems facing dialogue because the institutions themselves suffer internal problems; whether churches (not only Orthodox) or Islamic institutions. And even if there are people inside the institution who have the capacity and the will to engage in dialogue, they are being marginalized inside their institutions.[6]

In his interview with Amr Abdel Samea, the patriarch responded to those who complain about the bureaucratic/autocratic nature of the church:

> We organize the membership inside the Church. There are four kinds of membership: general . . . spiritual . . . working . . . and leadership. Had somebody who has no relation with the Church, its spirituality, its meetings, its religious life, its rituals, its service, come and demanded to suddenly jump on leadership positions of the Church, would that be accepted? If he does not make it, he makes troubles and asks for reform, which means but to be one of those who lead the Church (Abdel Samea 2001, 42).

When Abdel Samea proposed a more significant role of the congregation besides the hierarchy, the patriarch replied,

> Making use of the seculars does not mean abrogating the clergy because this is a Church system; otherwise we change the Church from orthodoxy to something else! We are a religious people; the Christian asks the blessing of the clergy, and the Muslim asks the blessing and prayers of Imams. Do they want the secular to dominate the religious man until he becomes his employee? (Abdel Samea 2001, 55).

The Underlying Sociocultural Competition

The collapse of civil society and its later invasion and domination by religious institutions makes it increasingly a space for competition rather than for understanding and cooperation. Unlike the 1911 Coptic and Islamic conferences, which were organized by secular Copts and Muslims, two conferences in 1977 were organized by the Coptic Orthodox Church and Al Azhar: one was chaired by the patriarch, the second by Sheikh Al Azhar. This reflected the decreasing secularism in Egyptian society. Other developments that demonstrate this competitive religious drive are the use of stickers that reveal the religious identity of a car owner, giving newborns names that reflect their religion, and the competition between Christians and Muslims for the domination of the Egyptian public sphere.

With the increasing Islamization of society, Copts have shown a sudden departure from using elements that could be interpreted as "Islamic." Using *As-Salamu Alaikum* instead of "good morning" as a greeting or wearing a headscarf rather than uncovering the head have become indicators not of social background but rather of religious identity. One interviewee listed the following social customs as threatening to Christians: Islamic signs, the forehead marking of a praying Muslim, the silver ring of Muslim husbands, the headscarf, and even the greeting of *As-Salamu Alaikum* ("peace be upon you"). In his book, Sameh Fawzi (1998, 117–19) lists some of the elements that are imposed to create a more Islamized society: the wearing of hijab, Al A'qiqa (a celebration that is held in the seventh day of the life of a new baby), the Islamic wedding, and the change of the oath of physicians.

The very practice of religion becomes loaded with perceived menace. Codes of ethics, social conduct, and dress become symbols of religious identity and, in some instances, cause for offense. Religious symbols are interpreted as having political meaning, and questions about comparative power become relevant. Whose symbols will dominate the social sphere? Whose gathering before the mosques or the churches will be larger? Whose religious audiocassettes will become more popular in the streets?

Blaming the State

Copts and Muslims both blame the state for problems relating to religious identity, but for different reasons. One interviewee considered the state, in terms of its security, as an obstacle to Muslim-Christian dialogue, stating, "Dialogue became a security issue not a cultural issue. This is very dangerous."[7] He is not against the state's role in the issue of dialogue; he just wants it to be kept away from the security apparatus. A second interviewee raised the same issue by saying, "I believe that security has played an important role in the development of sectarian violence, for many reasons. One of the reasons is that security always—by definition—wants to put an end to any sectarian activity, immediately."[8] He further elaborated that "it is dangerous to keep the file of Christian-Muslim relations in Egypt in the hands of security. As a very [sensitive] issue, it should be in the hands of the president."[9]

It is clear that there is ambivalence toward the state on the issue of Christian-Muslim relations. While some see state involvement as the problem, others see it as a solution. Reliance on the state is central to Copts. Rafiq Habib said (2001, 142), "Copts rely on the state because it owns power and therefore has to grant Copts their demands. It is the same relation between the church and the state, an institution asking a superior institution to pass down its rights or take care of its interests."

Negotiation and Compromise Strategies

Understanding the history of the Egyptian state is essential for understanding IFD in the country, because it was through the formation of the modern state in Egypt that Muslim-Christian relations and religious identities were contested and problematized. Furthermore, the peculiar history of the formation of the Egyptian state, as well as the Coptic demands, pushed the state to play a central role in shaping the agenda of dialogue and setting its regulations. It is important to understand that Egypt is neither a liberal democracy nor an autocracy. It is not a liberal democracy because of the absence of an independent bourgeois class. Capitalism and the bourgeoisie were created, maintained, and contained by the state. Even after Sadat's liberal policies, which were continued during Mubarak's reign, businessmen have allied themselves to the state and represented themselves through its ruling party, the National Democratic Party (NDP). Despite the reinstatement of a multiparty system, the NDP remains the political institution of the state, through which different classes and social groups compete and lobby for their interests.

Other political parties, as well as civil society, play the role of forums to develop, further, and campaign for specific agendas, be they liberal, nationalist, Marxist, or Islamist. Agendas are then represented, negotiated, and compromised through the political and administrative systems of the state. Even Islamists, whose political organizations are strictly banned and frequently crushed, occasionally have their agenda promoted and adopted through the state's institutions (Mosaad).

Egypt, as mentioned above, is not a democracy in the Western sense, where representatives of corresponding parties negotiate politics in the parliament and where the government is composed either of the majority party or a coalition. Egypt is also not an autocracy, where the will of the ruler and his regime is directly and oppressively imposed on opposition groups. The ruling party has, thus far, never displayed a specific ideology in contrast to the "opposition" ideologies. On the contrary, it demonstrates "compromised" ideology and policy. There is a constant negotiation process in which compromises are made. These compromises are not final; they change with global, regional, and local demands, which are reflected in the diversity of views held by political parties, social movements, and civil society organizations.

The dynamics of continuous internal negotiation and compromise have always shaped the nature of the Egyptian state: it is democratic and autocratic, secular and religious, liberal and socialist, conservative and progressive. The basis of Egypt's policies has been moderation and avoidance of radical solutions. The state has become a master of compromise.

The fact that Egypt is not an autocratic country means that demands of groups will not automatically be met once the ruler is convinced of their merit (Fawzi 1998). Additionally, civil society cannot be considered the solution. The fact that Egypt is not a democracy limits the ability of civil society to confront, lobby, or pressure the government. Egypt's socioeconomic reality does not provide the basic elements for a vibrant and independent civil society.

Unlike European Christianity, whose church sometimes played a political role, Sunni Islam has had no institution to represent itself in the political realm. But this does not mean religion was separate from the state. Religion, as a reference system of beliefs and actions, has always been a dominant political force in the Islamic world. In fact, secularization, in a European sense, has failed in the Islamic world, because there was no churchlike institution to be banned from politics. In Egypt, for instance, the creation of the modern nation-state was not the consequence of a failed Islamic system; it was expedited by and legalized through Islam.

It is important to note that the Coptic Church also expedited the state's creation. Mohamed Ali appealed to both Al Azhar and the patriarch to encourage Muslims and Christians to join the army. Since then, both religions have never failed to contribute to national negotiation and decision making through representing, not the voice of God, but the conscience of believers.

THE LEXICON OF INTERFAITH DIALOGUE

Before examining IFD in Egypt, we must question the language used to address this issue. An entire lexicon of concepts and meanings has been used to treat this topic: religious freedom, persecution, discrimination, conflict, conflict resolution, peace education, civil society, secularism, fundamentalism, and interfaith dialogue, to name a few. Such terminology frequently does not relate to the Egyptian reality and experience of IFD.

When IFD is attempted in Egypt, given all the local complexities, doubts and confusion increase. IFD, with its diverse labels and terminology, was not a local initiative; it was brought in by foreigners. In the *Dictionary of the Ecumenical Movement,* under the entry for "interfaith dialogue," Ariarajah (1991) wrote,

> Suspicion of interfaith dialogue among some Christians surfaced in the open controversy at the WCC's [World Council of Churches] fifth assembly (Nairobi 1975). For the first time, five persons of other faiths were invited to a WCC assembly as special guests and took part in the discussions of the section on "Seeking Community," where the dialogue issue was debated. Plenary discussion of the

report of this section highlighted the deep disagreement within the church on the issue of dialogue. Fears were expressed that dialogue would lead to the kind of syncretism against which the 1928 Jerusalem meeting warned, or that it would compromise faith in the uniqueness and finality of the revelation in Christ, or that it would threaten missions seen as fundamental to the being of the church itself.

When IFD is framed as a type of peacebuilding project, local Egyptians question the need for it, especially since there is no war.

Our interviewers in Egypt found that their main obstacle was the framing of the interview itself as research about IFD, because the concept itself was viewed with suspicion. Even those participating in interfaith activities outside Egypt do not feel totally at ease about it. There is a feeling among some that the concept of IFD is imposed from an alien, Western cultural context. One interviewee interrupted his interview in frustration asking, "Why interfaith dialogue? Because your friends outside of Egypt are interested in this? Why should we think of our problems and their solutions in their terms?"[10]

STATE SECURITY ROLE

A religious group in Egypt is officially recognized if it does not pose a threat, upset national unity, or disrupt social stability. Such recognition usually is done by the Religious Affairs Department at the Ministry of the Interior, after consultations with leading religious figures in the country, particularly the pope of the Coptic Orthodox Church and the sheikh of Al Azhar. The interference of the state in religion is apparent by the fact that the government controls mosques, appoints and pays the salaries of the imams who lead prayers in mosques, and monitors their sermons (U.S. Department of State 2003).

To approve the construction of places of worship, the State Security (SS) not only looks at the documents provided but also goes directly to the field, conducting long and thorough investigations and negotiations to uncover who finances each project, where each place of worship is built, and who builds it.

A CONCLUDING EXAMPLE

Mute tension between Muslims and Christians exists in Egypt, but rarely does it erupt into real violence. However, when violence does erupt, it reflects the sociocultural competition to dominate the public sphere. An example of just such a violent sectarian clash erupted in February 2002 in an Upper Egyptian village near the governorate of Maghagha. An eyewitness recalls, "I heard that the whole thing began when the exaggerated ringing of the church bells drowned out the call for the *fagr* [dawn] prayers coming from an adjacent mosque, something that provoked the Muslims. One thing led to another and the clashes happened" (Howeidy 2002). A local resident of a nearby village further commented on the factors that triggered these tensions: "The church was always there, but recent extensions have made it as high as fifteen meters. The adjacent mosque has similarly been extended upwards. On Sunday, instead of ringing the church bell briefly, Louka—a school secretary whose uncle is a priest—went on and on ringing. When some Muslims objected, he took his gun and shot at them. . . . Since then, armed men in green [antiriot squads] have occupied the village and enforced a curfew. It's been extremely tense" (Howeidy 2002). One Coptic resident stated, "We've always lived in peace with Muslims. This whole thing has been blown out of proportion. We live peacefully."[11]

What was clear in this incident was the politicization of the issue and its implications for security. Controlling the situation politically was the state's most important priority. While the state intensified the security in the villages, it also downplayed the danger and the intensity of the incident. One journalist observed,

> Heavy security forces have cordoned off Bani Wallnems since the clashes erupted preventing anyone from entering or exiting the village. . . . More than a dozen armed members of the Central Security Forces and assorted policemen blocked the entrance with the help of an armored vehicle. . . . A statement, issued by the Interior Ministry a few hours after the clashes, affirmed that the situation was "under control" and that the security apparatus succeeded in containing the violence which, according to the statement, was nothing more than a "minor incident" (Howeidy 2002).

In the days following the incident, ceremonial meetings were held emphasizing national unity and stressing that a minor incident will never crack the social solidarity of the Egyptian people. However, in reality, similar incidents and tensions could recur. The problem is a social one, and solving it through a political framework is therefore likely to be an inadequate solution. In addition to being places of worship, mosques and churches are also considered symbols of dominance, where communities compete with one another to dominate the social and culture spheres. Sociocultural approaches to the problem are needed—perhaps in the form of a dialogue that involves all stakeholders, not simply official representatives of the government and the religious institutions.

The politicization is not the sole responsibility of the state and its security institution. Many forces intentionally or unintentionally push the state to respond politically to the problem of Muslim-Christian relations. These forces include fundamentalist groups with a fanatical political agenda; the church, which claims to represent all Copts; the few emigrant extremist Copts who appeal to the international community, and especially to the United States, to intervene and put an end to the alleged murders and rapes against the Coptic minority; the United States, with its annual delegation to inspect "religious freedoms" in Egypt; and a national discourse that overemphasizes social harmony and national unity and reduces problems to "minor incidents." The state is an important party in dialogue between different communities. An interviewee describes the situation: "For the last thirty years, we have constantly been in a 'sectarian environment' filled with religious sectarian claims that have destroyed the roots of coexistence in the Egyptian society on both sides. We need dialogue to remove the unfounded fears and to get out of this environment."[12] The objective and focus of dialogue should not be how many churches are registered annually or how many Copts should be elected to the parliament. The core question is how to convert the competitive environment between Muslims and Copts into a cooperative one.

INTERFAITH ACTIVITIES IN EGYPT: APPROACHES

State of Dialogue in Egypt

Some of the leaders in the IFD movement emphasized that dialogue is very repressed in Egypt. Some felt that the religious authorities rejected dialogue and that the issue of dialogue was a taboo topic. One participant said, "There is no dialogue in Egypt; whenever there is an issue that is raised, it is immediately blocked the same way topics like Satanists or homosexuality are blocked."[13]

One possible reason for the lack of support for dialogue at the national level may have to do with the way it has been practiced thus far in Egypt. The tendency apparently has been to sugarcoat the process and avoid hot spots or authentic engagement. One seasoned veteran of IFD characterized the essentials of dialogue this way: "Set the exact agenda, tackle the real issues and declare the real opinions . . . then you are talking about a real problem and therefore dialogue can be fruitful. On the contrary the dialogues of 'protocol' or of 'celebration' make the people lose all faith in the credibility of dialogue, and so we can say we have now reached a very bad dialogue climate here [in Egypt]."[14] Many participants in Egyptian IFD feel that there is no earnest attempt to wrestle with "real" issues and differences, and thus the events are not dialogues so much as they are staged rituals.

Dialogues occurring on smaller, local levels are more likely to engender honest self-expression. The International Center for Studies (ICS) hosted a series of effective grassroots dialogues between Muslims and Christians. One organizer remarked, "We started a grassroots initiative of Muslim-Christian dialogue; we often met here at the ICS. . . . We also met elsewhere, like in the Maronite school, and we put on the agenda the 'hot issues' that affect the Muslim-Christian relationships in Egypt. And there was an important convergence with regards to the agenda, and that was translated to many important activities."[15] The organizer found that the process of building consensus on various topics became the basis for further cooperative efforts in the community.

Even though much of the dialogue in Egypt may seem surface level in comparison to efforts elsewhere, the fact that dialogue is seen by some as a positive contribution is promising. One sheikh commented,

Generally speaking, dialogue—when the world political factors are moderate—is the common human language. And God ordered the Muslims to communicate with the other whoever he may be, and this is a Quranic verse that expresses an Islamic duty; the necessity for the Muslim to communicate with all creatures or people. This communication should lead to acquaintance. This acquaintance should not be formal but should flourish into relationships that lead to the advancement and development of humanity on one hand, and on the other hand bring peace and prevent war. This is why if a person knows about a serious invitation for dialogue, he promptly responds to it as [if] he is accomplishing a duty.[16]

Unity Model

Most people do not readily associate Egypt with religious conflict. The relationship between the Muslims and Christians in Egypt rarely piques the attention of the Western press. Ignorance and denial of differences and conflict result from the unity model. Under this model, Egypt works hard to present a unified picture of solidarity among its people and hopes that the presentation will morph into reality.

On the surface, the desire to be nationally united is a profoundly important one. Egyptians fundamentally want peace and stability within their nation. Unfortunately, rather than examining the differences or roots of conflict, countries living under the unity mind-set move directly into enforcing unity. It appears that, within Egypt today, speaking about the need for dialogue between Copts and Muslims is seen as a kind of disloyalty to the country. It implies that something is amiss and contradicts the preferred image of strength and accord. Under the unity model, differences are suppressed or smoothed over, rather than explored, for fear of surfacing more conflict.

Even the way that most Egyptians define dialogue reflects the country's orientation toward the unity model. When asked to define dialogue, one author's answer is quite typical: "The 'cultural dialogue' highlights the common spaces, the common worries, and the common dreams. In Egypt for instance, Christians and Muslims have the same economic pressures, problems, and ambitions on the general level. This is what I mean by cultural dialogue, which highlights the importance of the value of tolerance in religion."[17]

The desire to appear united as a country is so strong that dialogue occurring between the Muslims and Christians is often hidden or unannounced because dialogue is viewed as an indicator of a divided Egypt. Many interviewees stressed finding common ground:

It is a dialogue between . . . not a dialogue between two religions, otherwise it becomes a dialogue of dogmas. . . . Consequently, what are the issues that are common to both sides? Moral issues or social issues or life issues . . . this is our approach to dialogue—to find the convergences and decrease or marginalize differences concerning these issues.[18]

Secondary or universal language is extremely important in the maintenance of this model of unity in Egypt. Issues of faith are closely associated with dogma or fundamentalism and are seen as a route to debates and clashes rather than to discussion.

Critical to the preservation of the unity model is the concept of equality. In Egypt, one important norm in the dialogue is the equality of both sides. Each side must see the other as a full partner in the discussion. At the same time, each culture wants to be recognized as unique and free from the imposition of the other's values. One Egyptian rejected the phrase "acceptance of the other" because he felt that it undermined the basic concept of equality too much.

> I absolutely refuse the term or concept "acceptance of the other." It is a concept that leads to exclusion and marginalization. . . . The other is someone who is highly different. Let's compare—although I don't like this comparison—the Christian personality and the Muslim personality. You will find that many things are common—except for religion, everything is common. It is therefore not an "other." Then what is an American, or a French person or a German? We have one culture, one language, one education; the things that are common are numerous.[19]

Usually in a mixed culture, the majority population will be more difference denying and unity emphasizing, while the minority population will more quickly point out differences. In Egypt, denial of difference is present among many in both the majority and minority populations. When asked to speak about dialogue in Egypt, one IFD leader said, "I want to start by saying that there is no dialogue between the Copts and Muslims because they have lived together and coexisted for 1,400 years. We are from the same family so the word 'dialogue' is not appropriate. . . . There are no two sides or two parties to engage in dialogue—so the word 'dialogue' is wrong."[20] A significant portion of the Coptic leadership rejects the idea that Copts are any different from the rest of society for a different reason—the fear of attracting too much attention to their community. One leader said, "We are citizens before all. We have complete rights and we have obligations to fulfill on the land of our country Egypt—as the Copts are not guests, we are not outside immigrants, our roots are Egyptian. Even Muslims are before all Egyptian. And so we are citizens before all."[21]

In the case of Egypt, the unity model functions on two different levels. The majority Muslim population denies that dialogue is needed because they do not want to appear to be oppressors, while the minority Christian population denies that dialogue is needed for fear of appearing to be traitors and attracting negative attention.

But one Coptic author is unafraid to dispute the unity model openly. "For the last thirty years we have constantly been in a 'sectarian ambience' filled with religious sectarian claims that have destroyed the roots of coexistence in the Egyptian society—on both sides. We need dialogue to elude the unfounded fears and get out of this condition."[22]

The American invasion and occupation of Iraq—as well as the British, Spanish, Dutch, Italian, Danish, and Australian support for the military action—has only deepened the power of the unity model in Egypt. The war created the belief that the only way for Egypt to survive if targeted for a second colonization by Western European governments is to stand strongly behind the national government, regardless of its possible faults. Any internal problems that might threaten national unity are currently muted by the need to be a strong Egypt.

Advocacy Model

Most Egyptians express a strong desire to see concrete results, in the form of improved social relations and development activities within Egypt, as an outcome of dialogue. One sheikh expressed that dialogue without action is neither desirable nor truly religious. He explained that the dialogues held in the United States and Europe had not changed the actions of citizens there and were thus pointless unless larger social change occurred. He said, "There must be fruits to dialogue, if there are no fruits other than celebrations and conferences and recommendations, you will find in fifty years we will be much weaker . . . and not advanced one step towards peace."[23]

In Egypt, religious institutions have become social service institutions as well as places of worship. Local places of worship meet the needs of their members by initiating private development projects within the mosque or church. Some Egyptians fear that this situation is shifting the loyalty of the people away from the state and toward their local religious institution. One active member of a political party said, "Everything is now transformed and related to the religious institution and the people are locking themselves in the religious institutions—mosque or church. They are gradually withdrawing from interaction in the society through public work to working for the benefit of the mosque or the church."[24]

While some Egyptians feel that the exclusive religious social service agencies are a problem, others do not see them as a barrier to interfaith relations.

> I think this [religiously based social service agencies] is a good thing [contrary] to what some people may say—that it divides people and provides services for the Christians only or the Muslims only. . . . there is no problem if some institutions serve the Christians only, as long as there is a healthy ambiance.[25]

Not everyone agrees. An Egyptian government official commented,

> I think this idea [of shared development projects] is dangerous because there are some very explosive places in Upper Egypt. . . . I think it is too explosive—there are tribal loyalties, fanaticism, and there is one essential suspicion with regards to interfaith dialogue and that is that I want you to become Christian or Muslim. The ordinary people are not qualified or prepared for that at all.[26]

The fear that development projects are a subtle form of conversion efforts is a barrier to the success of the advocacy model. Many Christians view development projects initiated by Muslims as subtle attempts to subject them to Shar'ia. Similalry, organizations like the Coptic Evangelical Organization for Social Services (CEOSS) have been working in social and economic development for many decades in many Egyptian rural areas and have faced such accusations in early stages, but they managed to build a certain level of credibility with local communities that allowed them to work effectively in a Muslim and Christian context.

But some Muslims feel that the Christians may be more adept in the field of social services because they have been working in the field longer and have more support from foreign funders. Therefore, these Muslims believe, the entire nation would benefit from the wider distribution of this expertise and access to resources.

The Role of Ritual

One arena where interfaith exchanges seem to be flourishing is in formal, ceremonious participation by religious leaders in one another's holidays. Much of the obvious contact between the religious leaders seems to occur at major religious ceremonies and holy days such as Easter, Ramadan, or Eid. On such occasions, the heads of religious institutions communicate their greetings to each other in recognition of their respective days of celebration. For a number of years now, the pope of the Coptic Church has dined with the Muslim community, breaking fast with them during their holy month of Ramadan. Similar gestures are also common from the Islamic community toward the Christian minority.

The practice of sharing rituals is extremely popular in the Egyptian interfaith dialogue movement. Around Ramadan, numerous Iftars take place with the participation of Christians. One organizer of such an event commented, "I organize each year an Iftar and invite a large group of Muslims and Christians. The Justice and Peace commission of the Catholic Schools also organize one, and they always invite them [Christians] and they have dialogues in those events—both sides are always present."27

It is important to restate, however, that the power dynamic between the ruling Muslim community and religious minorities deeply taints the perception of these gestures, often leading them to be viewed as insincere and patronizing.

Objectives of IFD in Egypt

The intended effects of IFD in Egypt are numerous. Most Egyptians interviewed seemed to agree that one of the primary objectives of IFD in their country should be to enable the citizens to begin to know one another better.

> Muslims do not know much about the Christians, there is ignorance with regards to the customs and traditions. . . . I don't know why they tattoo a cross on their hand. . . . I don't know many of their celebrations. And actually I should know the

differences between their different branches. . . . And the same thing for the Christians, they don't know about the differences in Islam.[28]

At the moment, Muslims and Christians tend to hold deep-seated fears about one another. Suspicion and misunderstanding abound. One Muslim admits, "The Christians fear the Muslims want to cut them to pieces . . . that they are infidels and ought to be killed or expatriated. . . . All these are unfounded fears but this atmosphere of fear does not help or encourage dialogue."[29] While many participants corroborated this societal fear of the other, one religious leader dismissed the idea, saying, "No, there is no fear. There is doubt with regards to its [IFD's] usefulness or a conviction that it is useless."[30]

Another commonly held objective of IFD is to open up more effective channels between the religious institutions and state institutions. One sheikh emphasized the need for an article in Egypt's constitution that generally recognized the value of religious institutions within the country. He stressed that this would not be a guarantee of religious freedom, but a way to give religious voices more power and credibility.

> The religious current must have a constitutional credibility rather than me dialoging with people who have no impact—it is useless. And so we need to invite [both] the people of dialogue on one hand and the State [government] on the other to recognize constitutionally not the right of the citizen to choose his creed but the recognition of the national and intellectual role of the religious people.[31]

At first glance, this statement may seem unrelated to the function of IFD in the state but it is, in fact, a strong indicator of the need to balance power relationships within Egypt. The religious leaders perceive themselves as being viewed as inferior to secular leaders. Thus, until there is some recognition of their importance in the state, they feel less able to work for change.

As previously mentioned, a primary objective of dialogue in Egypt is to create tangible positive change. The need for measurable advancement in areas of civil society is evident. One frustrated religious leader and burned-out dialogue participant stated,

> The effectiveness of any dialogue is measured by its fruits for humanity, and how it can be put to the service of humanity. The idea of dialogue started about a decade ago but did not give any fruits. . . . I consider your [the interviewer's] activity and mine in the field of advocacy as a way of distracting people from what the states [the government] are doing to them. What is the point of me preaching every Friday or you spending part of your time and knowledge to try and communicate with people here and there when they will in the end say "but what more can we do?"[32]

Unless a dialogue can produce substantial results that participants can see, they are likely to become frustrated and withdraw from the initiative.

Unfortunately many people are hesitant to join an IFD group because they see it as politically affiliated. They often fear that the dialogue is being held as a covert political operation by a government or institution. This fear is not unfounded; many dialogues do approach the conflict on political terms. While some Egyptians think IFD should be moving toward a democratic system, most Egyptians see the conflict between Muslims and Christians as sociocultural and consider the concern for democracy a distraction from resolving it. Politics is a hot topic. Some feel that politics strangle dialogue and should be avoided, that politics can only serve to stir up the people. Efforts within IFD to address politics are not directly forbidden by the government, but such efforts are frowned on.

IFD participants are often particularly concerned with the presence of fundamentalism in Egypt. Many see one of the objectives of dialogue as being to marginalize extremist and fundamentalist voices on both sides. Unfortunately, many of those creating terror and violence within Egypt pair their acts with religious language. This creates a further barrier to seeing religion as a source of reconciliation and dialogue.

Subjects and Topics of Dialogue

Aside from politics, the subjects of religion and Israel often feature in IFD in Egypt. Secular issues are seen as more "sensible" and "appropriate" topics for dialogue. One interviewee explains, "The Egyptian society has opened new files that are suitable for discussion: democracy, citizenship, participation, liberties, acceptance of the other. These are sociological and political issues that are easy to agree upon."[33] By dwelling more heavily on topics outside of religion, groups feel more comfortable getting to know one another without appearing to threaten national unity. In such cases, the use of secondary language can be very helpful in creating relationships and dispelling stereotypes about the other.

If religion is to be discussed, most feel that it is best left to the religious leadership. "In a country like Egypt, the religious issue is essential and therefore it is important that the mosque imams and church priests be aware of these questions and interact together."[34]

Egypt's close proximity to Israel/Palestine makes the topic impossible to ignore in a dialogue setting. One IFD participant went so far as to suggest that one of the objectives of dialogue in Egypt should be to strengthen a national vision and action plan on the issue of Palestine. Some dialogue participants believe that internal unity is necessary because Egypt needs to be able to "face" Israel. This is a double-edged sword. While some Egyptians see IFD as a necessary step in strengthening Egypt to live in a world with Israel, others see it as an unnecessary diversion that distracts the Egyptians from the topic of Israel.

Thus, the question is not whether IFD will in some way address the issue of Egypt's relationship to Israel, the question is how it will be addressed. If the issue of Jerusalem is addressed as a national issue—that Jerusalem should be a shared capital because such a situation would increase stability in the region —then the Christian population within Egypt actively engages in the dialogue.

But if the issue is addressed as an Islamic issue—that Jerusalem must be shared because Muslims want to retain control of Haram al-Sharif and al-Aqsa—then Christians are excluded and deterred from direct participation in the discussion. For most Egyptians, the question of how the topic of Israel should be addressed is answered again by the need for national unity. The approach most often taken is to discuss the holiness of Jerusalem to both Christianity and Islam, and the increased stability that a shared capital with the Jews would bring.

Who Participates? Secularists, Elites, and Youth

Participation in Egyptian dialogues must be balanced between the secularists and the religious believers. Often in the past, dialogues have tended to include more secularists than people of faith. Some participants in such dialogues demanded a more balanced representation, while others argued that the secularists must be present to keep the dialogue level-headed. One frustrated participant remarked,

> They [the organizers] discuss the issues from a secular point of view. And I get into conflict with them, I say this is a dialogue between religious people and they get a large number of secularists. But they started modifying this a bit. I told them this [too many secularists] would be a failure because the majority of the audience is religious—the Egyptian audience.[35]

Another imbalance to be redressed concerns class. Most IFD in Egypt involves the participation of the elite members of society only. One organizer admits, "We find that many of the dialogues are elitist, and so they share a common understanding but do not reach the grassroots."[36] While involving only elites in dialogue makes issues of specialized language or status within the group less problematic, such dialogues often fail to impact the masses outside the dialogue room. One participant in a prominent dialogue project withdrew after he observed that all the participants seemed to be friends and acquaintances. He claimed that the group purposely wanted to restrict membership and exclude people who were not in their inner circle of friends.

The religious elites of both the Muslims and the Christians control a significant portion of public opinion surrounding politics. Even among other intellectuals in society, the religious leaders hold important sway. Many intellectuals admit that their religious leaders tell them whom to vote for and encourage them not to form their own opinions.

In deciding to hold an IFD, there seems to be an elite class of people who must be invited. These are the nonofficial staples of the dialogue world: "those you have to approach if you want to engage in any dialogue," according to one participant.[37] These elites are seen as "knowing how to dialogue," "knowing the rules of dialogue," or being "better at dialogue than others."

Dialogue is not seen as an activity that is appropriate for the common person. The belief that special skills are necessary to participate may only contribute to the elite-centered nature of dialogue in Egypt. In many cases, these "nonofficial dialoguers" may be appointed or nominated by the state to take part in interfaith encounters. One Egyptian said such persons were "nominated by the state to take part in whatever dialogue as they know how not to make anyone angry—and they may be subjected to pressures. But this does not allow for serious dialogue—dialogue becomes formal and superficial and doesn't get into the depths."[38] The idea that professional government dialoguers are routinely participating in interfaith encounters may be enough to deter others who deem themselves less qualified. This dynamic of participation can become a cycle that only further confines dialogue to the elite members of society.

There is a sense among many in Egypt that it is time to move dialogue from the elite, institutional level to the popular, grassroots level. In an encounter between ordinary Muslims and ordinary Christians, there may be a greater opportunity for mutual empowerment and understanding. While dialogue between elites may create a rich intellectual contribution to the state of dialogue, the absence of a vibrant grassroots dialogue may be stifling other kinds of contributions. The elite and grassroots levels of dialogue are not mutually exclusive. Egyptian society need not choose one or the other. Engaging in both may be more deeply productive.

Another area having to do with inclusion across demographics concerns the typical age of participants. In Egypt, the gap between the generations is seen as both a resource and a liability. The older generation is seen as having the necessary experience to engage in dialogue, but do not because they are either too busy or too cautious. The younger generation has the will to dialogue, but is seen as lacking the necessary capacities, life experience, and skills. One interviewee told us,

> The older generation has the experience and has some answers . . . but they are depressed. They ask themselves what is the meaning and what is the point of doing anything. There must be cohesion of both generations for many things, including interfaith dialogue, and this can move the stagnant waters.[39]

While there are few dialogues occurring today involving the youth, many see them as the antidote to a world of IFD ruled by elites. One dialogue participant explained, "The important dialogue is the dialogue of youth who do not represent anyone. (Even true representatives do not truly represent anyone.) The problem is we are waiting for the representation while the representation is not necessary."[40] However, the young people also need some sort of training in dialogue. Dialogue is not easy work, and the youth need to be adequately prepared both emotionally and intellectually. They should be chosen based on an earnest desire to participate in getting to know people from the other side. Some Egyptians observe that the young people are volunteering to participate in dialogues outside of Egypt as a way to travel abroad. This angers those who see the urgent need for dialogue at home and who organize domestic dialogues in hopes of having a positive impact on society.

INTERFAITH ACTIVITIES IN EGYPT: ORGANIZATIONS

Al Azhar Committee for Dialogue

Despite acts of proclaimed egalitarianism on the part of the government, there is a long-standing, intimate relationship between the state and the official Islamic institution, Al Azhar. This unique rapport has often presented minority religious groups with a highly visible point of contention.

In 1997, Al Azhar created an interfaith committee called the Permanent Committee of Al-Azhar for Dialogue with the Monotheistic Religions. The committee is very official, concerned with neither grassroots activities nor local dialogue, but rather with addressing IFD from the perspective of religious and governmental organizations. Al Azhar representatives have met with Rabbi Samuel Sirat, former chief rabbi of France and vice president of the Conference of European Rabbis. Al Azhar officials have met also with government leaders of the United States of America, the United Kingdom, France, Germany, Norway, and the Czech Republic.

Religious Fraternity Association

The only official IFD NGO in Egypt is Al Ikhaa Al Dini, the Religious Fraternity Association. Its origins can be traced to 1938, when a group of Egyptian Muslims and Christians decided to launch a dialogue group called the Ikhwan Al Safa Group. The Religious Fraternity Association was officially established in 1978 as a simple initiative devised by a group of people who wanted to come to know one another better. Unlike many groups that form in the wake of a traumatic community event, this one was born out of the desire to talk to one another. This foundation for the group continues to affect the way that group members see themselves. In discussing the relatively long history of the group, one member reports, "The most important thing is that it wasn't a reaction to anything—because a reaction fades when the action is over—this is what happens to all the new associations you hear about."[41]

The group supports religious fraternity by organizing about nine seminars per year. The seminar is more of a cultural activity than a religious one, and religious differences are not a topic of conversation. One board member firmly stated, "We do not accept discussions on conflictual issues: whether the Christ was crucified or not, [nor] the Bernaba Bible predicting the arrival of [the] Prophet Mohammed. No one dares to tackle these subjects."[42] Discussions focus more on common values and morals; to discuss religious topics feels too close to fundamentalism. Only topics relating to Egypt are considered. The members acknowledge that there may be religious tensions in many other parts of the world, but they choose to focus only on Egypt so that they do not stray too far from their primary goal, which is religious fraternity within the country.

Membership currently stands at about 250 people—mostly elites of society, such as physicians, engineers, sheikhs, police officers, and priests. Members include prominent persons like Abdu Sallam, the former minister of health; Sheikh Ahmed Baqoury, the grand sheikh of Al Azhar; Bishop Samuel, the bishop of public services in the Catholic Church; Ahmed Al Wetaidy, the former president of the police academy and the former deputy minister of youth; and Abdul Fattah Shawqi, board member and treasurer of the Syndicate of Physicians. Membership is not open to everyone, and members are chosen carefully. An important criterion in the selection of members is that those who are chosen should not bring up sensitive issues in the discussion that might lead to conflict. The group does not want "troublemakers" within its ranks.

Muslim Brotherhood Group

In addition to the official initiative by Al Azhar, an Islamic group split from the Muslim Brotherhood Group (MBG) and founded the Al Wasat Party in 1995. The spokesman of the Al Wasat Party, Abu El Ela Madi, also directs a research center, the International Center for Studies (ICS), and cofounded an NGO called Misr Society for Culture and Dialogue (MSCD). It is through these three organizations that MBG pursues its political and cultural agenda. The ICS and MSCD have been the MBG's instruments for promoting a series of meetings to which it has invited representatives from across the Egyptian political and cultural spectrum. MBG had to be seriously engaged in a number of national dialogues in order to situate itself properly in the political and cultural arenas. MBG's ideological principles were based on the works and thoughts of a number of Islamic intellectuals, especially Mohamed Seleem El Awwa and Tarek El Bishri, who write about Muslim-Christian relations and participate in IFD activities. Unlike many of those who are involved in dialogue efforts in Egypt, MBG started its dialogue locally and later extended it regionally and globally.

MBG has not embarked on secular approaches or "liberal" Islamic interpretations to address Coptic concerns, but rather bases its work on fundamental Islamic interpretations.[43] It roots its views in accepted Islamic scholarship and the authenticated methodology of Ijtihad. MBG's spokesman noted,

> Some of the progressive ideas of people like El Awwa, El Bishri, and Hewaidi are not known and so I presented these ideas and clarified them [in dialogue meetings] and they got it. That was important for our Imams to be able to talk about citizenship in Islamic terms. These views are important not because they are the trend nowadays, or because they are Western, but because they represent a new Islamic discourse, a new Ijtihad.[44]

He added that imams have a problem of communication in dialogue because "they use a specific language derived from Fiqh."[45] MBG emphasizes that from the Shari'a point of view, there is no place today for concepts like *jizya* or *dhimma,* and that Copts are equal citizens who can be appointed as judges and can be elected to any office, including the office of presidency. Though the Al Wasat Party has never been recognized, MBG had the opportunity to practically implement their views and influence the last parliamentary elections; in 2000, Madi enthusiastically campaigned for Munir Fakhri, a Coptic candidate to the parliament.

It is important to note that MBG's work has been primarily an intellectual rather than a grassroots form of engagement and activism. This does not mean that its work is not important, but again points to the elite nature of IFD in Egypt.

Coptic Orthodox Church

The dialogue through the Orthodox Church has an impressive history grounded in an intrachurch clergy/laity dialogue. In 1985, a group of Coptic youth decided to found the Cultural Development Group (CDG). Samir Morqus, who used to write in *Al Ahali* (an Egyptian Marxist newspaper) before founding and leading this group, has written (2002, 2–3),

> This Group became the basis from which the Coptic Center for Social Studies (CCSS) emerged later in 1994. The Group and the Center could be considered as the two arms of the cultural and dialogical activities in the Coptic Church. Each one of them integrates the other; the Group works with the youth at the basic level under the umbrella of the Youth Bishopric and the Center works with the intellectual elite and the Egyptian research group under the umbrella of the Services Bishopric.

Morqus continues (2002, 4), "this activity [of the CDG] took into account that it does not reflect a specific political trend or intellectual school, but that it rather gets benefit from all human thought, achievement and experience through different ages and leaves it to the youth to decided for themselves what suits them."

A course on cultural development, with a primary focus on Muslim-Christian relations, was later designed according to the CDG's objectives:

1. Understanding the church history from a cultural view as well as giving it a more modern rereading
2. Rereading the Coptic history in the context of the history of the Egyptian national society
3. Studying the current reality with its many phenomena
4. Extending bridges of dialogue to the society and encouraging youth to vivid and effective participation
5. Developing thinking skills and gaining cultural skills (Morqus 2002, 4)

Besides Muslim liberals and Marxists, CDG invited Islamists, especially Emara, El Awwa, and El Bishri, to its lectures. It vehemently rejected both the religious Dhimmi and secular minority framing of Coptic issues and instead emphasized the notion of citizenship as the only accepted framework for the Coptic question (Morqus 2002, 14). To that end, CDG organized a number of lectures and, workshops, and invited Muslim and Coptic writers to participate.

By and large, the Coptic Orthodox IFD experiences are successful. Many factors contributed to this success:

- Cooperation and understanding between enthusiastic and wise young
- Copts like Morqus as well as clergy such as Archbishop Mousa, the archbishop of the Youth Bishopric
- Emphasizing the indigenization of dialogue, in terms of analytical concepts used, issues raised, and approaches
- Addressing the issue of national unity rather than pushing the dialogue toward sectarianism
- Raising important, and yet difficult, questions no matter how sensitive some people might consider them

Instead of the ceremonial meetings, in which dialogue sessions devolve into a celebration of national unity, the participants chose to get involved in hot and problematic issues that concern the Copts.

Some problems, nevertheless, still exist. Although Muslims are invited to speak, Muslim audiences have not been invited. This has meant that the greater number of people needed to further the dialogue have not been included. Morqus explained, "the audience is Christian, but the guests are Muslims. Because of objective reasons, the center's activities can include Muslims. Expanding a public invitation for Muslims to participate is, however, difficult in the church or cathedral."

One prominent CCSS leader said,

> There are some very good intellectual results, but the problem is that you cannot implement them. You find some excellent ideas coming out of sincere people who sat together and discussed and got real good results…but they only represent themselves; they have no means to implement these ideas. Now we can both of us find twenty ideas to create spaces for Muslims and Christians to interact and to calm down the environment, and even to solve the sectarian problems in Egypt, but what are our tools to implement this on the political level? This is the real obstacle against the intellectual dialogue. In the end, they have nothing but their thoughts and voices. The best they can do is to distribute these books on the largest number of people . . . given you don't find obstacles in the distribution of these books in the first place![46]

She hinted at two institutional problems, bureaucracy and conservatism, saying, "When there is an institution, you always have problems with dialogue because part of the institution's identity comes from its difference with the other. And this prevents it from being open, particularly when the institution is weak. . . . In the end I believe the conservatives get the upper hand—not the fundamentalists, but the conservatives."[47]

Coptic Evangelical Church

In addition to the Coptic Orthodox Church, the Coptic Evangelical Church has also promoted IFD activities via the Coptic Evangelical Organization for

Social Services (CEOSS). Originally started as a literacy project in 1950, CEOSS is now a social as well as development organization. Currently it is one of Egypt's largest development organizations and addresses needs such as health care; education; and economic, agricultural, and environmental development.

Dialogue is one of the three central tenets of CEOSS's work. Beginning in 1992, the organization worked to bring together Christians and Muslims to promote mutual understanding and tolerance between the two religions. CEOSS has a forum called the Forum for Intercultural Dialogue, which "brings together Christians and Muslims, clergy and lay people, intellectuals and individuals from the entire array of society for the sake of promoting mutual understandings on contemporary issues in religion, culture and civil society" (CEOSS Web site). The forum is very active: sixty-seven meetings and forty-five workshops have been held since its creation.

In 2003, the forum introduced a new program to break barriers separating East and West through collaboration with the Lutheran Evangelische Akademie in Loccum, Germany. Participants in this dialogue included a mixed group of religious leaders, Christians and Muslims, and influential intellectuals from Egypt and Germany.

One forum leader elaborated on an interesting program that started in 2000, the New Generation Program, which is a joint project with the Ministry of Awkaf/Endowment. He explains,

> The objective of the project is to create an environment of understanding between young priests/pastors and imams. When the sheikh and the priest coexist, this is transmitted to their communities. In the next phase, the sheikhs and priests will work together on developmental activities. The program tackles general issues such as plurality, citizenship, etc.[48]

The imams are invited through the Ministry of Endowment and the priests/pastors are invited from the three major churches of Egypt. The speakers have a diversity of secular and religious backgrounds, and the issues raised are social, cultural, and political. The forum launched a special program for Upper Egypt, where most of the violent events between Muslims and Christians take place. Additionally, it organizes Opinion Makers Round Tables, which bring Muslim and Coptic opinion makers together to discuss general social and political issues.

Roman Catholic Church

The Catholic Church in Egypt has demonstrated interest in promoting interfaith dialogue through forums such as the Egyptian Committee for Justice and Peace (ECJP). The ECJP invites Muslim and Christian participants to its national projects, through which a genuine dialogue is initiated to address real-world problems. It became clear through our interviews and research that participants in such dialogues usually belong to the intellectual elite and often do reshape their ideas and views according to the challenges they encounter in their work with the ECJP.

The ECJP called an interfaith meeting in 1995, which brought together a number of middle-aged Muslim and Christian intellectuals and activists. This group organized meetings in which participants were invited to present papers and discuss them. The meetings gradually stopped, but the work that was done was captured in a Catholic Church publication. The general secretary of Catholic schools in Egypt has also adopted IFD as one of his objectives. Muslim lecturers, some of them Islamists, are invited to its meetings and summer camps. Academically, both the Dominican Institute and the Human and Theological Sciences Faculty invite Muslim lecturers and writers to contribute to their academic work. The Jesuits also invite Muslim intellectuals to enrich their meetings and discussions.

Moral Rearmament Society

Some of the most prominent dialogues in Egypt are imports. One such imported organization for dialogue is Moral Rearmament (MR). MR first began in Europe after the Second World War as a way for people to arm themselves not with weapons but with morals. In Egypt, the initial founding members of the group were intellectuals. Their meetings were not religious, but were about morals. Internationally, the organization is now called Initiatives for Change. Egypt's group preferred to keep the old name. Initiatives of Change/Moral Rearmament is now registered as an international NGO.

The local founders—Muslims, Christians, and Jews—belonged to the Egyptian bourgeoisie or the agrarian aristocracy classes. Membership was composed of either Europeans or members married to Europeans. Members were expected to invite their families to the meetings and involve them in the activities. Initially, a Swiss couple in Alexandria hosted the meetings once a week, which later met in the homes or private gardens of group members to discuss life situations and how to deal with them. The focus was on moral standards, not on personal religious beliefs. Religion was not ignored, but the group chose to focus on the common ground shared by religions.

Most of the dialogues in which Egypt's MR participates take place outside of Egypt, usually in Europe. The focus is typically interfaith understanding, but the case of Egypt is not usually addressed directly. Discussions focus on broader Christian-Muslim understanding between the West and the East. The press is not invited to such interfaith meetings so that the people feel more free to speak openly.

In Egypt, MR is a registered organization, headed by Dr. Mohamed Hassoun. A few years ago MR organized a lecture on morals in sports in one of the sporting clubs and another one at the Nutrition Institute on morals against commercial cheating. After September 11, they called for a common prayer for peace—but there was no response from the larger community. However, a few months later, when the siege of Ramallah occurred in Palestine, Pope Shenouda and the sheikh of Al Azhar invited the group to a prayer in the cathedral, and one MR member helped to organize the event.

Although MR occasionally addresses IFD in Egypt, for the most part members claim that Egypt does not have the kind of problems that require dialogue. They focus more on supporting dialogue outside of Egypt between Christians and Muslims.

Today, the group is unfortunately decaying and holds irregular and infrequent meetings in the home of Nagia Said, usually whenever a European member is visiting Egypt. In the last three years, nevertheless, there was a small increase in its activities when a few members were invited to attend meetings in Switzerland and Malta.

Studio 206

A very small group called Comparative Religions meets in Studio 206, an art studio on Street 206 in the Ma'adi District of Cairo. The two founders explained that the objective is to use dialogue as "a tool to narrow the gap between religions." One founder explained how they both believe that "the essence of all religions is one. So we try to focus on this essence."[49] The other added that she has "read a lot of the Hindu religion texts, philosophy, etc. . . . It all points to a one Creator, the source of existence. And all the religions point to that, so the plurality of religions is just a question of flavors; different foods have different flavors."[50] Comparative Religions, which started as a Web-based discussion group, is inclined toward a humanistic approach that emphasizes psychological interpretations of problems and solutions, such as hatred, love, and unity. In their meetings, members do not discuss the social or legal systems of religions, or the social or political problems of religionists. They prefer talking about elements of the creed—like Heaven, Day of Judgment, Restoration—to demonstrate the diversity of interpretations displayed by different religions, and then trying to show how the essence in the end is one. The few meetings are frequented by youthful bourgeois.

Comparative Religions plays at most a minor role in Egypt; however, it is unique in that it displays the sort of discourse more common in the Western model of IFD. Unfortunately, such initiatives do not speak to the majority of people in Egypt.

The above list of forums of dialogue is not comprehensive. A number of other dialogue initiatives, unfortunately, have failed to continue or thrive in Egyptian society. Such initiatives usually have a short-term objective: they are created when violence erupts to emphasize national unity, propose ways of studying the problem, and try to radically solve it. Nevertheless, they gradually evaporate, although perhaps leaving a residue of positive relationships between Muslims and Copts, which could later grow and expand in other frameworks.

OBSTACLES TO INTERFAITH DIALOGUE

Four obstacles hinder IFD in Egypt: the overpoliticization of dialogue efforts, the deficiency of grassroots initiatives, the suspicion surrounding dialogue efforts, and the lack of a clear vision for dialogue. Despite the fact that these problems cannot be easily isolated from one another, it is important to try and explain them separately to shed light on their complexity.

Overpoliticization

The prevalent national unity discourse will satisfy neither Muslims nor Copts, who are engaged in a very competitive, albeit unnecessarily volatile, environment. There is a need to tackle the problem differently, promoting more cultural and social approaches. Unfortunately, numerous factors stand in the way of such approaches: Islamic radicalism, the negative role played by the immigrant Copts in the United States, and especially the pressure placed by the U.S. Congress through its monitoring of religious freedom. These factors stand in the way of removing IFD from an inflammatory political context.

Many Egyptians see the current state of politics within Egypt as a primary obstacle to dialogue. While state institutions insist that dialogue already occurs in the country, the facts on the ground are more complicated. Some have suggested that dialogue is merely a cosmetic exercise that has little connection to political and social realities. One prominent Egyptian declared,

> There is no clear and sincere recognition of the importance of dialogue. The existing dialogue is one of elites. The state institutions pretend they are capable of conducting dialogue, when in fact, they are not. Besides, they say there is dialogue when there isn't. Dialogue is no more than a good gesture, a décor. . . . Dialogue and interaction during social events and social celebrations is normal, it is a matter of ethics. What we need is a deeper dialogue, on the political and sociological problems. The Azhar and the Church are not even agreeing on the issue of normalization.[51]

Dialogue is seen as an issue of national security within Egypt. The Egyptian national security leaders want to put an end to any sort of sectarian activities within the country. The security arm of the state classifies dialogue as a sectarian activity; it encourages people to explore their identity as a member of one group in relation to another group.

Deficiency of Grassroots Initiatives

Civil society is essential to boost and support social activism. There must be a plethora of forums, societies, educational and research centers, institutions, and other organizations working to heal the bitter rift between Muslims and Christians. The lack of such cultural, educational, and social work is the second obstacle to IFD. The lack of serious grassroots activism to dispel the fears and doubts held by the respective sides and to build up bridges of confidence, understanding, and respect is a serious obstacle and must be overcome if any real change is to occur.

Building a vibrant grassroots effort is no easy task; establishing an NGO in Egypt requires a lot of work. One has to go through a battery of ancient laws and regulations that make such an endeavor almost impossible. Significant bureaucratic and administrative obstacles stand in the way. Moreover, any financial aid provided to these organizations is not tax deductible; such institutions might quickly run out of funds. Seeking foreign financial aid presents other serious problems, as the state and its media usually view such aid with suspicion. Recipients of foreign aid could find themselves suddenly either jailed by the state or accused and insulted by the media. Liberal NGOs that are financially supported by foreign aid became stigmatized as corrupt Westernized organizations founded by wealth seekers, entrepreneurs, and activists. There is also a lack of volunteerism in Egypt, which is grounded in the history of economic crises. Egyptians typically find little time for activism.

Suspicion and Separation

In Egypt several factors contribute to distrust and isolation. In a society divided by religious differences, members of either religion who seem comfortable with the other may be regarded with suspicion by their own group. One Muslim reported, "The frequency of my meetings with the Copts now started arousing some questions, as people say 'you are more with them than with us.' This makes me limit my participation [with the Copts]. This is a barrier . . . because you need to preserve your credibility."[52]

The Christians and Muslims often live quite separate lives from one another socially. Just as the religious institutions are taking on the role of social service institutions, so too are they taking on the role of social centers. The church and the mosque provide a variety of social activities and sports that encourage each group to keep to itself and isolate each from interacting with the other.

In Egypt, the organizer of an IFD must be careful to appear as honest and transparent as possible. A frequent obstacle to dialogue is that many participants harbor suspicions about the motivations behind the dialogue. The participants need to trust that the dialogue is not sponsored by a foreign institution that is attempting to intervene in Egyptian affairs. Many people fear that some invitations to dialogue are fronts for foreign political institutions involved in intelligence gathering.

Lack of Vision

The fourth major obstacle to IFD is the absence of a clear vision toward which grassroots activism could work. Many IFD initiatives did not move beyond trying to answer basic questions like what is dialogue and what does it involve. These philosophical questions are important, but the grassroots movement tends to require more concrete goals. Good intentions have always existed and are frequently expressed and emphasized. However, lack of clear objectives and models of best practice makes it impossible for noble intentions to be translated into action and social change.

AGENDA FOR THE FUTURE

Our research revealed that several adjustments need to be made to move forward. Ambitious IFD work should start with a process of "indigenization." The concepts, the problems and their theoretical framing, the approaches and proposed solutions, the objectives, and the organizations carrying out the work must be indigenous and rooted in Egyptian culture and experience. As we have seen, it is only when the dialogue is based locally and shapes its agenda through the daily encounter with Egyptian reality that it blooms and becomes fruitful. Such localized initiatives will be more successful than those imposed from the outside.

The rise of Islamism in the 1970s made the core question of interfaith relations in Egypt one of citizenship. Much effort, work, writing, and discussions situated the Coptic question in this framework. This conceptualization of the problem was good for the 1970s, but today, it risks adding to the undesired overpoliticization of dialogue. Social manifestations of sectarian conflict, which are currently considered minor or incidental, should be taken more seriously. The core question now is social relations; it is about the highly competitive social environment between Muslims and Christians. A political approach is necessary and important only if it is supported by social and cultural approaches as well.

CEOSS's successful experience of working through, not against, the state, in terms of its Ministry of Endowments, should be extended and reiterated. The state initiatives, like that of Al Azhar or the National Dialogue and Social Peace Committee of the parliament, are currently either ceremonial or too official. Such initiatives must be expanded to the grassroots, something that the state has the power and facilities to do. The question is how to properly communicate with the state to create and secure such spaces for dialogue. Cooperation between social/cultural forces and the state is important. What is required is a reduction of state bureaucracy to make such cooperation easier.

A plethora of dialogue forums and organizations must be created and encouraged to carry on the significant task of converting a competitive environment into one of cooperation and understanding. These organizations have to work at the grassroots level with all sectors of society. Besides these organizations, the religious civil society, instead of being recognized as a source of sectarianism, must be used to encourage dialogue.

It is important to remember that in Egypt, religion has played and will play a major and central role in daily life. Religious identity should not be disregarded in favor of national identity. It is through this religious identity that social unity has to be promoted. In this regard, Islamic and Christian organizations must be encouraged to conduct social services and joint projects together. They also should put IFD high on their agendas. "The maintenance of authentic and deep relations between Copts and Muslims," in Christian Van Nispen's words (1997, 32), "is not an automatic matter that can look after itself." A deliberate work to enhance such unity and carry it forward must be emphasized. It is through the local mosques and churches in every corner of Egypt that IFD must be conducted and maintained.

Living in a society with a Muslim majority, Copts have a reasonable degree of knowledge about Islam. However, Muslims' knowledge about Christianity in general and Coptic Christianity in particular is too scant. As Coptic initiatives to spread knowledge about Christianity have been perceived suspiciously as missionary work to convert Muslims, efforts to pursue and spread such knowledge must be initiated by Muslims. Popular writings, articles, booklets, curricula, and different audiovisual materials need to be created and put at the Muslims' disposal so that they can choose to learn more about their neighbors' history and legacy. Materials about Muslims and their heritage should also be made available to Copts, as such knowledge must be mutual.

The pull of national unity is at the moment silencing or marginalizing most efforts at Muslim-Christian dialogue. Those who advocate dialogue risk being portrayed as wanting to divide the greater nation of Egypt. Dialogue continues to be defined as a national security issue. Because of the perception that many dialogue efforts are the product of foreign institutions attempting to gain influence within Egypt's borders, the Egyptian government keeps a close eye on dialogue activity. If the nature of the relationship between Muslims and Christians is to change within the country, the government must stop seeing dialogue as a security issue and begin seeing it as a social issue.

Ultimately, IFD can help to open up relations between Muslims and Christians, but it may do little to change many of the country's problems. Dialogue may plant seeds of trust within the population, but these seeds will have to be watered with a more transparent political process and the lifting of institutional discrimination. Dialogue may provide a starting place for the exchange of ideas between religious leaders or political elites, but these ideas will have to be cultivated and nurtured by a public sector willing to implement them.

Despite efforts at a reduction in discriminatory actions on the part of the state, it remains to be seen whether economic conditions or legitimacy will be strengthened. Doing so would lead to the formation of an environment more conducive to dialogue, where people will see few economic differences as well as the presence of a universally enforced authority. This will help prevent conflicts of passion and frustration that are rarely rooted in differences of religion. As economic conditions worsen in Egypt and the income gap widens, interfaith disagreements stem increasingly from a sense of inequality. When this is combined with the fact that in most cases the distinguishing factor between Muslims and Christians is their faith and little else, religion becomes the focal point in the blame game that ensues.

It is encouraging many people are able to recognize this fact and make deliberate efforts at continuing to live in peace with their neighbors of a thousand years. Such efforts include shared nonprofit and humanitarian organizations at the local level, interfaith schools, sermons that preach tolerance and understanding, and the formation of committees and organizations dedicated to IFD. There exist so few examples of the latter that the need for an increase in the number of private and state-sponsored institutions of dialogue is quite clear. When faced with a rapidly growing grassroots Islamic revival, largely committed to nonviolence, it becomes all the more important that the state avoid antagonistic actions that destabilize interfaith relations (such as extrajudicial crackdowns on supporters of Islamic political parties, which can lead to their radicalization). With the vast majority of the Egyptian population being Muslim, and with the state's declaration of Islam as the national religion, responsibility for the enhancement of IFD falls largely on the state's shoulders. Local levels of dialogue also hold tremendous importance, but such efforts are often retarded and made fruitless by state policy.

The three-pronged core of the matter, our research concludes, is that interfaith work must be supported by the government as well as by the majority of the Egyptian population. It should extend beyond the boundaries of the church (and mosque) and include both Muslim and Christian participants. There is a need for additional venues for pursuing interfaith activities in civil society and for transferring the knowledge to a larger portion of society. Working on the grassroots level is of utmost importance.

6

INTERFAITH DIALOGUE IN JORDAN

Between International Host and Local Harmonizer

INTRODUCTION

When researching interfaith dialogue in the Middle East region, Jordan is an important country to study due to the proliferation of interfaith organizations and activities in the Kingdom. This chapter analyzes the state of IFD in Jordan by looking at the history of interfaith relations in the country; the scope of interfaith efforts; the goals, assumptions, and types of interfaith organizations; the approaches to IFD; and the challenges and obstacles facing such work. It further highlights some of the success stories narrated by interviewees active in the interfaith field and advances some recommendations for improving the field and the results of such work.[1]

Jordan's geographical location and past have played an important role in the shaping of its culture, history, and politics. Its close association with the Abrahamic faiths (Judaism, Christianity, and Islam) has contributed to its diversity as well as to the emergence of distinct loyalties among the inhabitants.

Jordan is a predominantly Muslim country with a population of 5 million. More than 95 percent of the population is Sunni Muslim (U.S. Department of State 2003). Official government figures estimate that Christians make up 4 percent of the population; however, government and Christian officials privately estimate the true figure to be closer to 3 percent. In addition, there are at least 20,000 Druze, a small number of Shi'ah Muslims, and fewer than 800 adherents of the Baha'i faith (U.S. Department of State 2003). Officially recognized Christian denominations include the Greek Orthodox, Roman Catholic, Greek Catholic (Melkite), Armenian Orthodox, Maronite Catholic, Assyrian, Anglican, Lutheran, Seventh-Day Adventist, United Pentecostal, and Presbyterian churches. Others, including the Baptist Church, Free Evangelical Church, Church of the Nazarene, Assembly of God, and Christian Missionary Alliance, are registered with the Ministry of Justice as "societies" but not as churches.

In addition to its native population, Jordan is home to large Egyptian and Iraqi immigrant populations. These populations contribute to the diversity of

Jordanian society, since some of the Egyptian immigrants are adherents of the Coptic Church, while the Iraqi immigrant community is made up of a number of Chaldean and Syriac Christians and Shi'ah Muslims. In general, the Jordanian population is scattered, with no major geographic concentrations of particular religious minorities. There are a few exceptions, however, such as the predominantly Christian towns of Husn in the north, Fuheis near Amman, and Madaba and Karak, south of Amman; the northern part of the city of Azraq, and Umm Al-Jamal in the city of Mafraq, which have a significant Druze population; Amman, Zarka, Irbid, and Aqaba, which also have a Druze population; and the Jordan Valley and the south, which are home to a number of nonindigenous Shi'ah.

HISTORICAL CONTEXT FOR MUSLIM-CHRISTIAN RELATIONS IN JORDAN

Nationalism strongly shapes the interaction between discrete groups in any country. National allegiances influence the behavior of competing groups toward either unity or discord. In the case of Jordan, it is important to understand the role of nationalism in order to understand the relations between Christians and Muslims in the country.

Because of Jordan's Ottoman and British colonial legacy, national identity was late in coming to the nation. When the area of the Transjordan (later to become the nation of Jordan) was first recognized as an independent entity, the people living within its boundaries had no sense of themselves as an independent political entity. Among the first efforts to shape the national identity of Jordan were the Law of Foreigners (or Aliens) of 1927 and the Nationality Act of 1928, which were two of the first official attempts to define what it meant to be Jordanian (Massad 2001). Jordanian historian Joseph Massad (2001, 27–28) writes, "Unlike most other nation-states whose formation is preceded by a nationalist movement or a sense of national identity, Transjordan experienced no such transformations. In fact, there was no country, territory, people or nationalist movement called Transjordan or Transjordanians prior to the establishment of the nation-state. The Transjordanian state, as a result, (albeit ambivalently at first) embarked on a number of policies, some of which intentionally aimed at fostering a sense of nationhood."

As Jordan became established as an independent entity, clearer divisions arose among the people as to who was or was not Jordanian. Herein lies the significance of nationalism and allegiance to interfaith relations in Jordan. While the division between Muslim and Christian Jordanians was not particularly relevant, the division between Jordanians and Jordanian Palestinians was highly charged. As the definition of national identity became territorialized, the differences between Jordanians and Jordanian Palestinians took on new significance. This reality is particularly important when considering interfaith relations because the majority of Jordan's Christian population also happens to be Palestinian. However, in examining the early attempts to establish national identity in Jordan, it appears that differences in religion were muted, while differences in country of origin were magnified.

The Organic Law of 1928 defined Transjordan geographically and proclaimed that the national religion of Jordan was Islam (Massad 2001). There was no mention of the role of Christians. The Law of Nationality made no direct reference to religion at all, thereby leaving open the possibility that membership in and allegiance to the Jordanian state had very little to do with one's faith. In the years that followed, both the 1946 and the 1952 constitutions explicitly forbade discrimination on the basis of religion.

While both ethnicity and religion were differences protected by the constitution, there was still tension within the country. Massad notes (2001, 222), "The presence of Palestinians in the country was crucial to the emergence of a specific configuration of Jordanian national identity and national culture which became increasingly exclusivist of large sections of the Jordanian citizenry with every passing decade." Jordanians increasingly sought to define themselves in opposition to the Palestinians within their borders. These efforts manifest themselves in seemingly small assertions of national character, such as the red-and-white *kaffiyeh* worn by many Jordanian men. Some Palestinian Jordanians donned black-and-white *kaffiyehs* as an affirmation of their distinct identity, while others who sought assimilation chose the red-and-white scarf (Massad 2001). Obviously, there are other national identity symbols, yet this seems one of the most visible.

It is not necessary for our purposes to go into great depth about the minutiae of Jordanian-Palestinian relations in the country. However, as we begin our examination of the scope and significance of interfaith relations in Jordan, it is important to keep in mind these early manifestations of national identity and the way that ethnic identity bears upon religious identity in this case. While Christians as a group were not singled out as "other" in the early days of Jordanian history, Palestinians certainly were. The fact that the majority of the Christian population in Jordan happens to be Palestinian seems to be of consequence to the way that interfaith efforts have progressed.

CONTEMPORARY STATE OF MUSLIM-CHRISTIAN RELATIONS IN JORDAN

Given the plurality within Jordan today, it is important to consider the constitutional rights granted to the different communities in the country, the treatment of religious groups in the educational system, and the existing institutions that formalize dialogue between the varied groups.

Article 2 of the Jordanian Constitution declares Islam the state religion. The Ministry of Religious Affairs and Trusts manages Islamic institutions and the construction of mosques, the appointment of imams, the provision of mosque staff salaries, the management of Islamic clergy training centers, and subsidization of certain activities sponsored by mosques. The government's control over religious matters also involves loosely monitoring sermons at mosques and requiring that speakers refrain from criticizing the royal family or instigating social or political unrest.

Article 14 of the Jordanian Constitution provides freedom of religion for Christian citizens on condition that their religious practices are consistent with "public order and morality." Non-Muslim citizens are permitted to profess and practice the Christian faith, although churches have to be accorded legal recognition through administrative procedures in order to own land and to perform marriages and other sacraments. Christian religious institutions, such as churches, that wish to receive official government recognition are required to apply to the prime ministry for registration. Furthermore, the prime minister unofficially confers with an interfaith council of bishops representing officially registered local churches on all matters relating to the Christian community, including the registration of new churches in the country (U.S. Department of State 2003). Churches applying for recognition must meet the following criteria: the faith does not contradict the nature of the Constitution, public ethics, customs, or traditions; the faith is recognized by the Middle East Council of Churches; the faith does not oppose the national religion (i.e., Islam); and the group includes Jordanian citizens among its followers (U.S. Department of State 2003). However, commenting on the role of the state in religious affairs, the government describes it as one limited to supervision, not control.

The Jordanian government constantly highlights the fact that Christians in Jordan maintain their religious, national, and communal identities and enjoy full citizenship and equal rights. Christians hold offices of legislative, executive, and judicial power in the government: they work side by side with Muslims in ministries; public institutions; economic, social, and cultural institutions; public security; armed forces; and so on. They also occupy high positions in academia as presidents of universities, professors, and Ph.D. advisers. Muslim-Christian relations in Jordan are often cited (by government officials and many Muslim and Christian leaders) as an example of coexistence and harmony based on friendship, mutual respect, and partnership ("Together in Defending the Nation" 2002, 43).

The Jordanian government does not recognize the Druze or Baha'i faiths as religions, but does not prohibit the practice of these faiths. According to the religious freedom reports issued annually by the U.S. State Department, Druze in Jordan experience official discrimination but do not complain of social discrimination. Baha'is in Jordan, by contrast, suffer both official and social discrimination in several ways. For example, the government does not record the bearer's religion on national identity cards issued to Druze or Baha'i. The Druze and Baha'i communities do not have their own courts to adjudicate personal status and family matters; such matters are heard in Islamic Shari'a courts. The government does not officially recognize the Druze temple in Azraq, and four social halls belonging to the Druze community are registered simply as "societies."[2] In addition, the government does not permit

Baha'i to register schools or places of worship. Similarly, Jordan does not recognize Jehovah's Witnesses, the Church of Christ, or the Church of Jesus Christ of Latter-Day Saints, although each denomination is allowed to conduct religious services and activities without interference (U.S. Department of State 2003).

The constitutional status of Islamic Shari'a as law in Jordan allows for the conversion of Christians to Islam, but prohibits Muslims from converting to any other religion. Muslims who convert do not fall under the jurisdiction of their new religion's laws in matters of personal status; they are still considered Muslims and subject to the jurisdiction of Shari'a courts in matters of family and property law. They may face social exclusion, threats, and abuse from their families and Muslim religious leaders. Despite these institutional restrictions, there are a few Muslims who do convert and, in addition to government sanctions, face societal discrimination. Neither the Jordanian government nor society approves of or accepts interfaith marriages. Couples who belong to different faiths normally convert or face social ostracism; some end up emigrating to other countries.

According to the Constitution, religious community trusts (*awqaf*) and matters of personal status—such as marriage, divorce, child custody, and inheritance—fall within the exclusive jurisdiction of the Shari'a courts for Muslims, and separate non-Muslim tribunals for each religious community recognized by the government. There is no provision for civil marriage or divorce. The head of the department that manages Shari'a court affairs (a cabinet-level position) appoints Shari'a judges, while each recognized non-Muslim religious community selects the structure and members of its own tribunal. All judicial nominations are approved by the prime minister and commissioned officially by royal decree. The Protestant denominations registered as "societies" come under the jurisdiction of one of the recognized Protestant church tribunals. There are no tribunals assigned for atheists or adherents of unrecognized religions. Such individuals must request one of the recognized courts to hear their personal status cases. Shari'a is applied in all matters relating to family law involving Muslims or the children of a Muslim father, and all citizens, including non-Muslims, are subject to Islamic legal provisions regarding inheritance.[3]

In general, minority groups in Jordan such as Christians are not subject to systematic persecution. "Christians are fully integrated into the national life of the country" (bin Talal 2001). Christians do hold high-level government and private sector positions and are represented in the media and academia approximately in proportion to their size in the general population. However, senior command positions in the military traditionally have been reserved for Muslims. The inclusion of Christians goes beyond the political system to public life. Distinguishing between people from different religions, however, is common in government positions and other jobs, as employment applications occasionally contain questions about the applicant's religion. Certain positions are restricted to Muslims, such as the minister of interior, governor, or general in the army. Other positions cannot be occupied by a Christian because certain official requirements or duties, such as going to the mosque for a religious holiday and overseeing tasks of Muslim religious clergy, are attached to the job (Ali 1999, 78).

In the Jordanian education system it is mandatory to include religious instruction in the curriculum for all Muslim students in public schools. Religious instruction for Christian students in public educational institutions was approved by the late King Hussein and the Ministry of Education in 1996 and an experimental program to incorporate Christian education in the public school system was launched by the government in 1998. In addition to the public school system, the Jordanian Constitution allows congregations the right to establish private schools for the education of their own members with the condition that they comply with the general provision of the law and be subject to the control of government in matters relating to their curricula and orientation.

There seems to be generally little discord between Muslim and Christian communities in Jordan. There have been both institutional and governmental efforts in promoting official engagement between the different religious groups. According to Prince Hassan bin Talal, "all of us living in Jordan and sharing the Jordanian experience are never really aware of there being an issue about Christian-Muslim relations. . . . I feel that our ethos in Jordan is very much a pluralistic one throughout the century. This is not a recent development, for the Hashemite movement itself has based its consensus on pluralism" (bin Talal 2001, 82). According to the executive director of the Jordanian Interfaith Coexistence Research Center, in Jordan "Christians and Muslims live together; everyone is free to perform their worships and rituals. We have a great record of fraternity between Christians and Muslims. In Jordan, we do not talk in terms of Muslims and Christians, we are all Jordanians" (Al-Dama 2004).

Perhaps the relative lack of tension between the Muslim and Christian communities in Jordan explains why the majority of the efforts at IFD target international scholars, intellectuals, and religious leaders and why they tend to discuss international and regional issues. There are two major government-sponsored institutions that promote interfaith understanding: the Royal Institute for Interfaith Studies and the Aal al-Bayt Foundation. Both institutions sponsor research, international conferences, and discussions on a wide range of religious, social, and historical questions from the perspective of both Muslims and Christians. Recently, new initiatives are emerging in this field of growing interest.

The September 11 attacks on the United States prompted an increase in interfaith activities in Jordan. Numerous lectures and meetings between Muslims and Christians—and sometimes Jews—have taken place in Jordan and abroad. Although interfaith activities were promoted in the country long before September 11, especially by former crown prince Hassan, King Abdullah's uncle, the media only recently focused its attention on the topic. The media's contemporary emphasis on interfaith can be attributed to several factors, including direct government and security apparatus orders to highlight interfaith harmony as part of overall strategies to fight Islamic extremism in the Kingdom; the Christian churches' attempts to combat radical Islamic movements; and the Arab Christian reactions in the Arab world, especially after the Iraq war and al Qaeda activities in Jordan and elsewhere.

THE SCOPE OF INTERFAITH DIALOGUE EFFORTS IN JORDAN

IFD has existed informally in Jordan since the creation of the country: people from different religions and sects have lived together and interacted in their daily lives. However, formalizing such dialogue only started to gain preponderance in the 1980s. Formal IFD has come a long way since then, but remains somewhat limited to a small number of people and activities. In an interview with the *Middle East Quarterly,* Prince Hassan emphasized that while Christian-Muslim interaction is a long-established dialogue, "efforts have been made to make it more formal and extend it into new areas" (bin Talal 2001, 83). Such planned conversations have been successful and proceed generally without problems despite the existence of some fears "at the fringes of the respective communities." According to Prince Hassan, Christian-Muslim dialogue is essential for fostering a culture of participation and interaction between the different communities, as it will allow people to get to know each other more and to "participate in each other's lives" (bin Talal 2001). In other words, the aim of dialogue is to promote truly communicative relations rather than simply passive coexistence between the communities.

In the past few years, publications on IFD and public expressions of coexistence between the two communities on the basis of mutual understanding and respect have increased. This was a result of a new curriculum, adopted by religious and academic institutions, that calls for the elimination of stereotypes and prejudices, and propagation of respect for the other. It also calls for moving away from ideological differences that cause separation and conflict (Ali 2000b, 3).

Jordan began assuming its regional and global role as a host for interfaith meetings and conferences in the early 1980s with the guidance and support of then-Crown Prince Hassan bin Talal. As the president of the Orthodox Society puts it, it was the aim of the government and royal family to illustrate "the ability of Muslims and Christians to come together in such discussions as a reflection of the coexistence between different religious communities in the Orient."[4]

For years, Jordan has been a participant and host for conferences on interfaith issues. Most focused internationally rather than reflecting on IFD in Jordan per se. Bringing together scholars and intellectuals from all over the world, many of these international meetings and conferences highlighted the unique role and function played by the royal family in this area. While avoiding interfaith issues in Jordan, these conferences addressed broader issues such as how Islam views Christianity and vice versa; peace in Christian and Muslim thought; Arab Christianity before Islam; Christianity in the Arab world; Christianity's contribution to Arab civilization; the history of Christian-Muslim relations; women, society, and religion in Jordan; experience of Muslim refugees in Europe; and more recently, Abrahamic (that is, Christian, Jewish, and Muslim) traditions and relations. In 2002, a conference entitled "Together in the Protection of the Nation" took place under the auspices of the first general conference of Christian Arabs. The participants emphasized the necessity of an internal dialogue to organize and unify the Arab-Muslim-Christian front ("Together in Defending the Nation" 2002, 38).

With the objective of promoting interfaith relations throughout the region and emphasizing the constructive role of religion in the Middle Eastern context, various Jordanian publications on IFD have emerged. They include articles—mostly published in the *Bulletin of the Royal Institute for Inter-Faith Studies (BRIIFS)*—on the representation and treatment of sects in Iraqi laws, new religious movements in the United States, forgiveness and mediation in Islam, Maronites and Lebanon, Bosnia and Herzegovina, dialogue between Muslims and Christians in Sudan, and dialogue between civilizations. Several organizers of IFD activities presented them as attempts to broaden the scope of knowledge and learn from different cases.

Jordanian support for interfaith efforts, in the Middle East and globally, is also reflected in the number of times Jordan hosted the World Conference on Religion and Peace (WCRP), the largest worldwide coalition of representatives of the major religions, founded in 1970. Prince Hassan is a moderator of the WCRP and has participated actively, along with Jordanian delegations, in various conferences. The WCRP brings together leaders of the world's religions to publicly acknowledge each other's differences and take common action to promote peace. WCRP has frequently recognized the Jordanian regime's openness to interfaith peacebuilding. For example, in May 2003, WCRP brought together in Amman representatives of each of Iraq's major religious groups—including Shi'ah, Sunni, and Christian leaders—in a meeting called "Rejecting Violence and Promoting Peace with Justice," to discuss ways of rejecting violence and promoting enhancement of peaceful relationships.

GOALS, ASSUMPTIONS, AND TYPES OF INTERFAITH ORGANIZATIONS

State and clerical support of interfaith activities in Jordan is primarily motivated by the assumption that IFD is a mission that all Muslims should undertake to deepen and broaden humanitarian relations with the "other" (Shamseddine 2001a, 4). Most Jordanian scholars assert that dialogue is at the essence of Islam, which recognizes plurality of religions and coexistence between them on the basis of just relations. The Quran, they explain, clearly legitimizes this view (Shamseddine 2001a, 4). A second primary assumption in interfaith work in Jordan according to the president of the Orthodox Society is that "Arab Christians are part of the Arab structure and culture. They are indigenous or native citizens, and their role in the development of the Arab culture should not be ignored."[5] Arab Christians share many cultural values with Muslims and there is no inherent conflict between all religions in Jordan. Several interviewees stressed the belief that most religious conflicts are not religious per se; they have political objectives and hence result in instability, enmity, and division between citizens of the same country or of neighboring countries (Ali 2000b, 3).

Recently, some Jordanian interfaith organizers began focusing on youth dialogue, stating that youth are the building blocks of the future. According to one organizer, "It is believed that youth are more open to new ideas and more accepting of differences and change."[6] For these reasons, the majority of IFD efforts now focus on this stratum of the population.

In general, the goals of interfaith activities carried out in Jordan are influenced by the elite nature of the sponsorship and institutional structures of the political and religious organizations that implement the activities. The heavy involvement of the government and royal family in the initiatives reveals an intention to create "top-down change," in which organizers aim to engage religious leaders, political leaders, and public opinion makers to spread messages of religious tolerance and pluralism. Among the few grassroots groups, activists (or organizers) described several primary goals of IFD. Nearly all saw it as a means for Christians and Muslims to better understand each other's religious beliefs. As one organizer stated, "It aims at mutual understanding and respect."[7] Interreligious dialogue provides a meeting point where the basis of a true relation of mutual respect and understanding can be built (Hamdan 2001, 3). As one professor at Yarmouk University said, "The goal from meeting and getting to know the other and his culture is to break down stereotypes and barriers."[8]

For grassroots organizers, this dialogue process should not be limited to the relationship of the individual with his religion alone, but should attempt to build relationships between individuals and bridges of rapprochement between religious communities. The objective of dialogue on the grassroots level is not merely to meet and discuss important theological issues (as does the elite or top-down approach adopted by the major interfaith organizations), but to build a strong basis of relationships by which people from different religions interact and discuss with each other even after the dialogue is over. According to a Muslim interfaith activist, a major goal of dialogue is "to listen to the other, to understand their feelings and ideas, and to love and respect the other as equal, despite the differences that exist."[9]

Organizers were careful to ensure that participants' religious identities remain intact; for them, the goal of dialogue is understanding, not conversion, as can be seen in these statements: "The goal is not to change people and preach them into changing their religion; it is an exchange of ideas through discussion of needs,"[10] "It does not mean that the participant must give up their Christianity or Islam,"[11] and "It is hoped that such dialogue will encourage coexistence with the other by understanding and respecting his/her differences."[12]

In addition to the internal focus of enhancing interreligious coexistence in Jordan, all organizations and organizers—Muslim, Christian, and interfaith —stated that improving the images of Islam and Arabs in the West had become an important goal of their work in the aftermath of the September 11 attacks on the United States.[13]

APPROACHES TO INTERFAITH WORK IN JORDAN

It was challenging for many interviewees to present a distinct model or theory of interfaith work in Jordan; several interviewees claimed that there is no model or theory of IFD. The archimandrite of the Ecumenical Studies Centers notes, "It is not like a medicine—you go to the doctor and he gives you a ready prescription for the disease or illness. Interfaith dialogue is built on numerous trials and theories, as life is one of experience and experimenting."[14]

Organizers find that each meeting takes on a form of its own depending on the participants involved and the topics discussed. One writer/journalist further notes that "there are no directive rules in dialogue. The person comes with an open heart and an open mind and there is no particular or specific curriculum or method."[15]

However, upon examination of interfaith activities in Jordan, several patterns become apparent, the most important of which is the emphasis on generating new cognitive knowledge on theological questions. This theological research is carried out mainly by the three major elite institutions and sponsored by the royal family and government. They aim to educate clergy and the public, through publications and seminars, so that religious differences will be tolerated and understood without leading to conflict and violence. This *theological* approach, involving elite clergy and scholars, was the dominant approach until the late 1990s.

Another approach to interfaith activities is the *dialogue of life* model. In the majority of grassroots meetings and conferences, there is no reference to ideological or theological issues; according to activists in dialogue, there is no point to discussing these topics. The issues that dominate dialogue are common concerns that affect daily life, such as coexistence, personal matters, coordination in protecting religious sites, funding for humanitarian and social projects, terrorism, and peace. According to an activist in the Orthodox Society, "The benefits from discussing such topics, rather than more theological/ideological ones, are tremendous. Most importantly, 'dialogue of life' allows you to get to know the others better rather than focus on the religious differences that are more difficult to agree on."[16] According to the World Council of Churches, "dialogue of life" encourages people from different religions to participate together in social activities. It is one that comes indirectly through building bridges between workers or participants in the same project or activity. The main assumption behind this type of dialogue is that working together toward a common aim eliminates the divisions between participants (Nielson 1997, 12).

Within the "dialogue of life" approach there is an emphasis on social issues related to family, education, and the social system without venturing into political issues. This is the reason why, according to one journalist and producer, dialogue does not have any direct effect on politics: "Such dialogue focuses on interaction between people as human beings—and not as belonging to a certain community or sect; it is often reflected in social work or services such as visits to elderly people's houses, to orphanages, etc."[17]

Another form of activity that aims to create more communal cohesion is the *ritual or ceremonial approach* to dialogue, which is also visible in Jordanian interfaith activities. Such dialogue does not require discussion groups, conferences, lectures or seminars. In these more unofficial types of encounters, leaders of different religious communities participate in each other's religious ceremonies or visit each other on religious holidays. These visits have not only a significant religious meaning, but social and cultural importance. Sometimes such efforts go even further, for example when a Catholic priest hosted a Ramadan Iftar (the meal to break the fast at the end of the day during the holy month of Ramadan) attended by hundreds of Muslims and Christians.[18]

However, total avoidance of political issues—especially global ones—is not always possible. Another type of interfaith work, the *unity* approach, brings Muslim and Christian participants from Jordan and the wider region together to issue a common statement or position on an international issue, such as the Palestinian question, the status of Jerusalem, the September 11 attacks, or the war in Iraq. Such statements aim to broadcast a political solidarity among the participants, regardless of their religious affiliation. Focusing on a common cause removes the discussion from the personal-individual level to the more general and thus releases the stress that can accompany interfaith encounters. However, as argued by some interfaith activists in Palestine, Lebanon, and Jordan, this type of approach, which fails to address internal differences, can generate an unhealthy avoidance of conflict.

MAJOR INTERFAITH ORGANIZATIONS IN JORDAN

Though Jordan does not lack for interfaith activities, three main organizations have been involved in interfaith issues and have dominated the field over the years. A fourth interfaith organization, the Jordanian Interfaith Coexistence Research Center, was established in June 2003 by an independent bishop, Fr. Nabil Haddad, and although it is not yet fully active, it seems to be preparing many activities. In addition to these organizations, a number of other bodies have sponsored numerous interfaith activities in the country or have hosted Jordanians in projects around the world.

The Royal Institute for Inter-Faith Studies (RIIFS) is the central institute that functioned as the hub for many international and local interfaith activities. It was established in July 1994 as a center for the study of Christian and Jewish traditions in the Arab world. RIIFS is officially recognized and is governed by a board of trustees chaired by Prince Hassan bin Talal. The prince's office funds RIIFS's activities; private donations make additional projects possible. Since its inception, RIIFS has broadened its field of academic interests from religion and religious diversity to covering other issues, such as humanities and social sciences related to cultural interactions, both in the regional and global context.

RIIFS encourages international participation in dialogue relating to religious and cultural diversity; it also encourages young Arab and other scholars to participate in its research projects regionally and locally. RIIFS brings lecturers from all over the world to discuss different topics and participate in workshops and exhibitions. The participants are intellectuals, academics, and interested elites from countries in the region. RIIFS has achieved certain academic standards and attracts leading professors from countries all over the world, who visit on their sabbaticals and contribute through their writings. RIIFS also has an Arabic program that focuses on the study and documentation of all subjects relating to Christianity and Muslim-Christian relations. In addition to its local and regional activities, it has sponsored numerous global conferences and activities on IFD.

Since 1994, RIIFS has been actively involved in organizing regional and international conferences, lectures, and workshops on a variety of issues, especially relating to different religions. In August 1995, RIIFS held its first international academic conference, "Christian Perceptions of Islam, Muslim Perceptions of Christianity: The Historical Record." The conference was attended by specialists in history and theology. Two years later, in August 1997, another international academic conference, "Muslim Arab Civilization: The Non-Muslim Dimensions," examined the significance of Christian and Jewish contributions to Muslim Arab civilization at different historical stages. In October 1998, the conference "Religion and Community: Cross-Cultural Patterns of Coexistence and Conflict in Contemporary Society" dealt with the nature and function of societies characterized by cultural pluralism in different parts of the world.

In addition to its own conferences, RIIFS cooperates with different organizations to organize meetings. An example of such coordinated work was the November 1999 Seventh World Assembly of the World Conference on Religion and Peace (WRCP), "Global Action for Common Living: The Role of Religions in the Next Millennium." The assembly, which aimed to promote and strongly establish dialogue between religions and confirm WRCP's role in promoting peace and coexistence in the world, was attended by more than a thousand political and religious leaders from religions and sects all over the world (*Al-Nashra* 1999, 4). RIIFS, along with the Jordan Institute of Diplomacy (JID) and in cooperation with the French Cultural Center in Amman, also hosted a lecture in March 2004, called "Christian Epiphany, Qur'anic Epiphany." Other conferences included "Islam and Science," organized in cooperation with the Rockefeller Foundation of New York in 2001, and "Common Dialogue between Islam and Christianity," organized in cooperation with the Swedish Church.

RIIFS is also active in the area of publications. It has an Arabic quarterly publication entitled *Al-Nashra,* which provides a forum for discussion of interfaith issues, particularly those that pertain to Arab and Islamic society. It presents topics that propagate knowledge about IFD and the role of religions in the dialogue of civilizations. It also publishes a biannual academic journal, the *Bulletin of the Royal Institute for Inter-Faith Studies,* or *BRIIFS,* in both English and French. Since its establishment in 1994, RIIFS has also published a number of books and articles on IFD and religious issues.[19]

The Aal Al-Bayt Foundation for Islamic Thought (formerly known as the Royal Academy for Islamic Civilization Research) is another important active organization in the field of IFD in Jordan. Aal Al-Bayt has a membership of one hundred Islamic scholars and clerics from countries around the world. It began its Muslim-Christian dialogue work in 1984 with the Independent Commission on Christian-Muslim Relations. This commission believes in the principles of cooperation and forgiveness and works for a world that is governed by values of love, justice, and peace (*Al-Nashra* 1999, 27). Aal al-Bayt's work is based on the belief that the objective of dialogue is to build confidence and foster mutual understanding between parties. In these dialogues, topics related to religious doctrines and ideologies are avoided, and the focus is on contemporary issues that are relevant to both Muslims and Christians in their daily lives (Aal al-Bayt Foundation 1999). The purposes of such Muslim-Christian dialogue and meetings are to look for common values between the participants from different faiths; to offer a space for people from different religions to come together and discuss issues and problems that affect everyone; to offer Muslims and Christians, especially youth, opportunities to meet and analyze these problems together; and to help in cementing the base of coexistence between the two communities (Aal al-Bayt Foundation 1999). At the basis of the foundation's work and approach is the belief that the power of religion should be used to solve problems, not to exacerbate conflict. Aal al-Bayt's members participate in such activities in their individual capacity, and not as representatives of certain communities; however, their main aim is to be able to get their message through to a larger portion of the population. One way to do that is through the media, which can play a major role in propagating the foundation's ideas.

Since its establishment, Aal al-Bayt has been a center for organizing conferences and workshops on interfaith issues. It has organized and hosted more than twenty lectures, seminars, and discussions during which working papers have been presented on topics such as faith, worship, treatment and relations of people, human rights and duties, the concept of liberty, and various social, economic, and political situations, to name a few. These topics were analyzed through different perspectives: according to their origins and backgrounds, their history and relations with the same fields in other religions as forms of comparative study, by pointing out the similarities and differences, or by correcting misconceptions and clarifying the ideologies behind the Abrahamic faiths. The foundation's work was conducted under the direct supervision of Prince Hassan bin Talal and has gradually expanded to include other religious institutes abroad.

In cooperation with the Orthodox Center of Switzerland, Aal al-Bayt organized a meeting in 1998 entitled "Muslims and Christians in Contemporary Society: The Image of the Other and the Meaning of Citizenship." The meeting was attended by seventy-five intellectuals, scholars, and youths, both Muslim and Christian, from Jordan, Switzerland, Libya, Iraq, Tunisia, Senegal, Palestine, Lebanon, Algeria, Egypt, France, Serbia, Cyprus, Greece, Bulgaria, Germany, Russia, and the United States. Discussions centered on issues of concern to people in their daily lives, issues that relate to values, and did not include religious ideologies ("The Muslim-Christian Meeting in Amman" 1998, 27). Aal al-Bayt's work expanded and included colloquia in cooperation with the Catholic Church, represented by the Pontifical Council for Interreligious Dialogue in the Vatican; the Orthodox Church; and the Evangelical Church. Each of these colloquia dealt with a clearly defined theme that presented both Christian and Muslim viewpoints. More than twenty such meetings have taken place, both inside Jordan and abroad, touching on issues such as secularism, reconciliation, pluralism, the educational system, religious education, women, rights, nationalism, human dignity, and peace (Aal al-Bayt Foundation 1999).[20]

The Jordanian Interfaith Coexistence Research Center, a nongovernmental organization, was founded in June 2003 by the efforts of Fr. Nabil Haddad, who has been actively involved in the issue of interfaith coexistence for the past sixteen years. Even though the center is portrayed as a nongovernmental organization, the Jordanian government is its foremost supporter. Fr. Haddad believes that he has a sacred duty to raise and advance the issue of coexistence and its values with his "Muslim brothers and sisters." He was motivated to establish this type of center by the words of Pope John Paul II during his visit to Jordan, when he said, "Muslims and Christians should live together." The center's board members are a diverse group of people, and they include senior religious Jordanian figures such as Sheikh Izzidin Al Khatib Al Tamimi, His Majesty King Abdullah's adviser for religious affairs, and a former Christian minister. Taking upon himself to promote the value of coexistence at the local, regional, and international level, Fr. Haddad established the Jordanian Interfaith Coexistence Research Center as a means by which he could transmit the idea in a scientific way. This was done through lectures, local campaigns, information technology, etc. With the main aim of fighting extremism and racism, the center focuses on living out one's values and the importance of religion in peacebuilding, conflict resolution, and education.[21] The center's main aim is to bring together Muslims and Christians to share and live their common values. It is an instrument by which these common values are "developed into some kind of a system that could be used to promote this coexistence and tolerance locally, regionally, and internationally."[22] The center, a civil, nongovernmental, nonecclesiastical organization, also aims to present Islam the "right way," as a religion and not as an ideology—something that became necessary after September 11. The center's primary objective is to "provide advice and assistance to governments and organizations regarding the issue of peacebuilding based on religious beliefs, the Jordanian model of peace and fraternal experience of coexistence and the new world human rights education for the purpose of creating and developing a better living environment." The center is a national initiative, not a religious one. Says Haddad,[23] "In the research, we do not talk dogma but talk about common and shared values." The reason for the center, as described by its founder, is to help present a clearer picture of the reality of coexistence between Muslims and Christians in the country and their cooperation in every aspect of life: economic, social, educational, and cultural. The center's numerous objectives include using the Jordanian model of coexistence to promote fraternity between people; conceptualizing Jordanian understandings of coexistence; solving humanitarian, social, and cultural problems and discussing them from a religious perspective; building cooperation with international organizations and institutions; and propagating respect and coexistence (Al-Dama, 2004, 17). The Jordanian Interfaith Coexistence Research Center tries to meet these objectives with a number of activities and efforts, including research, publications, conferences, and meetings.

Jordan Interfaith Action is registered as a youth organization related to IFD. It was founded in 2000 by Anas Al-Abadi and Mamoun Khuraysat, active participants in dialogue. According to this group, dialogue in the region faces many challenges due to the existing political problems and the Israeli policy in the area. However, despite the dominant view, "the group believes that religion is not the problem but rather could be the solution, or at least part of the solution, as religions call for peace."[24] The group works on dialogue among Muslims, Christians, and Jews—a sensitive and difficult task since the link between politics and religion in the area is very apparent and at times IFD swings toward politics. Jordan Interfaith Action receives funding annually from the United Religions Initiative and other sources, including the European Union.

The group has agreed upon certain principles, most important among them that IFD is not preaching. On the contrary, it calls for religious forgiveness, stating that there is no right religion and no wrong religion and that the aim is to know how each religion looks at a particular issue. Says Al-Abadi, "The question is whether it is possible for 'me' and 'you' to coexist in a peaceful way, while each one stays on his or her own religion." The aim is to get to know each other's faiths and beliefs and understand them; "interfaith dialogue is not in any way a call for a new global religion."[25] The aim of dialogue, according to Al-Abadi, is not to correct others, but to listen to the other in order to understand.

Al-Abadi says the group is conscientious about including new people in its activities. Some of these activities include Internet chat sessions between young men and women from Miami, Aqaba, and Chicago, as well as meetings and discussion sessions. It is important to note that religious dialogue as understood by this group is not really about religions; it takes place between average people and focuses on issues that are of interest to participants—issues mostly related to daily life and experiences. Despite its active involvement in interfaith dialogue, the group faces tremendous problems due to the inclusion of Jewish participants in their dialogue activities. For this reason, it tends to stay away from media attention for fear of being described as collaborating with the enemy.[26]

A social center that indirectly works in dialogue is Our Lady of Peace Center, Latin Vicariate, established for the service of Christians and Muslims with special needs. It is organized and run by the Missionary Service for Youth in collaboration with the Latin Vicariate of Jordan. The Committee for Our Lady of Peace Center was formed in 2002 by Bishop Salim Al-Sayyegh. Its main aim is to increase awareness among citizens about the rights of individuals with special needs to be treated with respect and dignity and have a decent life (Our Lady of Peace Center, Latin Vicariate, Web site). This is done through organized volunteer work, social activities, seminars, lectures, and so on. The center is divided into a section that provides basic medical services, a vocational training section, an educational and counseling section, a physiotherapy section, and an external services section. In addition to special-needs services, the center also has a pastoral and social activities section, where youth from different Christian congregations in Jordan and the Middle East come together. "The interfaith nature of the Center lies in the fact that it works in both Christian and Muslim environments; it caters to both Muslim and Christian individuals with special needs, and its volunteers, funders, and supporters also are adherents to both religions."[27] Hence, people from different communities interact and work together daily for a common cause, and they befriend and help each other. However, the difference in religion is not emphasized, as the belief is that both Muslims and Christians meet under one spiritual blanket and that God has created them equal (Our Lady of Peace Center n.d.). Through such practical work, dialogue between the two communities takes place away from ideological and abstract issues.

The General Islamic Congress for Jerusalem opened its office in 1953 following consultations among prominent scholars about the Palestinian question, the Jerusalem issue, and Muslim public affairs in general. The General Islamic Congress for Jerusalem's headquarter is in Jerusalem, with subsidiary offices in Jordan and other Arab and Muslim countries. Its basic principles include defending the Palestinian Arab cause, defending Holy Jerusalem, and establishing an Islamic fund for the defense of Jerusalem (General Islamic Congress for Jerusalem 2003, 2–3). Its main objective is to increase awareness about the Palestinian cause within global and international Muslim bodies and organizations. This is done through seminars, conferences, lectures, and other means. The subsidiary office of the General Muslim Congress for Jerusalem in Amman advances these objectives by publishing books, articles, flyers, and newsletters relating to the Palestinian question; organizing specialized conferences, cultural programs, lectures, and seminars; holding periodic and emergency meetings; publishing the magazine *Ard al-Isra;* publishing a non-periodical newsletter in Arabic and English, entitled *Nida' al-Quds;* and establishing a global body composed of local membership as well as the membership of a number of Muslim figures from around the world (General Islamic Congress for Jerusalem 2003, 3–4). The membership of the Congress is about 120 intellectuals and notables. It hosts a number of permanent projects such as local seminars on Jerusalem, educational competitions, and a mobile international exhibition. The financing of these activities is dependent upon donations from people interested in Islamic work and Muslim organizations and financial institutions (General Islamic Congress for Jerusalem 2003, 8).

The Middle East Council of Churches (MECC), the largest forum for Christians in the Middle East, has also contributed to Jordan's role as regional and global host of interfaith activities. In 1994, MECC held two four-day ecumenical conferences in Amman, Jordan, and in Cyprus to discuss the role of Christian ethics and morality in economic development. The conferences sought "to analyze the present economic situation, its causes and effects on the people of the region . . . and . . . to define the appropriate response of churches and the ecumenical movement" (Walz 1994, 70).

Another initiative supported by MECC is the Arab Working Group for Muslim-Christian Dialogue, which includes members from different countries in the region. The Arab Working Group convenes regularly to discuss an array of issues related to the goal of fortifying Christian-Muslim relations. The participants in the group are involved by their own personal conviction and do not officially represent any particular groups or communities. The discussions revolve around a process the group calls "dialogue of life," which takes place through intellectual research, shared work programs between the members of different religious communities, conferences on different issues, organizing meetings between Christian and Muslim youth in Egypt and Lebanon, and so on. The primary objective of the group is to strengthen shared living between people by emphasizing that religious differences do not contradict the unity of Arab culture. Furthermore, it stresses the importance of emphasizing national unity in the face of external interferences. Such dialogue is translated into practical programs that deal with the root causes of religious and sectarian tensions. An important objective of the group, reflected in its various activities, is to provide a unified Christian-Muslim Arab front in defense of shared Arab issues, such as the question of Palestine. According to one of the group's publications, dialogue is not an instrument of preaching and not an attempt to unify religions; it is a way to promote respect toward each other. Dialogue does not emphasize ideological debates and is not based on courtesy. An effective dialogue does not require one to relinquish anything from his or her beliefs or ideology. A dialogue, according to the group, should be one based on intellectual honesty (Arab Working Group for Muslim-Christian Dialogue 2001).

Amman is also the home of the United Nations University/International Academy, founded in 1995 and geared toward training potential leaders on issues of global concern. According to an interview conducted in February 1997 with Queen Noor, the chair of its advisory board, "the Academy [has] an interfaith component because we [are] bringing together leaders of different faiths and different cultures to identify common spiritual links as well as economic, political, social and cultural ones" (Noor 1997).

CHALLENGES AND OBSTACLES

Most of the people interviewed for this research claim that "there is nothing in Jordan that stands in the way of dialogue."[28] The president of the Orthodox Society, a participant in IFD, sees no deep-rooted challenges or obstacles to his work: "I do not remember that there were any obstacles in the face of dialogue. The political and social systems are open to the idea of dialogue and of the acceptance of the other; there is no religious or racial discrimination and Jordanians share similar culture. There are no specific obstacles [to dialogue] except that sometimes there will be an intense conflict with someone at the dialogue table."[29]

Despite these assertions by most interviewees, secondary data (publications and research) and a minority of the interviewees identified some strategic challenges to interfaith initiatives in Jordan. Chief among them is reaching a wider audience to disseminate the culture of dialogue and have a wider effect. This is the most pressing challenge facing Jordanian organizations and individuals. Even the Royal Institute for Inter-Faith Studies (RIIFS) is struggling with the issue and seeking ways to spread its materials and knowledge further. (bin Talal 2001).

This outreach problem is compounded by the typical quandary of dialogue groups: that many participants do not share what they have learned and experienced with their communities for fear of being labeled traitors. This fear, according to one organizer, has intensified the problem and difficulty of extending the reach of IFD to include more people.[30] Those who participate in dialogue are usually invited by the organization and represent only a small, targeted sector of the population. In addition to involving only a small number of participants, dialogue is also limited to a small number of conferences, symposia, academic circles, and publications, further restricting the propagation of a culture of dialogue at the grassroots level ("Together in Defending the Nation" 2002, 38). According to the bishop of the Roman Catholic Church and the founder of the Lady of Peace Center, such limited efforts do not represent true dialogue and do not advance the culture of dialogue: "Dialogue should be transferred to the grassroots level in the streets; it is important to include the masses and not limit dialogue to a group of professors and religious leaders"[31]

In terms of limits concerning substance, one writer/journalist believes that limiting dialogue to certain topics and avoiding others—such as ideological and dogmatic debates—limits the efficacy of dialogue and is done out of fear that there will be religious-ideological conflicts that will separate people. He believes that although focus should be on common values, common ground should be achieved by discussing conflictual issues and differences.[32]

An interfaith activist stated that "dialogue is something that is perpetual and continuous; it should not stop after a conference or a meeting, and should not remain constrained to the conference room and participants."[33] Yet there is no follow-up to most interfaith activities carried out by the major institutions; many have ended, as one interfaith activist puts it, "the moment the participants left the conference rooms." He believes that such obstacles could be overcome by including more people in dialogue, either through TV or radio, or even newspapers, as well as through common, shared projects between followers of different religions.[34]

The absence of structured preparation for IFD meetings also presents an obstacle. An Islamic scholar detected such fundamental limitation in interfaith meetings:

> Starting dialogue without guidelines or agreed-upon methodology might have a countereffect on the efficiency of dialogue and lead to more conflicts. The importance of having a structure does not mean that you enter into dialogue without being open to change your opinion. The structure is just to organize one's thoughts and not to limit one's capacity at going beyond what he/she originally believed. There should still be flexibility that will allow participants to make changes to the structure according to the context in which dialogue is taking place.[35]

Several interviewees dwelt upon participants' ignorance of the "other" as consuming a great deal of effort and energy during meetings. A writer in religious affairs described the dynamic: "None of the sides really understands the other; each person believes that his religion is the true one and judges people according to his religion—which becomes the measurement. This is the biggest obstacle in the way of dialogue."[36] Religious extremism was frequently cited as an obstacle to dialogue: "It is the cause behind conflicts and wars and makes it more difficult for people from different religious backgrounds to come together, respect, listen [to] and understand each other" (*Al-Nashra* 1999, 7). One TV producer and announcer accuses extremists and fundamentalists of attempting to change the reality of interfaith coexistence, so far unsuccessfully.[37] One Islamic scholar offers useful general advice on how to address these obstacles:

> What is necessary in order to overcome such obstacles is justice and time: justice is achieved by not permitting oneself to understand the other according to how one wants to understand him but to understand the other as he wants to be understood. Time is also important, as this is a lengthy process and does not happen overnight: it takes a lot of time to understand the other, his beliefs, and his behaviors deeply. [38]

In many countries, especially in the Middle East, activists describe politics as an obstacle to interfaith and peacebuilding work. Factors such as sponsorship, association with opposition, and foreign agenda are common challenges in the process and negatively impact the progress and nature of dialogue. In Jordan, according to a writer in religious affairs, it is the contrary: the political leadership is one of the most active in IFD in the world.[39] But politics affects dialogue in other ways. For example, as one Islamic scholar mentions, the political interests of the people involved in dialogue affect the dynamics of discussions and sometimes stop them.[40] On the international level, a writer in religious affairs told us that certain countries may refuse to grant visas for participants and thus block their participation in conferences and events.[41] Several of the interfaith active participants stated that tackling political issues in social, ideological, or intellectual dialogue often leads to conflict and undermines common values that exist between the communities.

According to one journalist, politicians are mostly disconnected from dialogue in the sense that it does not affect them or the course of policy.[42] However, politicians do interfere in such dialogue, directly or indirectly, by obstructing certain discussions (especially those related to inter-Jordanian relations) and types of dialogue while supporting others. A professor and interfaith activist believes, "Although we need an important party to encourage and support dialogue, we do not necessarily need a 100 percent official one that faces political issues. It is better if the party is independent and participates in interfaith dialogue in a general manner, unifies people, and brings the sides closer to each other."[43] In general, most Jordanian interviewees encourage the separation of political issues from religious conversations. "There should be separation between politics and dialogue of religions in the sense that interfaith dialogue should be a social activity and not a political one," says the bishop of the Roman Catholic Church, for example.[44] By contrast, there are a few voices of dissent who criticize the tendency of some interfaith organizers to emphasize the celebratory component of their interaction and utilize it mainly for publicity: "Dialogue most of the time is done as 'celebration,' for fame," notes the executive director of the Jordanian Interfaith Coexistence Research Center.[45]

The post–September 11 dynamics of religious polarization were identified as a source of difficulty for IFD activities, especially the perceived negative images of Arabs and Muslims in Western societies. The assistant director of Aal al-Bayt Foundation states, "Since then, differences between cultures and civilizations have been exaggerated and emphasized. People started to notice that they lack knowledge of the other."[46] Such negative images are exacerbated by issues such as the Palestinian question and the war in Iraq. These issues, according to the general director of the Department of Education at the Latin Patriarchate, present further difficulties and constant pressure on interfaith work and become a priority in such interactions.[47]

Although Jewish participation in interfaith meetings has been common in Jordan since Jordan signed a peace treaty with Israel in 1994, fear of the state security apparatus and fear of negative social repercussions make some citizens reluctant to meet with Jews or Israelis. According to an activist in the Jordan Interfaith Action group, this remains an obstacle in interfaith settings. "The participation of Israelis or Jews in dialogue presents an obstacle, as there is always doubt about their intentions," says the director of the Orthodox Society.[48] An active participant in dialogue goes further to explain that dealing with Jews is an obstacle because Jordanians and Arabs in general still do not have the necessary awareness for such interaction. One Christian organizer adds, "Most people do not feel comfortable participating in the presence of Jews and are not used to it."[49]

Lack of economic/financial resources also poses a major challenge to IFD in Jordan, especially for organizations other than the three main, government-affiliated groups. Dialogue projects require financial resources beyond those of most individuals and less influential institutions, according to a writer in religious affairs.[50] At a grassroots level, our sources suggested that sustainable funding is a major obstacle in interfaith initiatives: the lack of funding leads to shorter and, consequently, less meaningful, more superficial meetings. An Islamic scholar active in interfaith dialogue states that financial concerns usually prevent groups from organizing meetings that use a period of a few days to explore issues in depth, focusing instead on one-day meetings, which are economically feasible but tend to pack in issues one after the other with no time for deep discussions. In addition to its impact on local meetings, one interfaith participant from the Jordan Interfaith Action group states that "lack of funding limits the participation of Jordanians in international conferences, as it is difficult to provide tickets and lodging for those wishing to attend."[51]

A few interviewees expressed a contrary view, stating that despite the lack of funding, interfaith activities by their nature do not require huge amounts of resources and that small organizations can still accomplish a great deal. According to one activist, "Its [funding] absence should not be a reason for absence of such projects; it should not be considered a serious obstacle. One can prepare projects and activities that would not require a lot of money, and up to one's capacities and capabilities, and that could be as effective."[52]

As is the case with many other peace programs, few people recognize the value of IFD activities. According to a number of interviewees, many people, including scholars and religious leaders, do not believe in dialogue; some do not agree to participate in meetings when invited, others do not even respond to the invitation. However, due to the close affiliation of dialogue with the government and royal family, people rarely venture to criticize openly: "They do not attack the whole dialogue process in public," states an active participant from Aal al-Bayt Foundation.[53]

INTERFAITH SUCCESS STORIES

Measuring the success and effectiveness of IFD is a challenging task not only for Jordanian organizers, but for anyone involved in this field.[54] On a grassroots level, one participant in the Jordan Interfaith Action group believes that every meeting is a successful dialogue if it creates friendships. According to him, these are an important objective of dialogue and are measurable indicators of success: "By the mere fact that people from different communities sit together, a number of obstacles and stereotypes are overcome and broken. It is even more successful when participants from different religions become friends."[55] Similarly, one journalist and writer says, "A sign of dialogue accomplishment are these friendships that were born and created from such meetings throughout the years."[56] One Islamic scholar goes so far as to assert that any dialogue meeting or interfaith activity that takes place is respected and considered successful, whether or not it fulfills objectives beyond getting people together.[57]

The assistant director of the Aal al-Bayt Foundation conceptualizes success in terms of the extent of media coverage:

> We believe that every meeting that we have done is rather successful in achieving its objectives and I think the best success ever was when we had the chance to have real access to the mass media—for example, the extensive coverage of all activities on interfaith dialogue. This is important because people benefit from the experiences.[58]

But like others in this field, he admits to the difficulty of comprehensively evaluating interfaith work. He notes that there is no specific measure of success and that "the results or fruits of dialogue show up later and not directly."[59] One important sign is the impact that dialogue has on the community level, which is reflected in the coexistence between Muslims and Christians in Jordan and the very limited occurrence of problems or friction between religious groups. However, this argument can be reversed: Christian-Muslim relations in Jordan are not only a result of the dialogue, but "a solid base for such dialogue to take place and be that successful."[60]

Despite the statements of several interviewees, there is no evidence that proves that the low intensity of conflict and the apparent coexistence among

Christians and Muslims is attributable to the hundreds of interfaith activities carried out in Jordan, mainly by government-affiliated organizations. Other factors could explain the prevalence of the ethos of harmony among interfaith organizations and participants. First, Christians in Jordan constitute a very low percentage of the population and present no serious threat to the Muslim majority; thus the majority's leadership and elites actually encourage their presence and utilize it to reflect an international and local image of a diverse, pluralist kingdom. Second, since its inception in the 1950s, the Jordanian regime has adopted a policy of minority co-optation in which the small ethnic and religious groups—especially Circassians, Christians, and nomadic Bedouins—are rewarded for their loyalty and services by protection, placement in the military, and economic access.[61] Third, due to the privileges given to the various minority groups (especially Circassians and Christians), they develop a strong loyalty to the existing regime. These groups further benefit from the unity and harmony narrative that has been emphasized by authorities and elites through various governmental programs and policies, as well as by interfaith activities and organizations.

Whatever the merit of the various explanations, the Jordanian governmental elite and the Christian religious leadership have created a long-standing partnership and found a common voice. Both promote the message of interfaith pluralism to a degree rarely achieved in the Middle East. This message of tolerance is voiced and transmitted through most of the interfaith programs carried out by the three major organizations in Jordan. According to one Christian activist, their organizers mainly measure the success of their activities according to the opportunity that they create "for people to meet and be able to transfer knowledge to one another in order to eliminate misunderstandings."[62] He describes a successful conference that he organized in 2002, which was attended by 900 people. According to him, the conference was a success insofar as, after efforts to coordinate with different parties and sides, everyone participated: the staff officers of the Jordanian government, starting with the king; participants from all Christian sects; and participants from Syria, Lebanon, Israel, the West Bank, and Jordan.

Another success story is the Iftar banquet that a Catholic priest hosted and that was attended by a large number of Christians and Muslims. The priest finds this reassuring:

> The fact that a Catholic priest organized and hosted an Islamic Iftar to share in Muslims' Ramadan celebration, and the fact that more than 220 Muslims accepted the invitation, is a sign that there is no inherent conflict between Christians and Muslims, and that dialogue's success is reflected in the small activities and efforts that take place throughout the country.[63]

Such positive stories and thoughts on interfaith meetings are not universally held. A professor at the Jordan University does not believe that Jordanian IFD has succeeded:

All the efforts that took place so far and are still taking place have not led anywhere or produced visible positive results or changes. Dialogues do not have any impact on the social level, because they occur behind closed doors and their results don't reach the masses; they don't have an impact on the political level either, as the interests of individual politicians outweigh those of society.[64]

CHANGES AND RECOMMENDATIONS

It is obvious that successful IFD requires long-term commitment and sincerity among the organizers and participants. Most Jordanian interviewees viewed their involvement as a lifelong commitment; some even framed it as their individual, national, and human duty. One Christian active organizer and participant from the Ecumenical Studies Center told us that "Interfaith dialogue is a duty for everybody and it emerges from the belief that the human being does not live alone in the world and everyone has to be committed toward the other and towards understanding and respecting the different points of views."[65] The educational value and role of IFD was also identified as an important function in raising a generation trained in dialogue and discussion: "Education for dialogue, respect of other opinions, commitment, and honesty in dialogue are of utmost importance."[66]

For dialogue in Jordan to be more successful, participants and organizers made a few recommendations. First, a constructive dialogue between followers of the different religions should be based on the assumption of building on common values. It has been emphasized in written sources as well that dialogue should take place around these values rather than around theological issues and ideological debates (Abu Wendi 1997, 2). There should be some theological and ideological debates in which commonalities between religions are also emphasized, but this theological discussion should not take primacy over the secular social dialogue, and should be embarked upon only when participants have come to know each other and are mature parties to dialogue, in the sense of being open enough to accept each other's beliefs. Ideological and religious teachings should be taken into consideration in any IFD, but should not be the starting point or the central aim of such dialogue. The goal is not preaching or attempts by participants to convince the others of their own beliefs; dialogue is acceptance of differences. Abu Wendi (1996, 2) and Awad Ali (1997, 10) write that true dialogue is not a meeting between ideologies but interaction between people who share with one another the stories of their lives and their concerns and visions.

Second, all interviewees agreed that it is important for IFD to be characterized by honesty and openness. Knowing the other is one of the main objectives of such dialogue, and such knowledge does not take place in the absence of truthfulness, one activist states. Transparency is also an important condition for dialogue, and love, respect, honesty, and understanding are basic to success. An effective dialogue should be based on mutual respect, on equality between the participating parties, and on the acceptance of differences.

Third, participation in interfaith meetings must be expanded beyond the clergy and elites. Despite the fact that some believe that participation in IFD should be restricted to those who are equipped to conduct it properly, it is important to include the grassroots. One Christian organizer and participant holds that "whoever participates in dialogue has to be educated and cultured in religions and to have a deep understanding in his own religion."[67] But a writer in religious affairs points out that "religious education is not the only way that one can accept the different other and not try to convince him/her of the limitations of his/her religion."[68] All people who are open to differences can participate and will be able to accept the other. IFD is not only about religion. It actually is more often about other issues.

One writer agrees that dialogue should be given greater priority among a broader audience and describes his own sense that "It is important not to give up on dialogue and to participate in it whenever there is a chance, either through conferences or through writing articles and books on it; one should be as active and as patient as possible because in the long run, the results of dialogue will be clearer."[69] Dialogue should be raised from being marginal to being in the forefront. According to Nielson (1997, 11), its main aim should be to develop understanding between different religious communities in order to eliminate extremism and fundamentalism. He adds that religions should not be a source of conflict, but a means of reconciliation and forgiveness between different communities. To accomplish this result, dialogue must be comprehensive and occur at all levels and in a variety of settings: elite, academic, and in more ordinary social contexts (Nielson 1997, 12).

One strategy for increasing the profile of IFD and disseminating the practice to a wider audience is increasing media interest and involvement in the subject. Media should be mobilized and used for encouraging cooperation and respect of religious and intellectual freedom "Dialogue needs some kind of conscious advertisement for it to become more acceptable," says one participant.[70] Another activist continues,

> We need TV shows on the topic—for example a documentary to introduce interfaith dialogue, its nature, its goals and aims; to talk about common grounds between religions, values, and shared culture—to be presented in a way where more people can understand, both intellectuals and nonintellectuals, educated and noneducated. We need to have more announcements where events are taking place and make them more open to the public.[71]

Key to expansion will be reaching youth and making IFD available to people in every social strata ("Together in Defending the Nation" 2002, 38). IFD projects should be expanded to schools, media, and into every cultural domain to popularize the mentality of dialogue and understanding and to confirm the national values that Jordanians of every stripe share. The assistant director of Aal al-Bayt Foundation sees youth as most open to new ways of thinking and as important shapers of culture:

> Working with youth is especially important as they are the future generation and the basis on which the future is built. Dialogue can only be fruitful when it is uninhibited and carried out in a free atmosphere with no restrictions; it is also fruitful when and if all sectors of the society participate in it—especially youth and women.[72]

All interviewees support the view that dialogue should take place on the level of youth, because youth are more open to discussing issues together. The dialogue should deal with issues of interest to both Muslim and Christian communities, such as terrorism, abortion, and similar controversial issues. Al-Muqtabas ("Together in Defending the Nation" 2002, 39) emphasized the social qualities of youth: "Interfaith dialogue is a dialogue of living together, building together, facing challenges together, better mutual knowledge, accepting the other despite his differences, and this is something that is easier to accomplish through a younger generation."

Fourth, in terms of evaluation, there is a pressing need to systematically document the impact of interfaith activities and identify their potential. Obviously, it is important to make sure that evaluating or measuring one's success does not become the primary objective, but an instrument to facilitate more effective intervention. Some concerns regarding the difficulty of evaluating impact were voiced by a Jordanian organizer, who said, "Too much evaluation might reveal that you have not made as much progress as you think or wanted to achieve."[73] Furthermore, according to an Islamic scholar and a veteran interfaith dialogue participant, dialogue requires optimism among those who are participating: "Such optimism is the key for the continuation of such dialogue even if the results are not directly clear; one should be patient and should not give up on dialogue, as its results are not immediately noticeable. Dialogue is a long-term process and should be given the time it requires."[74]

Fifth, institutional flexibility and cooperation will prove indispensable to effective IFD. Due to the limited number of Jordanian participants who actually attend the various local and international interfaith activities, organizations should be in closer coordination and cooperation to try as much as possible to avoid redundancy in their projects, activities, and audiences. It is important to maintain diversity in organizations' coverage of discussion topics, states a participant from the Orthodox Society.[75] Planning for the future is equally strategic. There is a need to train a new and younger generation in the art of interfaith relations, and some interviewees, such as a parish priest of the Greek Orthodox community, even called for engaging new types of organizers or individuals who can excite and attract new audience:

> An important basis for the propagation of a dialogue culture is the presence of a powerful person or organization that will bring dialogue its splendor and brilliance. This will help to reinstate the organizational structures that used to work in dialogue and bring in people who are able to continue the path and replace the old crew. In addition to this, and especially if this person or organization enjoys governmental support, such projects will have more legitimacy.[76]

Governmental support is important for interfaith dialogue in Jordan, yet it is not sufficient to sustain it or spread it among the other sectors of the populace. For example, civil society groups have expressed very little interest in the subject. Several interviewees identified the importance of civil society in carrying the message in Jordan. Khalifeh wrote (2004, 8), "It should encourage political and intellectual pluralism and should not differentiate between citizens on the basis of their religions." Thus, coordination between government and civil society is also important so that they can expand the circle of dialogue.

Sixth, despite the narrative of harmony and discourse of national unity adopted by the government and interfaith organizers, it is obvious that there are certain tensions and concerns on the community level between Muslim and Christian communities and neighborhoods, fueled by a growing discourse of radical Islamism, especially after September 11. Interfaith meetings and programs can provide safe and appropriate forums to address these inter-religious concerns. The complete denial of such latent forces and dynamics in the Jordanian context can only be sustained for a short period; eventually these tensions and dynamics will surface in different manifestations, perhaps through local community disputes, polarized religious narratives, and further segregation. This latent threat emphasizes the urgency of expanding and improving the existing set of interfaith initiatives in Jordan.

CONCLUSION

Since the country's creation more than fifty years ago, there have not been any overt communal conflicts between Christians and Muslims in Jordan, except those surrounding the issue of intermarriage. The Jordanian government has done a great deal to try to eliminate religious and sectarian tensions. A significant step was the elimination of religious affiliation from the passport; however, one's religious identity remains on the family records as well as on the personal ID (Ali 1999, 78). Jordan is a country where Muslims and Christians live side by side; both are allowed to practice their religious rituals next to each other in full freedom and on the basis of mutual respect and religious tolerance (*Al-Nashra* 1999, 9). As one participant from Aal al-Bayt Foundation puts it, "Examples of plurality and coexistence are part of Jordanian daily life. Such values are supported by the government and always emphasized."[77] He further states that dialogue is not far from being a daily lived reality in Jordan: "Christians and Muslims live and talk together, sharing the same culture without legal enforcement. Therefore dialogue does not have to create coexistence, but simply to maintain it."[78] This can be done through more workshops on the grassroots level, more youth camps, and more shared social activities in which students participate. A Christian interfaith activist from the Orthodox Society reemphasizes that the results of dialogue are not immediately evident and its objectives are not easily met; however, it is important to persist.[79]

Prince Hassan reiterated Jordan's commitment to these values by stating that "we believe in diversity, which enriches the social, economic, and political process within the framework of values that contribute to the construction and stabilization of the region" ("Prince Hassan" 1990). Tolerance is in fact intrinsic to Jordanian identity, as indicated by this simple statement in the *Middle East Quarterly:* "Jordanians are part of a society with a long tradition of mutual respect" (bin Talal 2001). Jordan's reputation as a leading international and regional convener and promoter of interreligious harmony has been emphasized by the Jordanian government and media, which depict Jordan as being at the "vanguard" of dialogue that promotes "political and social pluralism" ("The House Speaker" 2004, 8).

That Jordan so proudly self-identifies as a champion of dialogue is natural given the Jordanian royal family's support and sponsorship of IFD. While this has strengthened IFD, it has also created a high level of dependency; IFD is vulnerable to shifts in the dynamics within the royal family. For example, because Prince Hassan was the main force behind most of the major IFD initiatives, the pace of interfaith activities dramatically slowed when King Hussein transferred succession from Hassan to his oldest son, Abdullah, the current king. A Christian participant in dialogue characterizes the current IFD landscape as calm. "There are no real big events and activities that are taking place because of the retreat of HRH Prince Hassan from the field."[80] One bishop concurs that IFD at the official level is at a halt and activity at other levels is also scant.[81]

Despite the fact that Jordan has distinguished itself internationally in the field of IFD, one participant feels that not enough progress has been made since the 1980s. "There is a lack of institutions that sponsor such type of work," he told us. "Those who work on this issue can be counted on the fingers and there is no media coverage of such events as well."[82] Because the field has not evolved to include the grassroots, IFD has remained behind closed doors, where academics, religious leaders, and elites talk about society's problems without including society in the discussion.

Both the sensitivity to changes in royal family politics and the slow growth of the field highlight the pressing need to expand Jordanian interfaith networks, participation, sponsorship, and organization to include nongovernmental groups. Such expansion would assist in institutionalizing the message of interfaith pluralism not only as a product of government and elite policy, but also as an internalized part of the social, cultural, and organizational fabric of Jordanian society.

7

THE NATURE AND TYPES OF INTERFAITH PEACE AND DIALOGUE EFFORTS IN THE MIDDLE EAST

A Comparative Perspective

Increased interest in interfaith dialogue is reflected in the recent upsurge of activities in Egypt, Jordan, Lebanon, Israel, and Palestine, as well as internationally. By looking closely at interfaith organizations, activists, and activities in each of these countries, our study attempted to highlight the state of dialogue, its objectives, success stories, challenges, and obstacles. Despite the peculiarities of each country and the different motivations that catalyzed IFD activities in each, common dynamics and principles are obviously the basis of this type of work. In chapter 2, we laid out a survey of the current literature on IFD, and in chapters 3 through 6 we explored the unique character of IFD in each of the countries under study. In this chapter we will synthesize the commonalities among the case studies, present a list of recommendations for improvement, and look at best practices in the IFD field in the Middle East.

The discourse of "peaceful coexistence" between people from the different Abrahamic religions has always been integral to life in the region. Daily interactions between people of different communities and religious backgrounds were always the norm.

Intentional interfaith interactions have also occurred as a part of daily life, not only as organized events. In addition, in Lebanon, Egypt, Jordan, and even in Palestine and Israel (especially among Christians and Muslims), there have always been certain religious leaders who regularly exchanged formal visits during their respective holidays, joined political rallies in opposing colonial powers, and spoke against religious and ethnic violence and hatred in times of crisis and confrontation. In fact, in each of these societies there is a deep-rooted narrative that "we always lived together peacefully, and there have been times in our history that we had very little problems or religious sectarian conflicts." This view of the past exists very clearly in the minds and collective memory of many members of these societies. Most of the interviewees made reference to such historical periods. Regardless of whether these collective memories are historically accurate or only nostalgic, they indicate the belief among interviewees that it is possible for their diverse religious groups to coexist peacefully with each other. Obviously, many of the interviewees and people will debate the causes of the current tension and its cure; however, they all agreed that once they had lived together more peacefully and cooperatively.

However, this type of interaction has recently been limited by quite a number of factors, including the emergence of political and postcolonial conflicts and violence, which have increased separation between communities. Nevertheless, despite the focus on negative and destructive interfaith interactions, we can still identify interfaith relationships across community boundaries. In fact, much of the work of interfaith peacebuilders in these societies has been to sustain existing relationships and initiate new ones toward rebuilding a closer and deeper understanding of each other's religious identity. In their pursuit of this task, these interfaith participants in these different societies have developed both unique and similar ways of conducting, framing, and evaluating their efforts. The following discussion captures the main patterns that characterize the IFD activities in each of these diverse societies in the Middle East. It is also an attempt to draw a set of lessons for future research and applications to improve and further institutionalize the work of these organizations and individuals who have made great sacrifices to promote the positive and constructive role of religion and religious actors in their society and the region.

COMMON IFD DYNAMICS AND PATTERNS IN MIDDLE EASTERN CONTEXTS

In comparing the operations of interfaith groups in these five societies, certain patterns and factors have emerged that affect the models, structure, processes, and perceptions of success. For example, the scope and nature of conflict are enormously important.

Interfaith Activities in Conflict Contexts

Lebanon, Palestine, and Israel are examples of cases where IFD takes place in a postagreement or active conflict zone. In these cases, different religious communities were or are locked in deadly violent conflict that has led to deep divisions and separations between the communities. In these societies, there is obvious competition among the various religious groups over political power. Participants in such meetings are more apprehensive and tense in their relationships. Their political differences and widely divergent views of the current reality cause most organizers to direct dialogue away from political issues to focus on "purely theological" debates and discussions or on simple social and cultural exchanges.

On the other hand, Egypt and Jordan are examples of places where conflict has not erupted as dramatically and where interfaith initiatives are not overshadowed by the memory or experience of violence. In Egypt, the conflict between Muslims and Copts surfaces occasionally through intercommunal skirmishes and attacks. Yet the government and IFD groups' discourses continue to emphasize national unity and harmony. Issues such as discriminatory policies, historical grievances, and national loyalties are mostly avoided in the interfaith conversation. Afraid of being perceived as divisive, many Christian interfaith activists frame issues in terms of cultural comparison or structure discussions around the criteria for constructive and inclusive citizenship for all Egyptians.

In the case of Jordan, relations between the different communities have not been framed as conflictual and there have not been any instances of overt violence. Thus, Jordanian interfaith participants and organizers present their case as a model for harmony and coexistence that other communities can emulate. The overwhelming majority of the interfaith workers in Jordan declared that there are no problems or tensions between Christians and Muslims in the country.

Interfaith work differs depending on whether one is working in a latent or an overt conflict context. It affects the ability to attract people from different communities who are willing to sit together in the same room and it impacts the issues discussed and the interpersonal dynamics during the meetings as well.

Improving the Religious Image

One of the most recent motivations for interfaith meetings and activities has been associated with the September 11 terrorist attacks on the United States and the aftermath of U.S. policy. As a result, a number of interfaith forums in the Middle East increased their activities to mend the image of Islam and Arabs. Such initiatives were not undertaken by Muslims alone; Christians in the region took this as their mission as well. But despite the increase in interfaith meetings, September 11 also made it more difficult for people to come together and meet, especially in an atmosphere of religious polarization in which differences between cultures were becoming increasingly emphasized.

Safe Space to Learn and Interact

In all the reviewed societies, interfaith meetings were identified as one of the rare forums to connect with people from other faith groups in a relatively safe environment. They provide a space for people to get to know and respect each other and learn about each other's religious beliefs objectively. It is through sitting together and discussing issues of common interest, as well as differences, that existing stereotypes are broken and genuine rapprochement with the other takes place—a process of utmost importance in diverse and pluralistic societies, especially when there is a high level of violence or sectarian divisions. Whether in Egypt, Lebanon, Palestine, Israel, or Jordan, there is a lack of intentional social and cultural setting for people to explicitly discuss differences or similarities. Interfaith meetings, regardless of their content and process, were simply appreciated for allowing structured and formal dialogues to take place.

Personal Conviction as Primary Motivation for Participation

What is apparent from all the case studies is that IFD in the region, especially on the grassroots level, is strongly motivated by efforts of individuals rather than well-established and institutionalized organizations or representatives of large or wider communities. Most interviewees pointed out that their involvement in IFD on this level stemmed primarily from personal conviction. All participants clearly stated that they represented themselves as individuals, not the community as a whole. The individualization of the process can be a limitation in the sense that participants can only make assertions for themselves and not on behalf of a larger group of people. As a result, there is less evidence to measure the extent to which the larger population is benefiting. Such need to reach out to wider audience of representation was especially important in the Lebanese and Israeli-Palestinian cases, where IFD was organized by the grassroots rather than by elite religious leadership and governments, as in Egypt and Jordan.

Role and Importance of Religious Clergy and Their Institutions

An important aspect of IFD in the region is the extent of involvement of religious leaders and institutions. A certain segment of both Muslim and Christian religious elites actively participate in dialogue as organizers, participants, or founders of interfaith organizations and initiatives. In Israeli-Palestinian theological dialogue, the Jewish organizers were in most cases not formally associated with Jewish religious institutions or clergy, but were individual rabbis who did not necessarily hold formal or institutional status. On the other hand, Christians and Muslims who took part in these meetings in Lebanon, Egypt, and Jordan were mostly members of religious institutions.

Middle-ranking religious leaders in these societies have a certain amount of legitimacy and are respected by their communities to varying degrees. Thus the assumption is that such meetings convened by these leaders have a greater chance of success in many cases. In Lebanon, for example, the Spiritual Summit that took place in the Maronite headquarters in Bkerke between the leaders of all sects contributed a certain degree of legitimacy and credibility to Lebanese IFD. In Egypt, when Sheikh al Azhar called for dialogue, respect for differences, and creating a committee for dialogue, the message reached more Egyptian Muslims. His stature may have influenced some to embrace the importance of such initiatives. Similarly, when Israel's chief rabbi attended and endorsed the Alexandria Declaration of Interfaith Coexistence and called for peaceful resolution, this resulted in greater media coverage—and recognition of the important role that religious leaders can play in the informal peace process.

Although the clergy's dominant role in interfaith initiatives provides legitimacy and credibility, if dialogue is primarily constructed around the clerics' role, such involvement may also reinforce the belief that they should be the only actors who provide "truth" and model the correct attitude one should have toward the religious other. In IFD, clerics are considered experts and are often relied on to provide theological knowledge in interfaith meetings. Because they occupy this place of privilege, most clerics, intentionally or unintentionally, play the role of gatekeeper. Unfortunately, this means that nominal believers and laypeople, especially women, are often not invited to forums focusing on theological issues.

Because of these considerations, several grassroots or academic/intellectual interfaith groups have deliberately avoided clergy as participants. Similarly, certain members of the clergy have restricted their interfaith group membership and discussion to "qualified" participants who can engage with the text.

Problem of Transferring a Culture of Dialogue to a Wider Audience

Our research indicated that the opportunity to participate in dialogue groups is limited to a few people or a particular stratum of the population. Those who participate are usually directly invited by organizers or are chosen in consultation with community leaders. The invitation of participants to conferences, meetings, and summer camps is not an open process. This dynamic presents a challenge in transfering the culture and benefits derived from IFD to a wider audience at the grassroots level. It is commonly believed that IFD should not be limited to a closed circle of elites—but rather transferred to a wider audience or population—but very little is done to actually accomplish this objective. In the cases of Jordan, Egypt, and Lebanon, it was obvious from the interviewees that the majority of participants in such activities are selected from middle- and upper-class people who have formed certain circles or networks.

This is a widespread and serious dilemma faced by interfaith activists in the region. One obstacle to inclusion stems from a bias organizers hold that if all the participants are at a certain intellectual level, a more balanced and meaningful discussion can take place. But there is a need to open IFD meetings beyond a small circle of people who all know each other. Many of these individuals or their organizations find themselves in competition for limited resources, or promoting one another's work through the same channels. In conducting the interviews, we noticed that interviewees repeatedly suggested the same names for additional interviews. Most interviewees admitted that there is a small interfaith community and they know each other's projects.

These closely knit webs of relationships, while positive in providing support and facilitating communication, hinder the wider development of IFD by constraining it within a small circle of people. Anyone who wants to enter the circle or introduce a new type of work or activity often faces a certain degree of resistance from the tight-knit interfaith field. Notably, despite this closeness, there is an absence of coordination among professionals in the field. There is no mailing list or database where all organizations and individuals working on IFD are listed. In Israel, several attempts have been made by various organizers to create a network for interfaith organizations, such as ICCI's effort to produce a directory of interfaith organizations and projects. Although the list includes many secular organizations that work on peace and intercultural relations, nevertheless it is an important step toward institutionalization and coordination among the interfaith initiatives in the country.

Lebanon is a prime example of the way the in-group dynamic continues to be constraining. In Lebanon, 150–200 individuals are known to be involved in dialogue and have become well acquainted with one another. Within this group, the dialogue participants are mainly limited to researchers, professors, professional and religious leaders, scholars, and intellectuals. For IFD to develop in the Lebanese context, it is crucial to find ways to open up participation to everyone interested instead of relying on those recommended by the religious leaders of each community.

The Egyptian interfaith group CEOSS struggled with this issue and has managed to accomplish some success by opening its forums to many ordinary Egyptian professionals and grassroot people when they created regional forums. In its fourth year of operation, CEOSS has reached out beyond the "usual dialogue suspects."

Limited Resources and Capabilities

The problem of funding is a very acute obstacle facing IFD in the region. It stands in the way of numerous exceptional, creative, and beneficial projects. Limits on resources and capabilities restrict the number and scope of the activities that are done. This lack of resources was emphasized by all interviewees and was blamed for the brevity, small size, and superficiality of the meetings. Instead of organizing meetings held over a period of days that would allow issues to be discussed deeply and comprehensively, financial restraints necessitate holding one-day meetings. Furthermore, the lack of funding makes it more difficult for participants from this region to travel abroad and participate in international conferences.

Even though it is essential to get funding for interfaith work, it is equally important to verify the sources of funding. This is a sensitive issue for all organizers, as donors might directly or indirectly attempt to influence and impact the process of dialogue (by choosing what type of work should be done, who should be invited, what issues should or should not be discussed, and so on). When available, government funding of interfaith activities, in all five cases, has produced the same pattern: manipulation of the agenda of IFD. Our research indicates that IFD work can be more effective in its credibility when it is funded by impartial local sources, not by governments, political parties, political tycoons, or foreign political agencies. Receiving funds from the American government was also cited as a sensitive issue for some interfaith peace workers in Egypt, Palestine, and Jordan. Information about such sources can be manipulated to delegitimize and pressure local interfaith groups or initiatives.[1]

Human resources are also limited. Most of those who work in dialogue do so on a voluntary basis. This lack further limits the continuity of dialogue, as organizers are not paid and have to make a living elsewhere. Working in IFD is thus a secondary job or priority, practiced only during one's spare time. Lack of appropriate resources to handle the demanding process of IFD has led, in most cases, to underdeveloped and underequipped organizations. This scarcity of time also constrains the professional development of the field of IFD, because organizers do not have the time to devote themselves entirely to advancing the theory or practice of dialogue in the region.

Despite the challenges posed by lack of resources, most IFD activists in the region make the best of what they have. "A lot can be accomplished with little funding" was a statement repeated by various actors in IFD. Regardless of the availability of funding, in general, religious actors who are involved in interfaith activities in these societies are persistent, highly committed individuals, willing to sacrifice their own resources and time for the sake of their ideological and religious beliefs in IFD and peace.

Problem of Cooperation and Coordination

Despite the small number of organizations and individuals involved in IFD, little effort is made to facilitate coordination or cooperation among them. On the contrary, often there is negative competition among them, especially when they reach a high level of institutionalization, as is the case in Israel. Even with an estimated 250–300 people involved in interfaith activities and organizations, there is no annual conference, professional network, or thematic or strategic coordination among the various organizers.

More regional and local cooperation and coordination is needed among IFD organizations to reduce repetition and redundancy in projects, activities, participants, and audiences. Also, coordination can increase the organizations' impact by giving them a broader reach and helping them appear as a larger and more coherent force in the process of social and political change.

Similar patterns exist at the regional level. Coordination and cooperation among interfaith organizations across societies could help consolidate their power and impact. Even basic actions, such as the creation of mailing lists, databases, and active communication between the participating centers, would be a valuable step toward institutional coordination. To this end, the United Religions Initiative (URI) has created several interfaith circles in Egypt, Lebanon, Jordan, and Israel. The regional meetings of these circles have become one of the few regional initiatives that involve all three religious traditions. Obviously, there is regional coordination within Christian denominations and sometimes between denominations (for example, the World Council of Churches), but their efforts remain confined to their own, relatively small church or group.

Importance of Youth in IFD

According to participants and organizers of IFD in our case studies, youth ought to be the first target of such activities. They are seen as the foundation of the future and perceived as more apt to offer understanding and acceptance and have greater interest in getting to know the other. It was generally recognized in the interviews and research that a bigger and more central role for youth in dialogue would strengthen the field considerably.

In Lebanon, the realization of the potential role of the youth has led to numerous activities or efforts to recruit them, such as summer or work camps in which youth from different communities live together for a time. These camps involve youth from all the countries under study and might be local (bringing together young people from different communities in the country) or regional/international (bringing together youth of different nationalities). The camps provide youth a space to meet, learn about each other's daily lives, discover the benefits of coexistence, learn the culture of the other, work together on joint developmental projects, listen to lectures on topics of interest to them, and discuss issues of concern—even controversial or political ones.

Similar patterns toward youth empowerment have been initiated in Egypt by the Coptic Church since the early 1990s. Intercultural youth meetings and forums were a primary tool for providing space for Egyptian Muslim and Christian youth to meet and learn about each other's cultural and faith identities. Involving the youth in such activities allowed the church to reach out to its community as well as engage wider audiences. However, like other interfaith meetings in Egypt, the organizers downplayed the religious and ethnic differences among the participants and insisted on framing the meeting within the narrative and discourse of national unity and harmony.

In Jordan, Israel, and Palestine, there has been less youth involvement in IFD.[2] The organizers have not yet turned their attention to youth or oriented their activities toward them. However, interviewees emphasized the importance and necessity of such action.

The Role of Government

In all of the cases under study, parts of government are directly involved in or influence IFD. The Jordanian government and royal family* representative have directed IFD efforts in the country since the 1980s. The Egyptian government offers its blessing and sponsorship to the internal ceremonial interfaith events (involving formal and government-affiliated Coptic and Muslim clergy). However, it distances itself from activities that recognize difference and have a joint Jewish, Muslim, and Christian focus or that are critique-oriented grassroots activities.

In general, politics and political leadership present an obstacle to the development and professionalization of IFD in a region where it is difficult to distinguish between IFD and politics. This negative impact emerges from the exploitation of religion for political purposes and interests. Governments have managed to co-opt the mainstream religious leadership to serve certain political ideologies or interests. Thus, when these leaders call for IFD and tolerance, they are immediately associated with the government, whose policies are often a primary cause of interreligious tensions or conflict.

An example of this arrangement was the Lebanese government's appointment of a religious dialogue and reconciliation committee in which all sectarian groups were appointed a religious representative. Similarly, when Israeli interfaith organizations refuse to take a stand against the occupation of the West Bank and Gaza or on basic human rights violations, many assume this reluctance is a result of government influence over these organizations. On the Palestinian side, many of the interfaith peace actors refuse to criticize the Palestinian Authority's internal policies and adopt the official line of the Palestinian National Authority in their political views. In Egypt, the religious leadership of Al Azhar often supports government policies regarding interfaith relations in Egypt. In addition, the Egyptian government has orchestrated an elite IFD arena and co-opted its leaders to serve the interests of the Muslim majority. There is very little critical examination of the Islamic majority's control of the narratives, including the Christian narrative, and very little effort to expand the space for internal critical examination.

In most of the interfaith processes in the five societies, political realities negatively affect the dynamics of interaction among individuals in the dialogue. Fearing that political debates might lead to conflicts between participants in the sessions, organizers avoid them and emphasize that IFD should be a social rather than a political activity. In addition, events sponsored and supported by various government offices may provide legitimate entry in certain forms of public discourse. In many cases, it is certainly safer for many participants to attend such events than those organized and funded by local or foreign NGOs. (The latter might be perceived as a forum to express opposition to government policies.)

In the case of Jordan, the government played an important role in promoting IFD. The most prominent organization, the Royal Institute for Inter-Faith Studies, was headed by Prince Hassan, the former crown prince. The prince was also directly involved with other prominent organizations working on IFD in the country and actively took part in their events. The Jordanian government is eager to highlight interfaith harmony in the country and wants to prove that Muslims and Christians are coexisting by showing that they are able to come together and discuss issues peacefully and rationally. There is a denial of any possible tension or differences in status between Christians and Muslims. It is clear that the top-down approach to IFD as reflected in the involvement of the government and the royal family has shaped the objectives tremendously. The political leadership in Jordan has proved helpful in pushing IFD to a level where it is widely accepted in the Kingdom; the active participation and sponsorship of the political leadership for this type of work gave it more public legitimacy. On the other hand, the extent of governmental control over the meetings and activities sometimes turns the involvement into a tool for religious co-option. The support of the Jordanian government might be helpful and important, but it runs the risk of creating a dependency that is vulnerable to the changes and dynamics within the royal family, thus affecting sustainability.[3]

In the case of Lebanon, the government does not directly or officially sponsor any interfaith activities or initiatives. However, at certain times, it has indirectly promoted or supported such interreligious understanding, especially by supporting the efforts of the National Committee for Christian-Muslim Dialogue, a committee that officially represents religious leaders of the different sectarian communities in the country.[4] Nonetheless, in a country where religion is politicized, all interviewees mentioned that it is better to stay away from politics and politicians, who can negatively affect the dynamics of the meetings and the interaction between participants. All interviewees in the case of Lebanon noted that they tend to avoid talking about politics as much as possible, but this proves to be difficult, as politics is directly related to the conflicts between the different communities and has a central role in the reconciliation process.

In Palestine, Egypt, and Jordan, very few activists or clergy in IFD feel safe enough to provide a solid critique of their own government and its role in IFD. (This may be true in the case of Israel, too, for only a few interviewees shared such critiques with us.) There are a variety of possible explanations for this situation, including the failure of field researchers to guarantee the safety of interviewees if they made such statements. Interviewees may not have been aware of their own government's role in perpetuating conflict, or may have a vested interest in restating and promoting the government line. However, security concerns were cited as the main reason for interviewees' hesitance to criticize the government; they voiced fears that they, as individuals, might be persecuted or that their initiatives might be banned. For example, in Lebanon, Palestine, and Israel, most interviewees were willing to participate and have their conversations recorded, whereas in Jordan and Egypt, field researchers faced greater resistance and more difficulties in getting access to interviewees.

Engaging the Media in Promoting Interfaith Work

In all of the cases, it was clear that media can play positive and negative roles in interfaith work. The media and its portrayal of the Israeli-Palestinian conflict negatively affected the dynamics and interactions among those who attended dialogue meetings. On the other hand, the Jordanian government-sponsored media's wide coverage of the interfaith events and initiatives led by Prince Hassan promoted positive images of religion as a way to reduce tension and conflict.

Media has been underutilized by the various interfaith organizers. Increased media attention could have a tremendous impact on IFD activities in the region by mobilizing and encouraging cooperation and respect for religious differences. Through shows, documentaries, and advertisements of IFD activities, a wider public could be reached. For example, increased attention to IFD emerged in Jordan after September 11, with more media coverage of IFD activities, despite the fact that such interfaith work had been taking place long before. It is through media (TV, radio, and newspapers) that dialogue might be transferred to more people and the effects of IFD meetings might reach beyond the conference rooms.

In Lebanon, sectarian media sources aired propaganda from different communities throughout the civil war.[5] Even a few years after the end of the war, the media was considered an obstacle to any prospect of interfaith rapprochement. However, in recent years, several media agencies have been promoting more diversified programming. In Israel/Palestine, the media was identified as an obstacle to interfaith work and has not been engaged in peacebuilding efforts. There is occasional newspaper coverage of interfaith activities, especially in the Israeli public media.[6]

Among the various interfaith organizations in the region, the CEOSS Intercultural Dialogue Forum is the most active in intentionally engaging formal and informal popular media in spreading the interfaith message. The organizers intentionally targeted and engaged many journalists in their various forums. One of their impressive success stories is the young imam who is hosting a weekly talk show viewed by millions. This particular imam was an active member of the Intercultural Dialogue Forum.

Difficulties in Evaluating or Measuring IFD Work

In all the case studies, there was a dilemma concerning how IFD or the interfaith field in general can be evaluated. All of those interviewed emphasized that the mere fact that dialogue occurred was itself an indicator of success. In a region where IFD is viewed suspiciously, being able to bring people together in one room to begin a process of breaking stereotypes and building friendships is a key first step toward positive change. Simply creating spaces for people to meet, interact, share knowledge with one another, and eliminate misunderstandings and stereotypes was considered a success, especially in contexts such as Lebanon, Palestine, and Israel, where segregation and division are widespread and common spaces are rare.

Surprisingly, none of the IFD organizers we interviewed possessed any system of evaluating, reporting, or systematically monitoring the impact of their work. Therefore, there were no established ways to measure these activities' effect on participants or the larger context. For example, even though interfaith organizations in Israel and Palestine have been active for almost two decades, no single evaluation report or body of research has attempted to examine their impact on the larger Israeli-Palestinian community or political processes. As in any area of conflict resolution and peace work, the nature of the intervention processes makes measuring IFD's outputs and impacts a challenging task.[7] Results of dialogue may only show up years later and in various manifestations, which may be captured only through longitudinal studies. Most IFD organizations lack the resources to carry out such studies.

Even if wide and comprehensive evaluation is not possible for many of these organizations, interviewees unanimously agreed that more systematic documentation of the impacts and potentials of IFD is possible and should be conducted in order to design more effective interventions and improve professional practices. Such documentation can be compiled from simple questionnaires or other evaluation tools at the end of every activity, to capture the participants' immediate responses.

Misperceptions of the Dialogue Process

Participants' perceptions of dialogue are also a common limitation to the advancement and progress of interfaith relations in the region. A number of participants in all five societies expressed serious concerns and a degree of cynicism regarding the real possibility of peace and the value of IFD. Some even considered it merely deceit or trickery, with no real results and benefits—"dialogue as only ink on paper," that is, just conversation that has no practical applicability on the ground. Also, some interviewees viewed dialogue activities as a tool used by certain active members to advance their own interests and power positions in the communities, rather than as a forum for building trust and sorting out differences. For example, one interfaith veteran in Israel/Palestine expressed that her motive for participation in an interfaith meeting was to gain credibility and public recognition in order to be elected to an official position.

On another level, participants in many IFD meetings were motivated by the need to defend their religion and faith; the dialogue space for them was mainly a forum to assert a positive image and remove negative perceptions of their faith among others. Attending dialogue in this sort of defensive mode may be counterproductive to learning and internalizing new information about the other. In fact, such an attitude might increase the rigidity of each side or move participants to focus mainly on similarities or only on positive images of their own religion.

Dialogue processes were viewed by certain participants and organizers as a mechanism to convey national harmony and unity among the participants, especially in the Egyptian and Jordanian contexts. Such emphasis on this type of dialogue process reduces its credibility and legitimacy as a viable alternative for dealing with conflict issues and intercommunal differences.

Professional Planning and Awareness of Systematic Intervention

The absence of ongoing structures and preparation for IFD activities constitutes an obstacle to effective IFD. Many interviewees (mainly in Palestine, Israel, Lebanon, and Egypt) described adding new members to their groups and sustaining activities over time as being difficult. Participants tend to leave the groups and activities after a few meetings. These conditions force organizers to accept newcomers without much preparation or proper criteria for selection.

The absence of professional facilitation in the interfaith initiatives was a common limitation in all the cases. Most organizers and directors involved in IFD in the region are intellectuals, scholars, or religious leaders who have no direct or formal training in conflict resolution, peace studies, or interfaith relations. Very few of them have been professionally trained for such work.

Professional expertise is needed to enhance the role of activists in grassroots peacemaking and the impact of interfaith activities locally and regionally.

None of the interviewees, when asked about the models used in their IFD initiatives, were able to describe any specific model applied, or even reference any of the theoretical assumptions underlying their interventions. The most common answer was that interfaith activities are conducted on a needs basis: that the way to approach dialogue depends on what the group wants at that particular time and place, as well as on the availability of resources.

Interviewees in all the cases were not familiar with the range of IFD models that could be used in their activities. Although we could apply some of the existing theory in the literature to the work that was being done, it was clear that the organizers themselves were not aware of the literature. Most interviewees asserted that there is flexibility in selecting processes and approaches, according to the participants and context. Some interviewees argued that IFD does not have any structure or directive rules or models; it is an open arena where the participants can come with an open heart and mind to discuss anything, without being constrained by a method or structure. Although interviewees in general were not aware of the explicit or implicit theoretical assumptions driving their interfaith programs, different models emerged as interviewees expressed their perceptions and described their activities.

MODELS OF IFD: PROCESS AND CONTENT

We found that in general IFD groups and their leaders had little knowledge or familiarity with various interfaith model and had difficulties articulating a clear theoretical rationale for their approach, especially when asked, "Why does your method work?" Most groups exhibited a mix of patterns and appeared to be drawing on several—and in some cases contradictory—principles or models.

However, when examined, most interfaith dialogues tended to be a mix of cognitive and affective, with the cognitive being more prevalent. Also, most interviewees tended to operate from a "minimization" mode or perspective, which avoids or minimizes religious differences. Such a perspective explains the wide acceptance of the IFD social and political functions in the region—reflected in the national unity model and the harmony model.

Another common feature to the case studies (except Israel), especially on the grassroots level, was the strong presence of sociocultural and political themes and processes (as would be found in any secular dialogue agenda), as opposed to a "pure" theological or religious dialogue. Interviewees believed that embarking on a theological or religious dialogue before participants know each other is dangerous and prevents open and mature dialogue. In addition, they believed that theological debates and explorations of the different faith groups can bring further divisions and misunderstanding, especially since laypersons are not qualified to discuss or explain theological matters. For interactions among clergy or intellectuals, the emphasis was on the theological issues, especially on the similarities and connectedness among the various faith groups in the dialogue. For example, such a rationale prompted certain Egyptian interfaith groups to formally decide to avoid all theological conversation and focus solely on current issues and concerns for Egyptian Christians and Muslims.

Prevalence of Intellectual/Cognitive and Informational Models of Dialogue

A common aspect of IFD in the region is the prevalence of intellectual, theological dialogue activities in the form of meetings, conferences, symposia, and lectures. The dominant style of dialogue is the information-based approach, which relates to a cognitive model that assumes that change occurs through learning and understanding the other and his or her religion. This model also assumes that misinformation and lack of information about the other religions (values, rituals, and symbols) are significant causes of conflict and interreligious tension.

Despite their advantages in terms of bringing about change in individual perceptions and knowledge, informational or cognitive models could be limited in that they exclude anyone who is not interested in these intellectual, academic, and "study circle" types of activities. This intellectual informational approach is reflected in the elite-level meetings and conferences that take place in Jordan and Israel, and in the proliferation of academic sessions/programs and conferences in Lebanon as well. The intellectual approach is also central in several Egyptian interfaith meetings organized by CEOSS and the Coptic Orthodox Chruch.

The intellectual/informational model of dialogue, which in most cases focuses on theological comparison, is also evident in the publication of books and articles on the topic of Christian-Muslim relations and IFD. A common practice, especially in Lebanon, is to publish the proceedings of interfaith meetings, like those that take place at the Saint Joseph University and the University of Balamand. This model assumes that publishing discussions among a few people will propagate a culture of dialogue to a wider audience outside the meeting room's doors. Similar assumptions are made by the Jordanian royal institutes, which host several high-level, prestigious international conferences to highlight the positive and constructive role of religion in dealing with conflicts around the globe. In Egypt, one interfaith project produced more than thirty books and monographs on a diverse set of social and theological issues. In none of these cases was there evidence of wide dissemination or impact of these publications beyond the small number of people who were involved in the discussion.

Thus, despite the immediate positive aspects of these publications for the discussion groups, they are limited to literate and intellectual audiences and do not reach most people at the grassroots level. A major limitation of this approach is the lack of organic linkages between these efforts and their wider audience. The publication of new materials and academic exploration of interfaith relations as a primary strategy for producing and promoting change was often cited as ineffective or limited in reaching the grassroots. The scope of this form of dialogue is limited to elite academic and theological circles. Thus, the nature and content of IFD in the region, especially in Lebanon, Jordan, and Egypt, inevitably have led in many forums to elite dominance.

Interfaith through the National Unity Model

One model that we had not captured in the literature review emerged quite prominently in our case studies: the national unity model. In Jordan, Egypt, and Lebanon, and between Muslim and Christian Palestinians, the underlying assumption behind dialogue had to do with emphasizing national unity. The participants' shared citizenship and loyalty to the same national group functioned as a sacred value, to which participants and organizers defaulted whenever there were major internal differences or intense debates.

Most important, the unity model emerged as a tool by which citizens of one country or collective emphasized their common stance on an external issue (such as the September 11 attack on the United States or the Israeli occupation of Palestine). Thus, displaying national unity became the first priority for participants in IFD meetings, especially when they were asked to present their group to outsiders.

This strategy or discourse of national unity has been adopted as a central approach to IFD among Christians and Muslims in the Middle East. The overemphasis on facing external threats has largely contributed to the delegitimization of an interfaith process that explores differences and conflict issues. Participants (in many cases from minority as well as majority religious groups) agreed that due to their shared national destiny and history, their current and future relationships ought to be explored without any emphasis on differences or conflicts.

This approach is especially true in the case of the Coptic and Muslim interfaith groups, which always praised their shared national identity and emphasized the prominent role that Copts played in the national liberation movement of Egypt from the British colonial powers. The unity imperative also provides a safety net, within which members of religious minority groups are able to articulate their views and critiques. For example, in Egypt a great deal of interfaith work has been done through the "one citizenship" narrative, thus downplaying existing cultural and religious differences.[8]

In the Palestinian case, Christian and Muslim interfaith groups and programs highlighted their mutual duty to the national liberation agenda of opposing Israeli occupation. The sense of shared victimhood was very strong among both Christians and Muslims. Some interviewees did not even see the need to explore differences or problems among the two groups until after the Israeli occupation ends. In fact, some have argued that one of the Israeli occupation policies is to stir division between Muslims and Christians as a part of the "divide and rule" strategy historically used by colonial forces.

In Jordan, this unified approach led to numerous common statements of positions on issues such as the Palestinian question, Jerusalem, September 11, and the Iraq war. A common position is promoted in facing difficult issues that might impact internal solidarity and stability. By showing solidarity between Jordanians and Arabs from different religious affiliations, internal differences that might lead to conflict are avoided. The focus on common causes releases the stress that some people might feel about participating in such meetings, as it moves the discussion to a more general level, away from a personal individual focus, which might make participants feel more personally exposed.

Emphasizing national unity also appears prominently in interfaith work in Lebanon. Discussions about local internal conflicts and differences are put aside, and the focus is mainly on the solidarity and unity between Muslims and Christians in the country, on the importance of coexistence and shared values. The common positions on any problem are assertively promoted abroad to show the world how similar Lebanese are and that there are no real conflicts between Christians and Muslims in the country.

In short, shared national identity is often utilized as a rallying point and manipulated to prevent exploration of internal problems and differences. Such an approach highlights unity in the face of external interference and provides a unified front on shared Arab, regional, and international issues.

The Harmony Model

An important trend in all the cases is the avoidance of discussion of differences through emphasis on similarities—the harmony model of IFD. We observed the majority of interviewees operating in the minimization mode identified in chapter 2. This minimization mode was expanded into a philosophy that tacitly seemed to guide the entire dialogue. Even though the majority of organizers recognize religious differences, they tend to deemphasize them in their activities. The goal of most of these initiatives is to highlight the commonalities among participants, usually by invoking national and religious unity and claiming, "We all worship the same God," or "We are all children of God." This approach, in short, assumes that emphasis on theological similarities and commonalities—sharing religious practices, ceremonies, and rituals —and building individual personal and social friendships are priorities for dialogue. The assumption is that seeking unity (national or theological) will provide different groups with a degree of cohesiveness.

Interfaith meetings often include ritualistic and ceremonial content to support the harmony model. This content usually takes the form of symbolic presentations of unity and diversity in the ways that different faith groups pray or worship, which allows participants to focus on similarities and harmony among themselves. The rituals can contribute to the creation of more communal cohesion. Often this format does not require discussion groups, meetings, or conferences, but is a more informal or unofficial type of encounter in which religious leaders participate in each other's religious ceremonies and visit each other during religious holidays.

In Jordan, an example of ritual as a form of dialogue is the Ramadan Iftar, attended by Muslims and Christians and hosted by Christian clergy. In addition, religious leaders participate in each other's religious celebrations, and people also help each other organize religious festivities and events. This form of interfaith meeting occurs frequently in countries where Christians and Muslims coexist in villages and small communities. In the case of Israel, an interfaith organization led by Yehuda Mclean utilized the *sulha* ritual as its main forum for convening Muslims, Christians, Druze, and Jews. This activity served both the ritual and the reconciliation purposes of dialogue outlined in chapter 1. *Sulha* involved a series of rituals, ceremonies, and cultural exchanges to facilitate peaceful interaction and promote the possibility of coexistence and reconciliation, especially among Arabs and Jews.[9]

Conflict and Diversity

Different from the harmony model is the conflict and diversity model, which assumes that religious/theological differences are as important as the similarities and need to be highlighted rather than ignored. This approach stems from the belief that dealing with differences will lead to more open, honest conversation and deeper understanding among participants, and that focusing exclusively on similarities and avoiding discussion of differences risks preserving existing power relations. As described in chapter 2, the participants in these dialogues tend to operate in the acceptance and adaptation modes of dealing with religious difference.

In the five interfaith settings, a small minority of participants and organizers stressed the need for an adequate level of awareness of religious difference, stating that this can help prevent the manipulation of religious beliefs to incite violence, hatred, or exclusiveness among the followers of different faiths. They provided many examples wherein religious leaders and participants who attended interfaith dialogue did not participate in urban or rural sectarian riots or violence. On the contrary, they acted as a buffer zone to separate perpetrators or stop the violence. Recent cases include Egyptian interfaith groups in Alexandria that intervened and mediated to stop the violence that erupted there. In another example, Lebanese religious leaders who were involved in interfaith forums were among the first to condemn sectarian violence. In Israel/Palestine, interfaith participants and leaders were among the first voices to call for *hudna* (ceasefire) between Hamas and the Israeli government.

According to such assumptions, these agreed-upon actions to stop violence are more likely to be reached by discussing and understanding conflictual issues and differences. Avoiding such discussion leads to structural limitations in the interfaith meetings and a diminishing efficiency of dialogue. There have been only a few attempts to operate or conduct interfaith meetings based on this model. For example, in Israel, ICCI initiated a project in which participants traveled to Northern Ireland and conducted a series of interfaith meetings focusing on their differences.[10]

Advocacy and Liberation Interfaith Approach

The advocacy and nonviolent resistance approach is based on a model of social action and liberation theology that assumes that understanding the structural violence perpetuated by political and religious institutions is key to creating peace and justice, and that such violence should be confronted through nonviolent actions and concrete resistance. Religious leaders in Latin America have led many resistance movements based on their interpretation of Christianity. Similarly, Quakers and Mennonites have adopted a unique role in promoting freedom and peacebuilding based on their interpretation of Christ's message. These religious groups have brought various faith groups to work together on actions to oppose injustice and oppression. Interfaith meetings based on such theology promote dialogue through action for social justice. Very few groups in the region were familiar with such practices. Only two organizations in Israel and Palestine (both unireligious organizations), Sabeel Center and Rabbis for Human Rights, were explicitly advocating such an approach to interfaith and intrafaith work.

Nonviolent resistance often requires the creation of a new religious consciousness that not only tolerates other religions but is not susceptible to the manipulation of religious identity for the purpose of escalating conflict dynamics. But in addition, it ventures into the process of exploration, recognition, even experience of the other's meaning system, and results in a commitment to stand and act against injustice. Such a level of awareness is essential for engagement in joint or separate religiously framed political actions. For these activists, "Dialogue is not enough!" (Abu-Nimer 1999). According to this model, interreligious dialogue as an end in itself is a framework that can contribute to the perpetuation of power imbalance and status quo. This notion was effectively expressed by a Palestinian participant in a women's interreligious dialogue group:

> Though some of the Muslim and Christian Arab women said they participate simply to know other religions and have others know their religion, a couple expressed disappointment that the group is not open to political discussion or action. They raised such subjects as roadblocks and military occupation, and dismay that their Jewish friends do not protest with them against injustices. On the flip side, a few of the Jewish women complained they feel pressured by the more political members of the group who try to change the agenda toward politics, and also by the sense that such suggestions only focus on what Jews, not Palestinians, should do differently.[11]

All the interfaith organizations in Israel/Palestine, Lebanon, Egypt, and Jordan are aimed at bringing some degree of religiorelative awareness to their participants. However, beyond this mere acceptance of differences and yet without becoming religiorelativists in their faith orientation, there is still possible space and potential for active peace and solidarity work.

For example, in Israel, a group that has conducted many peace activities and that has translated IFD into action is Rabbis for Human Rights (RHR). This grassroots organization was founded in 1988 "in response to serious abuses of human rights by the Israeli military authorities in the suppression of the Intifada. The indifference of much of the country's religious leadership and religiously identified citizenry to the suffering of innocent people seen as the enemy was a cause of concern to Rabbis for Human Rights organizers."[12] RHR is a small group of rabbis (ninety in all) from different streams of Judaism: orthodox, reformist, conservative, and constructionist. It is probably one of the most politically active religious peace groups in Israel. RHR operates from a Jewish moral standard that "every human being is created in the divine image." Its members are Israeli citizens with no affiliation with any political ideology or party. They are involved in ecumenical dialogue and educational activities, in addition to dealing with violations of the human rights of Israeli Arabs and West Bank Palestinians.

This group is not aimed at resolving or even exploring theological differences among Judaism, Christianity, and Islam, nor is it focused on the typical issues that other rabbis in Israel debate or address (such as kosher dietary laws, religious education, or Sabbath observance). As a unireligious group for action and solidarity, it emphasizes Jewish religious opposition to the occupation. Its uniqueness (in comparison to other interfaith or faith-based peace groups) is that its agenda includes solidarity actions with underrepresented groups and against injustice. Its members have protested Palestinian home demolition by Israeli authorities, opposed and challenged the siege of Palestinian villages for months and tried to penetrate these curfews, supported Jahhalin Bedouins uprooted from their traditional grazing land, lobbied for the rights of foreign workers, protested against government policy and its impact on poor communities, and undertaken hospital visits to be with the injured on both sides—a move that no other group in Israel/Palestine has taken. An active member of the group compares his RHR work with other interreligious peacework:[13]

> When I was young and participated in interreligious encounters, I was very optimistic, but now when I am older and more veteran in this field, I do not go to encounters with such high expectations. My work is more on human rights work. I bring volunteers and activists to Bedouin communities. The situation is very difficult and I bring people to see the reality and show them the picture to realize that they can and need to do something. That encounter is not made for the Bedouin or the Jewish visitors to know the family and the personal life of the Jew who comes, but to enter and leave with more realization of the situation.

One of the major political activities that RHR has taken is solidarity and action to protect Palestinian farmers during the olive harvest. As a form of collective punishment, the Israeli government often prohibited farmers from gathering their harvest. Some Jewish settlers also destroyed such harvests or actually uprooted trees and sold them in Israel. However, the most confrontational solidarity work that RHR has done is their challenge to the Israeli army's cutting off of entire villages with huge trenches and boulders. Rabbi Arik W. Ascherman describes the decision to challenge that immoral policy of collective punishment:

> I asked myself, what can I do so that if, one day, my infant daughter asks me what I did in these terrible times, I could answer her without shame. RHR decided to move from protest to nonviolent resistance, removing mounds of earth and filling in ditches near Palestinian villages, like Rantis. I was arrested close to ten times, interrogated but never jailed. But the army grew harsher in clamping down on dissidents, and our Palestinian partners were getting injured, so we decided to curtail these activities so as not to injure them. People called us "radicals," but most of us felt like middle-of-the-road citizens who were simply taking our religious values to their logical conclusion (Landau 2003, 22).

Sabeel Center in Palestine, too, has launched many educational and advocacy programs framed on liberation theology. Its actions have been characterized as "speaking truth to the powers." Although its interfaith initiatives have attracted Israeli and American Jews who are often considered outside the national Jewish consensus, it has nevertheless emerged as one of the few religious organizations to survive the various political crises. Many interfaith initiatives disappear with the eruption of violence or during wartime. Moreover, through its conferences, Sabeel has been able to provide space for Muslim, Christian, and Jewish scholars to explore their theological and political differences. It does not shy away from political controversies, either.

The above examples illustrate certain possibilities and potentials for interfaith peacebuilding activities in a Middle Eastern context. However, it is obvious that there are serious risks and costs that religious peace actors in such societies must consider before engaging in this type of nonviolent resistance. These calculations should be considered only by the local actors in each context. Nevertheless, religious peace activism is certainly a tool that might be explored by more interfaith groups in the Middle East.

Between Theological Dialogue and a Dialogue of Life

When theology was addressed in interfaith activities in the region, it was mostly indirectly—not through a discussion, but rather through panels conducted by intellectuals, scholars, or religious leaders with the aim of teaching participants about the different faiths and describing the different interpretations of theological concepts (such as the roots of Abraham, the meaning of jihad, or the comparative status of Mary in Islam and Christianity). Many Israeli-Palestinian groups, as well as those in Lebanon and Egypt, emphasize lectures by experts in their IFD approach. This reliance on experts and clergy limits change in attitudes, critical thinking, and new explorations of religious belief. It inherently disempowers the participants.

In all the cases, we observed religious leaders acting as gatekeepers, guarding the right to religious interpretation. Muslim imams and clergy discourage their followers from engaging in theological dialogues, as do Christian clergy. Several clergy interviewed emphasized the need to confine the theological dialogue to experts and exclude laypeople. One must ask how a layperson can be considered capable of working for peace if he or she is not considered competent to discuss the theology and interpretations of his or her own religion.

In Jordan, the primary modes of IFD were intellectual, with elite panel presentations and international conferences focusing on theological responses to issues of war, peace, and violence. Theological questions were central to these meetings, especially those hosted or sponsored by the royal families. Similarly, in Egypt, when Al Azhar and the Coptic Church convened interfaith events, the emphasis was on theological interpretations for peace and pluralism.

In Israel, several interfaith seminars were carried out by both academic research institutes and NGOs (namely, Truman, Herman, PASSIA, and ICCI). They focused on exploring theological differences among the three religious traditions with regard to a wide range of issues such as the status of women, war, jihad, and the status of the other. In fact, this form of interfaith theological exchange was dominant in many organizations in Israel until a decade ago, when new interfaith initiatives began working more on a grassroots level and less on academic or intellectual and theological levels (as in Yehuda Stolov's organization, for example).

The "dialogue of life" approach, by contrast, is one in which daily life issues occupy the center stage of the interfaith conversation. This is an affective model of dialogue in which every participant is an expert of his or her own life. In a dialogue of life, dogmatic and theological questions are avoided, but people are encouraged to think in terms of coexistence. Participants attend interfaith forums motivated by their faith, or operate from a faith-based identity, yet are primarily interested in exploring concrete social and political issues that relate to their daily concerns. Many participants in IFD in the five settings expressed interest in focusing more on issues of daily concern, such as the rights and duties of citizens, citizenship, democracy, and economy. Even though participants are chosen according to their religious background, their religious identity in these settings is downplayed and becomes a secondary factor in the conversation. This is sometimes reflected in the dynamics of the interaction, where the minority-majority dynamic emerges. In dialogues in Egypt, the Copts became more aware of their status as a minority when the Muslims adopted a majority attitude.

The organizers of this type of IFD claim that people get to know each other better by focusing on issues that are of relevance to all of them, rather than on theological issues that highlight religious differences, which are often the specialty of clergy. Similarly, in Palestine and Israel, there was a strong interest in IFD that focused on daily life issues and on a simple exploration of religious and cultural rituals and teachings. The dialogue of life approach is evident in Lebanon, where sectarian identity affects individual interactions and group dynamics at every level. In Jordan, too, at least one organizer emphasized the importance of addressing daily life issues, as opposed to focusing on theological issues.

Obviously, the above list of patterns is not a comprehensive or exhaustive treatment of interfaith dialogue work in these five societies. Much research and systematic analysis are needed to further the effectiveness and performance of the interfaith groups. Nevertheless, this discussion clearly points to an emerging field of practice in societies that are greatly in need of public and private efforts to explore the possible constructive role of religious identities and narratives in the ongoing processes of social and political change.

THE INTERFAITH PEACEBUILDING FIELD IN THE MIDDLE EAST: AN EMERGING AREA OF PRACTICE

In the five societies examined, it is clear that the interfaith field can play a role in promoting religious diversity and pluralism. However, organizers of such activities still face the difficulties and challenges typical of an emerging field. Among the most noticeable challenges are scarcity of the following:

- Clarity regarding the models or assumptions underlying interfaith work
- Critical evaluation of the activities, goals, and achievements of interfaith groups
- Professional and systematic planning for intervention
- Clear objectives and monitoring mechanisms of impact and effect
- Trained facilitators or trainers specialized in leading IFD groups
- Documentation and material to guide these groups and capture their work

Another problem concerns the continued control and manipulation of the organizations' approaches, perspectives, and activities by governments or political ideologies. Challenges specific to intense conflict zones like Lebanon and Palestine include the following:

- The civil war and post–civil war situation
- Traumas incurred as a result of ongoing conflict dynamics
- Massacres and violence
- Historical segregation and the limited spaces for interaction
- Basic ignorance of the other's tradition and culture

In most of the settings, interfaith work is isolated and its impact is confined to the micro level. Most of the activities involve a select group of individuals and lack systematic linkages to existing social and political movements operating in the same setting. For example, interfaith meetings in Lebanon are often conducted without coordination of the various political and social movements in Lebanon that work for greater tolerance through different venues and methodologies. The same problem exists in Israel/Palestine; interfaith initiatives operate independently of the hundreds of NGOs working there to improve Arab-Jewish relations. (In fact, there is a network of 250 organization funded by the Abraham Fund to coordinate the activities of these organizations.) Many members were not informed of activities in this field, and the organizers rarely manage to link their efforts with larger peacebuilding initiatives in the country.

Expanding IFD beyond closed-door forums (as in Lebanon, Egypt, or Jordan) to reach a wider audience of youth, women, and the public in general is a necessary step toward strengthening the role of interfaith peacebuilding, and thus achieving peaceful outcomes in the region. There needs to be a shift from elite-based to grassroots dialogue, and from a top-down dialogue that discusses theological issues to one that builds strong relationships between people and allows them to continue their interactions after the formal dialogue is over.

Success in IFD is modestly limited to the changes experienced by participants. In general, the impact of the dialogue initiatives in the region is mostly evident in the changes that take place within individuals' attitudes and perceptions. The criterion for success in most of these activities is for people to get to know and accept each other. When this measure is met and a basic subculture of trust, respect, and friendship is built, it might, in turn, lead to political and institutional change. The hope is that participants' new attitudes might then be conveyed through their interactions to the society as a whole.

But it is extremely difficult, and perhaps even impossible, to detect the impact of IFD at the macro level, in part due to the many other factors that affect interreligious relations. The impact IFD is having on the larger political level is not yet clear. In fact, many of these interfaith organizations avoid making any explicit references to any desire for political change, as such claims might constitute a high security risk for participants (especially in Jordan, Lebanon, and Egypt). In response to this criticism, IFD workers argue that macro-level changes have not taken place yet, because of the long years of violence and isolation.

IFD initiatives in these five societies have increased significantly throughout the last decade. However, such organizations are still extremely small, as is demonstrated by all our case studies. The proliferation of IFD activities in the region indicates a higher level of awareness of the need for religious peacebuilding. However, it is of utmost importance to sustain these activities and maintain professional standards to strengthen their impact and overcome the negative image of IFD as being about vacationing in hotels and traveling abroad. IFD needs to continue beyond the meeting halls; dialogue does not end once the participants leave the conference rooms. A follow-up mechanism is especially important and is missing in all these organizations.

There is a dearth of experts in Christian-Muslims relations and IFD in general, which can be traced to the limited enrollment in IFD educational programs. This, in turn, is due to the lack of job opportunities or future careers for those who major in these studies. Supporting interfaith projects in many sectors of civil society, instead of expecting smaller and less experienced interfaith organizations to carry the load, would be an important step toward strengthening the interfaith field. Religious peacebuilding is perhaps too important a process to be isolated or confined to the domain of faith-based organizations or individuals.

Finally, examining the state of the interfaith field in the region makes apparent the need for further clarity on the nature and type of processes that interfaith intervention can use to bring about change on attitudinal and social levels. Few of the interfaith organizers and participants were aware of the rationale for their intervention strategies and the phases in which change occurs among their participants.

Conclusion

Secular as well as religious people of all faiths have contributed in differing degrees to the manipulation of religion to fuel conflicts in the Middle East. Nevertheless, in the last decade, followers of the Abrahamic traditions in Israel/Palestine, Egypt, Jordan, and Lebanon have attempted to introduce religious beliefs and rituals as a positive and peaceful force.

There is a growing number of interreligious organizations and initiatives in these five societies. The majority of these organizations are still operating within a harmony and unity paradigm, and they are often isolated from wider political and social change movements. Anecdotal illustrations show that their impact tends to be confined to accomplishing attitudinal change at the individual level, raising the awareness of a small group of religiocentric individuals who become religiorelative, and hoping that their individual influence on the broader social collective will transmit this awareness to the general public on both sides. They contribute at least marginally to spreading a consciousness of tolerance and acceptance of religious differences, and confirm the notion that religion can be a source of peace instead of war and violence.

Focusing on dialogue and interreligious understanding is necessary for creating a culture of peace in divided societies. However, addressing gross injustices requires specific mechanisms and a different type of interreligious peacebuilding. When examining the impact of religious leaders on peace, it becomes clear that the religious nonviolent resistance teachings, movements, and leaders were highly effective in gaining moral authority for their causes of liberation, especially in violent contexts. Historically, figures like Martin Luther King Jr., Mahatma Gandhi, Abdul Ghaffar Khan, the Dalai Lama, Oscar Romero, and Desmond Tutu illustrate the crucial role that religious leaders can play in raising the profile of the justice discourse in the midst of oppression and violence. The Middle East is in need of a nonviolent religious resistance movement, one that is informed by Christian liberation theology and Judaic and Islamic teachings on nonviolence and justice. Such a movement might politically and religiously counter the effect of the militant religious groups that easily manipulate their faith groups and justify religiously based violence.

However, many of the interfaith organizations and initiatives in the region are still in the intitial stages of formation. The levels of professional development and performance vary from one country to the next. Supporting this development is essential to forming a reliable and influential field. Following are some of the areas in which further support of religious peacemaking is much needed.

First, the organization of a regional network through which interreligious peace organizations could exchange experiences and increase their level of coordination should be a priority. The network could provide technical support and host an annual meeting to share lessons from around the world.

Second, professional training for staff and directors of these organizations would build their capacities in the field of peacebuilding and conflict resolution and, most important, in the art of group facilitation.

Third, strategic and systematic linkages between these organizations and the existing local and regional social and political networks for change should be developed. For example, IFD should network with fields like human rights advocacy, democracy reform, and the peace movements.

Fourth, to expand the outreach of such organizations to a wider audience, new methods for accessing the general public through different forms of mass media should be explored.

Fifth, activities that include youth and younger generations in these efforts should be increased. Few youth interfaith programs exist in the Middle East. Expanding interfaith and peace into schools and informal education may provide a rare opportunity for peace workers to influence young people's perceptions of the role of religion.

Finally, it is obvious that researchers and evaluators need to provide concrete examples and illustrations of the contribution that the interfaith field in those five societies has made. Yet, the heroic day-to-day initiatives and actions that are carried out by the interfaith organizers and participants cannot be captured by statistics alone. The stories and personal sacrifices made by such people are the true reflection of the nature and contribution of the interfaith field in these societies. This study was a sincere attempt to capture some of the stories told by these peacemakers.

NOTES

2. IFD: Basic Concepts and Approaches

1. Track Two diplomacy is a term used by Joe Montville and John McDonald in their efforts to conceptualize the field of peace and conflict resolution and its various contributions to the formal peace process, which is often referred to as Track One diplomacy (see Diamond and McDonald 1996).

2. Studies have repeatedly shown that during the four centuries of the Ottoman Empire (1490–1916), different political and religious leaders utilized religious values and practices both to facilitate peaceful relations and to manipulate people to fight each other based on religious affiliation. The "millet system" supported a certain degree of religious tolerance by allowing different faith groups to administer their own religious affairs. Yet, the same system provided Muslims with dominant status in the empire. The massacre of Armenian Christians in Turkey is another example in which religion was used to politically manipulate various ethnic groups.

3. Abrahamic Discussion Group, 2003.

4. An earlier version of this article by Mohammed Abu-Nimer has been published in "Religion, Dialogue, and Nonviolent Actions in Israeli-Palestinian Conflict," *International Journal of Politics, Culture and Society* 17, no. 3 (Spring 2004).

5. It should be noted that the DMIS worldview stages described represent a modification of the original formulation of DMIS as developed by Bennett (1993) and are derived from findings presented in Hammer, Bennett, and Wiseman (2003).

6. The proposed model of interreligious awareness is adapted from Bennett's Developmental Model of Intercultural Sensitivity, which focuses mainly on how individuals react when confronted with cultural differences. Bennett's model avoids discussing religious differences as part of cultural identity, but Abu-Nimer (2001) has applied it in IFD and documented its shortcomings for that context. The data about specific reactions come from his field experience as a trainer and facilitator in IFD and training workshops in Israel, Palestine, and other conflict areas, where he has facilitated approximately five interfaith training workshops per year. In each workshop, there were twenty-five to thirty-five participants belonging to at least seven diverse religious traditions. Since 1998, the author has conducted dozens of IFD groups in which this model of interfaith awareness has been discussed and explored. The above reactions are based on interfaith meetings that took place at, among other places, Eastern Mennonite University in Harrisonburg, Virginia (1988–2003); the Mindanao Peacebuilding Institute (1999–2003); the Summer Peacebuilding and Development Institute at American University, Washington, D.C. (2001–3); and the United Religious Initiative (URI) Assembly conference in Rio, Brazil (August 2002).

7. Based on an IFD course offered in Mindanao Peacebuilding Institute (MPI), Davao City, Philippines, summer 2002.

8. Ibid.

9. In a similar context, Hindu and Buddhist religious practices were dismissed as heretical (Jerusalem, February 1999, conflict resolution workshop for Israeli and Palestinian civil societies).

10. Seminar on martyrdom in Islam and Judaism, Jerusalem, June 17, 2003, sponsored by the Interreligious Coordinating Council in Israel (ICCI).

11. United Religions Initiative (URI) Assembly conference, Rio, Brazil, August 2002.

12. Interview with a Muslim interfaith dialoguer in Galilee, July 30, 2003.

13. It should be noted that there is little empirical evidence to support the various manifestations of this phase in the intercultural developmental scale. Thus, scholars and practitioners have not addressed it fully, and further research is needed to explore the behavioral and perceptional changes in this phase.

14. Interfaith and peacebuilding evening in Washington, D.C., April 8, 2003.

15. According to the intercultural sensitivity developmental model embraced by these persons, individuals in the integration stage develop multiple cultural identities and frames of reference. However, according to this model, this multicultural person feels no obligation to one specific culture but is able to live in and adjust to many cultures. Symptoms of extreme alienation have been observed in certain teenagers who have embraced this mode, due to the lack of one solid identity base in a context where the external environment is religiously strictly divided (Bennett 1993).

16. Such tolerance and acceptance are especially needed if we consider the fact that in every conflict area, including Palestine and Israel, those who marry across faiths are often rejected by both communities.

3. IFD AND PEACEBUILDING IN ISRAEL AND PALESTINE

1. Interview with Palestinian woman from an IFD group, Jerusalem, July 2004.

2. Despite the fact that the Zionist leaders, such as Hertzel, co-opted religious sources and narratives to support their political claims, many Jewish religious groups continued to debate whether they would violate their religious belief if they joined the Zionist call to migrate to Israel. Orthodox Judaism, represented by Rabbi Kook, solved the paradox of waiting for the Messiah in the Diaspora, emigrating to the "promised land of Israel," and taking part in the Zionist project of state building. Despite their theological differences with Orthodox Judaism, Reform Judaism joined the Zionist project of state building and fully supported the state in the mid-1900s.

3. For example, Shas, the major religious politcal party, emerged in the early 1980s to become the largest party representing religious Sephardic Jews.

4. In fact, one of the major triggers for the current Intifada was the provocative visit of Ariel Sharon, with a few thousand policemen, to the Al Haram Al Sharif.

5. The Road Map was an initiative launched by several European countries and supported by the United States, too. It aimed at restoring the peace negotiations that collapsed in October 2000 (start of the second Palestinian Intifada) and followed the last intensive efforts of the U.S. president to reach an agreement or a settlement at Camp David.

6. Based on an interview with Abdul Salam Manasra, a Muslim community leader and veteran of interfaith dialogue, in Nazareth, July 2004. After issuing this call in 1989, Manasra received Rabbi Menahim Forman, who lives in one of the West Bank settlements. Rabbi Forman accepted the invitation, and the two ate together in

Manasra's house and launched a wide campaign to encourage religious peace among Arabs and Jews.

7. Interview in Jerusalem, spring 2003.

8. Cited in Landau 2003, 9.

9. By September 2004, there were 3,334 Palestinians and 847 Israelis killed. For more details on the updated numbers of causalities of this war, see www.palestinemonitor.org, and www.israel-mfa.gov.il.

10. Based on reports from local researchers (Aref Husseini and Kamal Kezel).

11. Interview in Jerusalem, spring 2003.

12. Interview with a Palestinian woman from the Women's Interfaith Encounter in Jerusalem, July 2003.

13. Interview with a Muslim woman, an organizer of interfaith activities in Israel, February 2003.

14. Interview in Majd Al Kurum, July 2004.

15. Interview in Nazareth, 2003.

16. Interview with Christian coordinator of Women's Interfaith Encounter, Jerusalem, 2004.

17. Interview in Jerusalem, October 2003.

18. Ibid.

19. Interview in Jerusalem, July 2004.

20. Yesodot is an interfaith organization that operates in Israel and involves Jews, Muslims, and Christians.

21. Interview in Nazareth, August 2003.

22. Interview in Jerusalem, February 4, 2003.

23. Interview in Jerusalem, June 2004.

24. Interview in Jerusalem, June 2004.

25. Interview in Jerusalem, July 2004.

26. Interview in Jerusalem, 2004.

27. Interview in Jerusalem, June 2003.

28. Interview in Jerusalem, August 2004.

29. Interview in Jerusalem, September 2003.

30. Interview with a Jewish interfaith woman participant from Haifa, April 2004.

31. Interview in Jerusalem, September 17, 2003.

32. Interview with David Neuhaus, Jerusalem, July 2004.

33. Interview at the Hartman Institute, Jerusalem, May 2004.

34. According to Sulha Peace Project, "Sulha is an indigenous, Middle Eastern way of reconciliation. Our goal is to rebuild trust among neighbors, Arabs and Jews, Israelis and Palestinians, heart to heart, as a contribution to peace in the Holy Land. In these critical times, we feel there is a need for a safe place to hear and appreciate each other's stories, hopes, fears, traditions, and cultures beyond a specific political agenda." www.Sulha.org. The Sulha Peace Project rituals are conducted by Rabbi E. Mclean's group.

35. Interview in Nazareth, July 2004.

36. Interview at the Hartman Institute, Jerusalem, May 2004.

37. Interview in Nazareth, 2004.

38. Ibid.

39. Interview in Jerusalem, August 2004.

40. Interview in Acre, February 2004.

41. Interview in Jerusalem, October 2003.

42. Interview in Jerusalem, February 2004.

43. Ibid.

44. Interview with Arab Christian leader, Galilee, July 2004.

45. Ibid.

46. Elana Rozenman describes the difficulties involved in managing this dilemma of political activism in an apolitical interfaith setting: "So we said we are nonpolitical, let's stick with this. And then she [the Arab participant] brought some fliers to the meeting, and we had a big problem because she stood up and started passing out fliers and announcing a political action. And I said, 'Look, we agreed we are not supposed to do this.' And she got very angry because she thought that I was embarrassing her in front of everyone and that I was trying to control her and that I was being the Jewish Israeli power. I felt very hurt and betrayed that after all of our talks and discussions, she is doing this anyway and kind of—what I felt—sabotaging the work. So anyways, this went on for a while, and she and I had to do a lot of work together individually and in front of the group to get over that and resolve that, and as a result of that she decided that she really wants to devote her time to Ta'ayush more." (Ta'ayush is an Arab-Jewish political protest group in Israel.)

47. Interview in Jerusalem, October 2003.

48. Interview with the director of IEA, Jerusalem, 2003.

49. Interview in Jerusalem, February 2004.

50. Ibid.

51. Interview in Jerusalem, October 2003.

52. Interview in Jerusalem, July 2004.

53. Interview with a Palestinian Christian woman, Jerusalem, July 2004.

54. Interview in Jerusalem, August 2003.

55. Arab and Jewish participants from Al-Fredese interfaith training, April 2003.

56. Interview with Jeremy Milgrom, Jerusalem, 2004.

57. Interview in Jerusalem, 2004.

58. Interview in Bethlehem, October 2003.

59. Interview at the Hartman Institute, Jerusalem, 2004.

60. Interview with Luci Thalgia, Bethlehem, 2003.

61. Interview with Saliba Tawil, Bethlehem, 2004. There are specific incidents cited mainly by some Christian interviewees regarding prejudice against them. For example, "A Christian woman was followed by Muslim kids in a refugee camp, and they threw stones at her because she wore a Christian cross as a necklace" (Luci Thalgia, Bethlehem, 2004).

62. Interview in Bethlehem, November 2003.

63. Interview in Jerusalem, October 2003.

64. Ibid.

65. Interview in Jerusalem, February 2004.

66. The book's seven chapters describe the three religions, and it utilizes eighty-nine different sources to explain and document religious interpretations.

67. Interview with Ghantus Ghantus, Tiberias, February 2004.

68. He even described Druze commanders who serve in the Occupied Territories as humane in dealing with the Palestinians. Based on an interview in Acre, July 2004.

69. Interview in Jerusalem, 2004.

70. Interview with Ibtisam Ibrahim, Tiberias, 2003.

71. Interview with a Muslim Sufi leader, Nazareth 2004.

72. Interview with David Neuhaus, Jerusalem, February 2004.

73. Interview in Jerusalem, February 2004.

74. Interview in Nazareth, 2004.

75. Interview with a Palestinian Christian woman, Jerusalem, 2003.

76. Interview in Jerusalem, 2004.

77. Interview in Haifa, 2004.

78. Interview in Nazareth, 2004.

79. Interview with Muslim coordinator for Women's Interfaith Encounter group, Jerusalem, 2004.

80. Interview in Nazareth, July 2004.

81. Interview in Jerusalem, August 2003.

82. Interview in Acre, February 2004.

83. Interview in Nazareth, July 2004.

84. Interview with a Palestinian Muslim woman, Jerusalem, July 2004.

85. Interview in Haifa, July 2004.

86. Interview in Jerusalem, October 2003.

87. Interview with PASSIA director, Jerusalem, 2004.

88. Interview in Jerusalem, February 2004.

89. Interview in Jerusalem, July 2004.

90. Interview in Jerusalem, February 2004.

91. Interview in Majd Alkurum, April 2004.

92. Interview in Jerusalem, February 2004.

93. Interview in Jerusalem, 2004.

94. Interview in Jerusalem, 2004.

95. Interview in Bethlehem, February 2004.

96. Interview in Nazareth, July 2004.

97. Ibid.

98. Interview in Bethlehem, October 2003.

99. Interview in Jerusalem, October 2003.

100. Yehuda Stolov from IEA cited this event as part of a successful activity carried out on February 2, 2003.

101. Interview in Jerusalem, July 2004.

102. Interview in Haifa, July 2004.

103. Interview in Jerusalem, October 2003.

104. Interview with a Palestinian Christian participant, Jerusalem, 2004.

105. Interview in Bethlehem, 2003.

106. The Jewish interviewee recalled the story as an illustration of concrete success of his interfaith group activities in the late 1970s. Interview in Jerusalem, 2004.

107. Bishop Muneeb Yunan cited several other stories in which he was called to help Muslims (individuals and communities) due to his IFD involvement and religious status. Interview in Jerusalem, 2004.

108. Elias Jabour is a well-known Palestinian Christian community leader who is active in traditional dispute resolution and interfaith circles. Interview in Shefa'mr, October 2003.

109. Interview with David Rosen, Jerusalem, 2004.

110. Interview of a Muslim leader in Nazareth, 2003; interview of a Christian priest in Jerusalem, October 2003.

111. Interview with Jeremy Milgrom, Jerusalem, 2003.

112. Since 2001, the Abraham Funds has supported the creation of a network for Arab-Jewish coexistence organizations, which managed to serve more than 250 organizations that work on improving Arab-Jewish relations in Israel (see www .coexnet.org.il).

113. "There is a difference: Arabs and Jews are not killing each other in Israel. . . . Even though incidents do happen, such as the killing of thirteen Arabs. We are done with that, there was the Or Commission." Interview with the ICCI director, Jerusalem 2003. The Or Commission was established by the Israeli government to investigate the killing of thirteen Arabs from Israel during the events of October 2000, when massive demonstrations and protests erupted in response to Israeli security measures and Sharon's visit to the Al Aqsa Mosque in Jerusalem. These events marked the beginning of the second Palestinian Intifada.

114. Interview in Jerusalem, May 2004.

115. A Christian priest and others have observed similar patterns when working with Muslim, Christian, and Jewish participants on an interfaith educational curriculum for schools. Interview in Jerusalem, October 2003.

116. Interview in Tiberias, February 2004.

117. Interview, June 2004.

118. Interview in Jerusalem, October 2003.

119. Interview with a Palestinian Muslim and religious scholar, Bethlehem, 2003.

120. Interview in Jerusalem, February 2003.

121. Interview with a Muslim community leader, Nazareth, 2004.

122. Ibid.

123. Interview with a Palestinian Muslim scholar, Bethlehem, 2004.

124. Interview in Acre, 2004.

125. Interview in Nazareth, July 2004.

126. Interview in Tiberias, 2003.

127. Interview in Jerusalem, April 2004.

128. Interview in Tiberias, February 2004.

129. Ibid.

130. Interview with a Palestinian Christian coordinator for Women's Interfaith Encounter group, Jerusalem, 2004.

131. Personal interview, Upper Galilee, 2004.

132. Interview with the PASSIA director, Jerusalem, 2004.

133. Interview in Jerusalem, 2004.

134. Interview with a Christian interfaith organizer, Jerusalem, 2004.

135. Interview in Jerusalem, October 2003.

136. Interview in Bethlehem, 2003.

137. Interview with a Christian organizer of IFD, Jerusalem, 2003.

138. Interview with an Arab Muslim woman coordinator of an interfaith group, Tiberias, 2004. The same statement was echoed by other interfaith participants, especially the Palestinians.

139. Interview in Jerusalem, Hartman Institute, 2004.

140. Interview in Bethlehem, 2004.

141. Interview in Bethlehem, 2004.

142. Interview in Bethlehem, July 2004.

143. In several encounters observed by the researchers, representatives of Muslim and Druze communities were not present or were identified in last-minute efforts.

144. Interview in Bethlehem, July 2004.

145. Interview in Jerusalem, 2004.

146. Interview with Hisham Najar, Bethlehem, 2004.

147. Ibid.

148. Interview in Bethlehem, 2004.

149. Ibid.

150. Interview in Jerusalem, 2004.

4. IFD IN LEBANON: OVERCOMING SECTARIAN DIVIDES

1. The duration of the Lebanese civil war is an issue of contention among different people and researchers. While some have it at fifteen years—from 1975 until 1990 (the signing of the Taef Agreement)—others believe it lasted for sixteen years, since the war did not effectively stop at the signing of the Taef Agreement but continued until 1991.

2. Interview in Beirut, July 2003.

3. Ibid.

4. For more information on the Jewish community in Lebanon, see Kirsten Schulze, *The Jews of Lebanon: Between Coexistence and Conflict* (Brighton: Sussex Academic Press, 2001).

5. Interview with Shiite scholar and interfaith activist, Beirut, July 2003.

6. Interview with Maronite Christian activist and member of the National Committee for Christian-Muslim Dialogue, Beirut, July 2003.

7. Interview with Christian activist in Moral Rearmament, Beirut, August 2003.

8. Interview in Beirut, July 2003.

9. Interview with a Druze intellectual, businessman, and interfaith activist, Beirut, July 2003.

10. Interview with a Sunni journalist and interfaith activist, Beirut, July 2003.

11. Interview in Beirut, July 2003.

12. Interview with an Orthodox priest, Aley, August 2003.

13. Interview with a Muslim scholar, Beirut, July 2003.

14. This group is also sometimes referred to as the National Committee for Islamo-Christian Dialogue.

15. Interview with a Maronite interfaith activist, Beirut, July 2003.

16. Interview in Beirut, July 2003.

17. Ibid.

18. Interview with a Christian interfaith activist, Beirut, August 2003.

19. Ibid.

20. Interview with director of MECC, Beirut, July 2003.

21. Interview with a Christian interfaith organizer, Beirut, July 2003.

22. Following the Cairo meeting, the group officially registered itself in Lebanon as a nonprofit civic organization.

23. Interview, Beirut, July 2003.

24. Ibid.

25. Interview in Beirut, August 2003

26. Ibid.

27. Ibid.

28. Interview with an Armenian interfaith activist and organizer, Beirut, July 2003.

29. Ibid.

30. Interview with a Christian interfaith participant and activist, Beirut, August 2003.

31. Ibid.

32. Interview in Beirut, August 2003.

33. Ibid.

34. Ibid.

35. Interview in Beirut, December 2003.

36. Interview with the director of the IEIC, Beirut, July 2003.

37. Ibid.

38. Interview in Beirut, July 2003.

39. Interview with a Muslim scholar and activist, Beirut, July 2003.

40. Among the center's publications, *Al-Marqab Journal* is its scholarly mouthpiece. It addresses current issues concerning Christian-Muslim coexistence in Lebanon. The center also publishes the proceedings and results of its sessions, conferences, and seminars, as well as other books dealing with the issue. The center's publications include *Role and Vision* (1996), the proceedings of the consultancy session; *Towards an Enhanced Dialogue; Christianity and Islam: Mirrors of Encounter; Mutual Views and Changing Relations between Christians and Muslims* (1997); *Studies in Christian-Muslim Relations* (Mahmoud Ayoub, translated into English by Catherine Srour, 2000); *Towards a Better Debate: Christian-Islamic Dialogues; The Coming Goods: Looking at the Christian-Muslim Rapprochement; Religion, Globalization and Pluralism* (the proceedings of the fourth summer session); the two volumes of Mahmoud Ayoub, *On Christian-Muslim Relations* and *Religion and World* (proceedings of the first summer session).

41. Interview with the Center for Christian-Muslim Studies, Aley, August 2003.

42. Interview with the general supervisor of Al-Ishrak, Beirut, December 2003.

43. Ibid.

44. Ibid.

45. Interview with a Catholic bishop, Al-Rabwa, July 2003.

46. Interview with an activist in WCRP, Beirut, August 2003.

47. Interview with the director of the Lebanese Conflict Resolution Network (LCRN), Beirut, July 2003.

48. Other types of IFD can also be found in the Lebanese context, for example, *dialogue through discussion,* in which participants learn about each other's religions and seek common moral values; *dialogue of experiences,* which puts forth the view that Islam and Christianity worship the same God in different but complementary ways (Center for Christian-Muslim Studies 1996, 14–15); *dialogue of words* (sometimes also called *dialogue of ideology, mind, or thoughts*), which attempts to cultivate mutual knowledge and discovery of the other; *dialogue of hearts,* which is based on the idea that relationships based on affection, friendship, and harmony might facilitate better dialogue than the dialogue that occurs between two who are not linked by friendship; and *dialogue of silence,* which is listening to the voice of God, who speaks inside each person and helps one accept the other (Ghazzal n.d., 3–4).

49. Interview in Beirut, July 2003.

50. Interview in Beirut, July 2003.

51. Interview in Beirut, July 2003.

52. Interview in Aley, August 2003.

53. Interview with a Muslim activist, Beirut, July 2003.

54. Interview in Beirut, August 2003.

55. Interview in Beirut, August 2003.

56. Interview in Beirut, July 2003.

57. Interview with a Christian organizer and activist, Beirut, August 2003.

58. Interview with Muslim activist, Beirut, August 2003.

59. Interview with Christian participant and lawyer, Beirut, August 2003.

60. Interview in Beirut, July 2003.

61. Interview with a Christian participant and organizer, Beirut, December 2003.

62. Interview in Beirut, July 2003.

63. Interview in Beirut, July 2003.

64. Interview with Catholic bishop, Al-Rabwa, July 2003.

65. Interview with Christian priest, Beirut, July2003.

66. Ibid.

67. Interview in Beirut, July 2003.

68. Interview with a Muslim scholar and activist, Beirut, July 2003.

69. Ibid.

70. Interview with Christian organizer, Beirut, July 2003.

71. Interview in Beirut, August 2003.

72. Interview in Beirut, July 2003.

73. Interview in Beirut, July 2003.

74. Interview in Beirut, August 2003.

75. Interview in Beirut, December 2003.

76. Interview in Beirut, July 2003.

77. Interview with a Muslim activist, Beirut, August 2003.

78. Interview with a Shiite scholar and activist, Beirut, July 2003.

79. Interview with a Muslim activist, Beirut, August 2003.

80. Ibid.

5. IFD IN EGYPT: NATIONAL UNITY AND TOLERANCE

1. The percentage of the Copts in Egypt is always a controversial figure, however. Van Nispen (1997) wrote that Copts are "today closer to 6 percent." In the *Annual Report on International Religious Freedom,* released by the Bureau of Democracy, Human Rights, and Labor (U.S. Department of State 2003), Copts are estimated as 8–10 percent of the population.

2. "People of the land" is the expression used by A'mr Ibn El-Aas in his messages to Caliph Omar Ibn El Khattab to describe the Copts. Kelada uses the same expression here to describe the Egyptians, whether Copts or Muslims, to emphasize his argument.

3. The debate was quoted in detail in *The Muslims and Copts in the Framework of the National Society* (El Bishri 1988, 171–74).

4. Interview in Cairo, 2003.

5. Interview in Cairo, November 8, 2003.

6. Interview in Cairo, November 10, 2003.

7. Interview in Cairo, October 25, 2003.

8. Interview in Cairo, 2003.

9. Ibid.

10. Interview in Cairo, November 1, 2003.

11. Interview in Cairo, November 2, 2003.

12. Interview in Cairo, October 25, 2003.

13. Interview in Cairo, October 28, 2003.

14. Interview in Cairo, November 8, 2003.

15. Interview in Cairo, November 8, 2003.

16. Interview in Cairo, November 29, 2003.

17. Interview in Cairo, November 3, 2003.

18. Interview in Cairo, November 8, 2003.

19. Interview in Cairo, November 4, 2003.

20. Interview in Cairo, December 20, 2003.

21. Interview in Cairo, November 10, 2003.

22. Interview in Cairo, October 25, 2003.

23. Interview in Cairo, November 29, 2003.

24. Interview in Cairo, 2003.

25. Interview in Cairo, October 28, 2003.

26. Interview in Cairo, 2003.

27. Interview in Cairo, November 8, 2003.

28. Interview in Cairo, October 28, 2003.

29. Interview in Cairo, October 28, 2003.

30. Interview in Cairo, November 29, 2003.

31. Interview in Cairo, November 29, 2003.

32. Interview in Cairo, November 29, 2003.

33. Interview in Cairo, October 25, 2003.

34. Interview in Cairo, November 8, 2003.

35. Interview in Cairo, November 8, 2003.

36. Interview in Cairo, November 8, 2003.

37. Interview in Cairo, October 25, 2003.

38. Interview in Cairo, October 25, 2003.

39. Interview in Cairo, October 28, 2003.

40. Interview in Cairo, October 25, 2003.

41. Interview in Cairo, December 20, 2003.

42. Interview in Cairo, December 20, 2003.

43. Fundamentalism in Islam does not mean sticking to certain ancient interpretations, but, on the contrary, getting rid of all interpretations and going back to the two "fundamentals": Quran and Sunna. Naturally, the two fundamentals need interpretations that would be contextualized in the current history. Western media and research centers have often called "Salafists" fundamentalists. Salafists are those who would rather stick to old interpretations. Here, and once again, we can see the confusion raised from using Western lexicon to read local reality.

44. Interview in Cairo, November 8, 2003.

45. Ibid.

46. Interview in Cairo, November 10, 2003.

47. Ibid.

48. Interview in Cairo, October 28, 2003.

49. Interview in Cairo, December 16, 2003.

50. Interview in Cairo, December 16, 2003.

51. Interview in Cairo, November 4, 2003.

52. Interview in Cairo, November 8, 2003.

6. IFD in Jordan: Between International Host and Local Harmonizer

1. To obtain firsthand information about IFD in Jordan, fieldwork was done in Jordan and interviews were conducted with activists and participants in IFD. Printed material about the projects and activities collected from the different interfaith organizations was reviewed to supplement the interviews. As will be elaborated on in the chapter, a major challenge facing the interfaith field in Jordan is how to expand IFD to the grassroots—something considered of real importance to all those involved.

2. While the Druze, a minority faith, are recognized in Israel/Palestine, Lebanon, and Syria as independent and separate congregations with a parallel status to Islam and Christianity, in Jordan they are treated as a sect of Islam with no separate court system.

3. In the past two decades there have been several political developments in which Islamic political groups managed to gain public support and even representation in Jordanian parliamentary elections. Their agenda and narrative have been focused on establishing and enforcing Jordanian Shari'a laws. King Hussein and his successor, Abdullah, and the Jordanian authorities have been trying to curb the growth of these groups and on various occasions they jailed their political leaders, dissolved the parliament, or directly intervened in local elections. In addition, there have been several violent incidents or attacks carried out by Jordanians (who adopted militant political Islamic ideology) against foreign diplomats, including the recent bombing in the Amman hotel.

4. Interview, 2003. The Jordanian government's strong support of such meetings is demonstrated by the granting of government facilities and services for hosting such activities.

5. Interview in Amman, 2003.

6. Interview in Amman, 2003.

7. Interview in Amman, 2003.

8. Interview in Amman, 2003.

9. Interview in Amman, 2003.

10. Interview in Amman, 2003.

11. Interview in Amman, 2003.

12. Interview in Amman, 2003.

13. Interview in Amman, 2003.

14. Interview in Amman, 2003.

15. Interview with a journalist, Amman, 2003.

16. Interview in Amman, 2003.

17. Interview with a journalist, Amman, 2003.

18. Interview with a Catholic priest, Amman, 2003.

19. RIIFS's publications include `*Isa wa Maryam fi al Qur'an wal Tafasir* ("Jesus and Mary in the Quran and Quranic Exegesis"), by Yusuf K. Khoury and Royal Institute for Inter-Faith Studies Arabic research staff; *Sirat al-Sayyid al-Masih li-Ibn*

`Asakir al-Dimashqi (1105–1176)* (a biography of Jesus by Ibn `Asakir of Damascus, 1105–76); a Muslim interpretation of Jesus as a prophet of Islam, written by a Damascene scholar during the period of Crusader rule in Syria, edited by Suleiman Ali Mourad; Père Michel Lelong's *Al-Kanisa al-Kathulikiyya wal-Islam* ("The Catholic Church and Islam"); *The Druze Heritage: An Annotated Bibliography,* by Talal Fandi and Ziyad Abi-Shakra; *Al-Nasara fi al-Qur`an wal-Tafasir* ("The Christians in the Quran and Quranic Exegesis"); *Al-Kana`is al-`Arabiyya fil sijill al-canasi al-`Uthmani 1869–1922* ("The Arab Churches in the Church Register of the Ottoman State, 1869–1922"), by Abdul-Rahim Abu Husayn and Saleh Sa`dawi ir Abduh; and *l-Suryan qadiman wa hadithan* ("The Syriac Christian Community Past and Present"), to name but a few.

20. In addition to its activities, the foundation publishes a number of books, papers, and articles. Its publications include *Model of Historical Co-Existence between Muslims and Christians and Its Future Prospects; Common Humanitarian Ideals for Muslims and Christians; Religious Pluralism; Annotated Index of Muslim-Christian Meetings (1954–1997),* 3rd edition; *The Educational System in Islam and Christianity;* and *Perspectives of Cooperation and Participation between Muslims and Christians on the Eve of the New Century.*

21. Interview with Haddad, Amman, March 2003.

22. Ibid.

23. Ibid.

24. Interview with Al-Abadi, Amman, Jordan, 2003.

25. Ibid.

26. Ibid.

27. Interview with Keldani, Amman, 2003.

28. Similar statements or assumptions were voiced by most of the interviewees in Jordan.

29. Interview in Amman, 2003.

30. Interview with a writer, Amman, 2003.

31. Interview with a Roman Catholic bishop, Amman, 2003.

32. Interview in Amman, 2003.

33. Interview in Amman, 2003.

34. Ibid.

35. Interview with Muslim scholar, Amman, 2003.

36. Interview with a writer, Amman, 2003.

37. Interview in Amman, 2003.

38. Interview with an Islamic scholar, Amman, 2003.

39. Interview in Amman, 2003.

40. Interview with an Islamic scholar, Amman, 2003.

41. Interview in Amman, 2003.

42. Interview in Amman, 2003.

43. Interview in Amman, 2003.

44. Interview in Amman, 2003.

45. Interview in Amman 2003.

46. Interview in Amman, 2003.

47. Interview in Amman, 2003.

48. Interview in Amman, 2003.

49. Interview in Amman, 2003.

50. Interview in Amman, 2003.

51. Interview in Amman, 2003.

52. Interview in Amman, 2003.

53. Interview in Amman, 2003.

54. See Renee Garfinkel, "What Works? Evaluating Interfaith Dialogue Programs," United States Institute of Peace Special Report no. 123 (Washington, D.C.: United States Institute of Peace, July 2004).

55. Interview in Amman, 2003.

56. Interview in Amman, 2003.

57. Interview in Amman, 2003.

58. Interview in Amman, 2003.

59. Ibid.

60. Ibid.

61. An online Arabic newspaper reported, "According to estimates, approximately 125,000 Jordanians are members of the Circassian ethnic community. All of them are Muslims. Circassians originally came to Jordan from the Caucasus area, fleeing Tsarist repression in 1875. Most of them today are middle class. It is worth mentioning that the Circassian and Chechen communities have, according to the quota system, three seats in the Jordanian parliament. The Circassians are careful to preserve their own language, tradition, and heritage. The chairman of the Circassian society in Jordan stressed that preserving their culture does not conflict with their integration in the Jordanian society. The Circassian community in Jordan asserts that its primary loyalty and commitment are to Jordan rather than the original Caucasian homeland" (*Jordan, Culture,* 1/12/2004; www.arabicnews.com).

62. Interview in Amman, 2003.

63. Interview with Christian priest, Amman, 2003.

64. Interview in Amman, 2003.

65. Interview in Amman, 2003.

66. Ibid.

67. Interview in Amman, 2003.

68. Interview in Amman, 2003.

69. Ibid.

70. Interview in Amman, 2003.

71. Interview in Amman, 2003.

72. Interview in Amman, 2003.

73. Interview in Amman, 2003.

74. Interview in Amman, 2003.

75. Interview with a Christian participant in Amman, 2003.

76. Interview in Amman, 2003.

77. Interview in Amman, 2003.

78. Ibid.

79. Interview in Amman, 2003.

80. Interview in Amman, 2003.

81. Interview in Amman, 2003.

82. Interview in Amman, 2003.

7. IFD IN THE MIDDLE EAST: A COMPARATIVE PERSPECTIVE

1. A typical question posed to many peace workers in these places: "Is this a CIA-funded project?" In the post–Iraq war reality, there is even greater suspicion and threat attached to any initiative associated with U.S. foreign policy.

2. In Israel, the *sulha* rituals, as organized by the interfaith organization led by Yehuda Mclean, have drawn considerable numbers of youth. ICCI conducts a few face-to-face, faith-to-faith youth programs, but in general there are no systematic initiatives for religious pluralism among youth in or outside the Israeli formal educational system.

3. Several interviewees pointed out that the interfaith field has suffered greatly since Crown Prince Hassan stepped back after the death of King Hussein.

4. Lebanese political discourse, led by sectarian leaders, uses sectarianism to create conflict and animosity between people. Yet, however divisive the confessional system may be, more emphasis on unity has been apparent on the level of the people, as well as on the part of some politicians, since the assassination of former prime minister Rafik Hariri in 2005. This outpouring of unity and national feeling was reflected in the huge demonstrations after his death, a unity festival to revive downtown Beirut, and a festival to commemorate the thirty-year anniversary of the beginning of the civil war. Despite this slight change in public discourse, the political leadership in the country continues to politicize religious affiliation and does not support interfaith unity.

5. In Lebanon, sectarian political and community groups have launched their own radio and television stations and newspapers.

6. Search for Common Ground's Media and Conflict Department has been developing several programs in various media sources (Palestinian and Israeli TV and newspapers), but very few of these programs relate to interfaith peacebuilding.

7. For further details on evaluation of interfaith dialogue, see United States Institute of Peace Special Report no. 123, *What Works: Evaluating Interfaith Dialogue Programs*, Renee Garfinkel, July 2004.

8. Taking the internal dynamics of Egyptian politics into consideration, these organizers and participants in IFD shied away from religious dialogue in their activities. They did not want to emphasize their religious differences and identities, fearing that this would eventually backfire and hurt the dialogue initiatives. The unity model was considered the safest approach.

9. *Sulha,* an Arab traditional reconciliation ritual, is utilized by this interfaith group to bring Arabs and Jews together in an attempt to facilitate peaceful cultural and social contacts.

10. Based on an interview with Ron Kronish, director of ICCI, Jerusalem, 2004.

11. Lauren Gelfond, "Girl Talk, Underground: In quiet gatherings, religious Jewish, Muslim, Druze and Christian women deal with the hostilities and hatred by turning to, instead of against, each other," *Jerusalem Post*, March 14, 2003.

12. Based on their Web site, www.rhr.israel.net/profile/index.shtml.

13. Interview in Jerusalem, August 5, 2003.

APPENDIX A:
LIST OF ACRONYMS

AWGMCD	Arab Working Group on Muslim-Christian Dialogue
CCSS	Coptic Center for Social Studies
CDD	Circle for Development and Dialogue
CDG	Cultural Development Group
CEOSS	Coptic Evangelical Organization for Social Services
ECJP	Egyptian Committee for Justice and Peace
IC	Initiatives of Change
ICCI	Interreligious Coordinating Council in Israel
ICS	International Center for Studies
IEA	Interfaith Encounter Association
IEIC	Institute for Islamo-Christian Studies
IFD	interfaith dialogue
JID	Jordan Institute of Diplomacy
LCRN	Lebanese Conflict Resolution Network
LED	Lebanese Encounter for Dialogue
LICD	Lebanese Islamic Committee for Dialogue
MBG	Muslim Brotherhood Group
MECC	Middle East Council of Churches
MR	Moral Rearmament
MSCD	Misr Society for Culture and Dialogue
PASSIA	Palestinian Academic Society for the Study of International Affairs
RHR	Rabbis for Human Rights
RIIFS	Royal Institute for Inter-Faith Studies
URI	United Religions Initiative
WCC	World Council of Churches
WCRP	World Conference on Religion and Peace
WSCF	World Student Christian Foundation

APPENDIX B:
LIST OF ORGANIZATIONS

<small>IsRAEL/PALESTINE:</small>

Al Liqa' Center for Religious and Heritage Studies in the Holy Land
Address: Hebron Road, Bethlehem
P.O. Box 11328, Jerusalem
Phone: 02-2750134; 02-2742321
Fax: 02-2750133
E-mail: al-liqa@p-ol.cm
Web site: www.al-liqacenter.org

Association for the Promotion of Interreligious Education in Israel
Address: P.O. Box 7972, Jerusalem 91079
Fax: 02-5376699
E-mail: tsevi@netmedia.net.il

Clergy for Peace
Address: 8A/3 Gad St., Jerusalem 93622
Phone: 053-371144
Fax: 02-5663865
E-mail: abu-maor@inter.net.il

College of Shari'a and Islamic Studies
Address: P.O. Box 124, Baqa El-Gharbiah 30100
Phone: 04-6382780/2457
Fax: 04-6383676
E-mail: college@macam.ac.il

Ecumenical Theological Research Fraternity in Israel
Address: P.O. Box 249, Jerusalem 91002
Phone: 02-6254941
Fax: 02-6724237
E-mail: ecu_frat@netvision.net.il

Elijah School for the Study of Wisdom in World Religions
Address: 9 Yehoshua Bin Nun Street, Jerusalem 93145
Phone: 052-780029
Fax: 02-5671674
E-mail: info@elijah.org.il
Web site: www.elijah.org.il

Elijah School Interfaith Academy
Address: 10 Caspi Street, Jerusalem 93554
Phone: 52-780-069
E-mail: admin@elijah.org.il

House of Hope—International Peace Center
Address: P.O. Box 272, Shefar'am 20200
Phone: 04-9868558
Fax: 04-9861211
Web site: www.hohpeacecenter.org

Interfaith Encounter Association (IEA)
Address: P.O. Box 3814, Jerusalem, 91037
Phone: 02-6510520
Fax: 02-6510557
E-mail: office@iea-encounter.org
Web site: www.interfaith-encounter.org

Interreligious Coordinating Council in Israel (ICCI)
Address: P.O. Box 8771, Jerusalem 91086
Phone: 02-561-1899
Fax: 02-563-4148
E-mail: iccijeru@icci.co.il

Israel Interfaith Association
Address: P.O. Box 7739, Jerusalem 91077
Phone: 02-6203251
Fax: 02-6203388
E-mail: msyuda@mscc.huji.ac.il; mskrupp@mscc.huji.ac.il

Melitz Center for Interfaith Encounter with Israel
Address: 19 Yishai St., Abu Tor, Jerusalem 93544
Phone: 02-6734441
Fax: 02-6733447
E-mail: oyarden@cc.huji.ac.il; overseas@melitz.org.il

Mercaz Ami—Jerusalem Center for Biblical Studies and Research
Address: P.O. Box 8017, Jerusalem 91080
Phone: 02-5636375
Fax: 02-5638426
E-mail: ami_jc@netvision.net.il

Oz VeShalom/Netivot Shalom
Address: P.O. Box 4433, Jerusalem 91043
Phone: 02-6730196; 02-6788925
Fax: 02-6788925
E-mail: ozshalom@netvision.net.il
Web site: www.ariga.com/ozveshalom

Palestinian Academic Society for the Study of International Affairs (PASSIA)
Address: 18, Hatem Al-Ta'i Street
P.O. Box 19545, Jerusalem
Phone: 02-6264426
Fax: 02-6282819
E-mail: passia@palnet.com
Web site: www.passia.org

Pontifical Biblical Institute
Address: 3, Paul Emile Botta Street, Box 497, Jerusalem 91004
Phone: 02-6252843
Fax: 02-6241203
E-mail: dmoore@netvision.net.il; pbijer@netvision.net.il

Pontifical Institute Ratisbonne—Christian Center of Jewish Studies
Address: P.O. Box 7336, Jerusalem 91027
Phone: 02-6257068/6259171
Fax: 02-6259172
E-mail: ratisbon@netvision.net.il
Web site: www.ratisbonne.org

Rabbis for Human Rights (RHR)
Address: Rehov Harekhavim 9, Jerusalem 93462
Phone: 02-5637731
Fax: 02-5662815
E-mail: info@rhr.israel.net
Web site: www.rhr.israel.net

**Sabeel Ecumenical Liberation Theology Center
(Ecumenical Centre for Theological Research at Tantur)**
Address: P.O. Box 49084, Jerusalem 91491
Phone: 02-532-7136
Fax: 02-532-7137
E-mail: sabeel@sabeel.org

Shalom Hartman Institute
Address: 12 Gedalyahu Alon, P.O. Box 8029, Jerusalem 93113
Phone: 02-5675320
Fax: 02-5611913
E-mail: shi@shi.org.il
Web site: www.hartmaninstitute.com

Sisters of Sion
Address: P.O. Box 19056, Jerusalem 91190
Phone: 02-6277292
Fax: 02-6282224
E-mail: oeccehomo@inter.net.il
Web site: webmaster@sion.org/eccehomo.htm

Swedish Theological Institute
Address: P.O. Box 37 Jerusalem, Israel
Phone: 02-6253822
Fax: 02-6254460
E-mail: sti@swedtheol.co.il
Web site: http://skm.svenskakyrkan.se/STI

Tantur Ecunemical Institute for Theological Studies
Address: P.O. Box 19556, Jerusalem 91194
Phone: 02-6760911
Fax: 02-6760914
E-mail: tantur@netvision.net.il
Web site: www.come.to/tantur

United Religions Initiative
Address: P.O. Box 29242, San Francisco, CA, USA 94129
Phone: 415-561-2300
Fax: 415-561-2313
E-mail: office@uri.org

Wiam Center for Conflict Resolution
Address: P.O. Box 1039, Bethlehem, West Bank via Israel
Phone: 02-2770513
Fax: 02-2777333
E-mail: alaslah@planet.edu
Web site: www.planet.edu/~alaslah/

Women's Interfaith Encounter
See Interfaith Encounter Association

Yakar Center for Torah, Tradition and Creativity
Address: Halamed Hei 10, Jerusalem 93661
Phone: 02-561-2310
Fax: 02-563-2917
E-mail: info@yakar.org
Web site: www.yakar.org

Yesodot—Center for the Study of Torah and Democracy
Address: Rehov Rivka 11, Jerusalem 93461
Phone: 02-671-5950
Fax: 02- 671-6092
E-mail: yesodot1@netvision.net.il
Web site: www.icci.co.il/YESODOT.htm

LEBANON:

Al-Ishrak Intellectual and Cultural Association/Transcendental Theosophy Institute: Theoretical and Practical
Address: Beirut, Autostrade Sfeir, Abu Ta'am Building, 1st Floor
Phone: 1-822232; 1-845094; 3-221803
Fax: 1-822232; 011-961-1-845094
E-mail: al_ishrak@hotmail.com

Al-Makassed Higher Institute of Islamic Studies
Address: Mseitbeh, Uthman bin Affan St., Beirut
P.O. Box 11-5832,
Riad El-Solh, Beirut 1107-2200
Phone: 1-377533
Fax: 1-377285
E-mail: makcicr@cyberia.net.lb; islamicstudies@makassed.org
Web site: www.makassed.org.lb/islamicstudies.html

Arab Working Group for Muslim-Christian Dialogue
Address: Makhoul Street, Deeb Building, P. O. Box 5376, Beirut
Phone: 1-344896; 1-742088; 1-353938
Fax: 1-344894
E-mail: mecc@cyberia.net.lb

Center for Christian-Muslim Studies, University of Balamand
Address: Center for Christian-Muslim Studies, University of Balamand,
P.O. Box 100, Tripoli
Phone: 3-335683, ext. 149
Fax: 6-400742
E-mail: ccms@balamand.edu.lb
Web site: www.balamand.edu.lb/CCMS/CCMS.html

Circle (or Center) for Development and Dialogue
Address: Majdalyoun, Sidon
Phone: 7-753525
Fax: 7-753522
E-mail: cddsl@hotmail.com

Lebanon Conflict Resolution Network (LCRN)
Address: Tayyar Center, Sin al-Fil, P.O. Box 55215, Beirut
Phone: 1-490561; 1-490566; 3-918067
Fax: 1-490375
E-mail: abalian@lcps.org.lb

Middle East Council of Churches (MECC)
Address: Makhoul Street, Deeb Building, P. O. Box 5376, Beirut
Phone: 1-344896; 1-742088; 1-353938
Fax: 1-344894
E-mail: mecc@cyberia.net.lb

Université Saint Joseph (USJ), Institut d'études Islamo-Chrétiennes (Institute for Islamo-Christian Studies)
Address: Faculte des Sciences Religieuses, Campus des sciences humaines, Rue de Damas, B.P. 17-5208, Mar Mikhael, Beirut 1104 2020
Phone: 1-611 456, ext. 5807
Fax: 1- 611-365
E-mail: ieic@usj.edu.lb
Web site: www.ieic.usj.edu.lb

EGYPT:

Al Ikhaa Al Dini (Religious Fraternity)
Address: Dar El Salam Church, Sheikh Youssef St., Garden City, Cairo
Phone: 2-205-1631

Coptic Center for Social Studies/Orthodox Coptic Church
Address: Mohamed Yousef Mousa St. (near the Sayeda El Azraa Church)
P.O. Box 4019, Nasr City
Phone: 2-260-3495
Fax: 2-260-5999

Cultural Dialogue Program/Coptic Evangelical Organization for Social Services (CEOSS)
Address: P.O. Box 162-11811, El Panorama, Cairo
Phone: 2-297-5901/2/3; 202-297-5872/3/4
Fax: 2-297-5878
E-mail: int.relatns@ceoss.org.eg
Web site: www.ceoss.org.eg

Egypt-URI CC (United Religions Initiative)
Address: P.O. Box 151, October City
Phone: 2-587-5864
Fax: 2-587-5864
E-mail: mmosaad@uri.org
Web site: www.uri.org

International Center for Studies (ICS)
Address: 51 Kasr El Aini Street, Cairo
Phone: 2-364-6016
E-mail: ics@internetegypt.co

Misr Society for Culture and Dialogue (MSCD)
Address: 93 Nozha St., Nasr City, Cairo
Phone: 2-414-9953; 2-418-8819

Moral Rearmament (MR-Egypt)
Address: 49 Giza St., Giza
Phone: 2-572-9644
E-mail: a_m_farahat@yahoo.co.uk

Permanent Committee of Al-Azhar for Dialogue with Monotheistic Religions
Address: 15 Abu Al-Feda, Cairo
Phone: 2-737-4286
Fax: 2-735-0236
Web site: www.alazharinterfaith.org

South Group for Research
Phone: 1-051-04530
E-mail: Post111@yahoo.com

JORDAN:

Aal al-Bayt Foundation for Islamic Thought (previously known as the Royal Academy for Islamic Civilization Research)
Address: P.O. Box 950361, Amman 11195
Phone: 6-5539471
Fax: 6-5526471
E-mail: aalal-bayt@nets.com.jo

Amman Center for Peace and Development
Address: P.O. Box 3435, Amman 11181
Phone: 6-5664651
E-mail: acpd@index.com.jo

Ecumenical Studies Center
Address: P.O. Box 410286, Amman 11141
Phone: 6-5673067
Fax: 6-4788557
E-mail: ecumenicalcenter@hotmail.com

General Islamic Congress for Jerusalem
Address: P.O. Box 2074, Amman 11181
Phone: 6-5511722
Fax: 6-5511733
E-mail: gicj@arabia.com

Jordanian Interfaith Coexistence Research Center
Address: P.O. Box 811633, Amman 11181
Phone/Fax: 6-4623057
E-mail: frnabil@nol.com.jo; frnabil@prayjordan.org

Latin Patriarchate, Department of Education
Address: P.O. Box 9525, Amman 11191
Phone: 6-5933885
Fax: 6-5933874
E-mail: kildani@hotmail.com

Orthodox Society
Address: P.O.Box 910665, Amman 11191
Phone: 6-4625161
Fax: 6-4628167
E-mail: raouf.abujaber@abujaber.com
Web site: www.orthodoxsoc.org

Our Lady of Peace Center, Latin Vicariate
Address: P.O. Box 851379, Amman 11185
Phone: 6-5931162; 6-6929546
Fax: 6-5920548
E-mail: info@ourladyofpeacecentre.org
Web site: www.ourladyofpeacecentre.org

Royal Institute for Inter-Faith Studies (RIIFS)
Address: P.O. Box 830562, Amman 11183
Phone: 6-4618051
Fax: 6-4618053
E-mail: riifs@go.com.jo
Web site: www.riifs.org

BIBLIOGRAPHY

Aal al-Bayt Foundation. 1999. "Overview on Dialogue Symposiums between Muslims." Brochure.

Abboud, Hamzeh, Ramzi Ayoub, Hassan Mroueh, and Emile Iskandar. 1995. *Circle for Development and Dialogue.* Beirut: Bolsiah Publishing (in Arabic).

Abdel Samea, Amr. 2001. Copts and the Difficult Figures. Cairo: Public Egyptian Association of Books (in Arabic).

Abu-Amr, Ziad. 1994. *Islamic Fundamentalism in the West Bank and Gaza: Muslim Brotherhood and Islamic Jihad.* Bloomington: Indiana University Press.

Abu-Nimer, Mohammed. 1999. *Dialogue, Conflict Resolution and Change: Arab-Jewish Encounters in Israel.* Albany: State University of New York Press.

———, 2001. "Conflict Resolution and Religion: Toward a Training Model of Interreligious Peacebuilding." *Journal of Peace Research* 38, no. 6: 685–704.

———, ed. 2001. *Reconciliation, Justice and Coexistence.* Lanham, Md.: Lexington.

———. 2002. "The Miracles of Transformation through Interfaith Dialogue: Are You a Believer?" In *Interfaith Dialogue and Peacebuilding,* ed. David Smock, 15–32. Washington, D.C.: United States Institute of Peace.

———. 2003. *Nonviolence and Peacebuilding in Islamic Communities.* Gainesville: University Press of Florida.

———. 2004. "Religion, Dialogue, and Nonviolent Actions in Palestinian-Israeli Conflict." *Politics, Culture, and Society* 17, no. 3 (Spring): 491–511.

Abu-Nimer, Mohammed, Abdul Aziz Said, and Lakshitha Prelis. 2001. "Conclusion: The Long Road to Reconciliation." In Abu-Nimer, ed. 2001, 339–49.

Abu Wendi, Riad. 1996. "The Value of Religious Dialogue." *Al-Nashra,* no. 2: 2 (in Arabic).

———. 1997. "The Common Values of Religions." *Al-Nashra,* no. 4: 2 (in Arabic).

Ajouz, Elie. 1999. "Citizenship and Coexistence." *MECC NewsReport* 11, no. 1 (Winter/Spring): 31.

Al-Ajlani, Ibrahim. 2004. *Al-Kitabiyon in the Shadows of Islam.* Amman: Al-Rai Center for Research and Information.

Al-Dama, Mohammed. 2004. "The Jordanian Interfaith Coexistence Research Center: An Experience in the Culture of Religious Forgiveness, Dialogue of Civilizations, and Human Rights." *Asharq Al-Awsat* (August 2): 17 (in Arabic).

Al-Hewar Center. 1997. "Dr. Yvonne Haddad Speaks at Al-Hewar Center about Christian-Muslim Relations." December 17. www.Alhewar.com/Haddad .htm (accessed February 3, 2003).

Al-Hiwar.Net. http://hiwar-net.usj.edu.lb. Website of the Center of Dialogue/ Islamic-Christian Dialogue Committee, Institute of Islamo-Christian Studies, Saint Joseph University (accessed February 3, 2003).

Ali, Awad. 1997. "A Dialogue with Tarek Mitri, Executive Secretary for Christian-Muslim Dialogue in the World Council of Churches." *Al-Nashra,* no. 2: 8–10 (in Arabic).

————. 1999. *The Arab Christian Today.* Proceedings of two dialogue sessions held in Amman, September 16–17, 1997, and December 13–14, 1997. Amman: Royal Institute for Inter-Faith Studies.

————. 2000a. "Publications to Deepen Dialogue and Coexistence." *Al-Nashra* (Summer): 3 (in Arabic).

————. 2000b. "Religious Conflicts and the Dangers of Division." *Al-Nashra* (Spring): 3 (in Arabic).

Ali, S. A. 1998. "Christian-Muslim Relations: Ushering In a New Era." In Bryant and Ali 1998.

Al-Ishrak Intellectual and Cultural Association/Transcendental Theosophy Institute: Theoretical and Practical. n.d. Brochure.

Al-Makassed Philanthropic Islamic Association of Beirut, Makassed Higher Institute of Islamic Studies. www.makassed.org.lb (accessed February 3, 2003).

Al-Mawla, Saoud. 1997. "Muslim-Christian Dialogue: A Preliminary View." *Al-Nashra,* no. 4: 8–10 (in Arabic).

————. September 11–13, 1998. "Christian-Muslim Dialogue in Lebanon: History and Problems." Presented at the Religion between Violence and Reconciliation Conference. German Oriental Institute, Beirut. http://hiwar-net.usj.edu.lb (in French, accessed February 3, 2003).

————. 2001. "Christian-Muslim Dialogue: A Necessity and an Adventure." http://hiwar-net.usj.edu.lb (in French, accessed February 3, 2003).

————. 2002. "Post-War Lebanon." Lecture, French Cultural Center, Beirut, March 14. http://hiwar-net.usj.edu.lb (in French, accessed February 3, 2003).

————. 2003a. "Abbas El-Halabi in Dialogue and Reconciliation: The Arab Druze, the Muslim, the Lebanese, in the Balance and Dialogue." *An-Nahar* (August 10): 11 (in Arabic).

————. 2003b. *Justice in Coalescence.* Dialogue Notebooks Series, no. 2. Beirut: Center for Dialogue, Institute for Islamic-Christian Studies, Saint-Joseph University (in Arabic).

————. 2003c. "The Maronite Meeting and the Courage of Self-Criticism: Muslim Synod Demanded." *Al-Najwa* (June 16): 15–19 (in Arabic).

Al-Nashra. 1998. "The Muslim-Christian Meeting in Amman." No. 9 (Fall): 27 (in Arabic).

————. 1999. "Special Edition: The Seventh Assembly of the World Conference for Religion and Peace." No. 12 (Fall): 4–27 (in Arabic).

Al-Sammak, Mohammed. 2002. "Religion and Politics: The Case of Lebanon." In *Lebanon's Second Republic: Prospects for the Twenty-First Century,* ed. Kail C. Ellis. Gainesville: University Press of Florida.

————. 2003a. "Similarities in Islam and Christianity: The Divine Honoring of the Human." *An-Nahar* (July 20): 11.

————. 2003b. "The Arab Working Group for Muslim-Christian Dialogue: A Movement in the Right Direction." *An-Nahar* (May 18): 11.

Amin, Samir. 1984. "Contradictions in the Capitalist Development of Egypt: A Review Essay." *Monthly Review Foundation* 9.

An-Nahar. 2003. "'The Lebanese Dialogue Group' Discusses the War on Iraq. Jarjour: A New Colonization Rejected by All Churches." (February 25): 5.

Appleby, Scott. 1998. *The Ambivalence of the Sacred: Religion, Violence, and Reconciliation.* New York: Rowman and Littlefield.

Arab Working Group for Muslim-Christian Dialogue. 2001. *Dialogue and Unified Living: An Arab Muslim-Christian Covenant.* Cairo.

Arab Working Group for Muslim-Christian Dialogue. 2002. *Dialogue and Coexistence: An Arab Muslim-Christian Covenant.* Beirut: Ace Design and Printing Center.

Arian, Asher, and Michal Shamir, eds. 1999. *The Elections in Israel.* New York: State University of New York Press (with Israel Democracy Institute).

Ariarajah, S. Wesley. 1991. "Interfaith Dialogue." Entry in the *Dictionary of the Ecumenical Movement,* ed. Nicholas Lossky, José Bonino, John Pobee, Tom Stransky, Geoffrey Wainwright, and Pauline Webb. Geneva: WCC Publications; and Grand Rapids, Mich.: Wm. B. Eerdmans.

Arinze, Francis Cardinal. 1986. "Some Projects for International WCRP Sponsorship." In *Religions for Human Dignity and World Peace,* ed. John Taylor and Gunther Gebhardt, 58–60. Geneva: World Conference on Religion and Peace.

———. 2002. *Religions for Peace: A Call for Solidarity to the Religions of the World.* New York: Doubleday.

As-Sa'igh, Ziyad. 2003. "Muslims and Christians Facing Present Challenges Together: A Symposium of the MECC and the Arab Working Group on Muslim-Christian Dialogue (Cairo, December 17–20, 2002)." *MECC NewsReport* 14, nos. 3–4 (Winter): 12–17.

Assefa, Hizkias. 2001. "Coexistence and Reconciliation in the Northern Region of Ghana." In Abu-Nimer 2001, 65–185.

Ayoub, Mahmoud. 2000. *On Christian-Muslim Relations.* Vol. 1. Trans. Catherine Srour. Balamand, Lebanon: Center of Christian-Muslim Studies, University of Balamand.

———. 2001. *On Christian-Muslim Relations.* Vol. 2. Trans. Catherine Srour. Balamand, Lebanon: Center of Christian-Muslim Studies, University of Balamand.

Ayoub, Rita. 2003. "Youth of Lebanon: Let's Live Together." Proposal for a dialogue project submitted to the Center of Dialogue, Institute of Muslim-Christian Dialogue at the Saint Joseph University (unpublished paper, in French).

Baagill, H. M. 1984. *Christian Muslim Dialogue.* Jeddah, Saudi Arabia: Islamic Education Foundation.

Bakradouni, Karim. 1997. "A New Hope for Lebanon." *Al-Nashra,* no. 5: 7–10 (in Arabic).

Barber, Benjamin. 2001. *Jihad vs. McWorld.* New York: Ballantine Books.

Barnes, Michael Anthony. 2001. "Between Rhetoric and Reticence: Theology of Dialogue in a Post-Modern World." In Singh and Schick 2001, 134–53.

Baskin, Gershon, and Mohammad Dajani. 2006. "Israeli-Palestinian Joint Activities: Problematic Endeavor, Necessary Challenge." In *Bridging the Divide: Peacebuilding in the Israeli-Palestinian Conflict,* ed. Edy Kaufman, Walid Salem, and Juliette Verhoeven. Boulder, Colo.: Lynne Rienner.

Bennet, Milton. 1993. "Towards Ethnorelativism: A Developmental Model of Inter-cultural Sensitivity." In *Education for the Intercultural Experience,* ed. R. M. Paige, 21–71. Yarmouth, Me.: Intercultural Press.

Bennett, Clinton. 2001. "Christian Trinity and Muslim Attributes: An Invitation to Spiritual Exploration." In Singh and Schick 2001, 265–70.

Bijlefeld, Willem. 2001. "Christian-Muslim Relations: A Burdensome Past, a Chal-lenging Future." In Singh and Schick 2001, 154–72.

bin Talal, HRH Prince Hassan. 2001. Interview. *Middle East Quarterly* 8, no. 1. www.meforum.org/article/20 (accessed July 11, 2005).

Brink, Paul. 2003. "Debating International Human Rights." *Brandywine Review of Faith and International Affairs* 1, no. 2 (Fall): 13–20.

Bryant, M. Darrol. 1998. "Can There Be a Muslim/Christian Dialogue Concerning Jesus/Isa?" In Bryant and Ali 1998.

Bryant, M. Darrol, and S. A. Ali, eds. 1998. *Muslim-Christian Dialogue: Promises and Problems.* St. Paul, Minn.: Paragon House.

Center for Christian-Muslim Studies. 1996a. *Religion and World in Christianity and Islam.* Proceedings of the First Summer Session. Balamand, Lebanon: University of Balamand (in Arabic).

———. 1996b. *Role and Vision.* Araya, Lebanon: Catholic Printing Press.

———. 1997. *Mutual Views between Christians and Muslims in the Past and Present.* Proceedings of the Second Summer Session. Balamand, Lebanon: Center of Christian-Muslim Studies, University of Balamand (in Arabic).

———. 2000. *Religion, Globalization, and Pluralism.* Proceedings of the Fourth Sum-mer Session. Balamand, Lebaonon: University of Balamand (in Arabic).

Center (or Circle) for Development and Dialogue. n.d. Brochure (in Arabic).

Chahine, Jerome. 2000. "Coexistence and Religious Unrest: Muslim, Christian Thinkers Meet to Consider the Causes of Violence in the Arab World." *MECC NewsReport* 12, no. 2 (Spring/Summer): 4–5.

Challenges to Mutual Understanding: Muslim and Christian Students Face to Face. 2002. Muslim-Christian Interaction Series, no.1. Beirut: Saint Joseph Univer-sity, Institute of Muslim-Christian Studies, Dar Al-Mashreq (in Arabic).

Chehab, Hicham. 2003a. "Proposal for Creating the Center for Reconciliation and Democracy." E-mail sent to author, July 10, 2003.

———. 2003b. "My PT in Switzerland." E-mail sent to author, August 2003.

———. 2003c. "Speech at Caux." E-mail sent to author, August 2003.

"Christian-Muslim Dialogue: Five Conferences." 2002. *MECC NewsReport* 14, no. 2 (Autumn): 34.

Cilliers, Jaco. 2002. "Building Bridges for Interfaith Dialogue." In Smock 2002.

Coptic Evangelical Organization for Social Services. www.ceoss.org.eg/ Dialogue.htm (accessed August 20, 2004).

Cox, Brian, and Daniel Philpott. 2003. "CFIA Task Force Report: Faith-Based Diplo-macy." *Brandywine Review of Faith and International Affairs* 1, no. 2 (Fall): 31–40.

Dagher, Carole H. 2000. *Bringing Down the Walls: Lebanon's Postwar Challenge.* New York: St. Martin's Press.

Davis, Eric. 1984. "Ideology, Social Class and Islamic Radicalism in Modern Egypt." In *From Nationalism to Revolutionary Islam,* ed. Said Amir Arjomand. Albany: State University of New York Press.

Diamond, Louise, and John McDonald, eds. 1996. *Multi-Track Diplomacy: A Systems Approach to Peace.* West Hartford, Conn.: Kumarian Press.

Donahue, John J. 1996. *Muslim-Christian Relations: Dialogue in Lebanon.* Occasional Paper Series. Washington, D.C.: Center for Muslim-Christian Understanding: History and International Affairs, Georgetown University.

Dyck, David. 2001. "Islam and Christianity as Sources of Conflict and Resources for Peace on the Island of Mindanao in the Philippines: A Case Study of Two Interfaith Peace-building Initiatives." In Singh and Schick 2001, 470–99.

"Ecumenism: Voices of the Middle East." 1999. Interviews with His Holiness Mar-Ignatious Zakkâ I Iwâs and His Eminence Bishop Boulos Matar. *MECC News-Report* 11, no. 1 (Winter/Spring): 4–8.

Eisen, Robert. 2002. "The Complexity of Jewish Identity and Inter-religious Dialogue." Unpublished paper presented at the USIP Conference on Abrahamic Traditions.

El Bishri, Tarik. 1988. *The Muslims and Copts in the Framework of the National Society.* Cairo: Dar El Shorouk.

El-Halabi, Abbas. 2002. *On Dialogue, Reconciliation, and Civil Peace.* Dialogue Notebooks Series, no.1. Beirut: Center for Dialogue, Institute for Islamic-Christian Studies, Saint-Joseph University (in Arabic).

———. 2003. "Reconciling Sectarian Relations in Lebanon." Lecture at Initiatives for Change, Washington, D.C., February.

El-Kadi, Rashid. 2003. "On Dialogue, Reconciliation and Civil Peace by Abbas El-Halabi: Dialogue Is Demanded around the Issue of the Lebanonization of Lebanon." *An-Nahar* (March 2): 9 (in Arabic).

Ellis, Kail C., ed. 2002. *Lebanon's Second Republic: Prospects for the Twenty-first Century.* Gainesville: University Press of Florida.

Faour, Mohammed. 1997. "Factors of Agreement and Friendliness in Lebanese Society." *Al-Nashra,* no, 3: 12–14 (in Arabic).

Fawzi, Sameh. 1998. *Copts' Concerns.* Cairo: Ibn Khaldoun Center for Developmental Studies.

Feiler, Bruce. 2002. *Abraham: A Journey to the Heart of Three Faiths.* New York: HarperCollins.

Fitzgerald, Michael F. April 10, 2000. "Christian Muslim Dialogue—A Survey of Recent Developments." www.sedos.org/english/fitzgerald.htm (accessed April 10, 2004).

Frangieh, Samir. 2003. "An Invitation to Agree on the Meaning of Lebanon: A Pact for Dialogue and Cooperation for a New Lebanese Meeting." Unpublished paper (in Arabic).

General Islamic Congress for Jerusalem. 2003. Introductory leaflet.

Ghazzal, Salim. 1989. "A Song of Hope Amidst Torment: Testimony on Islamo-Christian Coexistence during the events in South Lebanon." Prepared for the Seventeenth Session of the Roman Days, September1–7 (in French).

———. 1992. "Islamo-Christian Dialogue: Lived Testimony." Paper presented at the Forum of International Development, Paris, June 7 (in French).

———. 1995. Speech at the Circle for Development and Dialogue. Sidon, Lebanon (in Arabic and French).

———. October 3, 2000. "The Church and Social Work: Spiritual Perspectives and Personal Testimony." Unpublished paper (in Arabic).

———. September 6, 2002. "On the Topic of Coexistence as Insurance to National Unity." Lecture at the National Library, Baakline (in Arabic).

———. February 26, 2003. "The Position of the Church from the War on Iraq." Beirut, Lebanon (in Arabic).

———. n.d. "Coexistence: Personal Experiences and Dialogue Bases." Unpublished paper (in Arabic).

Goddard, Hugh. 1995. *Christians and Muslims: From Double Standards to Mutual Understanding.* Richmond, UK: Curzon Press.

Gopin, Marc. 2000. *Between Eden and Armageddon: The Future of World Religions, Violence, and Peacemaking.* New York: Oxford University Press.

———. 2002. "The Use of the Word and Its Limits: A Critical Evaluation of Religious Dialogue as Peacemaking." In Smock 2002.

Grose, George B., and Benjamin J. Hubbard, eds. 1994. *The Abraham Connection: A Jew, Christian and Muslim in Dialogue.* Vol. 6 of *The Church and the World* series. An encounter between Dr. David Gordis, Dr. George Grose, and Dr. Muzammil Siddiqi, moderated by Benjamin Hubbard. South Bend, Ind.: Cross Cultural Publications.

Habib, Rafiq. 2001. Interview in Abdel Samea 2001.

Halbertal, Rabbi Moshe. February 16, 1990. "The Role of Religious Values in the Search for Peace." Panel discussion moderated by Joseph Montville, Boston College.

Hamdan, Marwan. 2001. "Dialogue Is the Basis of Civilization." *Al-Nashra,* no. 18: 3 (in Arabic).

Hammer, M. R., and M. J. Bennett. 1998. *The Intercultural Development Inventory (IDI) Manual.* Portland, Ore.: Intercultural Communication Institute.

Hammer, M. R., M. J. Bennett, and R. Wiseman. 2003. "Measuring Intercultural Sensitivity: The Intercultural Development Inventory." *International Journal of Intercultural Relations* 27, no. 4 (July): 421–43.

Hanna, Milad. 2001. Interview in Abdel Samea 2001.

Hanson, Paul. 1992. "Study and Experience: Two Dimensions of Jewish-Christian Dialog." In *Overcoming Fear between Jews and Christians,* ed. James Charlesworth. New York: Crossroad.

Havemann, Axel. 2002. "Historiography in 20th-Century Lebanon: Between Confessional Identity and National Coalescence." *Bulletin of Royal Institute for Inter-Faith Studies* 4, no. 2 (Autumn/Winter): 49–69.

Hitti, Philip K. 1957. *Lebanon in History: From the earliest times to the present.* London: Macmillan.

"The House Speaker in His Speech to the Conference. Al-Majali: Jordan Is at the Head of Those Who Call for Deep-Seated, Deep-Rooted Peaceful and Civilizational Dialogue." 2004. *Ad-Dustour* (June 28): 8.

Howeidy, Amira. 2002. "Putting Out the Fire." *Al-Ahram Weekly,* no. 573 (February 14–20).

Hroub, Khaled. 2000. *Hamas: Political Thought and Practice.* Washington, D.C.: Institute for Palestine Studies.

Hubbard, Amy. 2001. "Understanding Majority and Minority Participation in Interracial and Interethnic Dialogue." In Abu-Nimer, ed. 2001.

Ibrahim, Saad Eddin. 1994. *Religions, Traditions, and Ethnicity.* Cairo: Ibn Khaldoun Center for Developmental Studies.

———. 1998. "Introduction." In *Copts' Concerns,* ed. Sameh Fawzi. Cairo: Ibn Khaldoun Center for Developmental Studies.

"Impact of the September 11 Events on Coexistence: Youth from Different Countries, Religions Come Together to Work and Study." 2002. *MECC NewsReport* 14, no. 2 (Autumn): 22.

Initiatives of Change. 2002. *Breaking the Chain of Hate: Visit to the UK of Lebanese Former Militiamen, April 19–25.* Brochure. London: Agenda for Reconciliation, Initiatives of Change.

———. February 6, 2003. "Breaking the Chain of Hate." Lecture with Abbas El-Halabi and Hicham Chehab, Washington, D.C.

———. n.d. *Frequently Asked Questions.* Handout.

Institute of Muslim-Christian Studies. 2003–2004. "Course/Program of the Certificate of Research in Muslim-Christian Studies" (DARIC). Handout (in Arabic and French).

———. n.d. *Origin and Project.* Brochure. Beirut: Center of Dialogue, Saint Joseph University (in French).

Iskandar, Emile. 1991. *A Look at the Church of the South (through the work of Father Salim Ghazzal and the Apostolic Movements 1962–1990)* (in Arabic).

Islamic-Christian National Dialogue Committee. n.d. Unified Working Paper (sent to author by Mr. Al-Sammak).

Jarjour, Riad. October 28–30, 2002. "For a Better Cooperation between Peoples and Religions." *The Tenth Round of the Christian-Muslim Dialogue Conference: Research and Working Papers,* Bahrain (in Arabic).

Jewish-Palestinian Dialogue Group. November 15, 1997. *Building a Common Future.* Evening program and reconciliation resource.

Johnston, Douglas, and Cynthia Sampson, eds. 1994. *Religion: The Missing Dimension of Statecraft.* New York: Oxford University Press.

Jordanian Constitution. www.mfa.gov.jo/uploads/const.pdf (accessed July 11, 2005).

Kasimow, Harold, and Byron Sherwin. 1991. *No Religion Is an Island: Abraham Joshua Heschel and Interreligious Dialogue.* Maryknoll, N.Y.: Orbis.

Kataregga, Badru, and David Shenk. 1980. *Islam and Christianity: A Muslim and a Christian in Dialogue.* Grand Rapids, Mich.: Eerdmans.

Kelada, William Soliman. 1994. *The Birth of the Citizenship Principle in Egypt.* Cairo: Coptic Center for Social Studies.

———. 1998. "The Creation of Citizenship Principle in Egypt." In *Citizenship: Historically, Constitutionally and Legally,* ed. Abd Allah, Ismaeil Sabri, et al. Cairo: Coptic Center for Social Studies.

Khalifeh, Ezzeddine. 2004. "Announcing the Establishment of the World Conference for Islam 'Wasatiya.'" *Ad-Dustour* (June 30): 8.

Khodr, George. 2000. *Ideas and Opinions on Christian-Muslim Dialogue and Coexistence.* Beirut: Al-Boulsia (in Arabic).

Khoury, Souha. 2000. "Muslim and Christian Youth Work, Learn Together." *MECC NewsReport* 12, no. 1 (Winter): 21.

Kimball, Charles. 1991. *Striving Together. A Way Forward in Christian-Muslim Relations.* Maryknoll, N.Y.: Orbis.

———. 2002. *When Religion Becomes Evil.* San Francisco: Harper.

Kimmerling, Baruch. 2001. *The Invention and Decline of Israeliness: State, Society, and the Military.* Berkeley: University of California Press.

Kimmerling, Baruch, and Joel S. Migdal. 2003. *The Palestinian People: A History.* Cambridge, Mass.: Harvard University Press.

Kolvenbach, Peter-Hans, and Joseph Pittau. 1999. *Understanding and Discussion: Approaches to Muslim-Christian Dialogue.* Rome: Editrice Pontificia Universita Gregoriana.

Kronish, Ron. 1997. "Understanding One Another in Israel." *Brandeis Review* (Spring).

Labib, Hany. 2000. *The Crisis of Religious Protection: The Religion and the State in Egypt.* Cairo: Dar El Shorouk.

Landau, Yehezkel. 2003. *Healing the Holy Land: Religious Peacebuilding in Israel Palestine.* Peaceworks Series. Washington, D.C.: United States Institute of Peace.

"The Lebanese Forum for Dialogue, Third Meeting." 2001. *MECC NewsReport* 13, nos. 3–4 (Autumn): 14.

"The Lebanese Meeting for Dialogue Discussed the War on Iraq. Jarjour: A New Colonization Rejected by All Churches." 2003. *An-Nahar* (February 25): 5.

"Lebanese Muslims and Christians Establish 'Caucus on Dialogue.'" 2001. *MECC NewsReport* 13, no. 2 (Summer): 27.

"Lebanese Muslims, Christians Respond to Pope's Call for Peace." 2003. *MECC NewsReport* 14, nos. 3–4 (Winter): 17.

Lebanon Conflict Resolution Network (LCRN). n.d. "An Introduction." Handout.

Liechty, Joseph. 2002. "Mitigation in Northern Ireland: A Strategy for Living in Peace when Truth Claims Clash." In Smock 2002.

Lustick, I. 1980. *Arabs in the Jewish State: Israel's Control of a National Minority.* Austin: University of Texas Press.

Massad, Joseph. 2001. *Colonial Effects: The Making of National Identity in Jordan.* New York: Columbia University Press.

Massouh, George. 2003. *The Coming Goods: Views in the Proximity of Christianity and Islam.* Balamand, Lebanon: Center for Christian-Muslim Studies, University of Balamand (in Arabic).

Massouh, George, and Catherine Srour. 1997. *Towards a Better Debate: Muslim-Christian Conversations* (with Bishop George Khodr and Dr. Mahmoud Ayoub).

Araya, Lebanon: Center of Christian-Muslim Studies, University of Balamand: Catholic Publishing Press (in Arabic).

Masters, Bruce. 2001. *Christians and Jews in the Ottoman Arab World: The Roots of Sectarianism.* New York: Cambridge University Press.

Mbillah, Johnson. 2002. "Towards Peace and Reconciliation between Christians and Muslims in Africa: The PROCMURA Initiative." *Journal of the Henry Martyn Institute* 21, no. 2.

McCarthy, Kate. 1998. "Reckoning with Religious Difference: Models of Interreligious Moral Dialogue." In *Explorations in Global Ethics: Comparative Religious Ethics and Interreligious Dialogue,* ed. Sumner B. Twiss and Bruce Grelle. Boulder, Colo.: Westview Press.

Messarra, Antoine. 1998. *Prospects for Lebanon: The Challenge of Coexistence.* Oxford, UK: Centre for Lebanese Studies.

Mezvinsky, Norton. 1988. "Reform Judaism and Zionism: Early History and Change." In *Anti Zionism: Analytical Reflections,* ed. Roselle Tekiner, Samir Abed-Rabbo, and Norton Mezvinsky, 313–41. Brattleboro, Vt.: Amana Books.

Middle East Council of Churches (MECC). 2002a. "Dialogue: Necessity and Adventure." *Al-Muntada* (December): 42.

————. 2002b. "Impact of the September 11 Events on 'Coexistence': A Youth Work Camp by the Church Coordination Committee for Development and Relief." *Al-Muntada* (December): 46–47 (in Arabic).

Mitchell, Donald W. 2000. "John Paul II and Interreligious Dialogue." Book review of *John Paul II and Interreligious Dialogue,* ed. Byron L. Sherwin and Harold Kasimow. *Buddhist-Christian Studies* 20: 300–11.

"The 'Montreux Statement' Muslim-Christian Dialogue Meeting." 2001. Montreux, Switzerland, June 16–20, 2001. *MECC NewsReport* 13, no. 2 (Summer): 27.

Morqus, Samir. 2000. *Protection and Punishment: The West and the Religious Question in the Middle East.* Cairo: El Dar El Masriya Lil Tebaa'a.

————. October 30–31, 2002. "The Coptic Center for Social Studies: The Experience of the Citizenship-Based Islamic Christian Dialogue, Program for Dialogue of Civilizations." Conference Proceedings. Cairo University, Faculty of Economics and Political Science.

Mosaad, Mohamed. 2002. "Islam and Postmodernity: The New Islamic Discourse in Egypt." Master's thesis, the American University in Cairo.

"The Muslim-Christian Meeting in Amman." 1998. *Al-Nashra,* no. 9: 27 (in Arabic).

"Muslim-Christian Relations: One Muslim Woman's Views." 2000. *MECC NewsReport* 12, no. 2 (Spring/Summer): 5.

"Muslim-Christian Working Group." 1999. *MECC NewsReport* 11, no. 1 (Winter/Spring): 24.

National Committee for Muslim-Christian Dialogue. n.d. Handout.

Neuhaus, Richard John. 1985. "What the Fundamentalists Want." *Ethics and Public Policy Reprint 61.* Latham, MD: Ethics and Public Policy Center.

Nielsen, Jorgen S. 1997. "Between Rocks and Sadness: The Value of Dialogue between Religions." *Al-Nashra,* no. 5: 11–12 (in Arabic).

———. 2000. "The Contribution of Interfaith Dialogue Towards a Culture of Peace." Paper given at the International Conference on Dialogue of Civilizations, Institute of Islamic Studies, London, October 27, 2000. *Current Dialogue* 36 (December).

Noor, HM Queen. February 4, 1997. Transcript of an interview with Ms. Samar Daoud, for *Al-Mushahid Assiyasi,* at Al-Nadwa Palace on the United Nations University/International Academy. www.go.com.jo/QNoorjo/main/ivmsh.htm (accessed March 29, 2004).

"On the Sharkas Community in Jordan." January 12, 2004. *Jordan Culture,* www.arabicnews.com/ansub/Daily/Day/040112/2004011209.html (accessed February 1, 2004).

Osseiran, Sanaa. 1995. *The Bikfaya Training Report.* Unpublished report.

Our Lady of Peace Center, Latin Vicariate, Jordan. n.d. Leaflet.

Our Lady of Peace Center. www.ourladyofpeacecentre.org.

Panikkar, Raimon. 1999. *The Intra-religious Dialogue.* New York: Paulist Press.

"Prince Hassan Receives Aziz, Patriarch Sfeir." October 11, 1990. *Jordan Times.*

Royal Institute for Inter-Faith Studies (RIIFS). www.riifs.org/ (accessed April 2, 2004).

Sachedina, Abdul Aziz. 1990. "The Role of Religious Values in the Search for Peace." Panel discussion moderated by Joseph Montville, Boston College, February 16, 1990.

Said, Abdul Aziz. 2002. "Moving Towards a Transnational Consciousness." *Spirituality and Reality* 2, no 1: 6–7.

Said, Edward W. 1979. *Orientalism.* New York: Vintage Books.

Saif, Walid. 2000. "An Assessment of Christian-Muslim Dialogue." Paper given at a Christian-Muslim Consultation sponsored by the WCC, Amersfoort, Netherlands, November 8, 2000. *Current Dialogue* 36 (December).

Sampson, Cynthia. 1997. "Religion and Peacebuilding." In *Peacemaking in International Conflict,* ed. William Zartman and Lewis Rasmussen, 273–319. Washington, D.C.: United States Institute of Peace.

Sayah, Paul Nabil. May 8, 1998. "Relations between Christians and Muslims in the Middle East." Presented at a symposium on Asian Church Concerns sponsored by SEDOS-Servizio di Documentazione e Studi (Center for Documentation and Studies) in Rome. *UCAN Report* (May 13).

———. 2002. "Muslim-Christian Relations in Lebanon: A Christian Perspective." In *Lebanon's Second Republic: Prospects for the Twenty-First Century,* ed. Kail C. Ellis. Gainesville: University Press of Florida.

Schirch, Lisa. 2001. "Ritual Reconciliation." In Abu-Nimer, ed. 2001.

Scott, David. 1995. "Buddhism and Islam: Past to Present Encounters and Interfaith Lessons." *Numen* 42: 141–55.

Scudder, Tom. 2001. "Muslim-Christian Relations." *MECC NewsReport* 13, nos. 3–4 (Autumn): 4–11.

Shamseddine, Sheikh Mohammed Mahdi. 2000a. "Christianity in the Current Cultural Islamic Understanding." *Al-Nashra,* no. 15: 4–8.

———. 2000b. "Christianity in the Current Cultural Islamic Understanding." *Al-Nashra,* no. 16: 9–12.

———. 2001a. "Christianity in the Current Cultural Islamic Understanding." *Al-Nashra,* no. 18: 4–7.

———. 2001b. "Christianity in the Current Cultural Islamic Understanding." *Al-Nashra,* no. 19: 4–8.

———. 2001c. "Christianity in the Current Cultural Islamic Understanding." *Al-Nashra,* no. 20: 4–8.

Shenouda III, Patriarch. 2001. Interview in Abdel Samea 2001.

Singh, David, and Robert Schick, eds. 2001. *Approaches, Foundations, Issues and Models of Interfaith Relations.* Delhi: Henry Martyn Institute of Islamic Studies.

Smith, Jane. 1998. "Christian-Muslim-Jewish Dialogue in Denver." In Bryant and Ali 1998.

Smock, David. September 28, 2002. "Clash of Civilizations or Opportunity for Dialogue?" *The American Muslim.*

———, ed. 2002. *Interfaith Dialogue and Peacebuilding.* Washington, D.C.: United States Institute of Peace Press.

Steele, David. 2002. "Peacebuilding in Former Yugoslavia." In Smock 2002.

Stendahl, Bishop Krister. 1990. "The Role of Religious Values in the Search for Peace." Panel discussion moderated by Joseph Montville, Boston College, February 16, 1990.

Swidler, Leonard. 1998. *Theoria-Praxis: How Jews, Christians and Muslims Can Move Together from Theory to Practice.* Leuven, Belgium: Peeters.

Tabshouri, Bassam. 1992. *Between Dust (or Earth) and Spirit: How Lebanese Religious Communities Evaluate and Define the "Human Other."* Beirut: Dar Al-Mahreq (in Arabic).

Takieddine, Sleiman. 2002. "The Arab Pact for Muslim-Christian Dialogue: The Dialogue of Life Is Wealthier in the Shadow of a Just State." *An-Nahar* (March 10): 11 (in Arabic).

Thistlethwaite, Susan. 2002. Preparatory paper and speech delivered to United States Institute of Peace, Second Abrahamic Trialogue Meeting, Washington, D.C., October 14–15, 2002.

Thomas, Kenneth. 2001. "The Place of the Bible in Muslim-Christian Relations." In Singh and Schick 2001.

"Together in Defending the Nation: The First General Conference of Christian Arabs." 2002. *Al-Muqtabas* (February/March): 36–43 (in Arabic).

Turner, Bryan S. 2002. "Orientalism, or the Politics of the Text." In *Interpreting Islam,* ed. Hastings Donnan. Thousand Oaks, Calif.: Sage Publications.

UNESCO–Lebanese National Commission. 2002. *Coexistence in Islam and Christianity.* Beirut: Modern Publishing Center (in Arabic).

"A Unique Meeting between Students from Christian and Muslim Religious Schools." 1999. *Al-Nashra,* no. 11: 30 (in Arabic).

U.S. Department of State. 2001. *Annual Report on International Religious Freedom.* Submitted to the Committee on International Relations, U.S. House of Representatives, and the Committee on Foreign Relations, U.S. Senate.

———. 2002. *Annual Report on International Religious Freedom.* Submitted to the Committee on International Relations, U.S. House of Representatives, and the Committee on Foreign Relations, U.S. Senate.

———. 2003. *Annual Report on International Religious Freedom.* Washington, D.C.: Bureau of Democracy, Human Rights and Labor. www.state.gov/g/drl/rls/irf/2003/24454.htm (accessed March 23, 2004).

United States Institute of Peace (USIP). July 2–3, 2002. "USIP Abrahamic Trialogue Summary." From a conference of the United States Institute of Peace, Washington, D.C.

University of Balamand. 2001. *The Center for Christian-Muslim Studies.* Brochure. Balamand, Lebanon: Lezard (in Arabic).

———. n.d. www.balamand.edu.lb/CCMS (accessed February 3, 2003).

Van Nispen, Christian. 1997. *Changes in Relations between Copts and Muslims (1952–1994) in the Light of Historical Experience, in between Desert and City: The Coptic Orthodox Church Today.* Oslo: Instituttet for sammenlignende kulturforskning.

Volkan, Vamik. 1997. *Bloodlines: From Ethnic Pride to Ethnic Terrorism.* New York: Farrar, Straus and Giroux.

Volkan, Vamik, and Norman Itzkowitz. 1994. *Turks and Greeks: Neighbors in Conflict.* Huntingdon, UK: Eothen Press.

Waardenburg, Jacques, ed. 2000. *Muslim-Christian Perceptions of Dialogue Today: Experiences and Expectations,* Leuven, Belgium: Peeters.

Walz, L. Humphrey. 1994. "Christianity and the Middle East: MECC Holds Conferences on Middle East Economics and Ethics." *Washington Post Report on Middle East Affairs* 13, no. 1: 70. http://gateway.proquest.com/openurl?url_ver=Z39.88-2004&res_dat=xri:pqd&rft_val_fmt=info:ofi/fmt:kev:mtx:journal&genre=article&rft_dat=xri:pqd:did=000000592496101&svc_dat=xri:pqil:fmt:text&req_dat=xri:pqil:pq_clntid=31806 (accessed March 30, 2004).

Watt, William Montgomery. 1991. *Muslim-Christian Encounters: Perceptions and Misperceptions.* New York: Routledge.

Wessels, Antonie. 1995. *Arab* and *Christian? Christians in the Middle East.* Kampen, Netherlands: Kok Pharos.

Winslow, Charles. 1996. *Lebanon: War and Politics in a Fragmented Society.* London: Routlege.

"A Workshop of Conflict Resolution." January 27, 2003. *LCRN Newsletter.*

Zeineddine, Sleiman. 2003. "On Dialogue, Reconciliation, and Civil Peace by Abbas El-Halabi: Ideas that Solidify the Principle of Accepting the Other and the Right to Differ." *An-Nahar* (June 20): 17 (in Arabic).

Zisser, Eyal. 2002. "Lebanon: State, Diaspora, and the Question of Political Stability." In *Middle Eastern Minorities and Diasporas,* ed. Moshe Ma'Oz and Gabriel Sheffer, 231–47. Brighton, UK: Sussex Academic Press.

INDEX

ABOUT THE AUTHORS

Mohammed Abu-Nimer, an associate professor at the American University School of International Service, International Peace and Conflict Resolution Program (IPCR), is an expert on interfaith dialogue for peace. His publications include *Nonviolence and Peacebuilding in Islam: Theory and Practice* (Gainesville: University Press of Florida, 2003); *Dialogue, Conflict Resolution and Change: Arab-Jewish Encounters in Israel* (Albany, N.Y.: SUNY Press, 1999); and two edited volumes: *Positive Approaches to Peacebuilding* (Washington, D.C.: PACT, 2003); and *Reconciliation, Justice, and Coexistence: Theory and Practice* (New York: Lexington, 2001). As a practitioner of peacebuilding, Abu-Nimer has been conducting conflict resolution, dialogue, and diversity training workshops since 1982 in many countries, including the United States, Israel, Palestine, Jordan, Egypt, Sri Lanka, and the Philippines.

Amal Khoury is a visiting assistant professor at McDaniel College. Her work focuses on international relations, conflict resolution, the nexus between peacebuilding and development, and internal displacement, with a focus on the Middle East in general and Lebanon in particular.

Emily Welty has a master's degree in International Peace and Conflict Resolution from the American University and currently works for the Association for Conflict Resolution. She has worked on conflict and human rights issues in Israel/Palestine, South Africa, and Northern Ireland.

UNITED STATES INSTITUTE OF PEACE

The United States Institute of Peace is an independent, non-partisan institution established and funded by Congress. Its goals are to help prevent and resolve violent conflicts, promote post-conflict peacebuilding, and increase conflict-management tools, capacity, and intellectual capital worldwide. The Institute does this by empowering others with knowledge, skills, and resources, as well as by its direct involvement in conflict zones around the globe.

Chairman of the Board: J. Robinson West
Vice Chairman: María Otero
President: Richard H. Solomon
Acting Executive Vice President: Patricia Powers Thomson
Vice President: Charles E. Nelson

Board of Directors

J. Robinson West (Chairman), Chairman, PFC Energy, Washington, D.C.

María Otero (Vice Chairman), President, ACCION International, Boston, Mass.

Betty F. Bumpers, Founder and former President, Peace Links, Washington, D.C.

Holly J. Burkhalter, Vice President of Government Affairs, International Justice Mission, Washington, D.C.

Chester A. Crocker, James R. Schlesinger Professor of Strategic Studies, School of Foreign Service, Georgetown University, Washington, D.C.

Laurie S. Fulton, Partner, Williams and Connolly, Washington, D.C.

Charles Horner, Senior Fellow, Hudson Institute, Washington, D.C.

Mora L. McLean, President, Africa-America Institute, New York, N.Y.

Barbara W. Snelling, former State Senator and former Lieutenant Governor, Shelburne, Vt.

Members ex officio

Barry F. Lowenkron, Assistant Secretary of State for Democracy, Human Rights, and Labor

Robert M. Gates, Secretary of Defense

Richard H. Solomon, President, United States Institute of Peace (nonvoting)

Frances C. Wilson, Lieutenant General, U.S. Marine Corps; President, National Defense University

UNITY IN DIVERSITY

This book is set in Adobe Garamond; the display type is Arial Narrow. The Creative Shop designed the book's cover; Katharine Moore designed the interior. Helene Y. Redmond made up the pages, and EEI Communications, Inc., prepared the index. The text was copyedited and proofread by EEI. The book's editor was Michael Carr.